FAIRY TAIL

フェアリーテイル

38

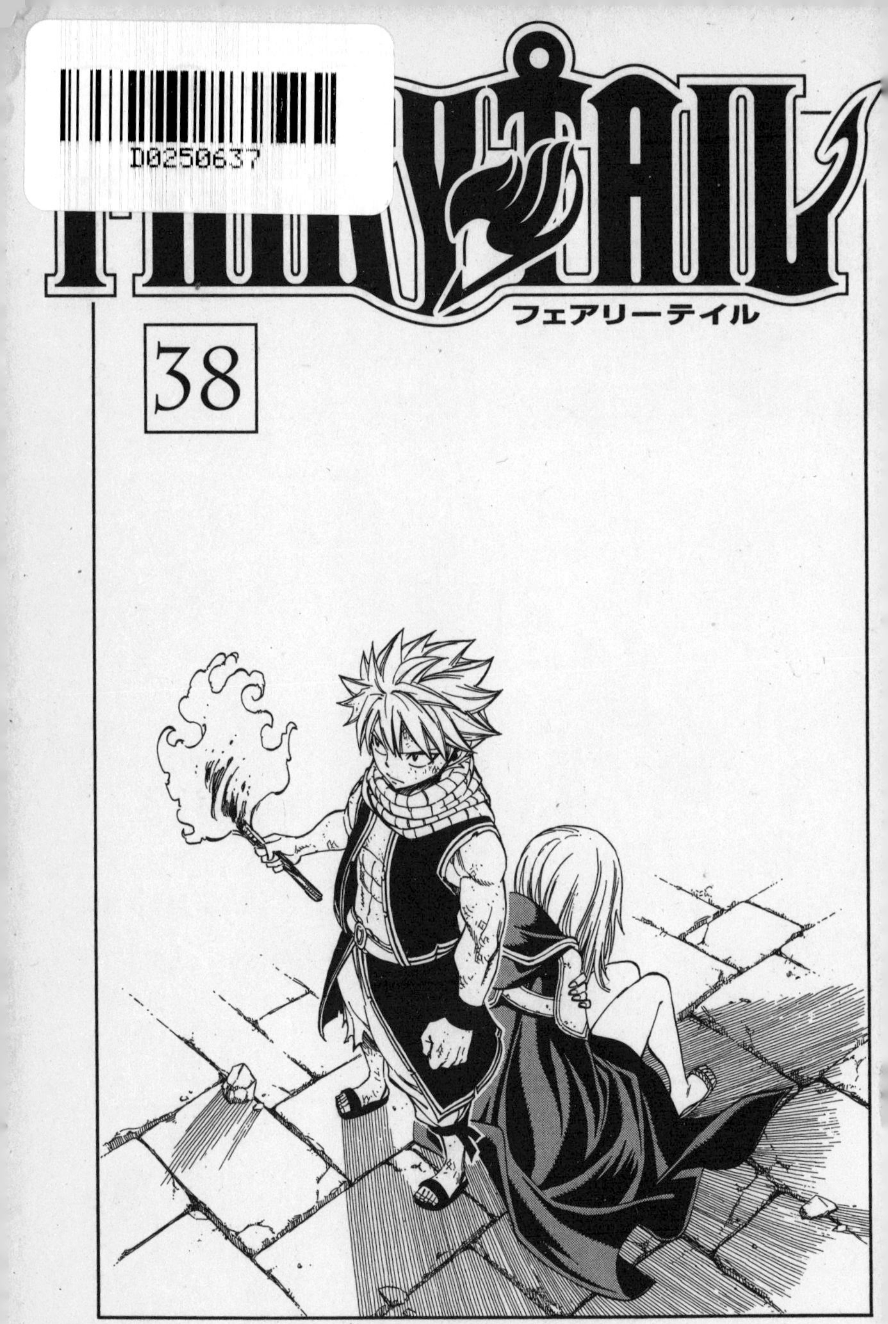

HIRO MASHIMA

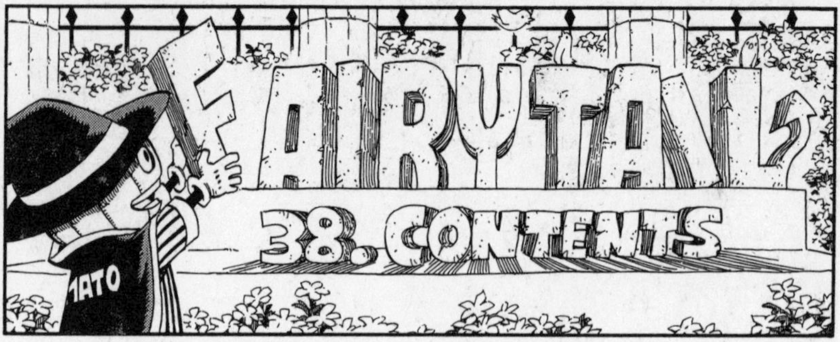
FAIRY TAIL
38. CONTENTS

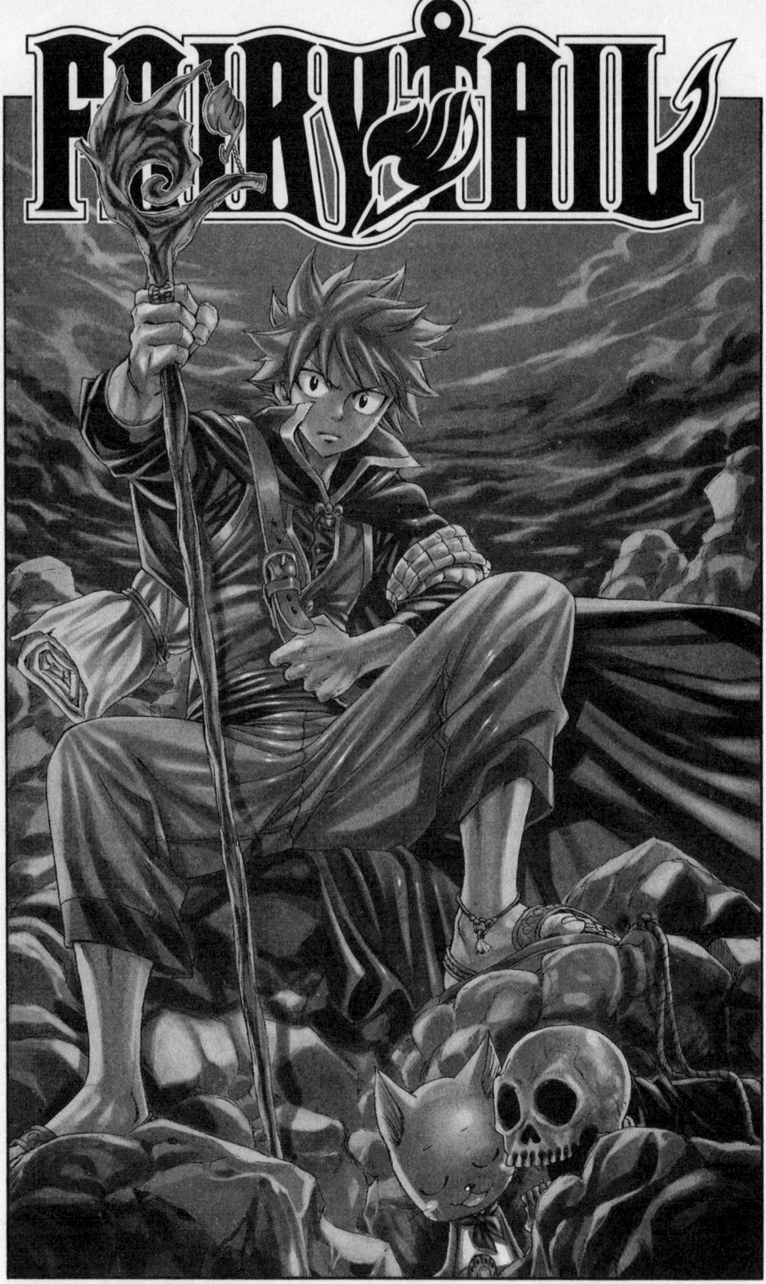
FAIRY TAIL

Chapter 318: Gajeel vs. Rogue

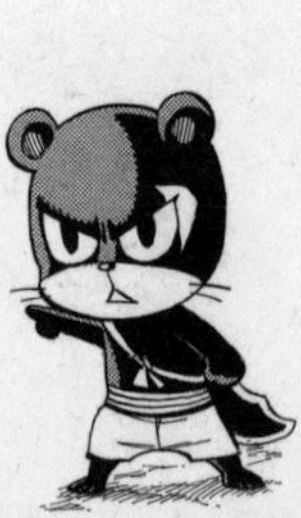

FAIRY TAIL

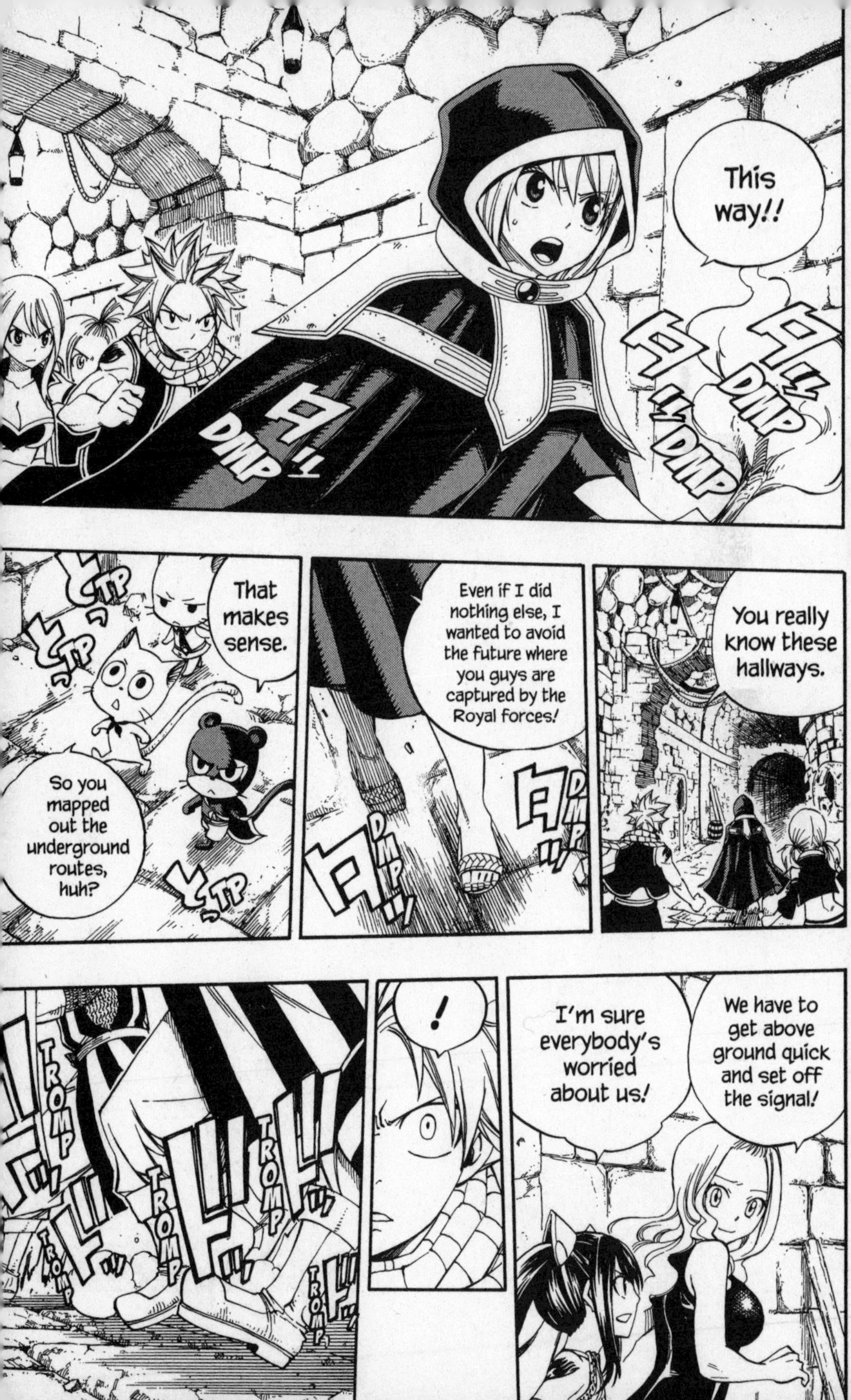
This way!!
DMP
DMP
DMP
You really know these hallways.
Even if I did nothing else, I wanted to avoid the future where you guys are captured by the Royal forces!
DMP
DMP
That makes sense.
TP
TP
So you mapped out the underground routes, huh?
TP
We have to get above ground quick and set off the signal!
I'm sure everybody's worried about us!
!
TROMP
TROMP
TROMP
TROMP
TROMP

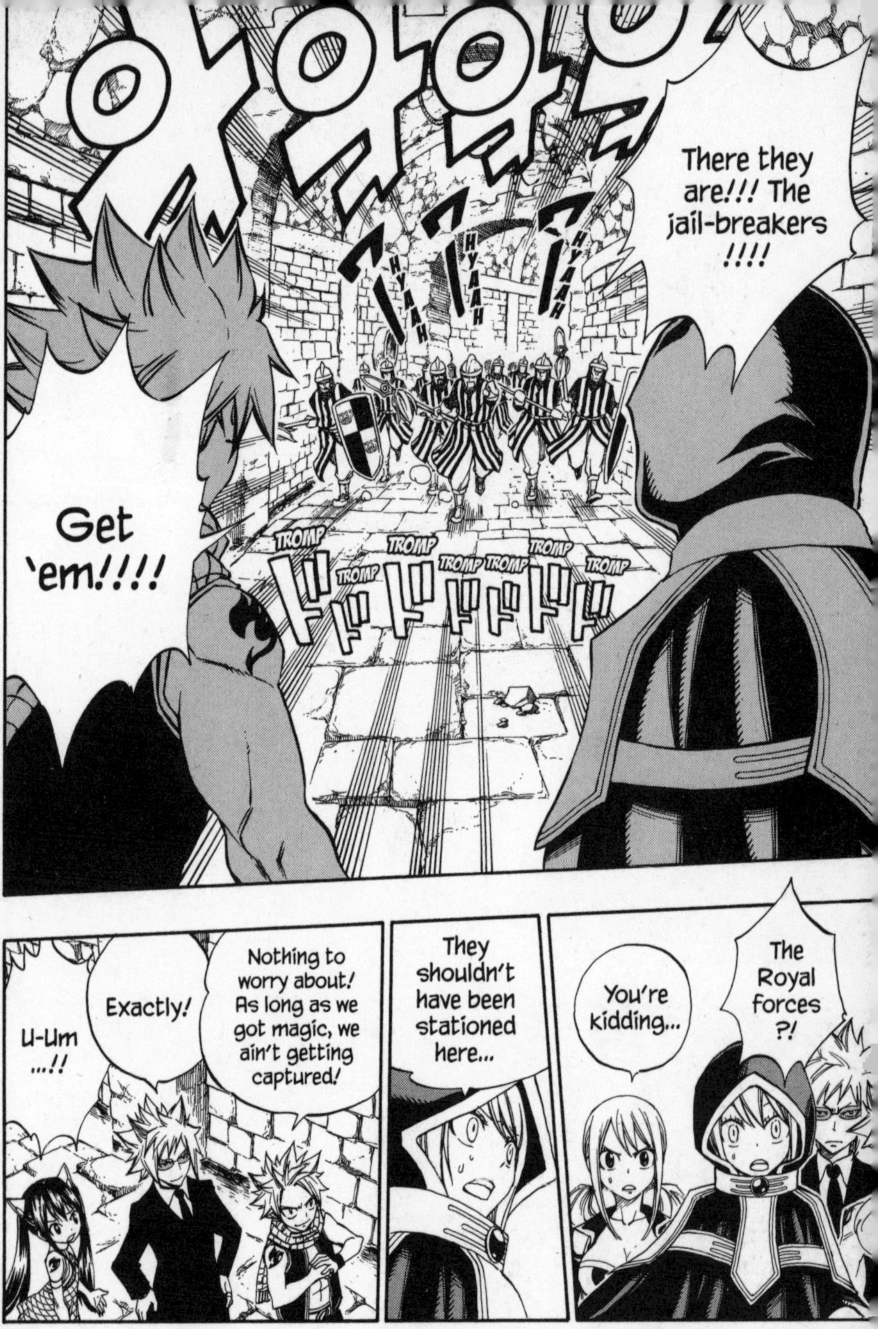
There they are!!! The jail-breakers !!!!
HYAAH
HYAAH
HYAAH
Get 'em!!!!
TROMP
TROMP
TROMP
TROMP
TROMP
TROMP
TROMP
The Royal forces ?!
You're kidding...
They shouldn't have been stationed here...
Nothing to worry about! As long as we got magic, we ain't getting captured!
Exactly!
U-Um ...!!

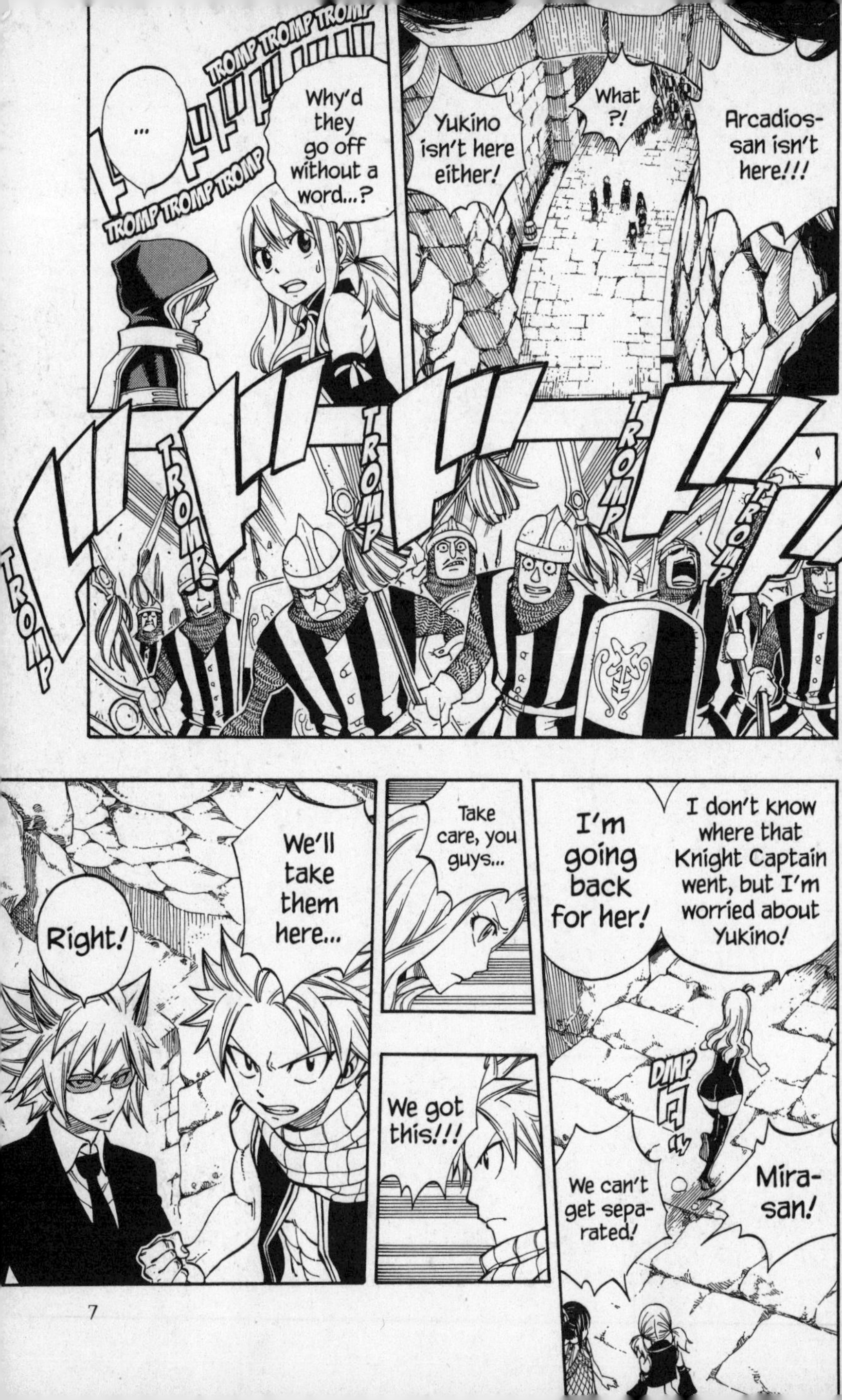
Arcadios-san isn't here!!!
What ?!
Yukino isn't here either!
TROMP TROMP TROMP
Why'd they go off without a word...?
...
TROMP TROMP TROMP
TROMP
TROMP
TROMP
TROMP
TROMP
I don't know where that Knight Captain went, but I'm worried about Yukino!
I'm going back for her!
DMP
Mira-san!
We can't get separated!
Take care, you guys...
We got this!!!
We'll take them here...
Right!

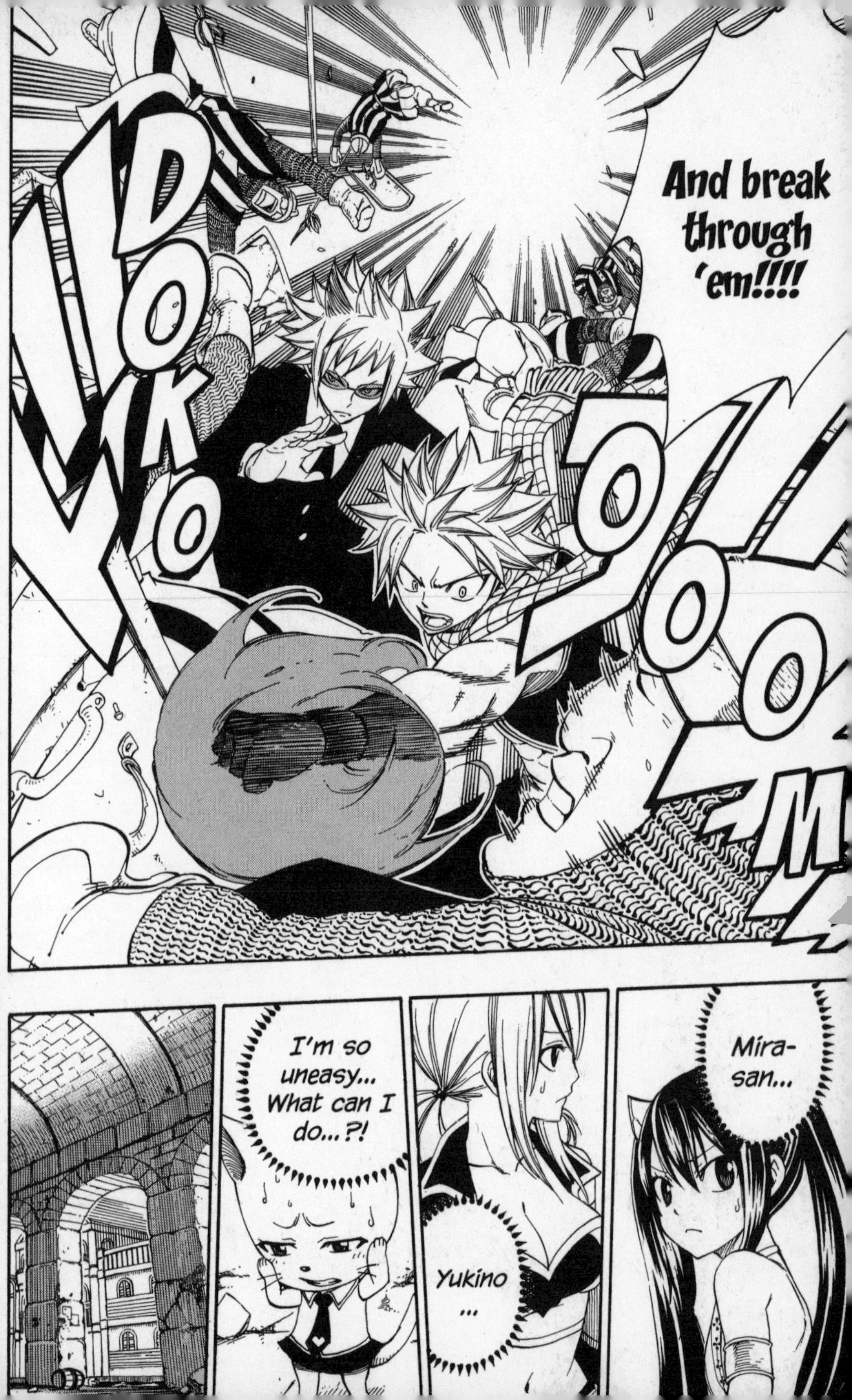
And break through 'em!!!!
Mira-san...
Yukino ...
I'm so uneasy... What can I do...?!

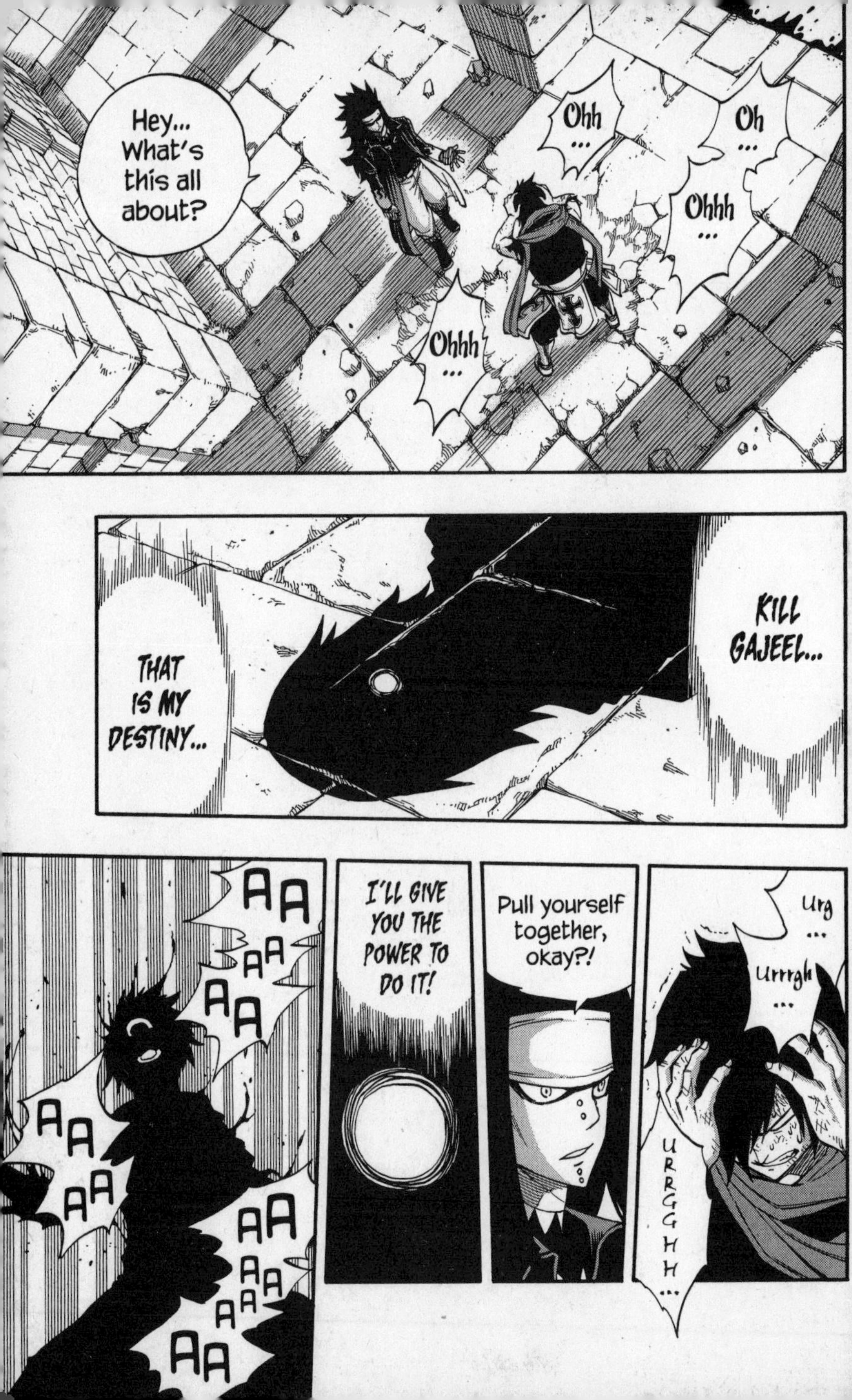
Oh...
Ohh...
Ohhh...
Ohhh...
Hey... What's this all about?
KILL GAJEEL...
THAT IS MY DESTINY...
Urg... Urrrgh...
URRGGHH...
Pull yourself together, okay?!
I'LL GIVE YOU THE POWER TO DO IT!
AAAAAA
AAAA
AAAAAAAA

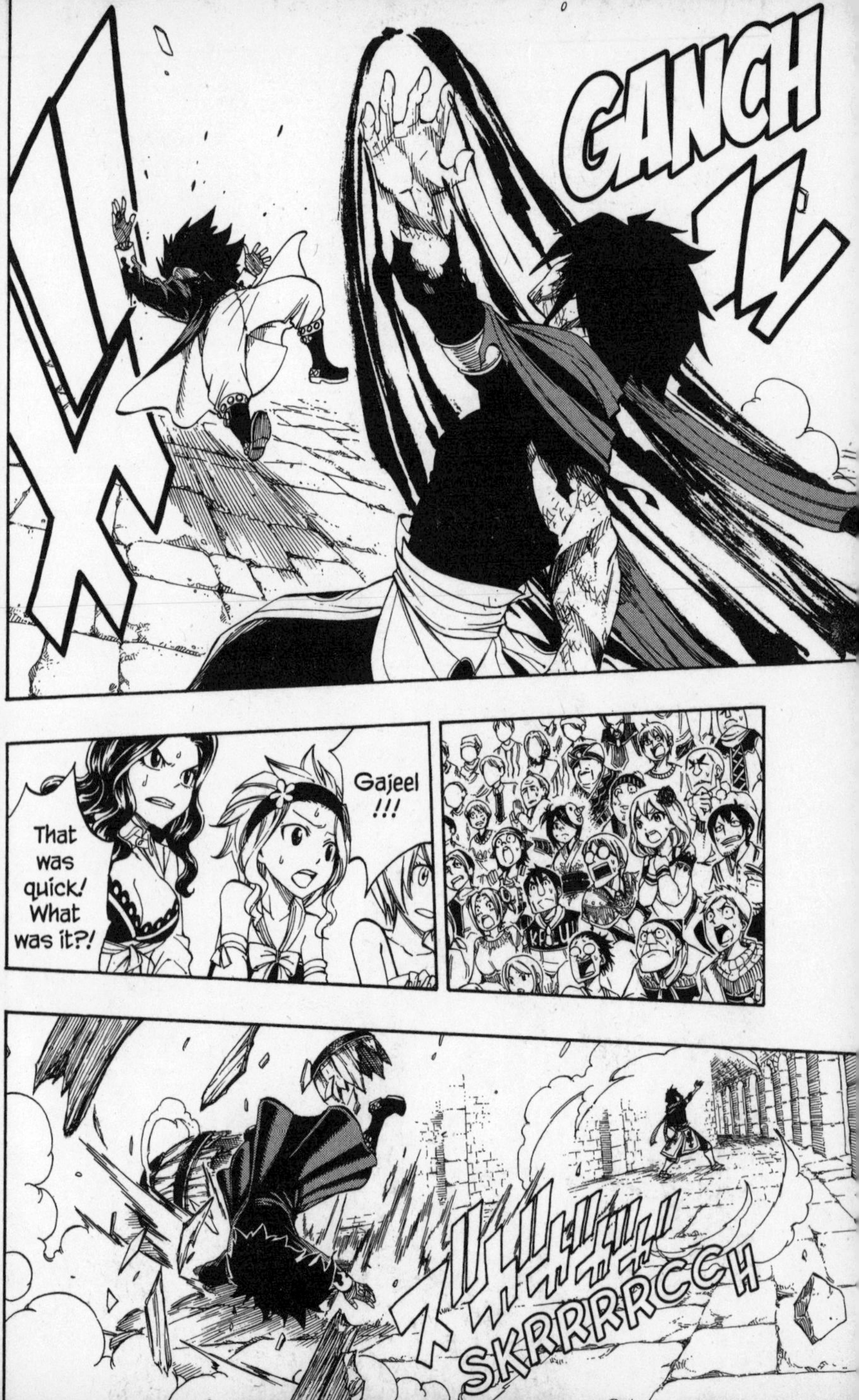
GANCH
Gajeel!!!
That was quick! What was it?!
SKRRRRCCH

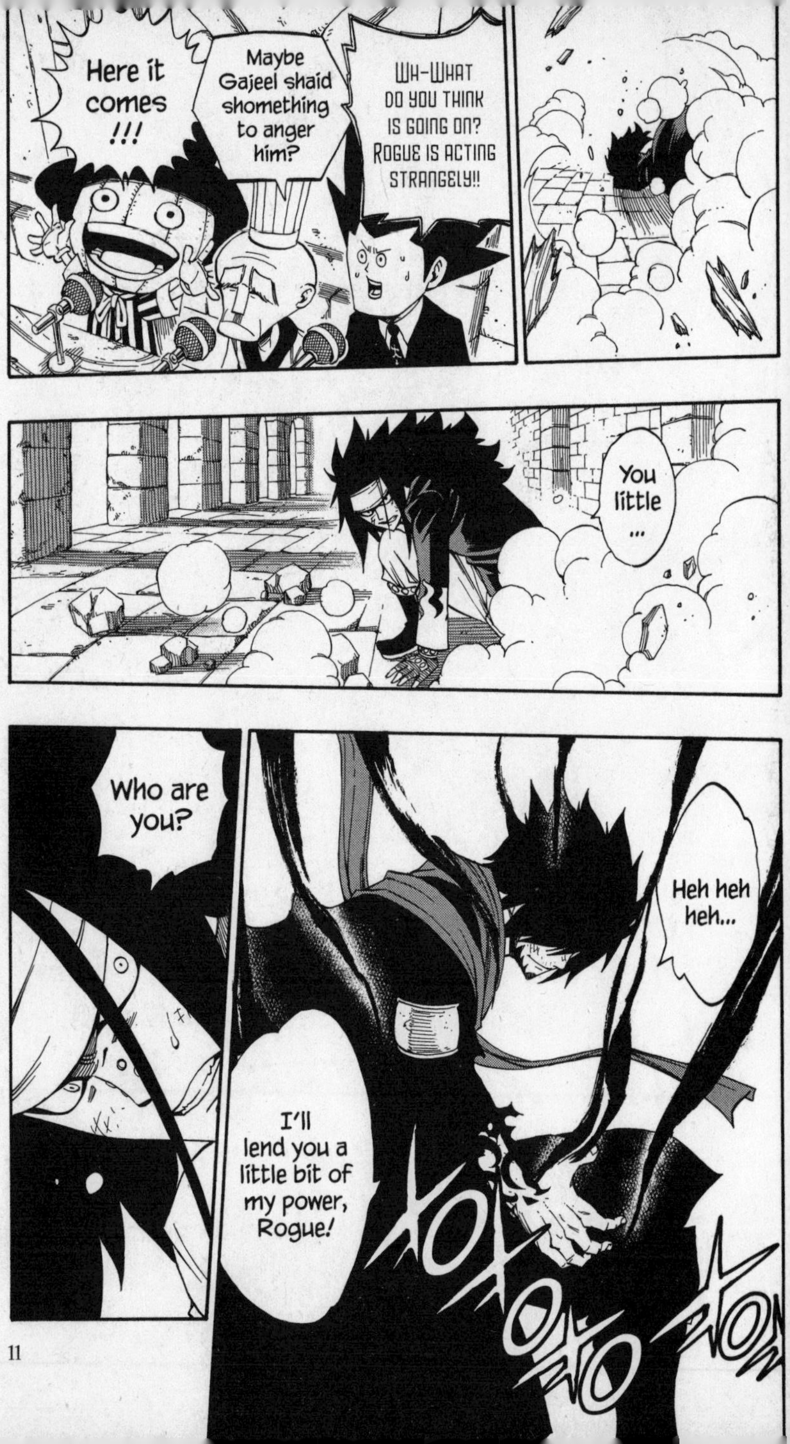
Wh-What do you think is going on? Rogue is acting strangely!!
Maybe Gajeel shaid shomething to anger him?
Here it comes!!!
You little...
Heh heh heh...
I'll lend you a little bit of my power, Rogue!
Who are you?

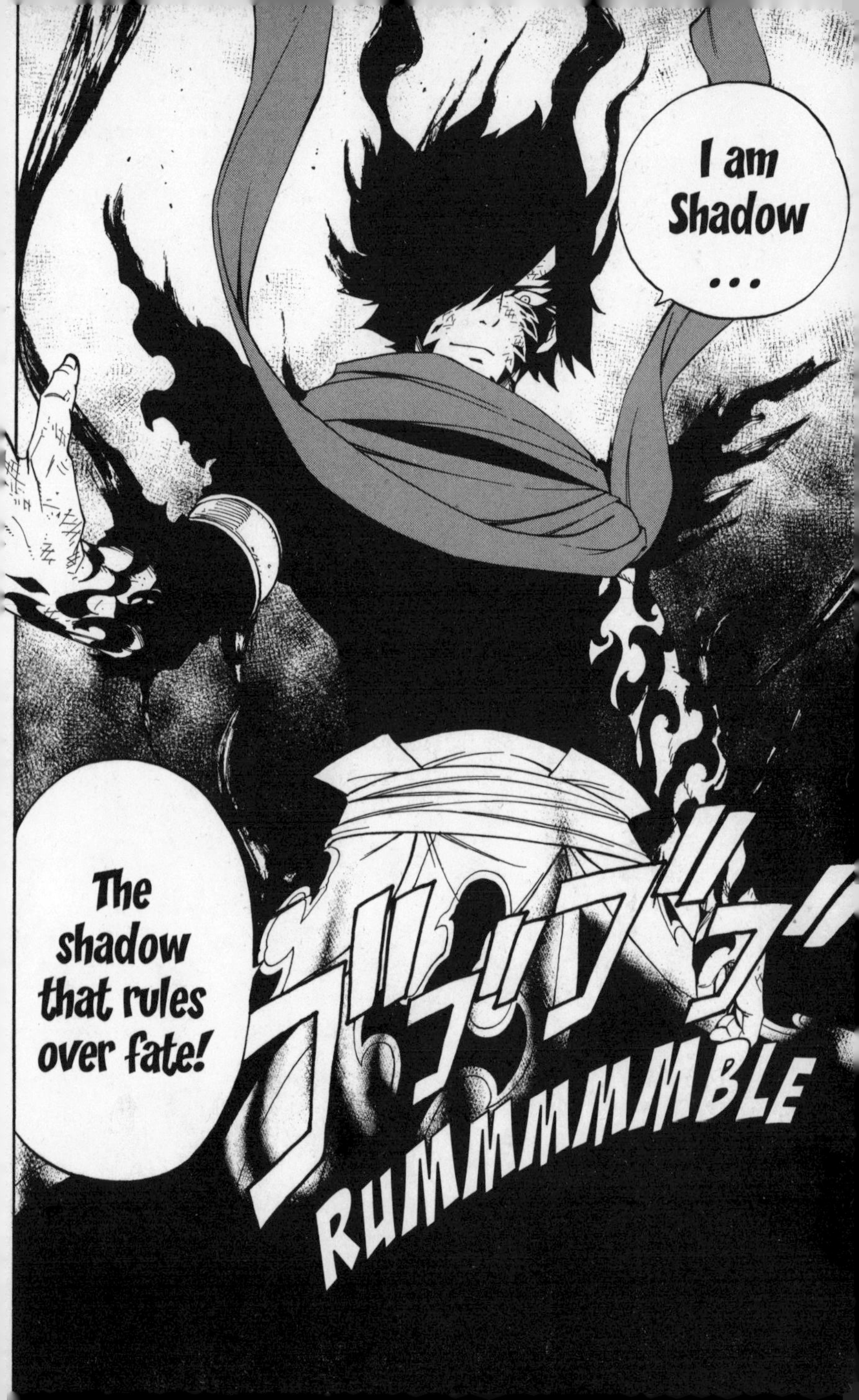
I am Shadow ...
The shadow that rules over fate!
RUMMMMMBLE

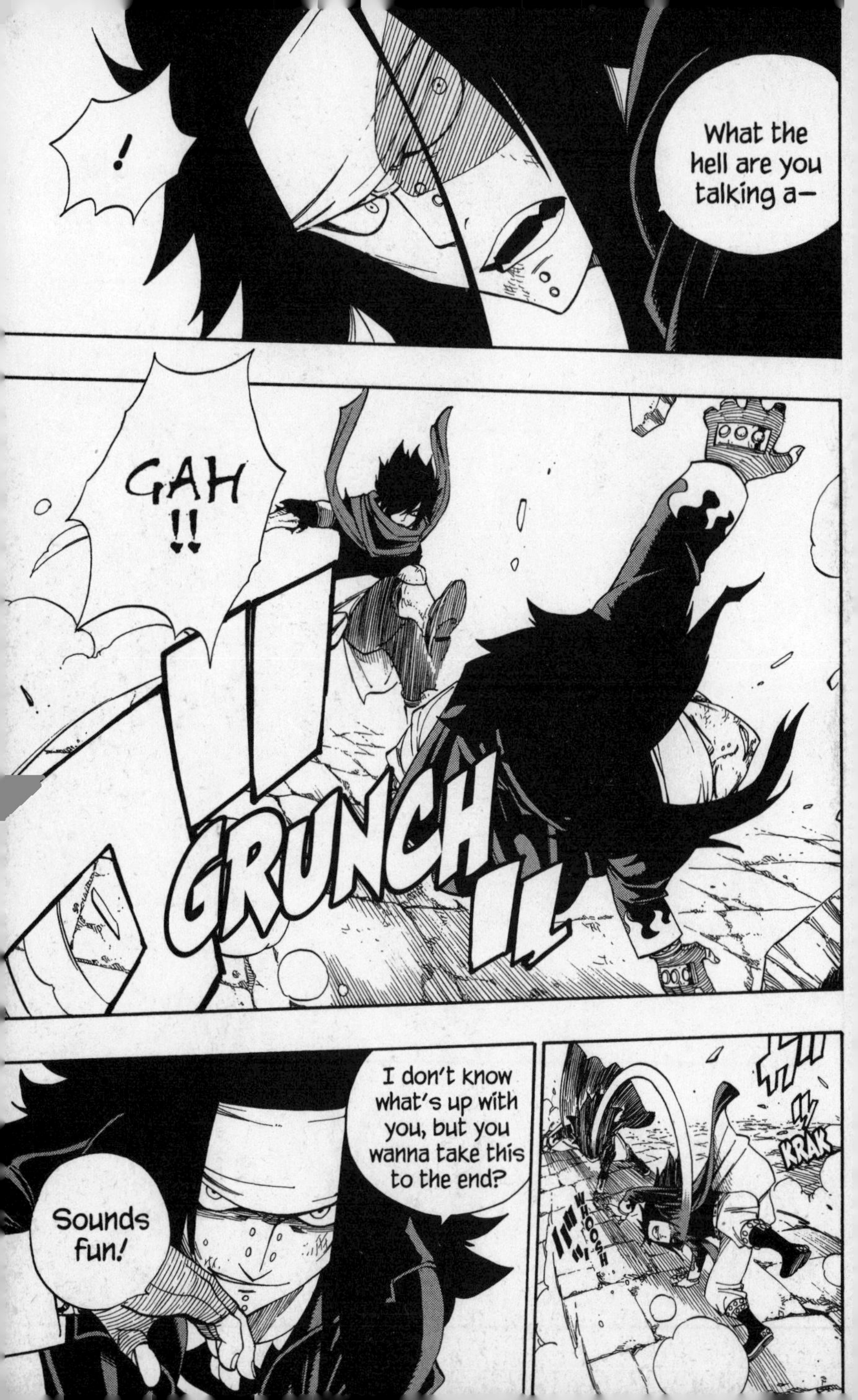
What the hell are you talking a—
!
GAH!!
GRUNCH
KRAK
WHOOSH
I don't know what's up with you, but you wanna take this to the end?
Sounds fun!

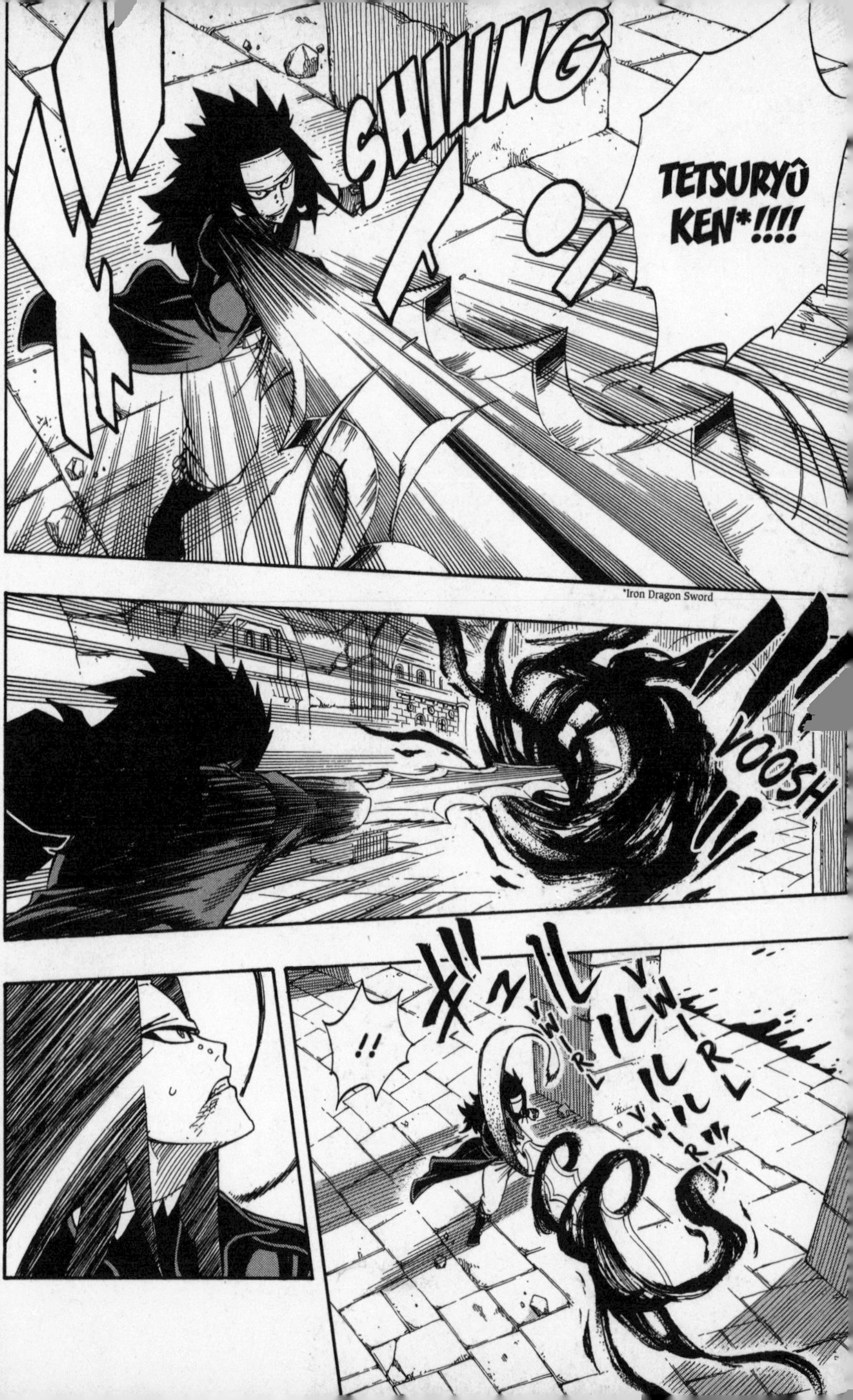
TETSURYÛ KEN*!!!!
SHIIING
VOOSH
!!
VWIRL
VWIRL
VWIRL
*Iron Dragon Sword

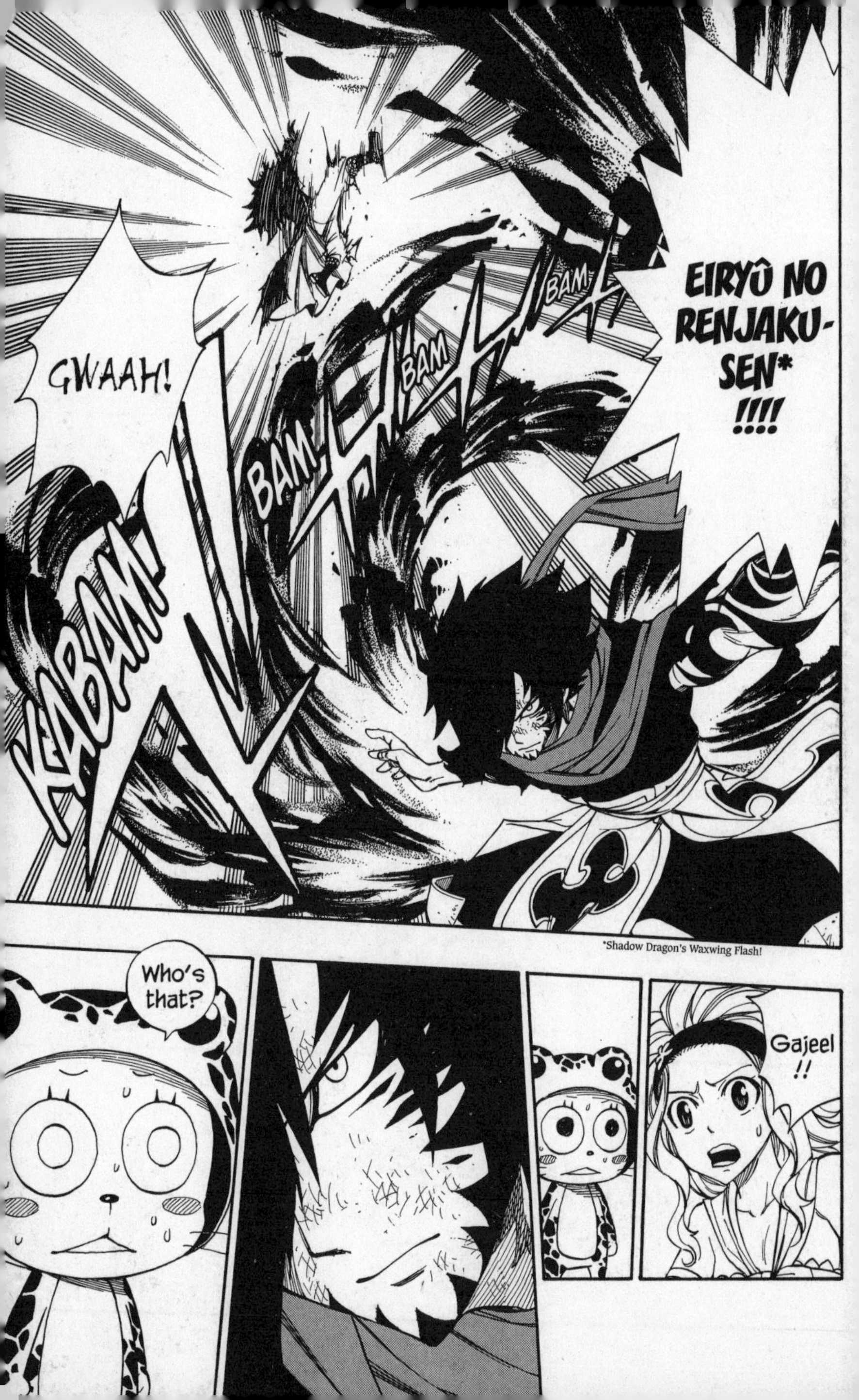
EIRYÛ NO RENJAKU-SEN* !!!!
BAM
BAM
BAM
BAM
KABAM!
GWAAH!
Gajeel!!
Who's that?
*Shadow Dragon's Waxwing Flash!

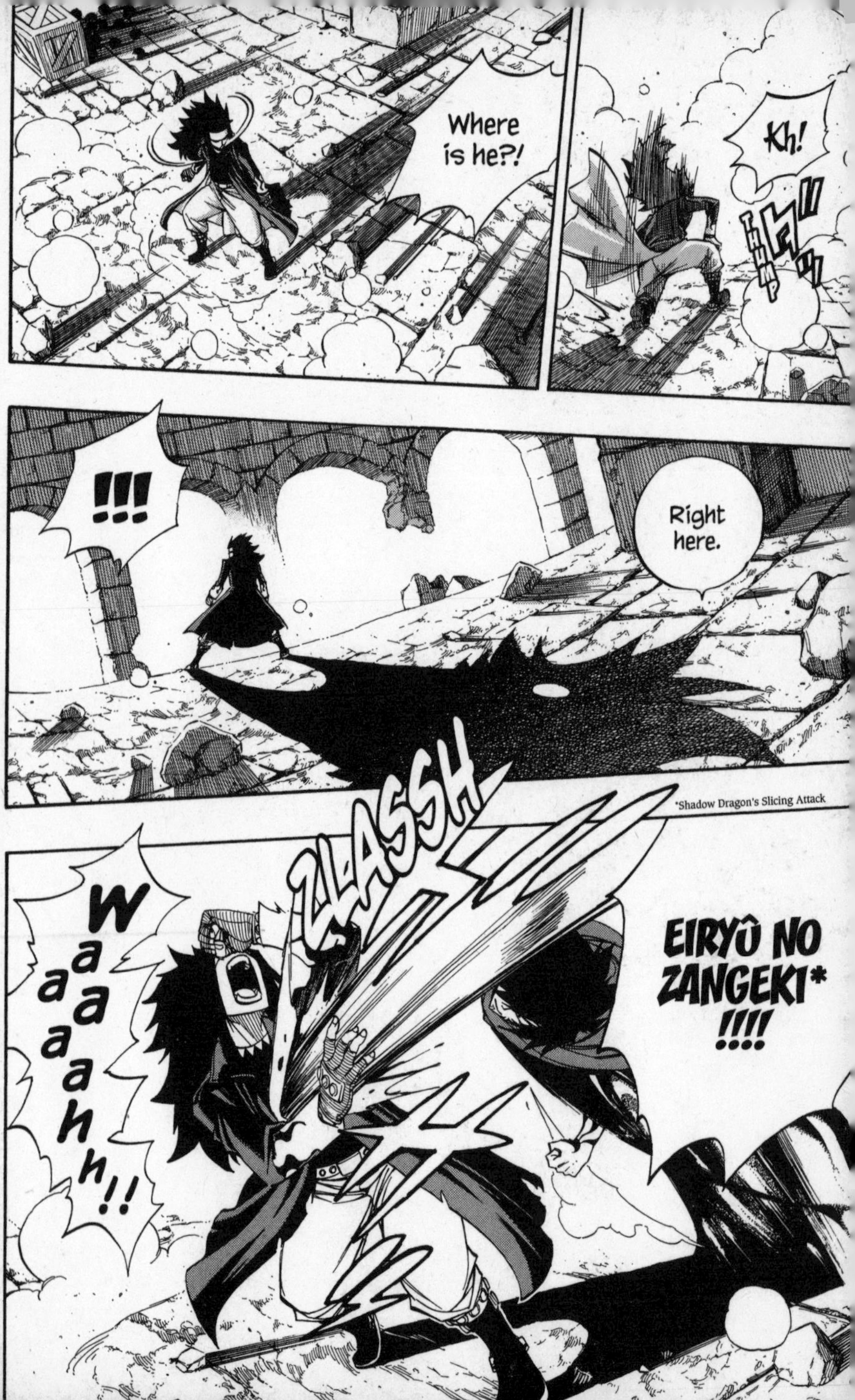
Kh!
THUMP
Where is he?!
Right here.
!!!
EIRYÛ NO ZANGEKI* !!!!
ZLASSH
Waaaaaaahhh!!
*Shadow Dragon's Slicing Attack

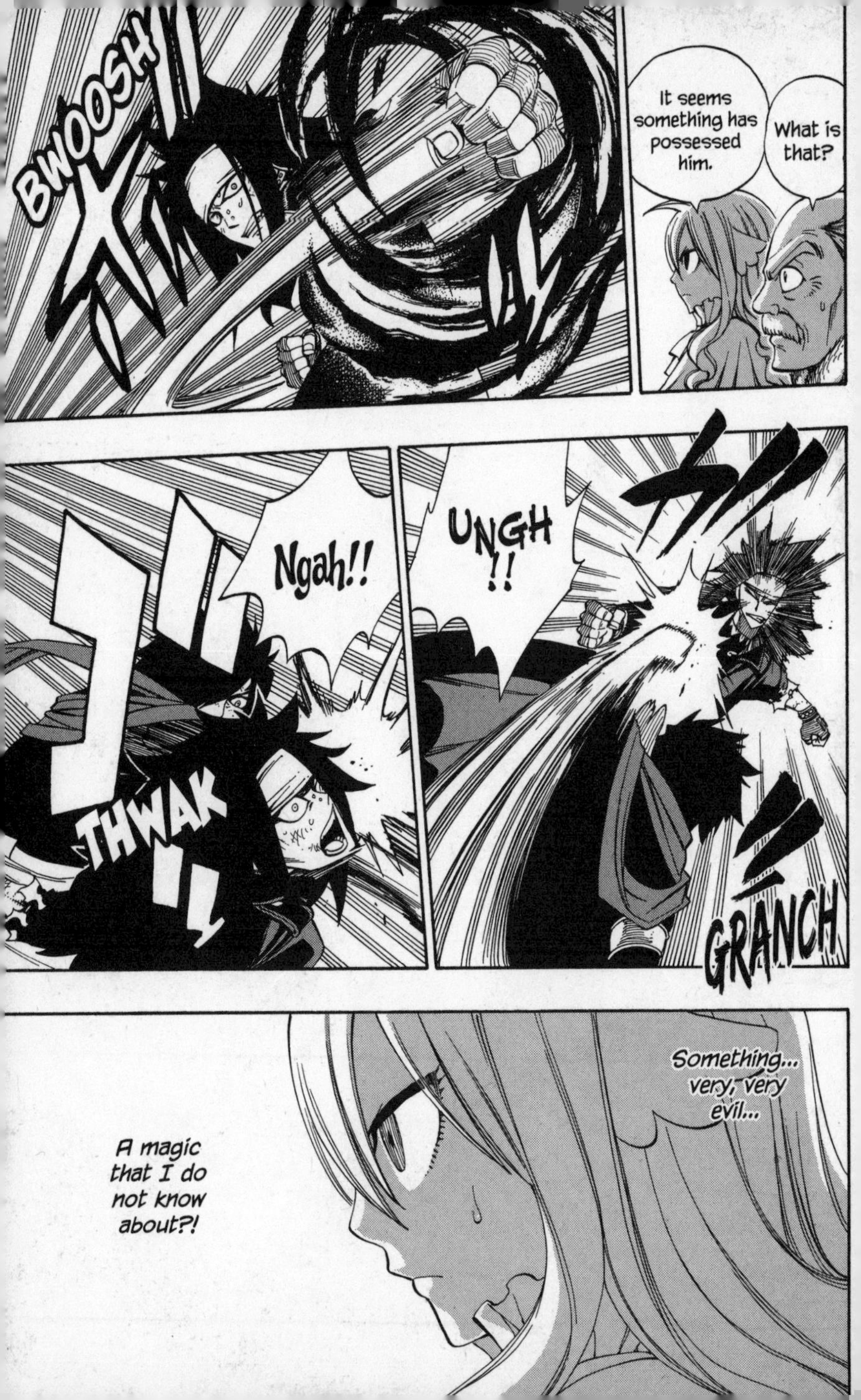
What is that?
It seems something has possessed him.
BWOOSH!!
UNGH!!
GRANCH
Ngah!!
THWAK!!
Something... very, very evil...
A magic that I do not know about?!

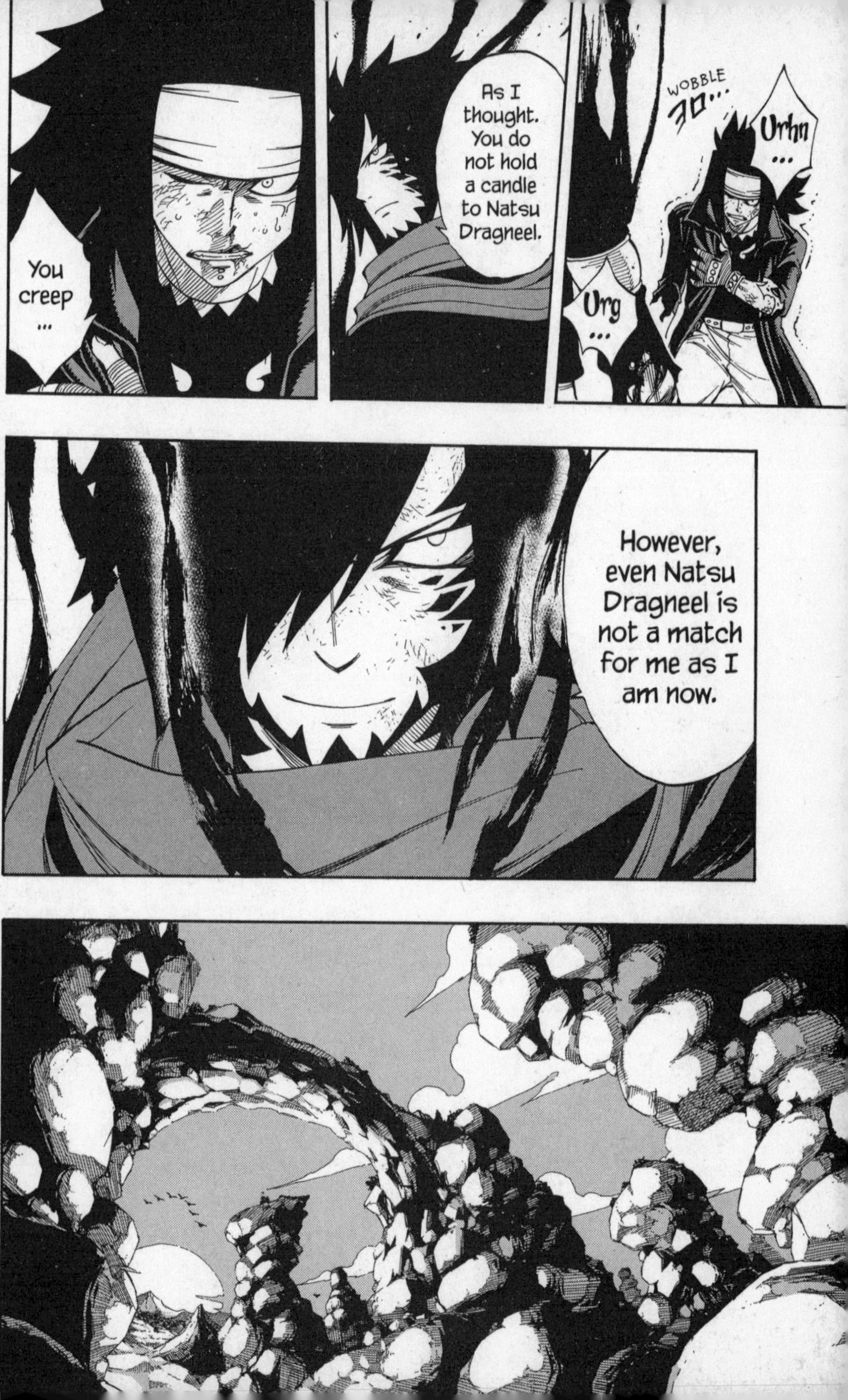
Urhn ...
WOBBLE
ヨロ…
Urg ...
As I thought. You do not hold a candle to Natsu Dragneel.
You creep ...
However, even Natsu Dragneel is not a match for me as I am now.

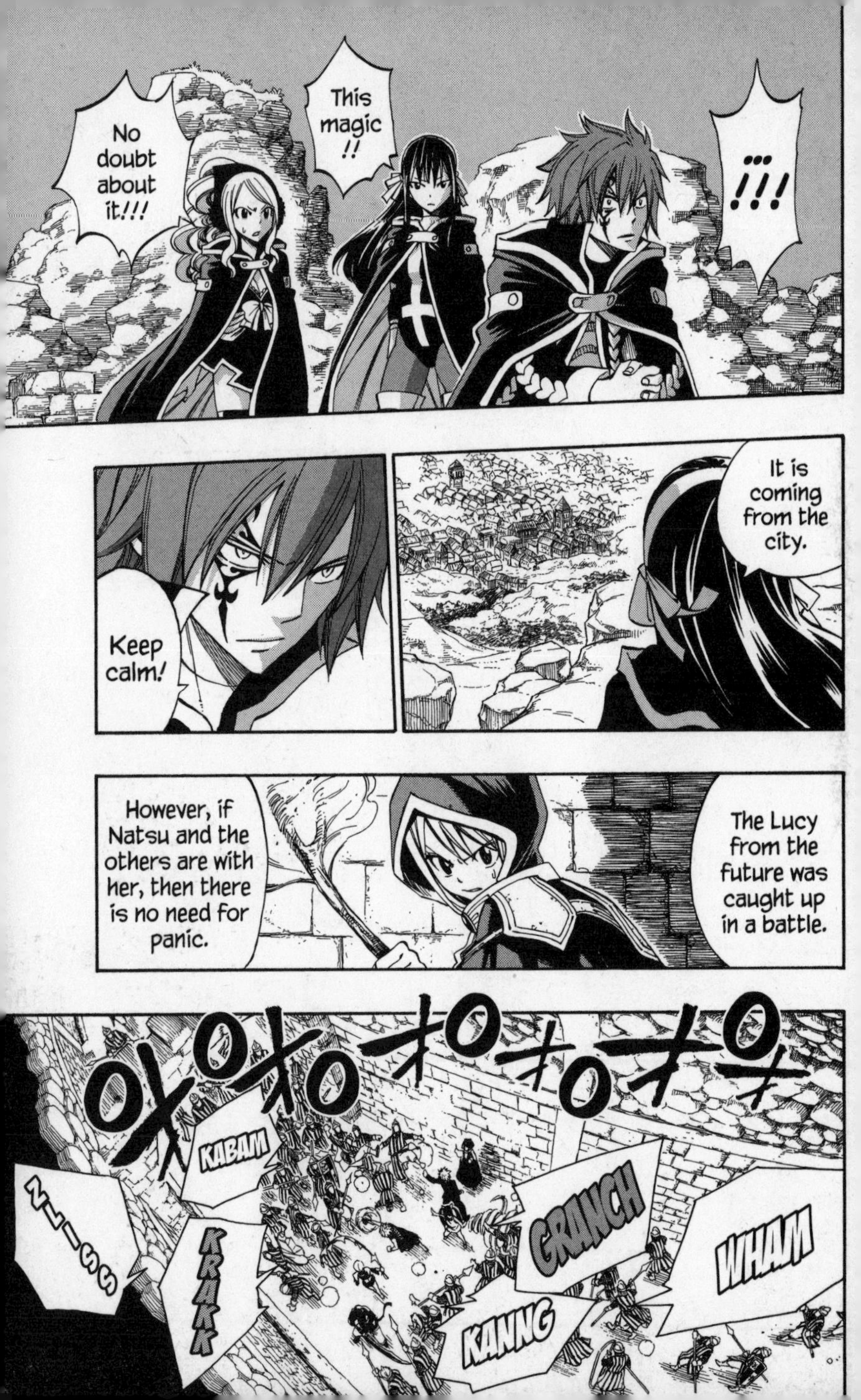
...!!!
This magic !!
No doubt about it!!!
It is coming from the city.
Keep calm!
The Lucy from the future was caught up in a battle.
However, if Natsu and the others are with her, then there is no need for panic.
WHAM
GRANCH
KANNG
KABAM
KRAKK

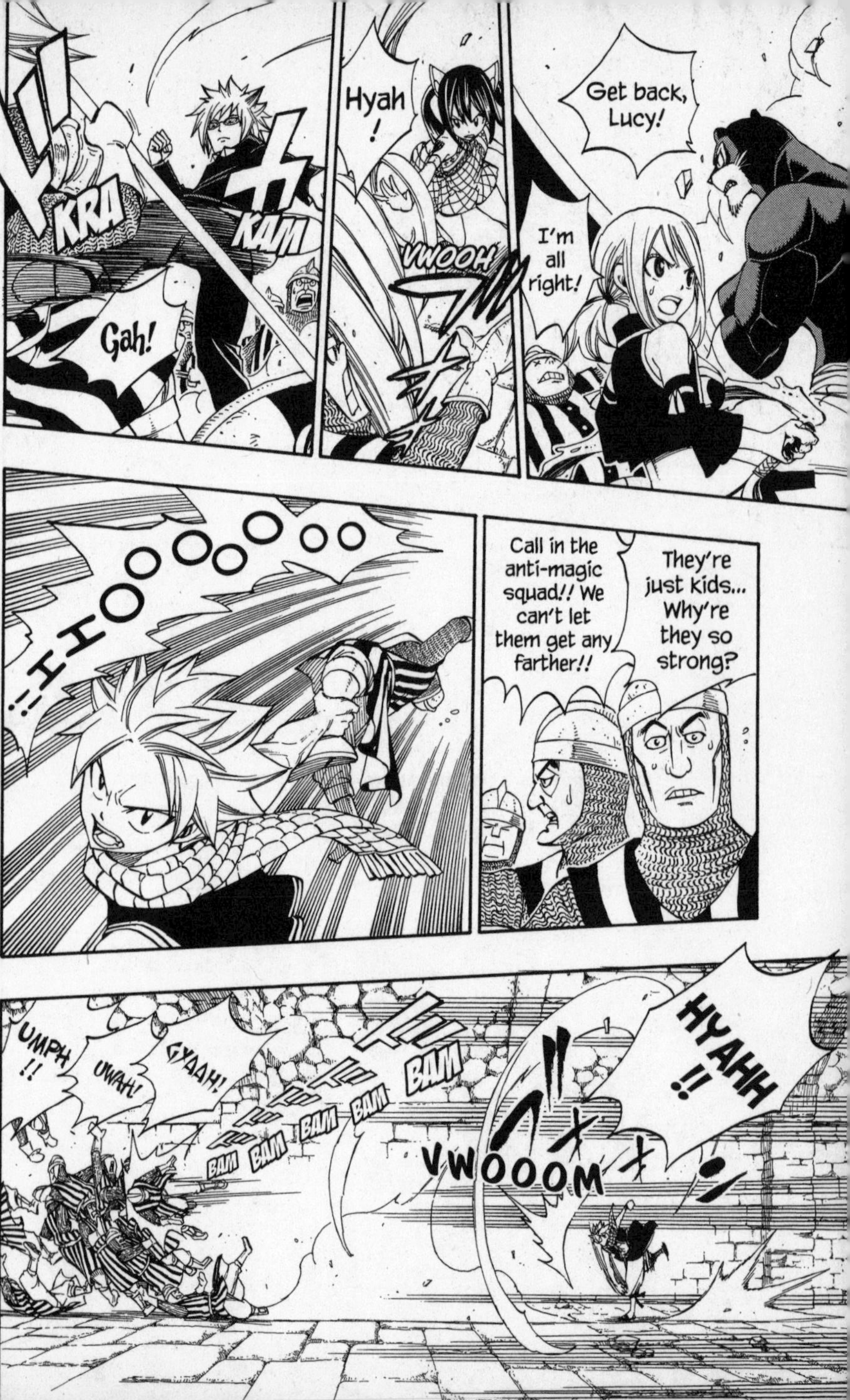
Get back, Lucy!
I'm all right!
Hyah!
VWOOH
KRA
KAM
Gah!
They're just kids... Why're they so strong?
Call in the anti-magic squad!! We can't let them get any farther!!
HIOOOOOOOO!!
HYAHH!!
VWOOOM
BAM
BAM
BAM
BAM
BAM
GYAAH!
UWAH!
UMPH!!

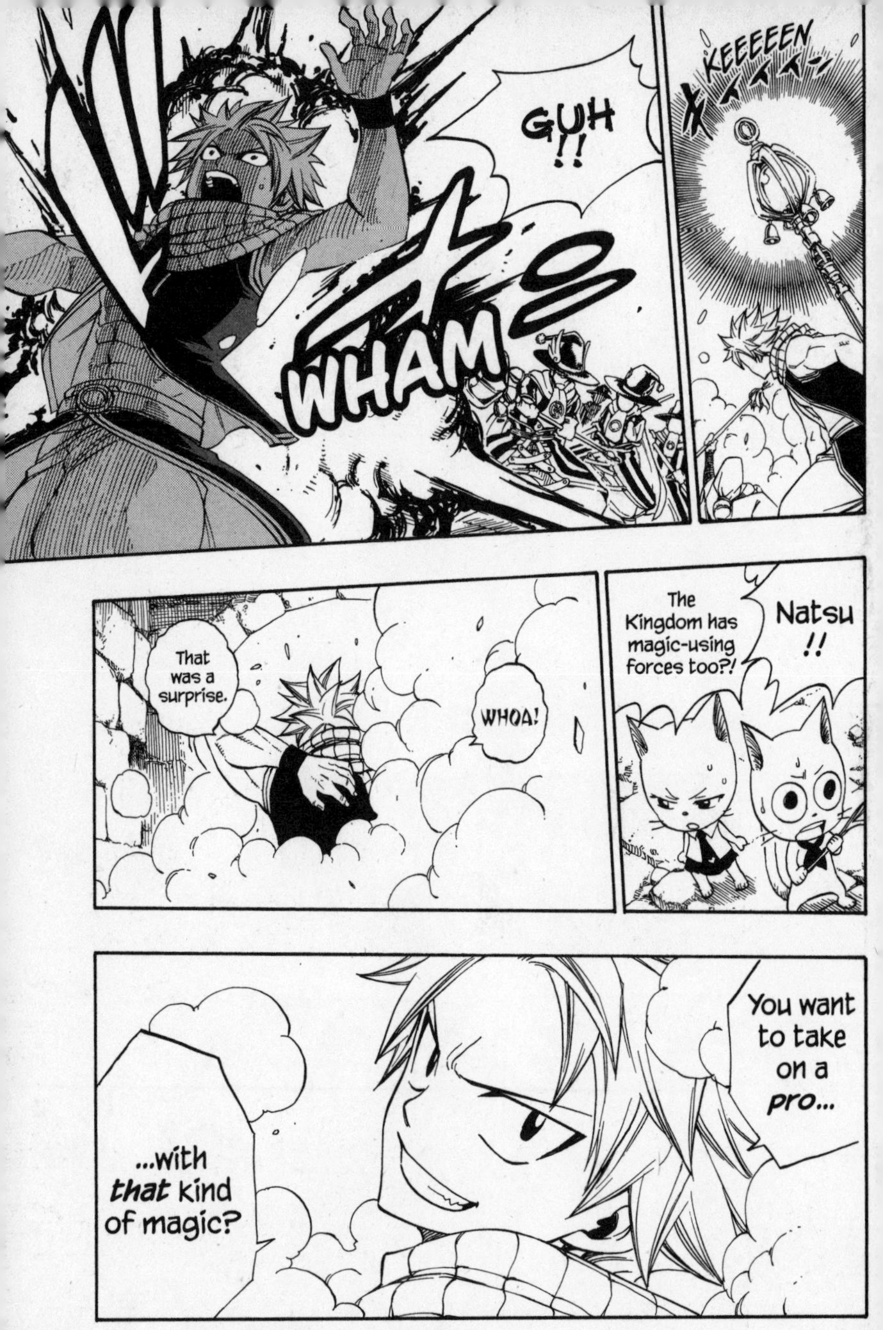
KEEEEEN
GUH!!
WHAM
Natsu!!
The Kingdom has magic-using forces too?!
WHOA!
That was a surprise.
You want to take on a *pro*...
...with *that* kind of magic?

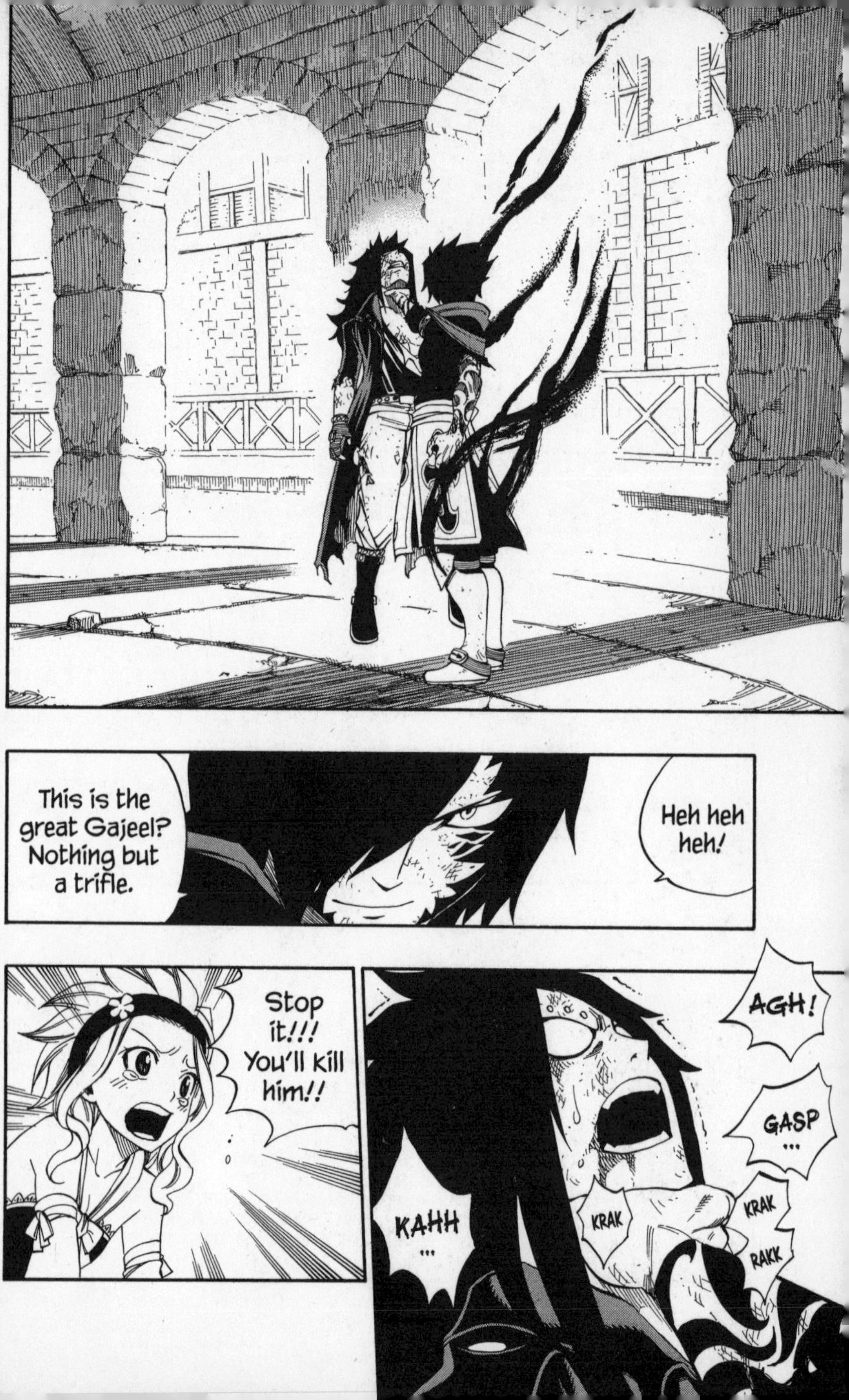
Heh heh heh!
This is the great Gajeel? Nothing but a trifle.
AGH!
GASP ...
KRAK
KRAK
RAKK
KAHH ...
Stop it!!! You'll kill him!!

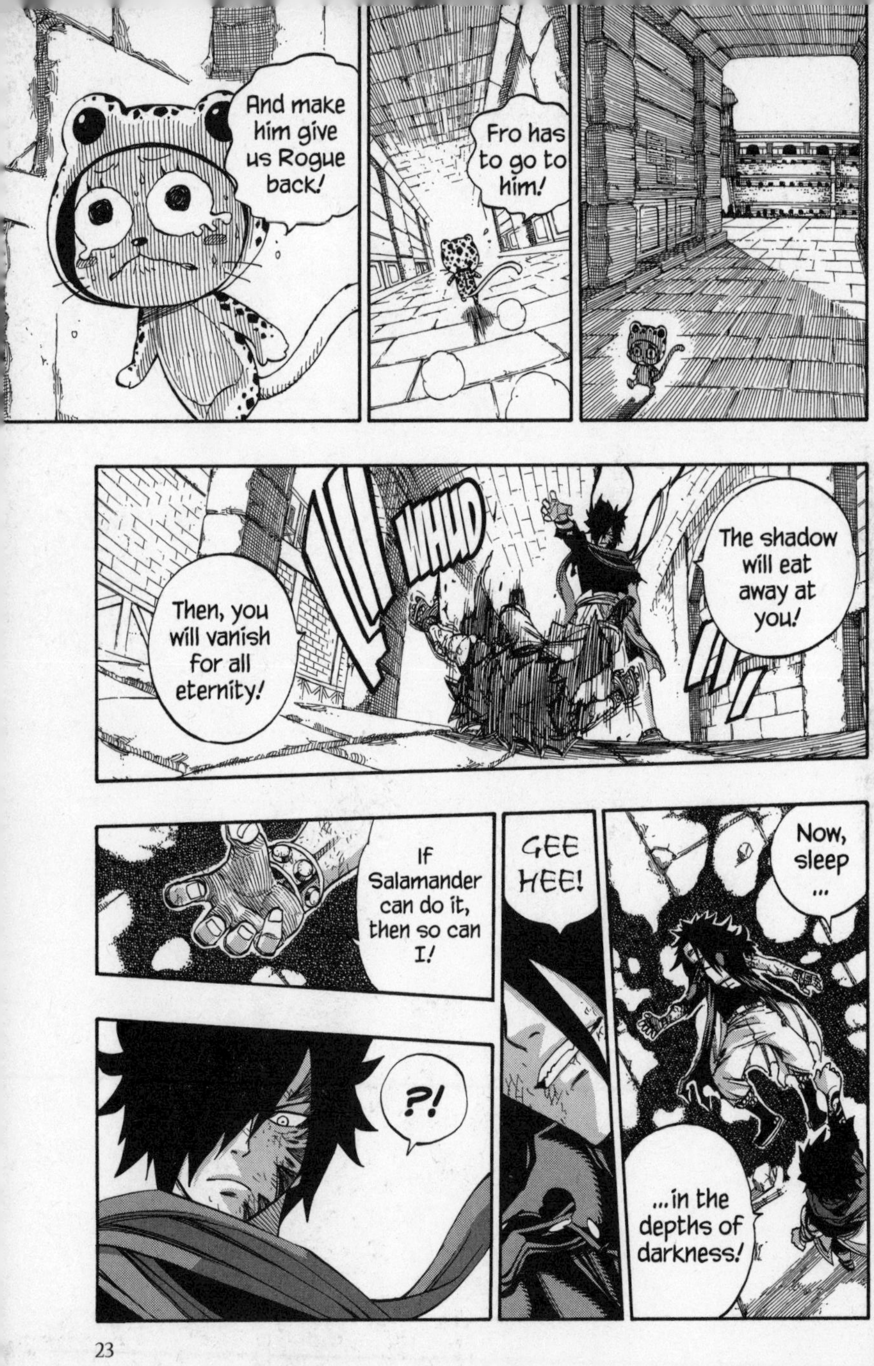
Fro has to go to him!
And make him give us Rogue back!
The shadow will eat away at you!
WHUD
Then, you will vanish for all eternity!
Now, sleep ...
...in the depths of darkness!
GEE HEE!
If Salamander can do it, then so can I!
?!

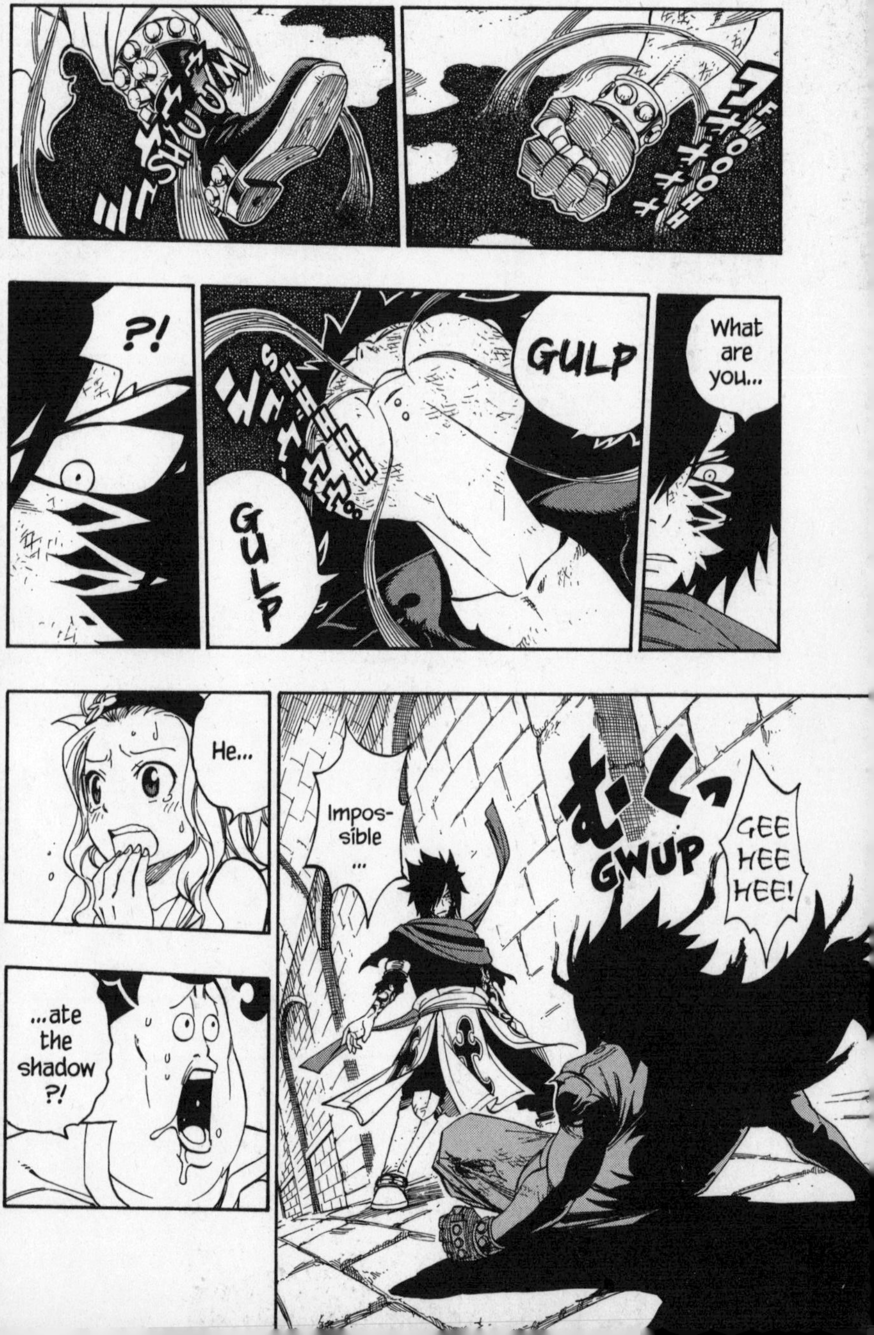

FWOOOOOSH
SHOOM
What are you...
GULP
SHHHHH
GULP
?!
GEE HEE HEE!
GWUP
Impos-sible...
He...
...ate the shadow?!

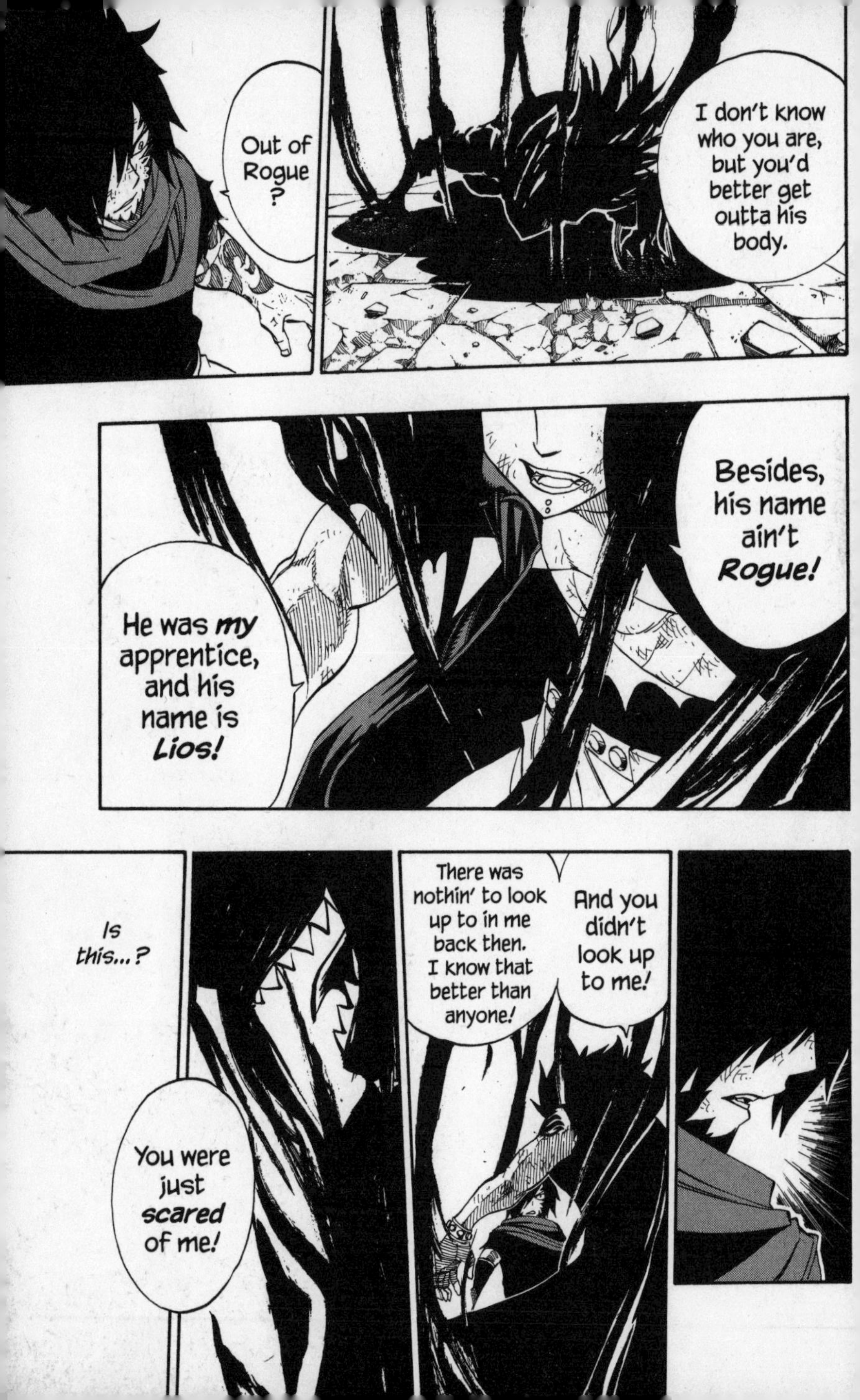
I don't know who you are, but you'd better get outta his body.
Out of Rogue?
Besides, his name ain't ***Rogue!***
He was ***my*** apprentice, and his name is ***Lios!***
And you didn't look up to me!
There was nothin' to look up to in me back then. I know that better than anyone!
You were just ***scared*** of me!
Is this...?

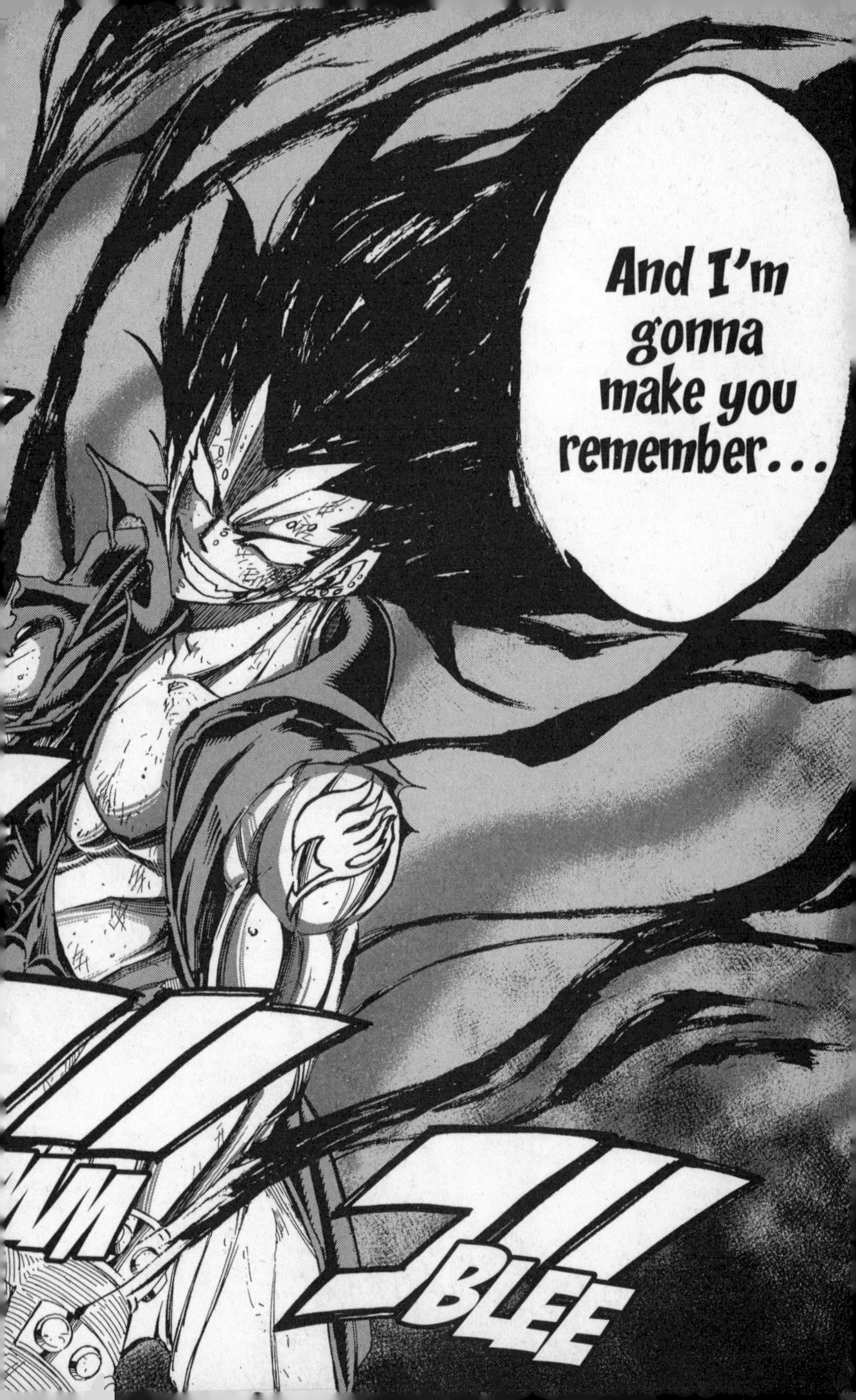
And I'm gonna make you remember...
BLEE

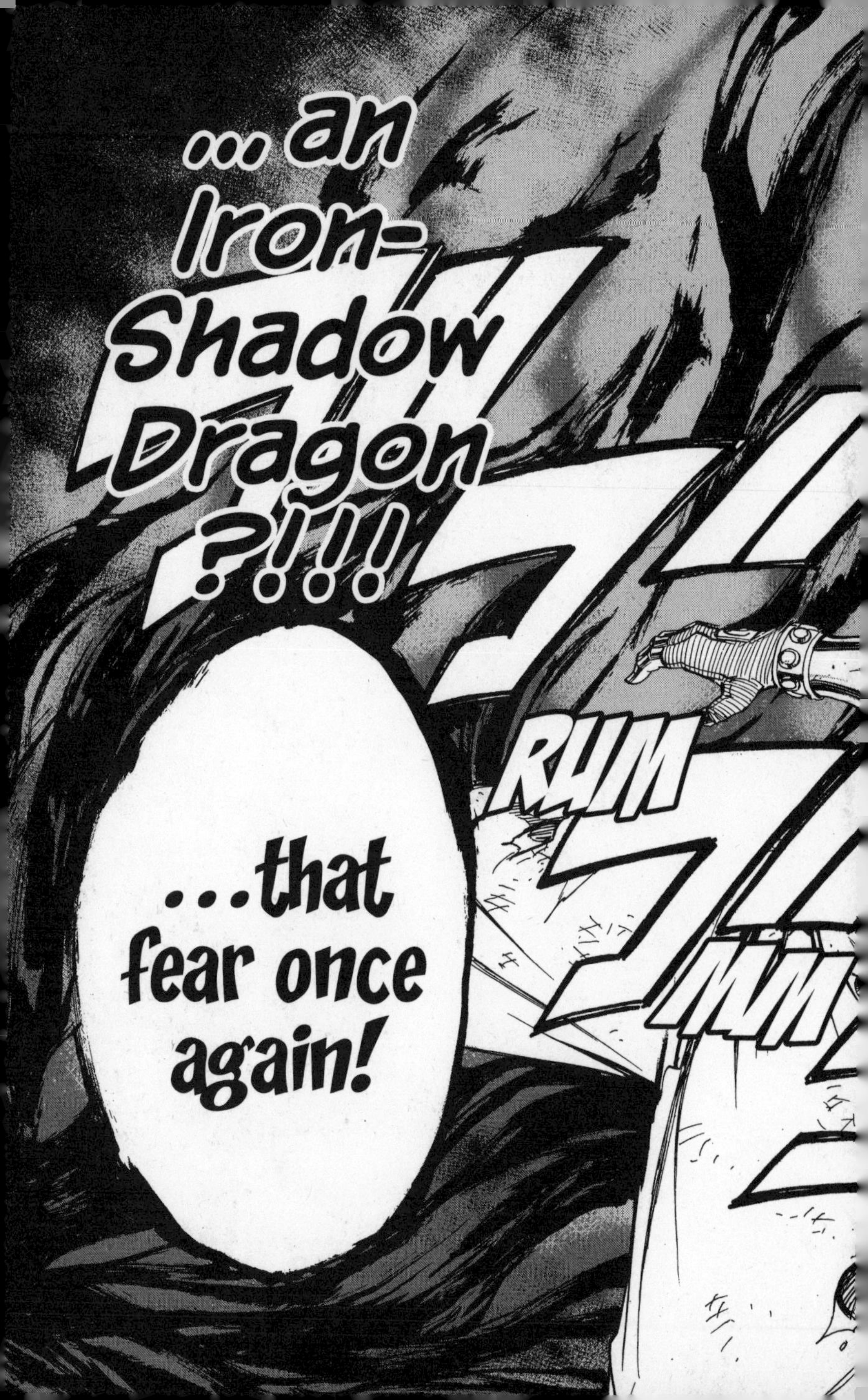
...an Iron-Shadow Dragon?!!!
...that fear once again!
RUM
MM

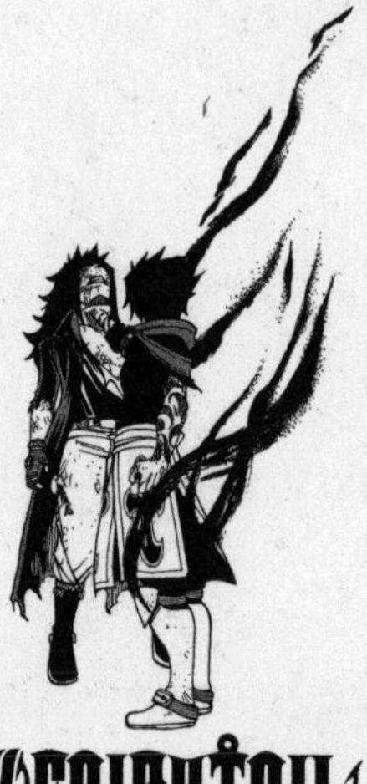

FAIRY TAIL

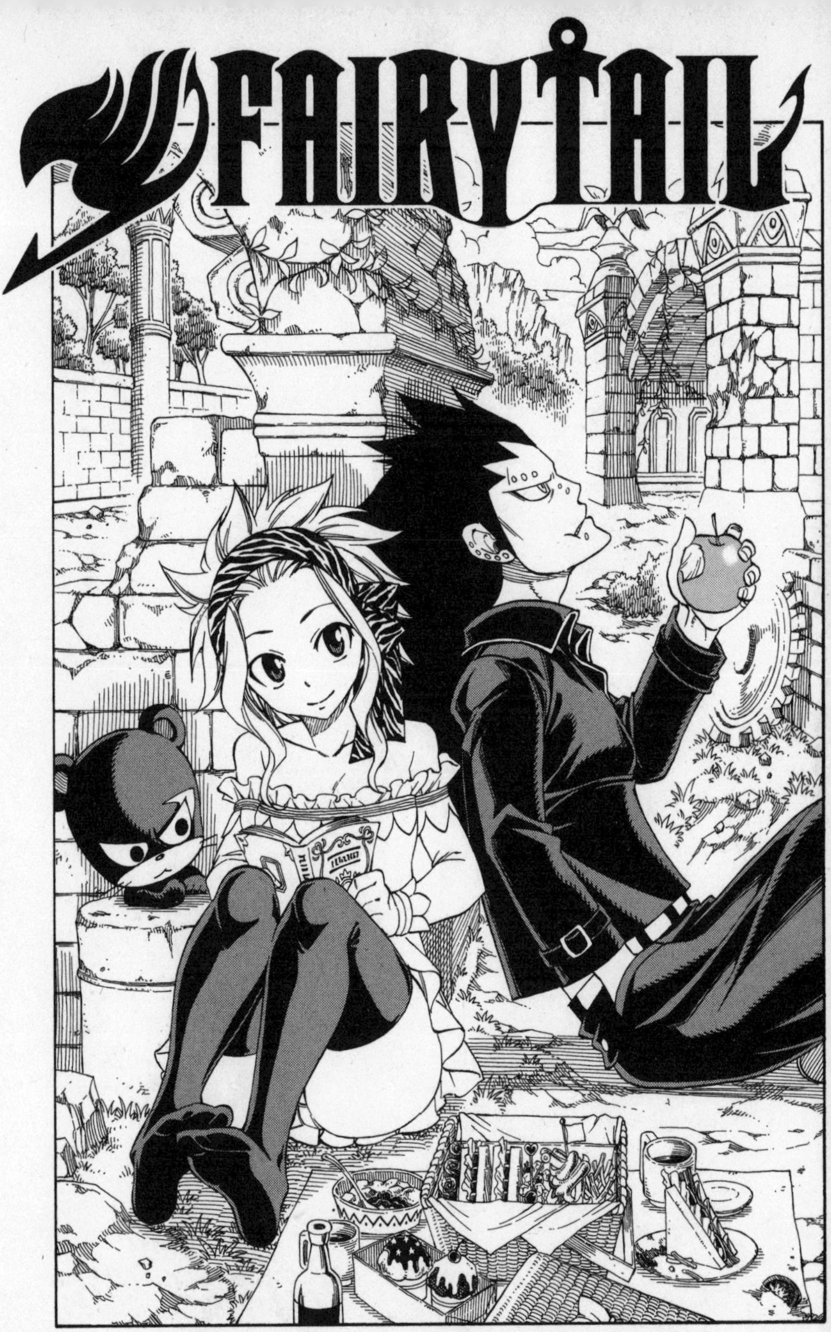
FAIRY TAIL

Chapter 319: White Knight

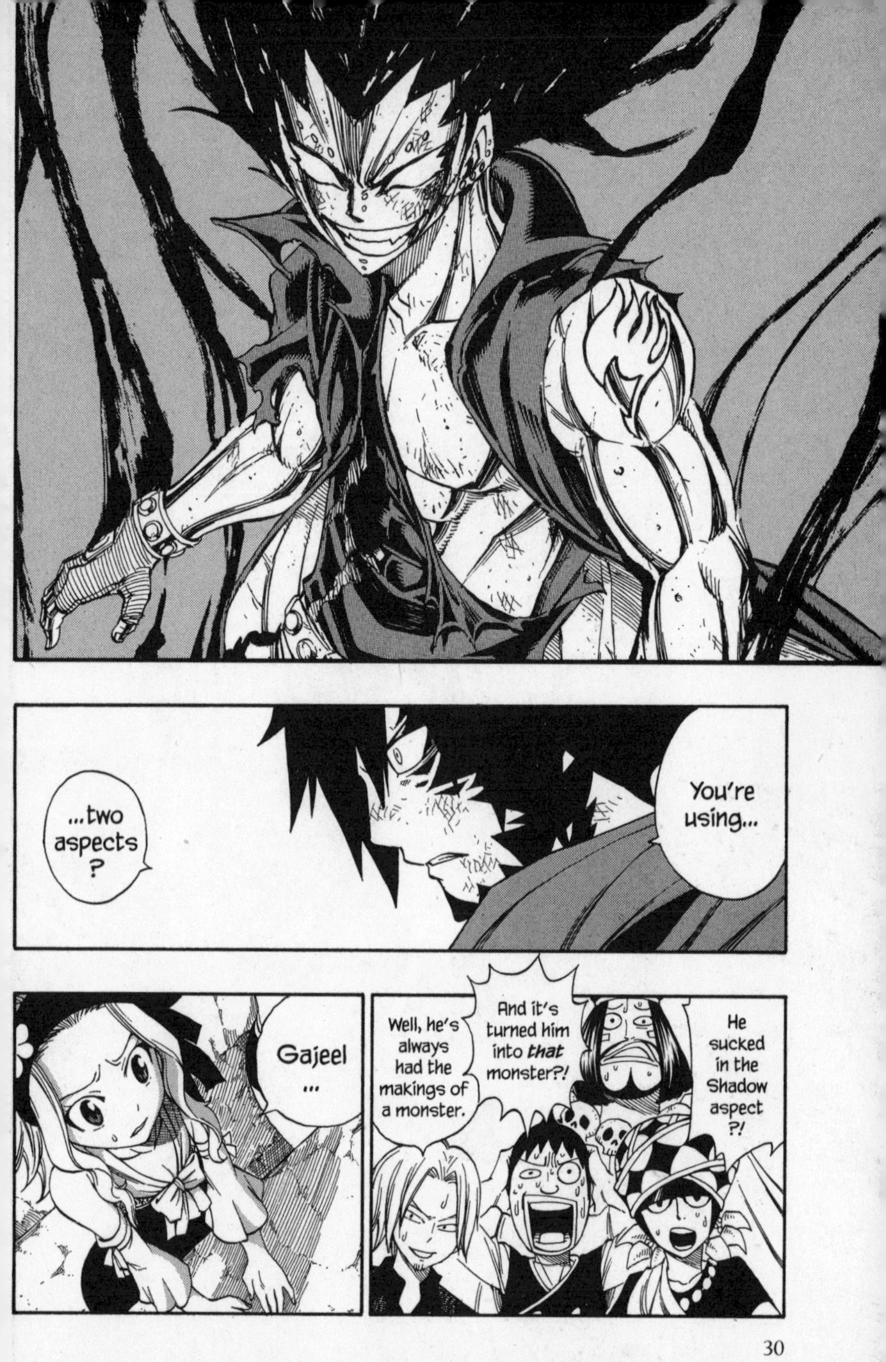
You're using...
...two aspects?
He sucked in the Shadow aspect?!
And it's turned him into *that* monster?!
Well, he's always had the makings of a monster.
Gajeel ...

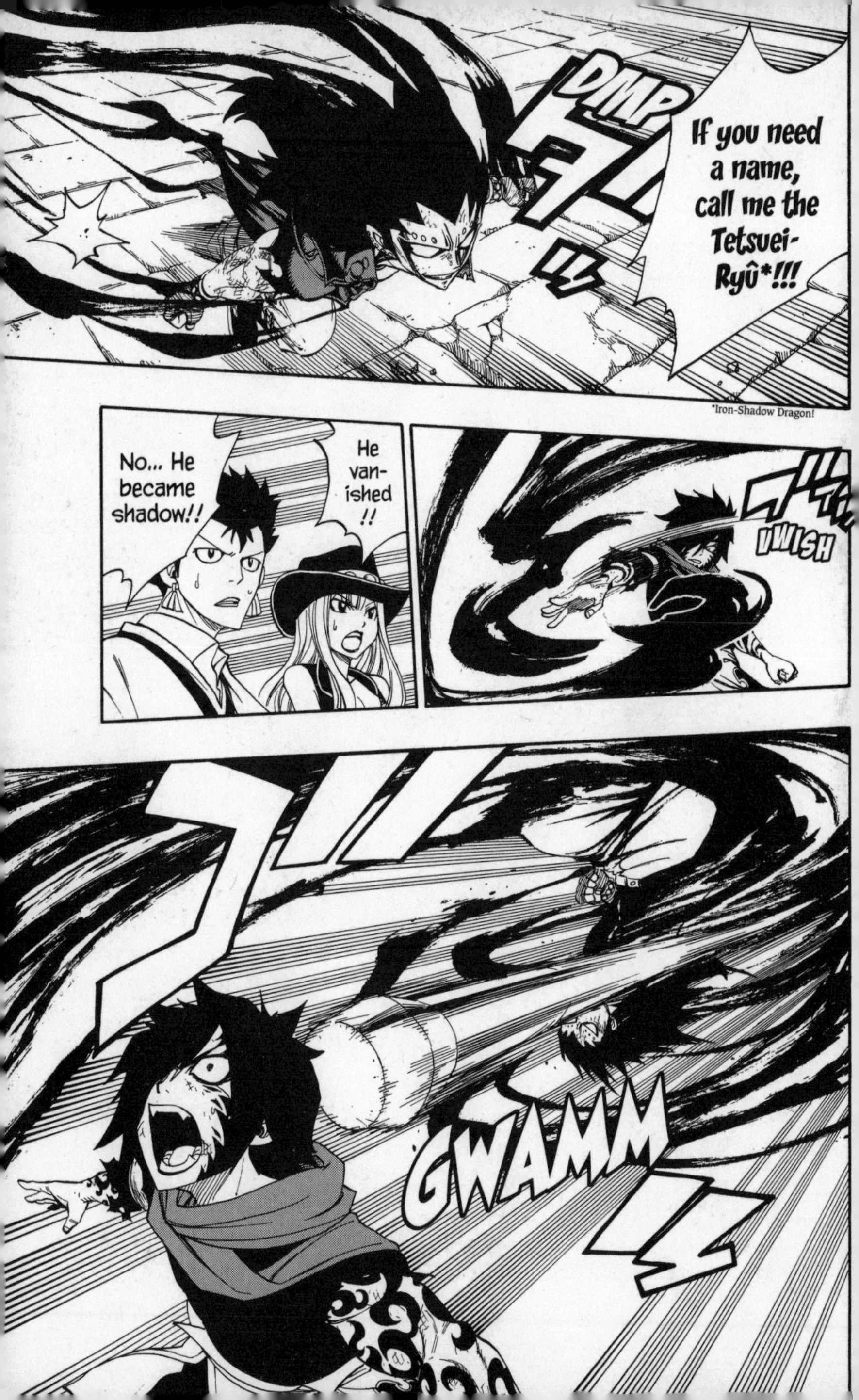
DMP
If you need a name, call me the Tetsuei-Ryû*!!!
VWISH
He van-ished!!
No... He became shadow!!
GWAMM
*Iron-Shadow Dragon!

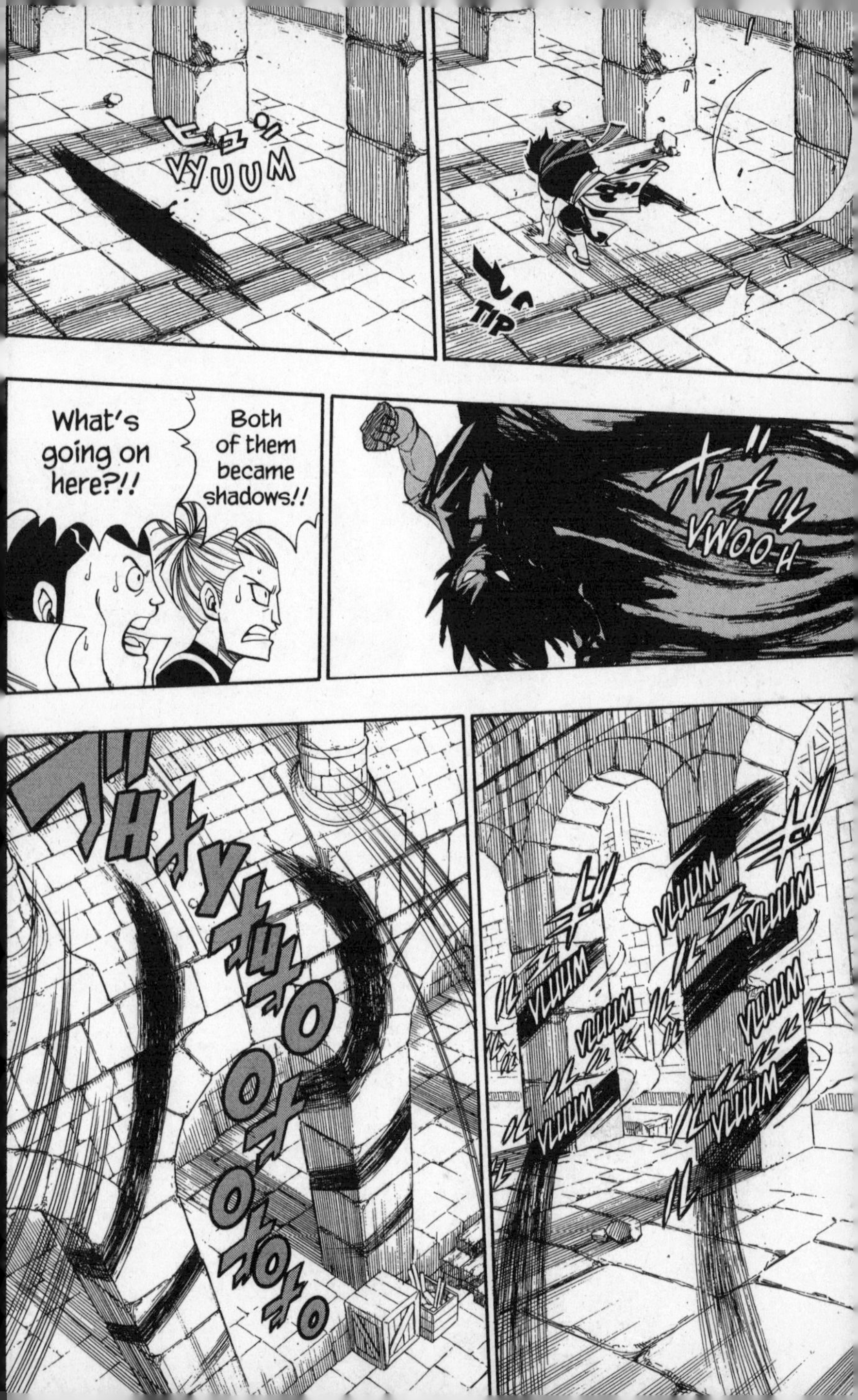
TIP
VYUUM
VWOOH
Both of them became shadows!!
What's going on here?!!
VLUUM
VLUUM
VLUUM
VLUUM
VLUUM
VLUUM
VLUUM
VLUUM

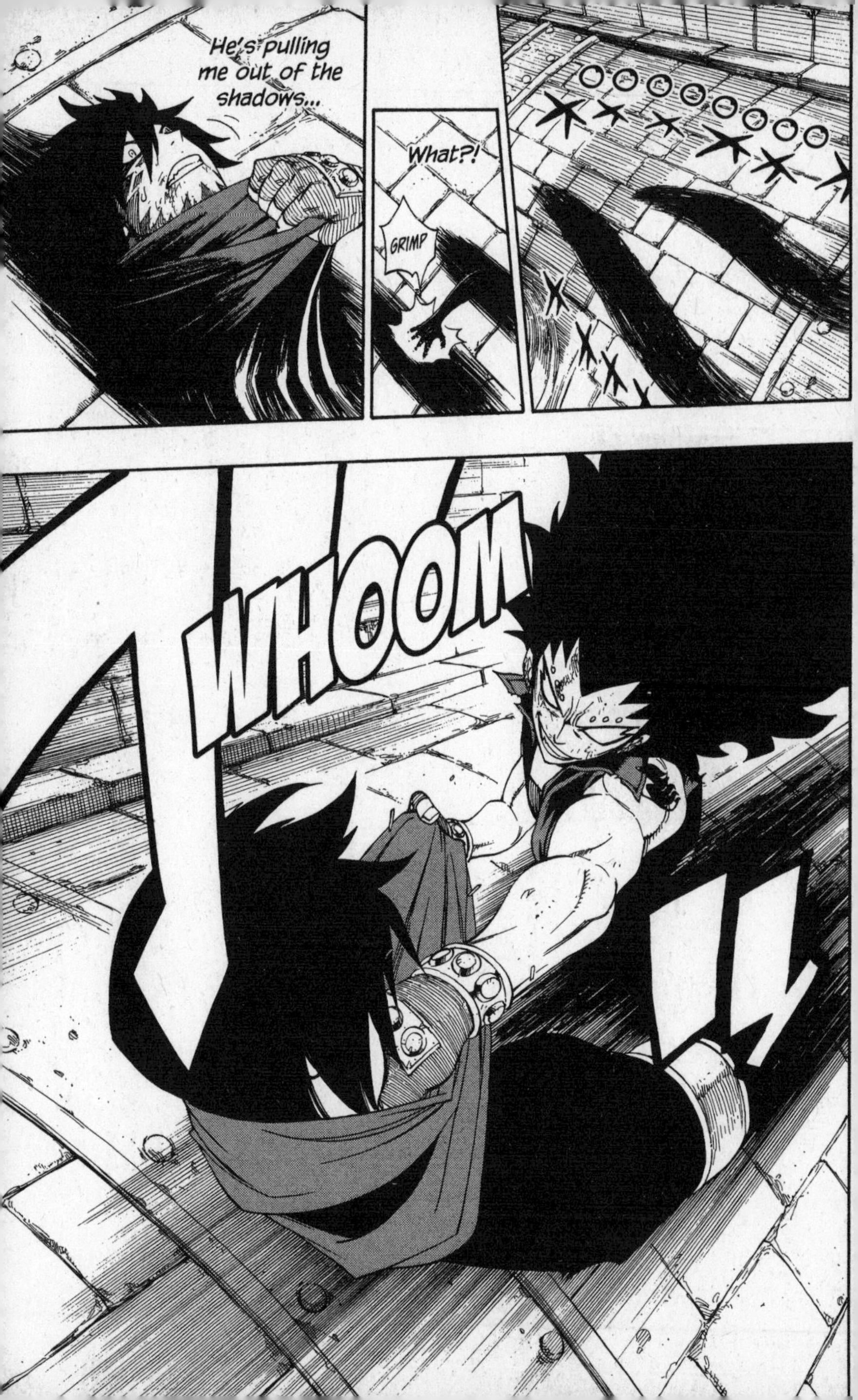

What?!
GRIMP
He's pulling me out of the shadows...
WHOOM

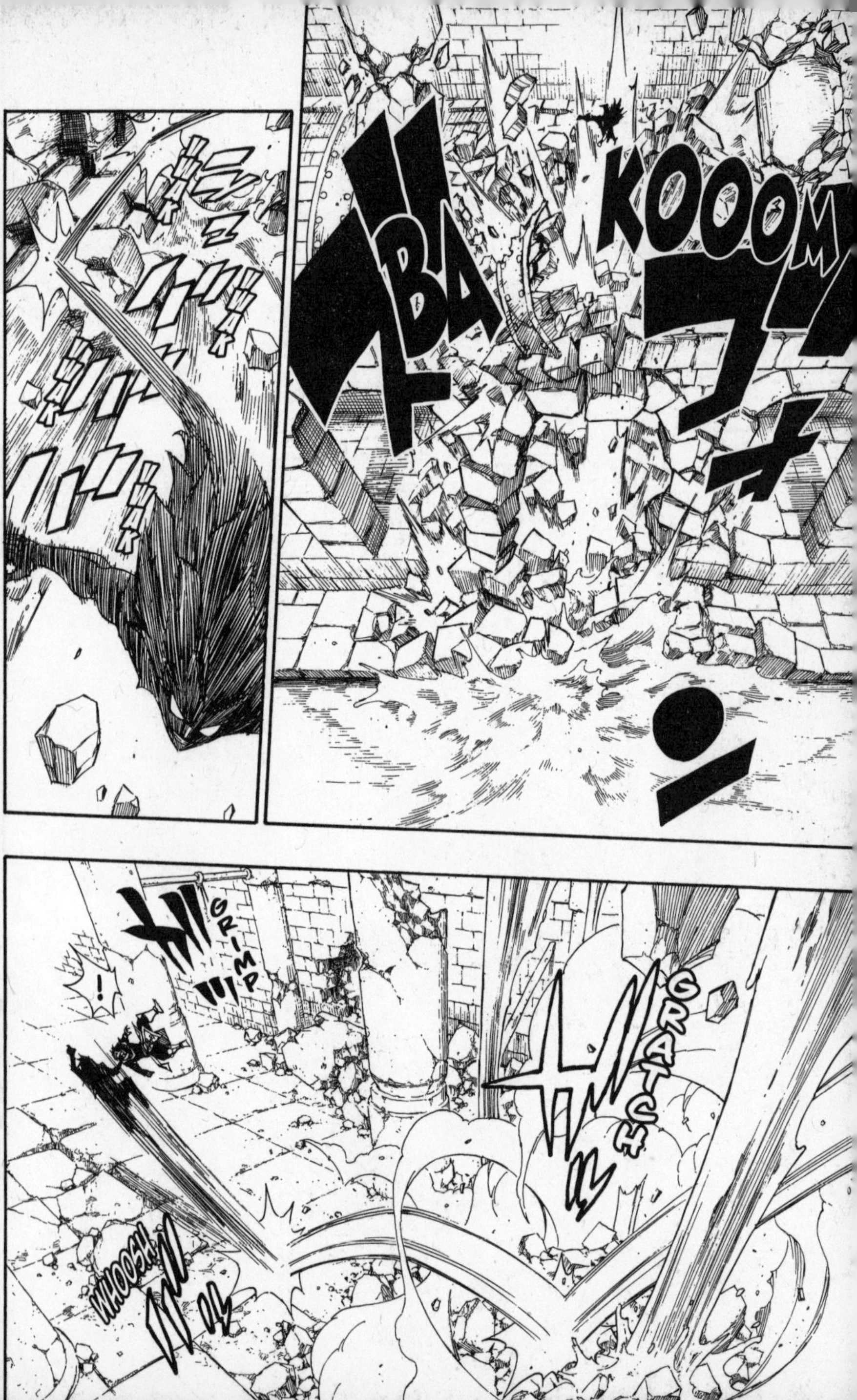

BA
KOOOM
KWAK
KWAK
KWAK
KWAK
GRATCH
GRIMP
!
WHOOSH

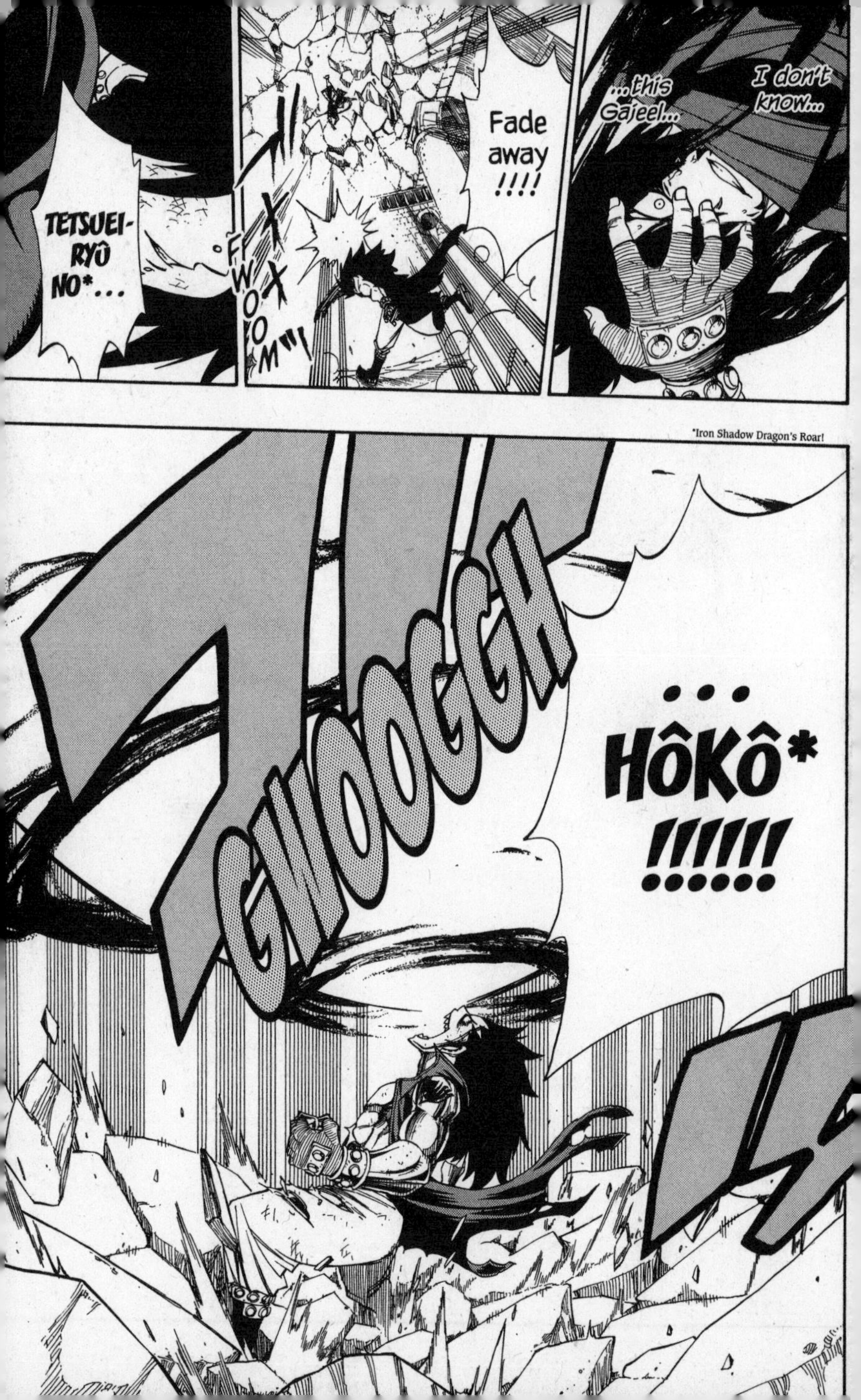
I don't know...
...this Gajeel...
Fade away!!!!
FWOOM
TETSUEI-RYÛ NO*...
GWOOGGH
...HÔKÔ* !!!!!!

*Iron Shadow Dragon's Roar!

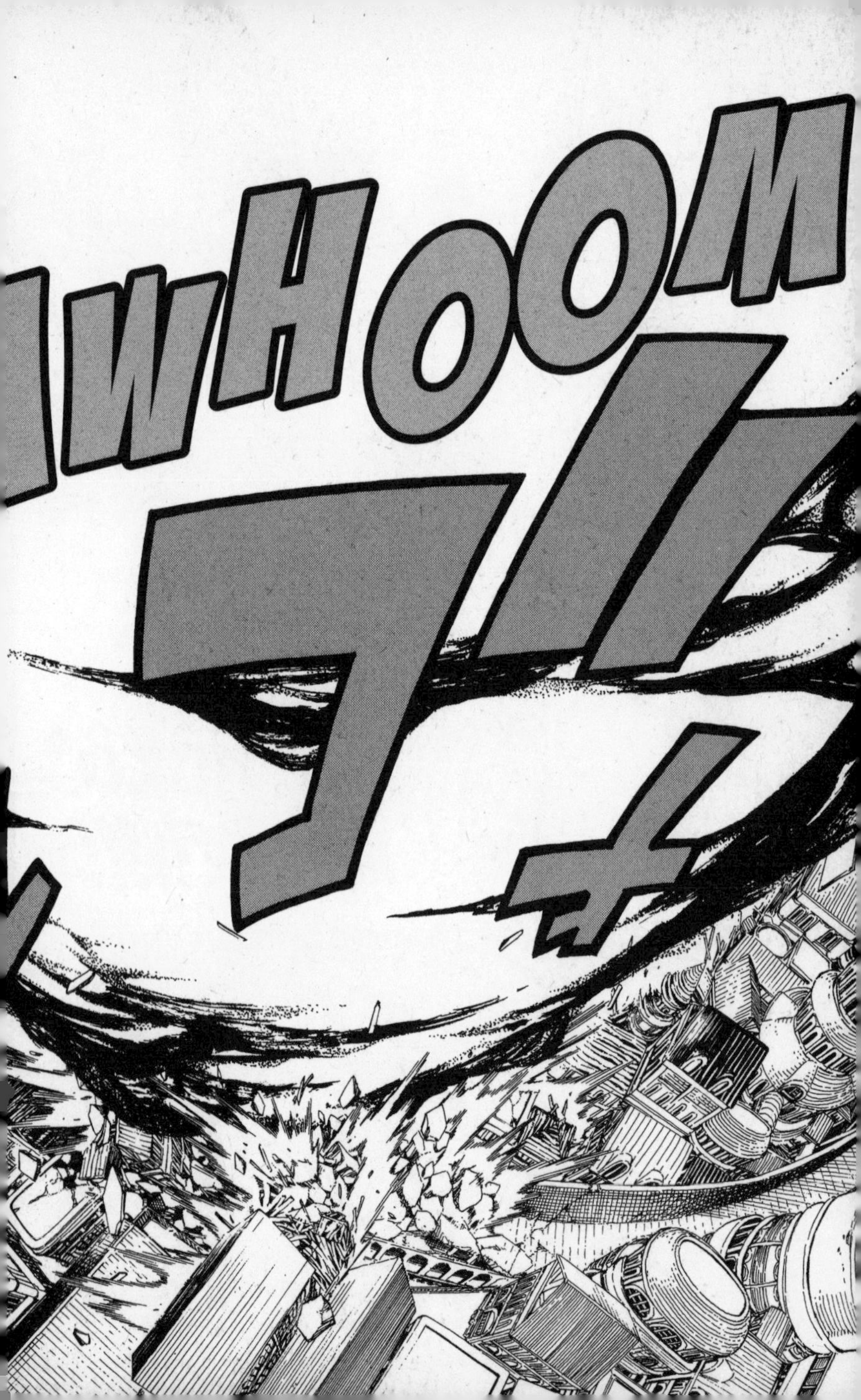
WHOOM

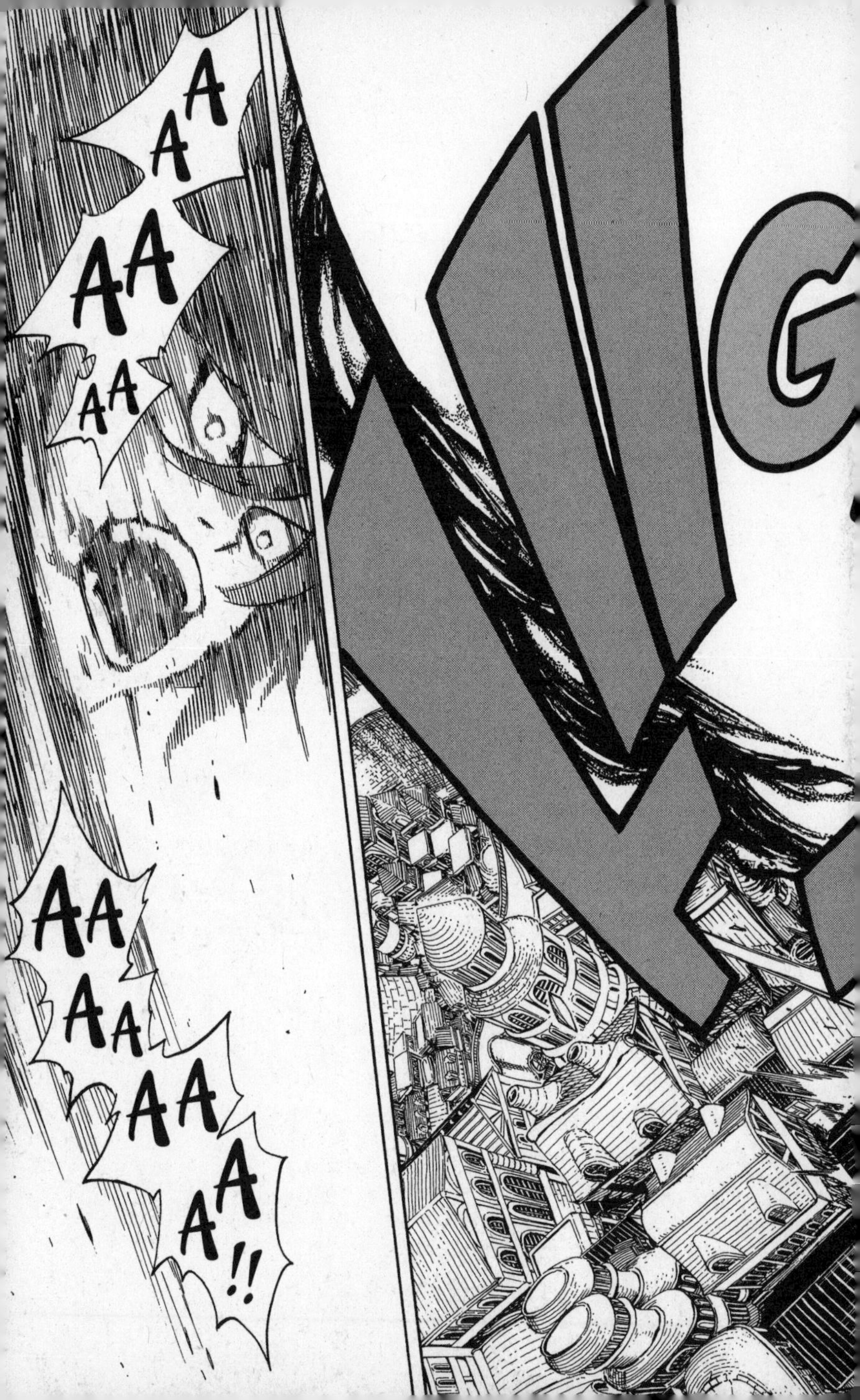
G
AAAAAA
AAAAAAAA!!

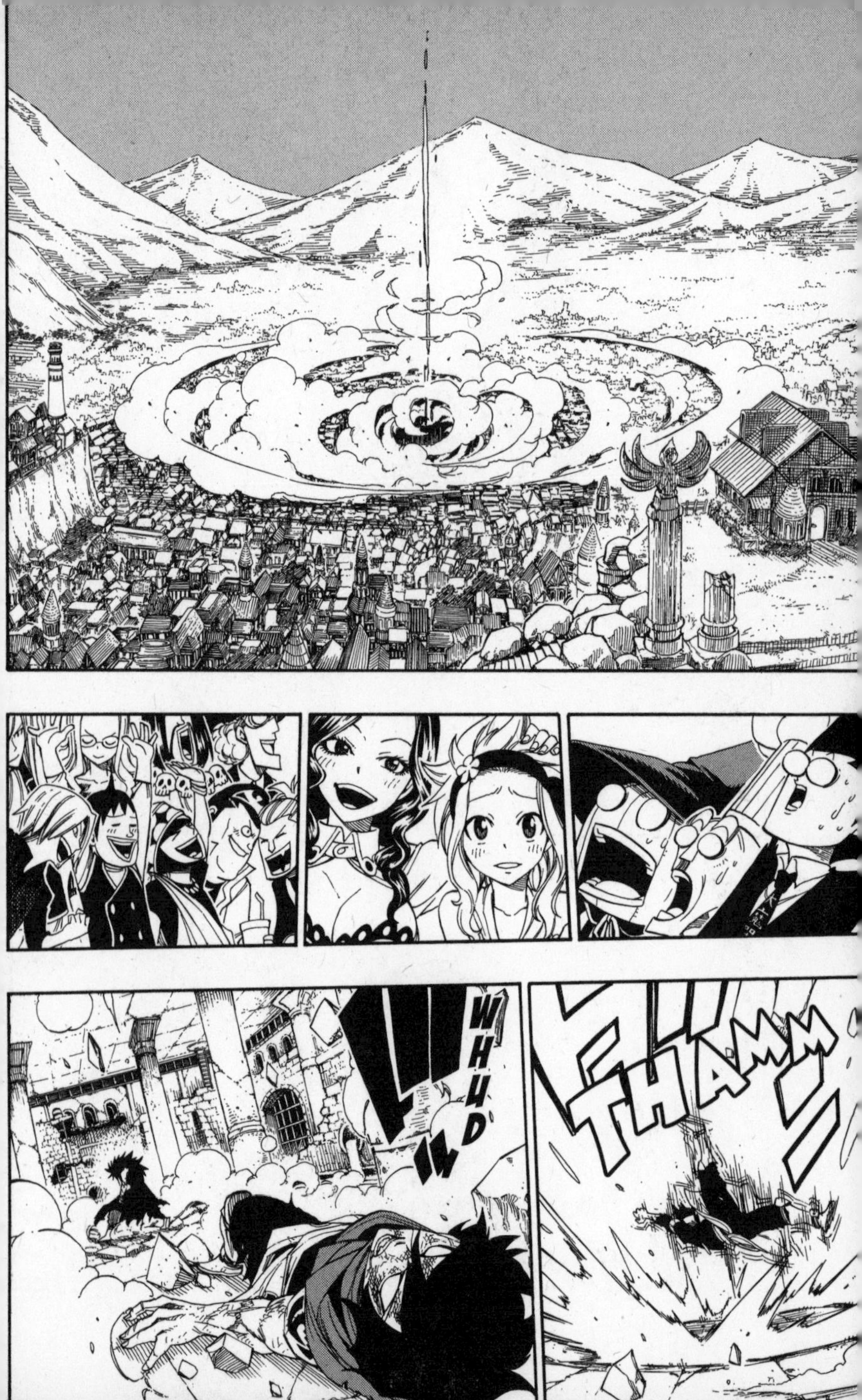
THAMM
WHUD

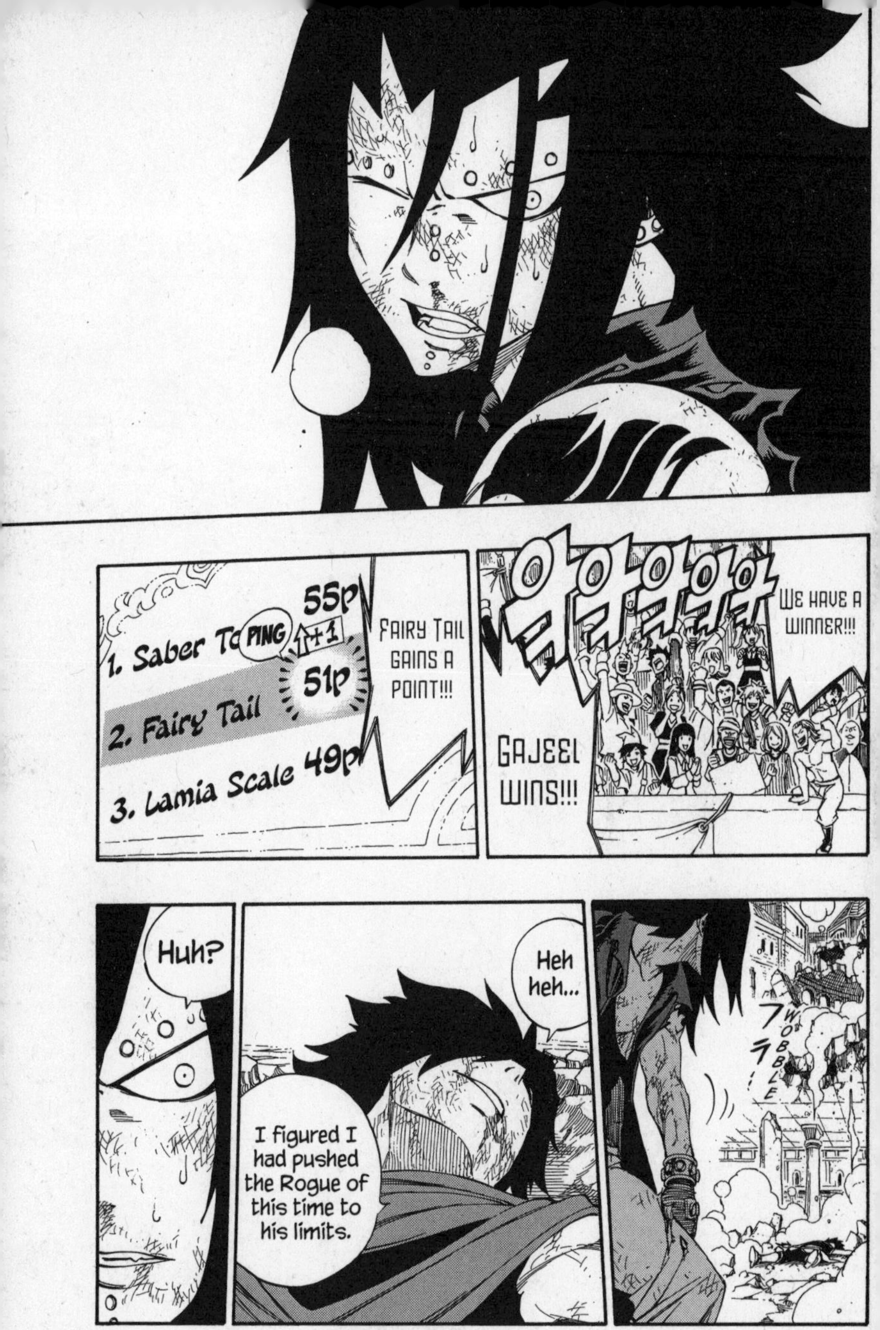
WE HAVE A WINNER!!!
GAJEEL WINS!!!
FAIRY TAIL GAINS A POINT!!!
1. Saber To
PING
55p
+1
2. Fairy Tail
51p
3. Lamia Scale 49p
WOBBLE
Heh heh...
I figured I had pushed the Rogue of this time to his limits.
Huh?

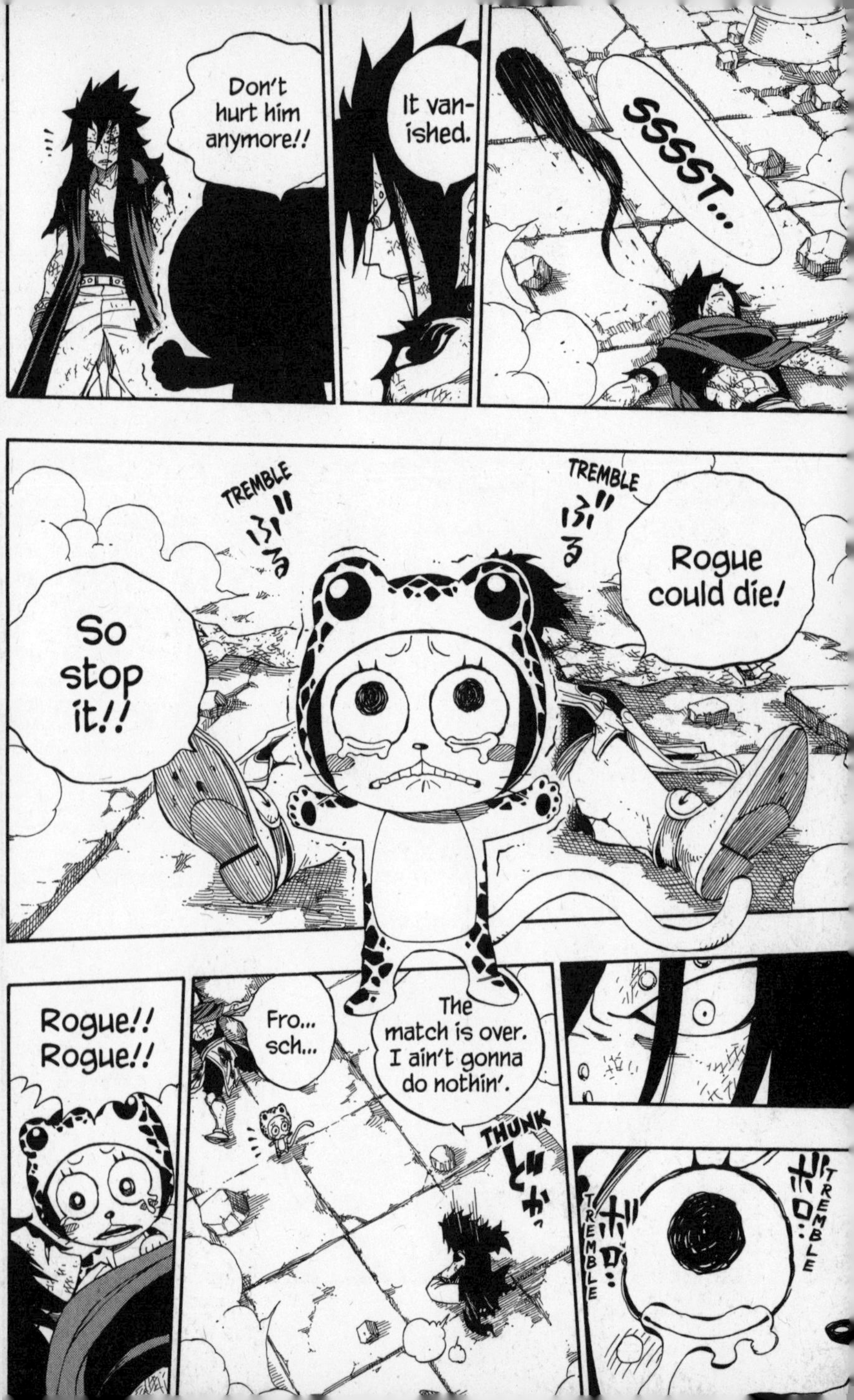
SSSST...
It van-ished.
Don't hurt him anymore!!
TREMBLE
ぶる
Rogue could die!
TREMBLE
ぶる
So stop it!!
TREMBLE
TREMBLE
The match is over. I ain't gonna do nothin'.
Fro... sch...
THUNK
Rogue!! Rogue!!

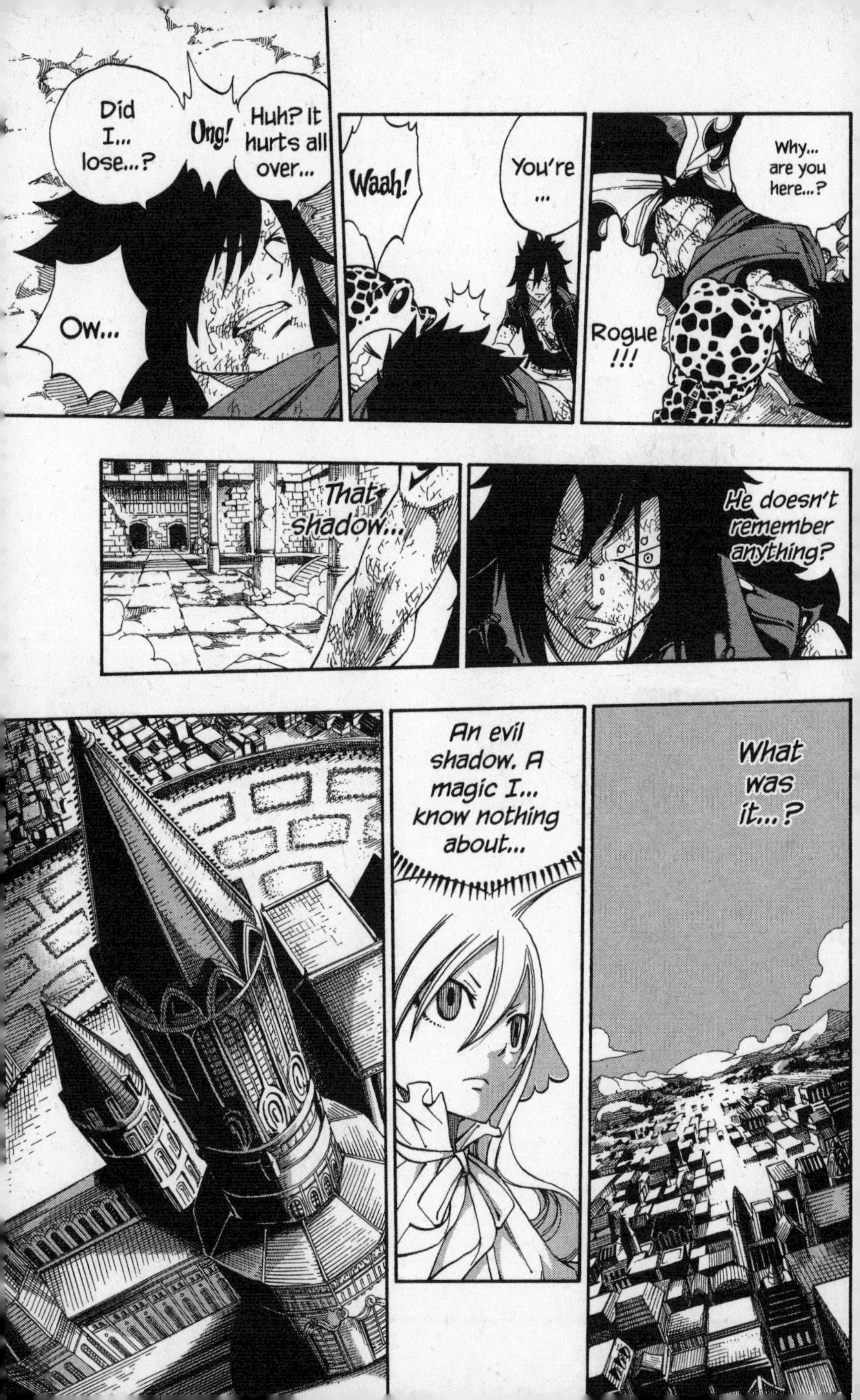
Why... are you here...?
Rogue !!!
You're ...
Waah!
Huh? It hurts all over...
Ung!
Did I... lose...?
Ow...
He doesn't remember anything?
That shadow...
What was it...?
An evil shadow. A magic I... know nothing about...

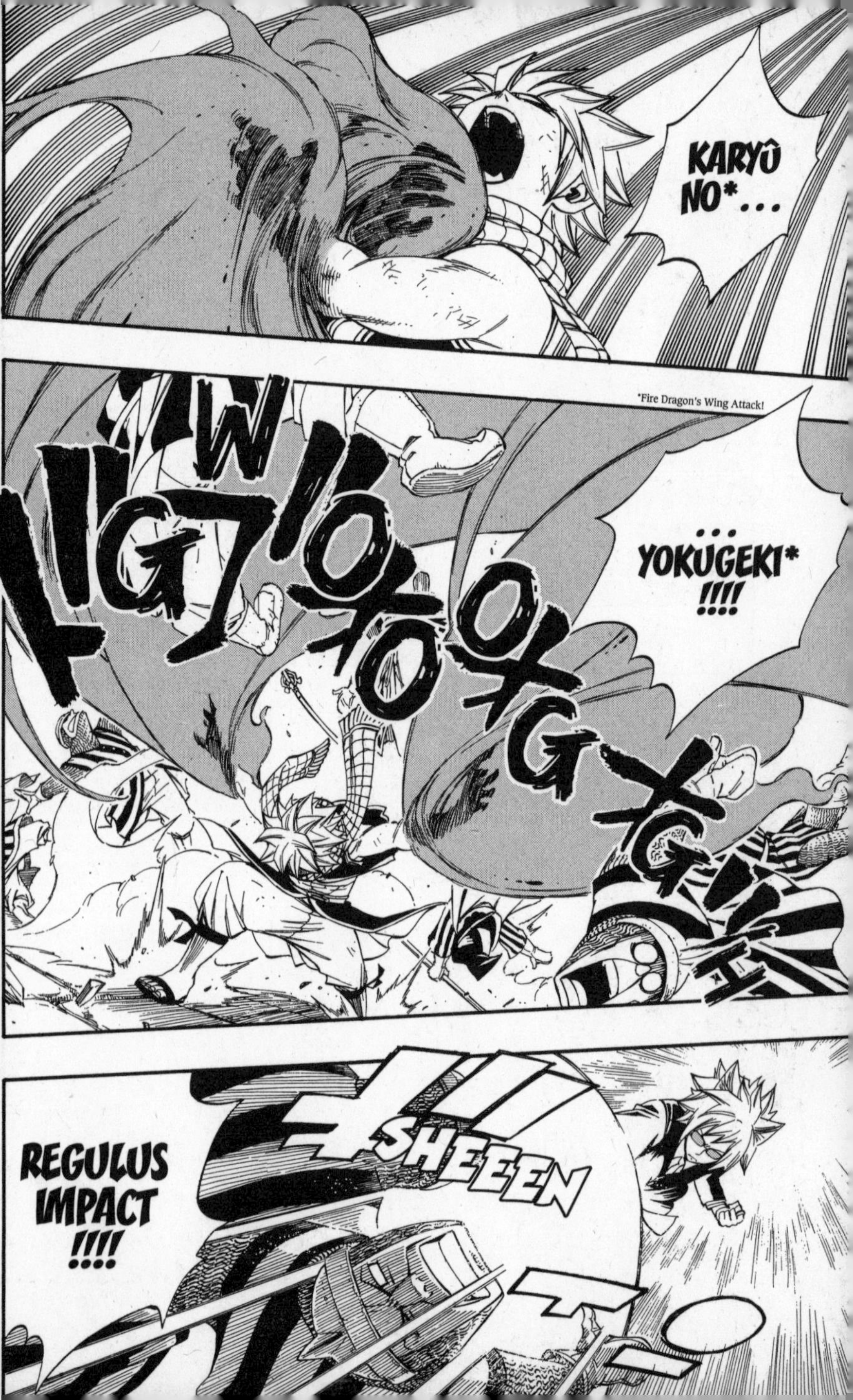

KARYÛ NO*...
...YOKUGEKI* !!!!
SHEEEN
REGULUS IMPACT !!!!

*Fire Dragon's Wing Attack!

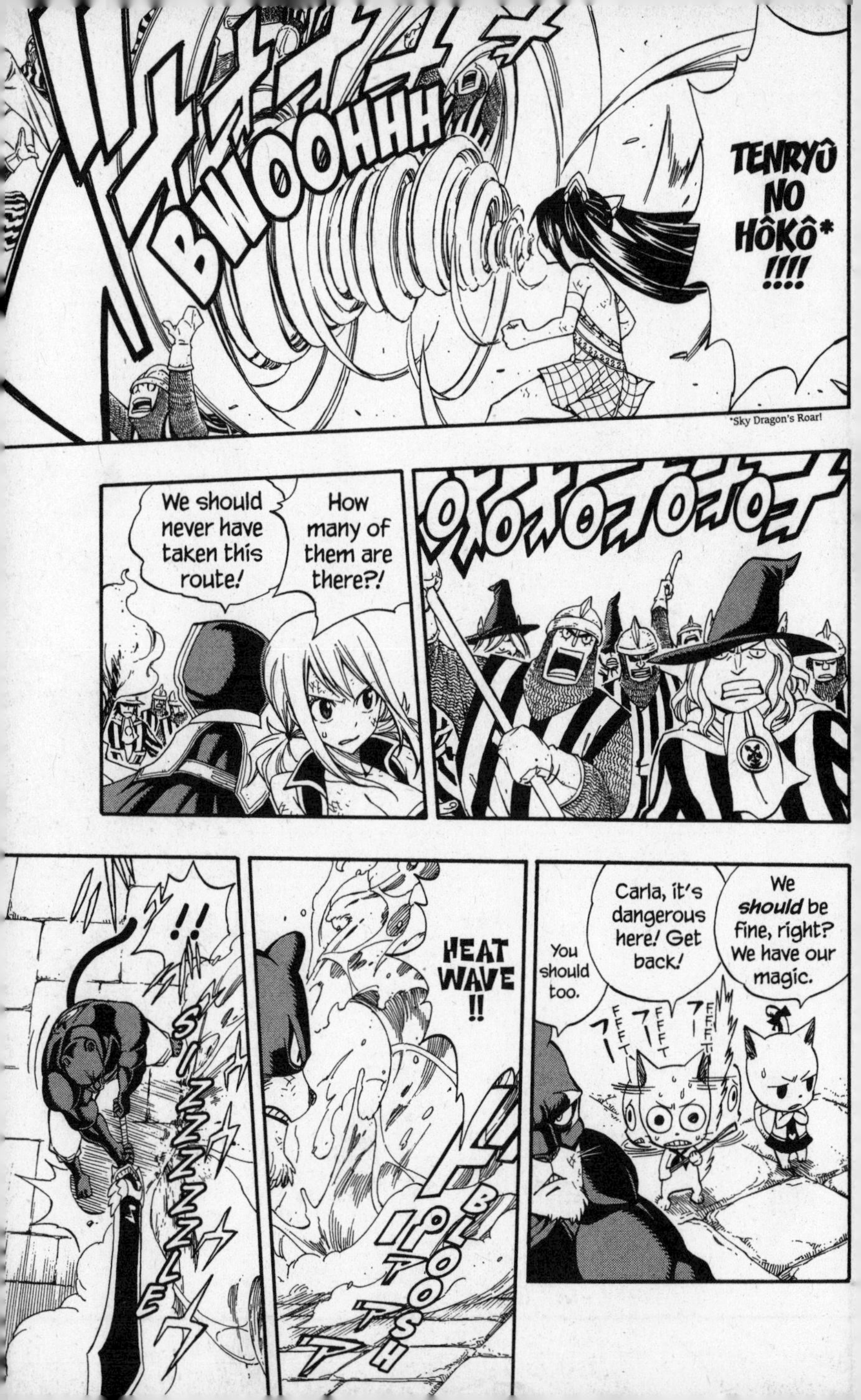
TENRYÛ NO HÔKÔ* !!!!
BWOOHHH
How many of them are there?!
We should never have taken this route!
We *should* be fine, right? We have our magic.
Carla, it's dangerous here! Get back!
You should too.
FFFT
FFFT
FFFT
HEAT WAVE !!
BLOOOSH
!!
SIZZZZZZLE
*Sky Dragon's Roar!

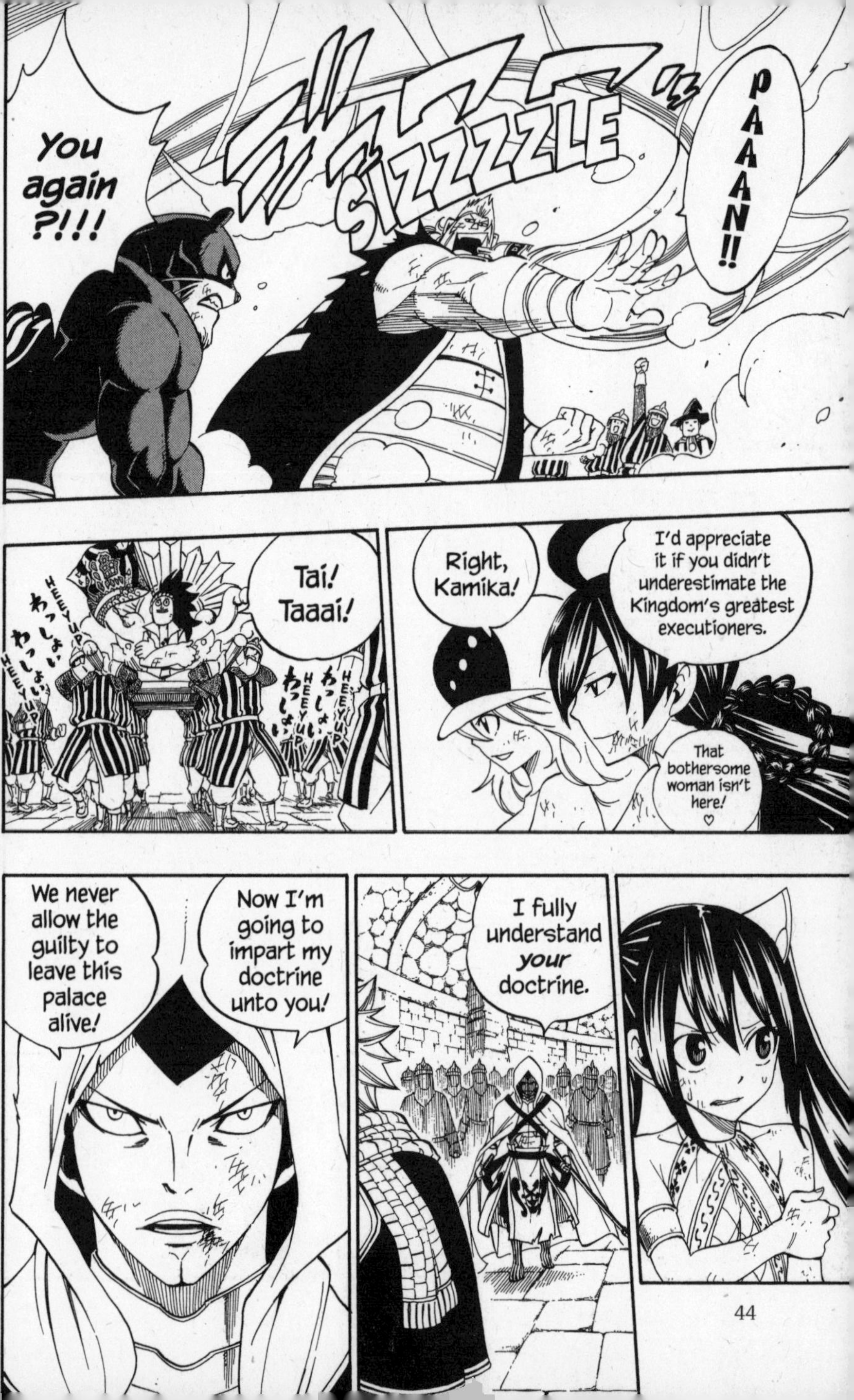
PAAAAN!!
SIZZZZLE
You again?!!!
I'd appreciate it if you didn't underestimate the Kingdom's greatest executioners.
Right, Kamika!
That bothersome woman isn't here! ♡
Tai! Taaai!
わっしょい HEEYUP
わっしょい HEEYUP
わっしょい HEEYUP
わっしょい HEEYUP
I fully understand *your* doctrine.
Now I'm going to impart my doctrine unto you!
We never allow the guilty to leave this palace alive!

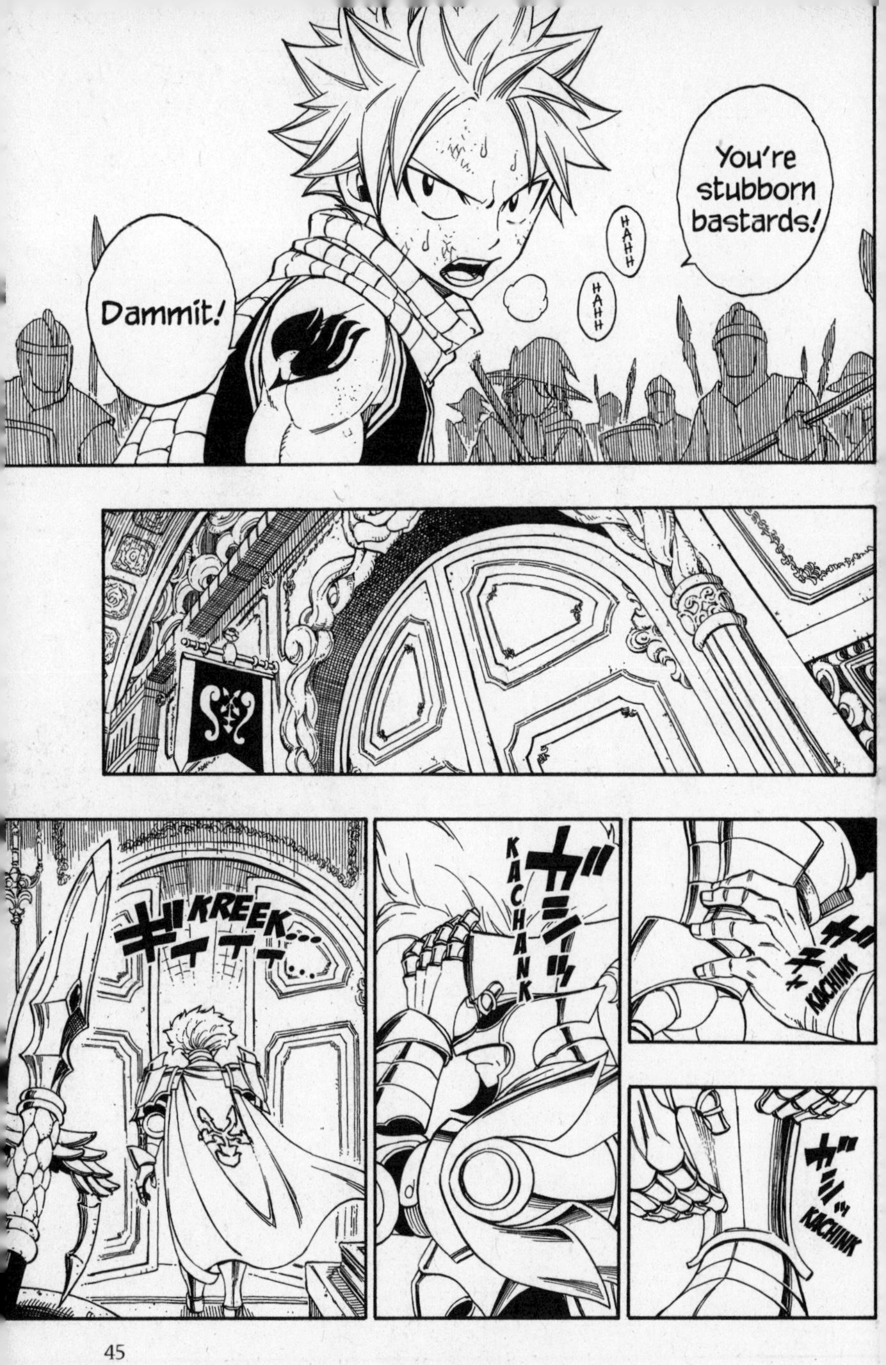
You're stubborn bastards!
HAHH
HAHH
Dammit!
KACHINK
KACHINK
KACHANK
KREEEK...

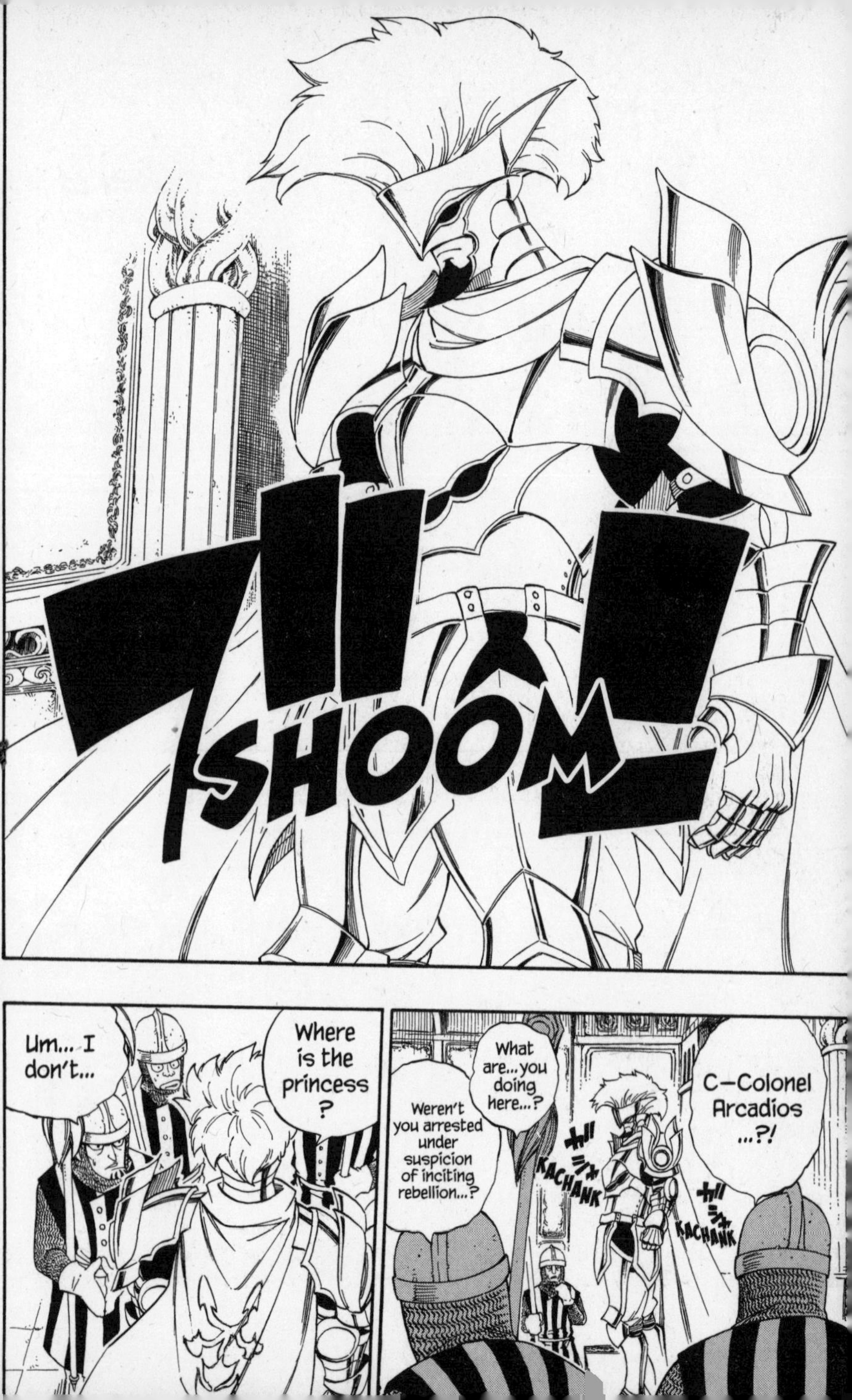
SHOOM
C-Colonel Arcadios ...?!
What are...you doing here...?
Weren't you arrested under suspicion of inciting rebellion...?
KACHANK
KACHANK
Where is the princess?
Um... I don't...

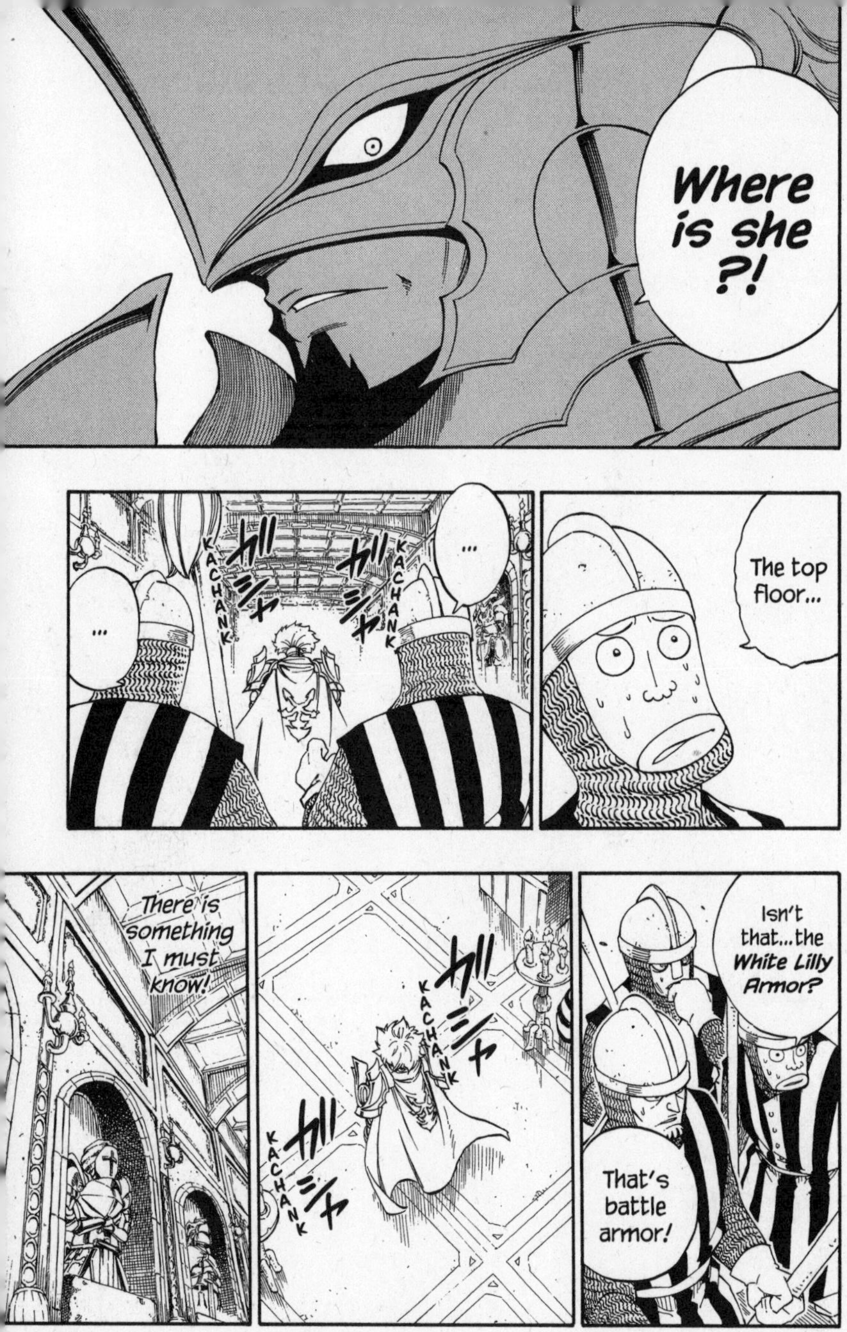
Where is she ?!
The top floor...
...
KACHANK
KACHANK
...
Isn't that...the White Lilly Armor?
That's battle armor!
KACHANK
KACHANK
There is something I must know!

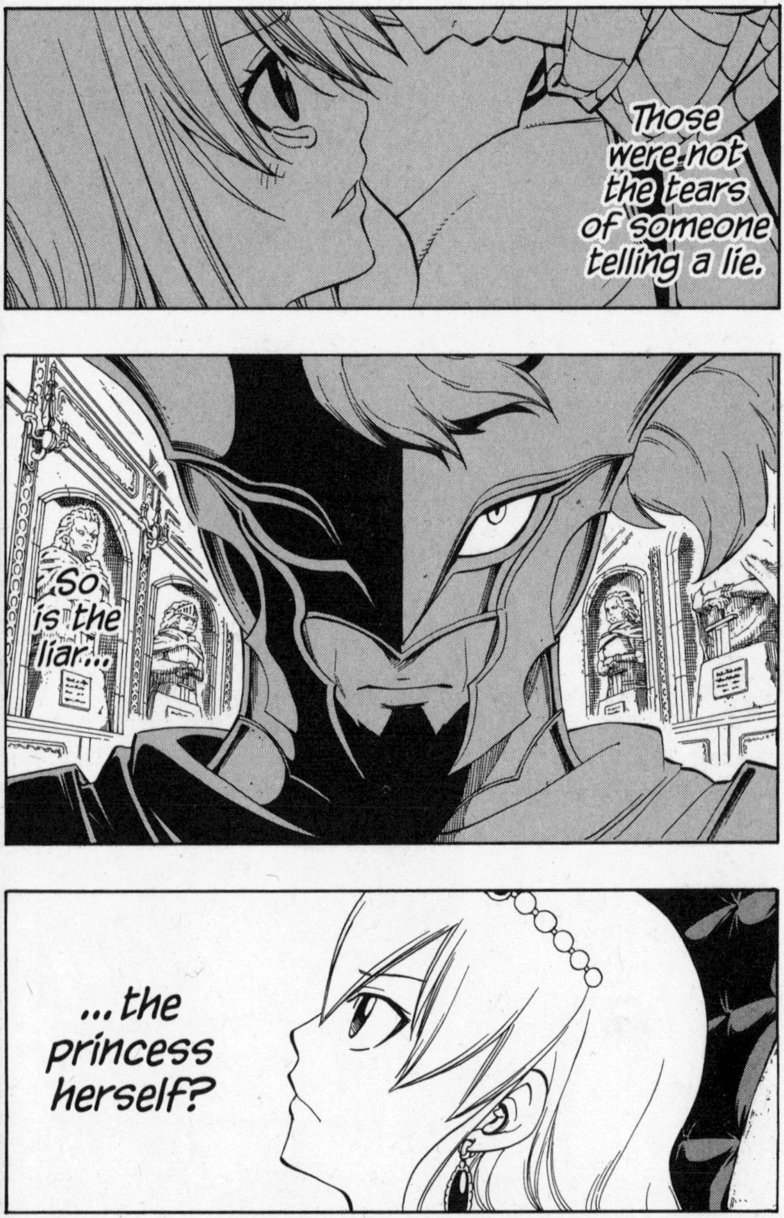
Those were not the tears of someone telling a lie.
So is the liar...
...the princess herself?

FAIRY TAIL

フェアリーテイル

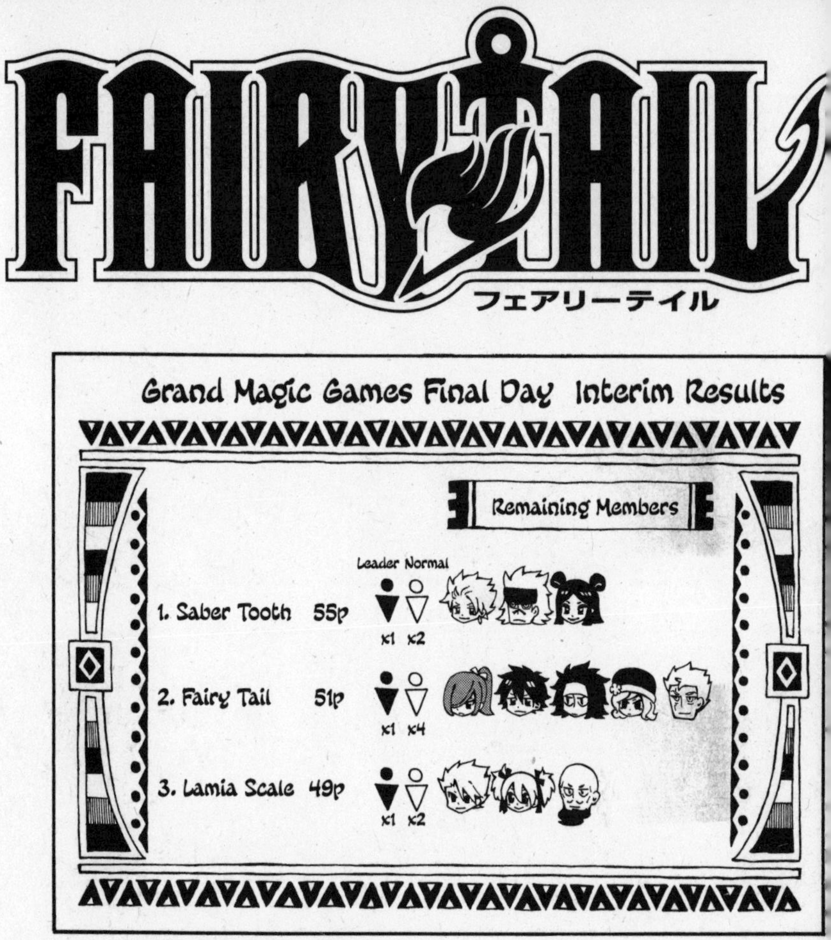
Grand Magic Games Final Day Interim Results
Remaining Members
Leader Normal
1. Saber Tooth 55p
x1 x2
2. Fairy Tail 51p
x1 x4
3. Lamia Scale 49p
x1 x2

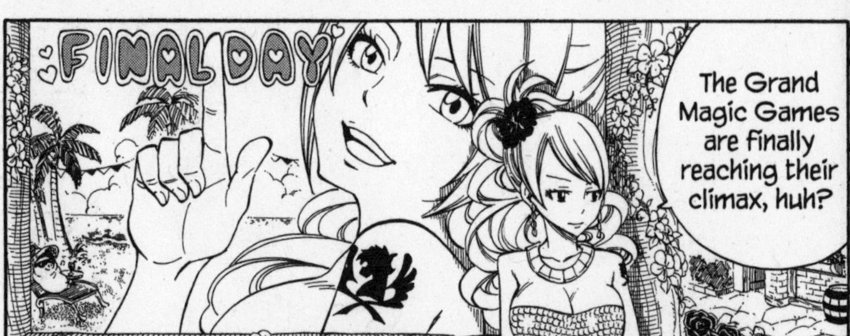
FINAL DAY
The Grand Magic Games are finally reaching their climax, huh?

Chapter 320: Attacking Lightning

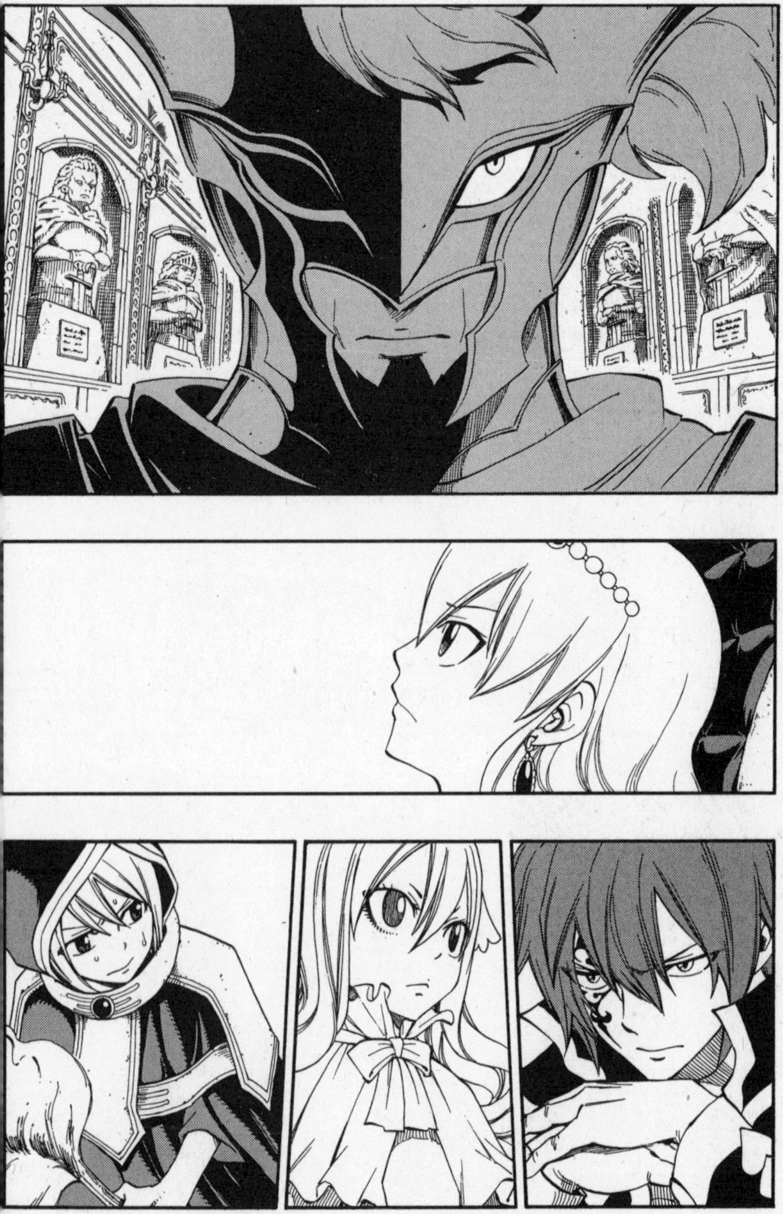

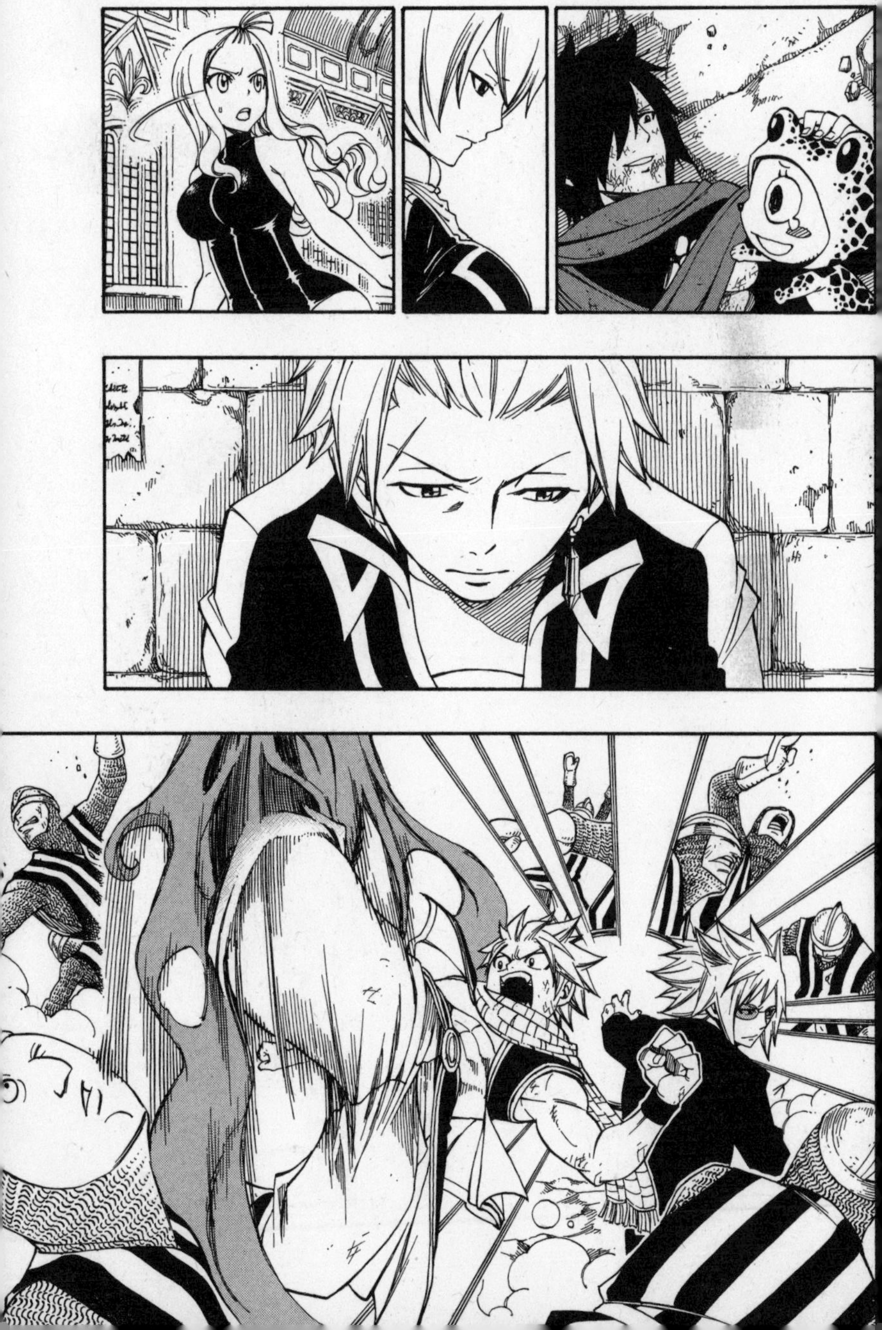

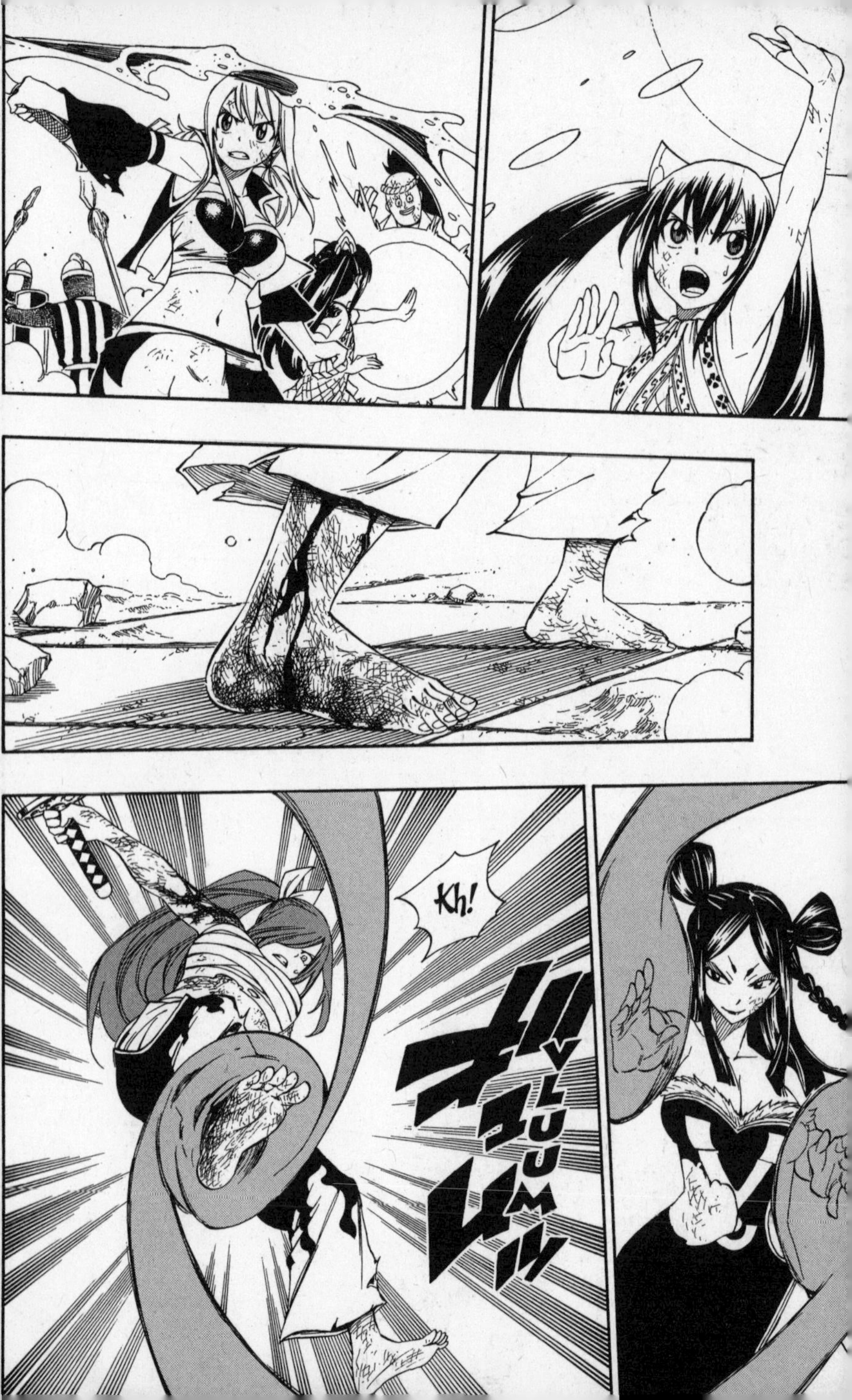
Kh!
VWUUMM!!

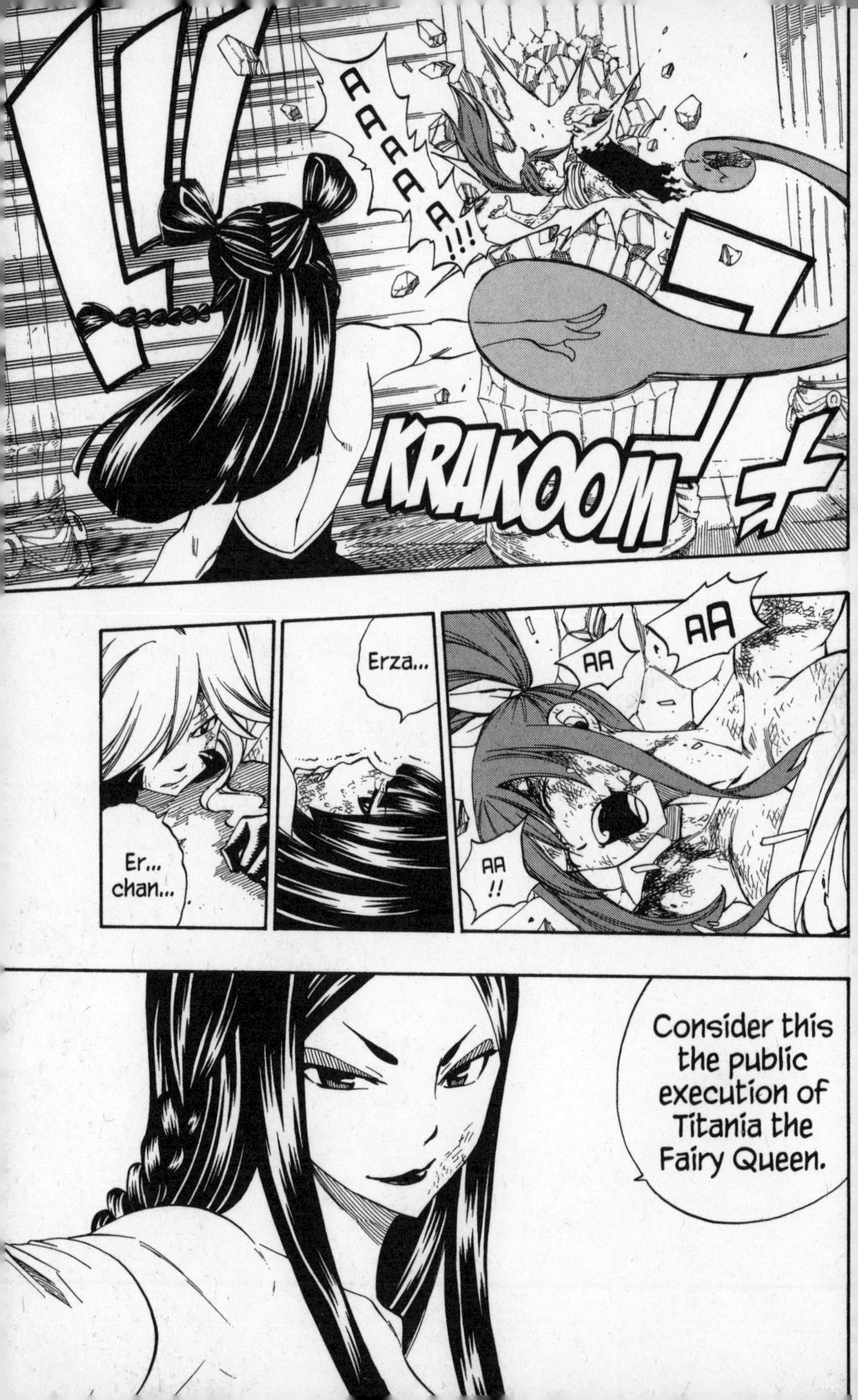
AAAAA!!!
KRAKOOM
AA
AA
AA!!
Erza...
Er... chan...
Consider this the public execution of Titania the Fairy Queen.

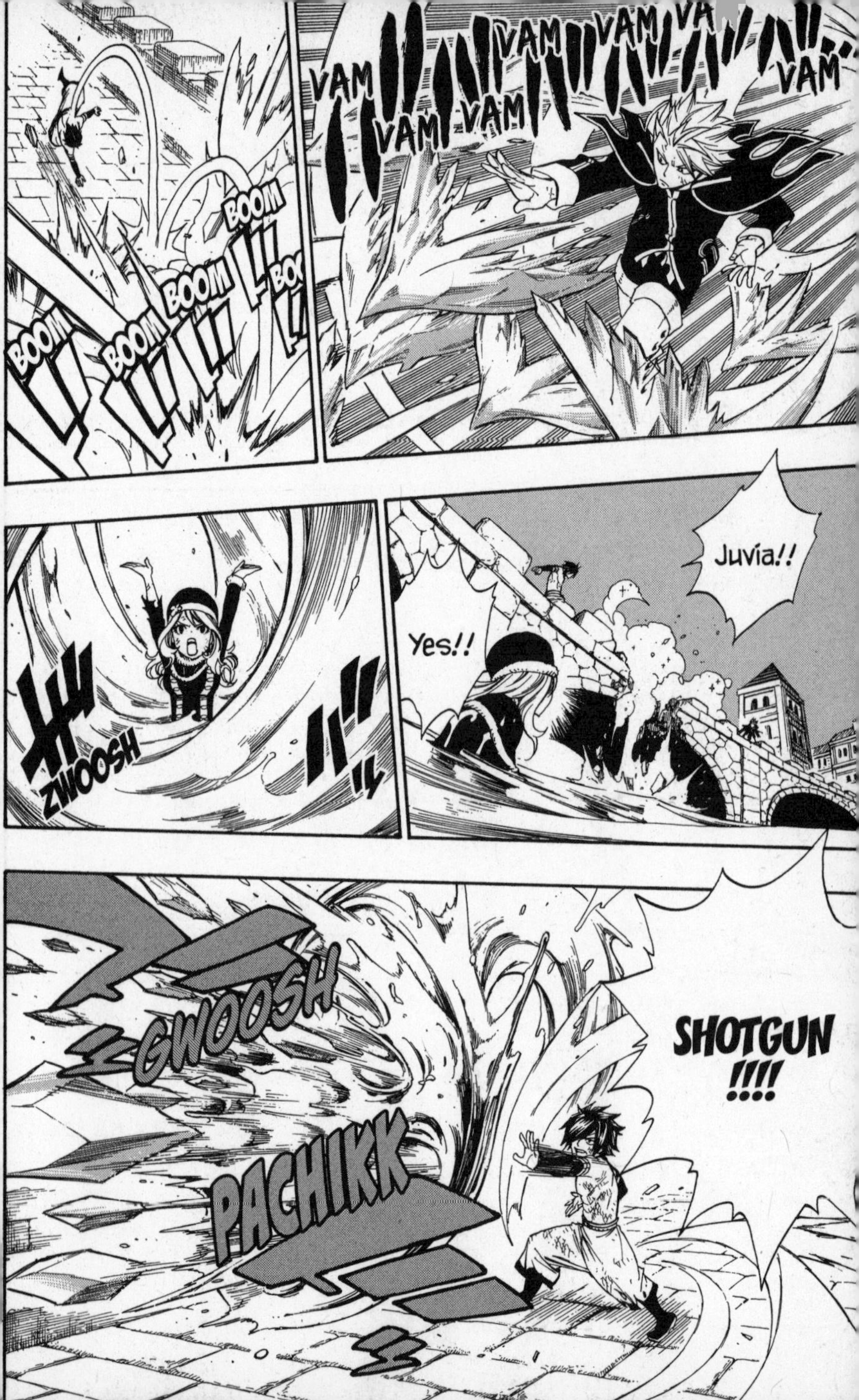
VAM
VA
VAM
VAM
VAM
VAM
VAM
BOOM
BOOM
BOOM
BOOM
BO
Juvia!!
Yes!!
ZWOOSH
SHOTGUN !!!!
GWOOSH
PACHIKK

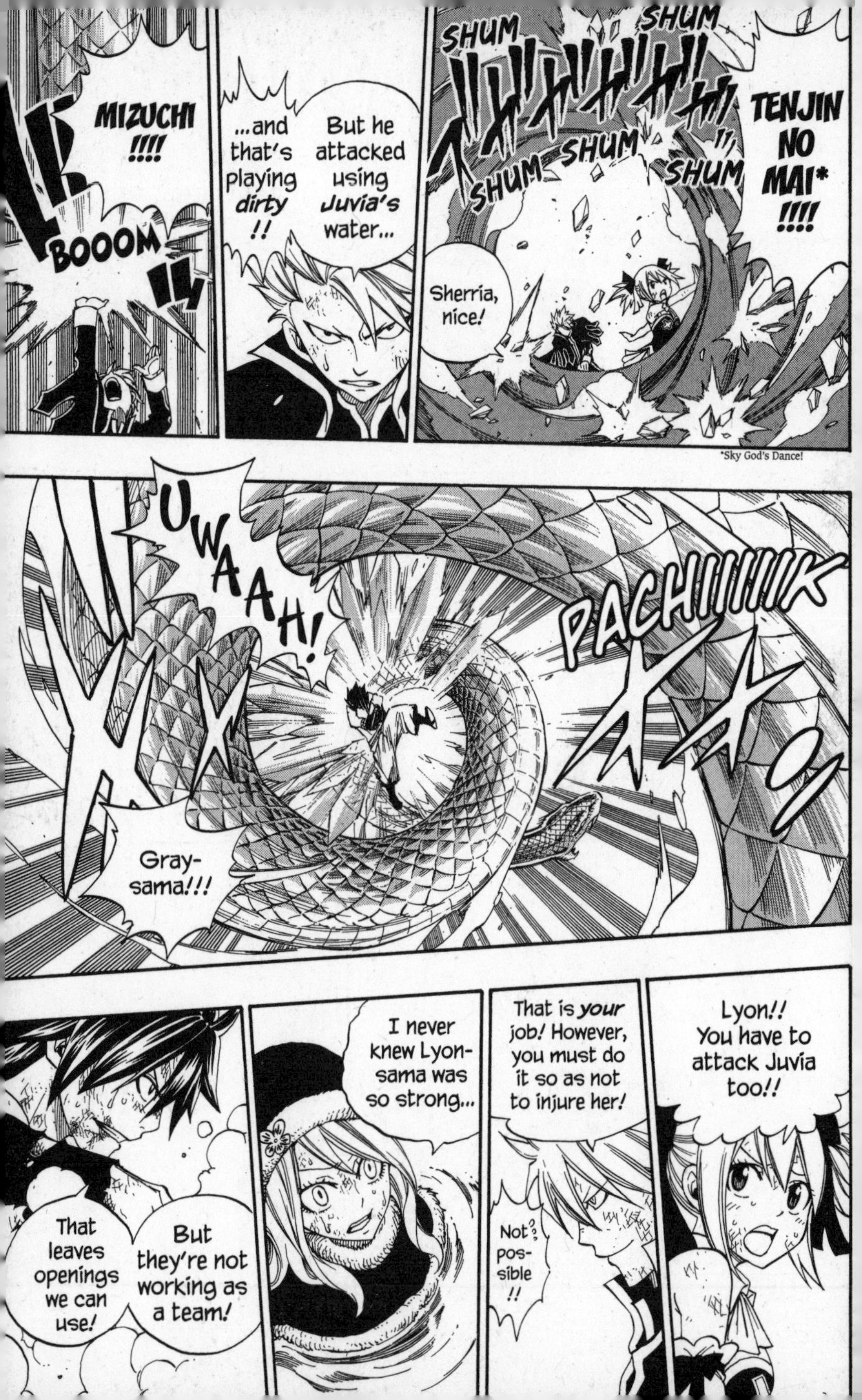
SHUM
SHUM
TENJIN NO MAI* !!!!
SHUM SHUM
SHUM
SHUM
Sherria, nice!
But he attacked using Juvia's water...
...and that's playing dirty!!
MIZUCHI !!!!
BOOOM
PACHIIIIIK
UWAAAH!
Gray-sama!!!
Lyon!! You have to attack Juvia too!!
That is your job! However, you must do it so as not to injure her!
Not possible!!
I never knew Lyon-sama was so strong...
But they're not working as a team!
That leaves openings we can use!

*Sky God's Dance!

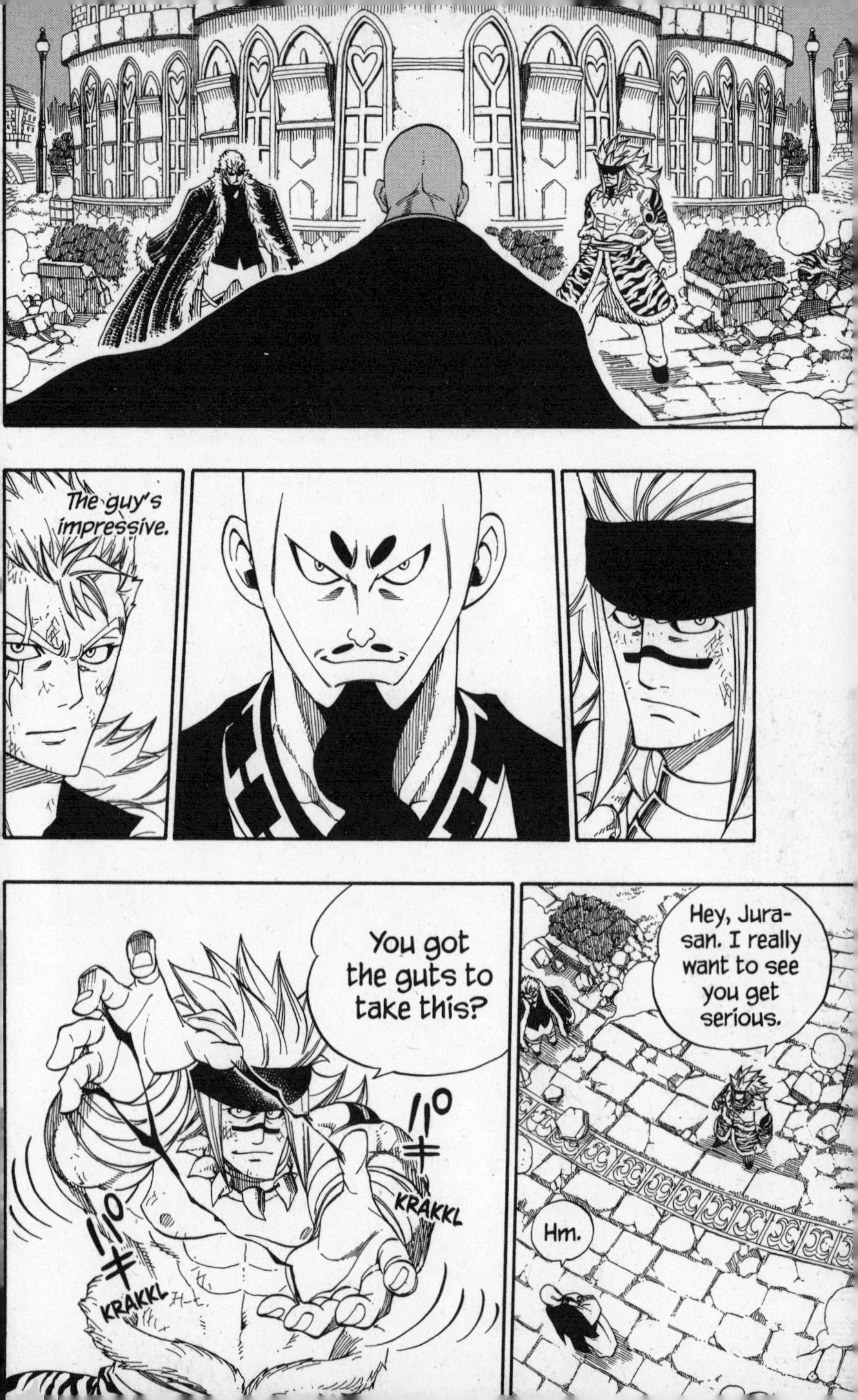
The guy's impressive.
Hey, Jura-san. I really want to see you get serious.
Hm.
You got the guts to take this?
KRAKKL
KRAKKL

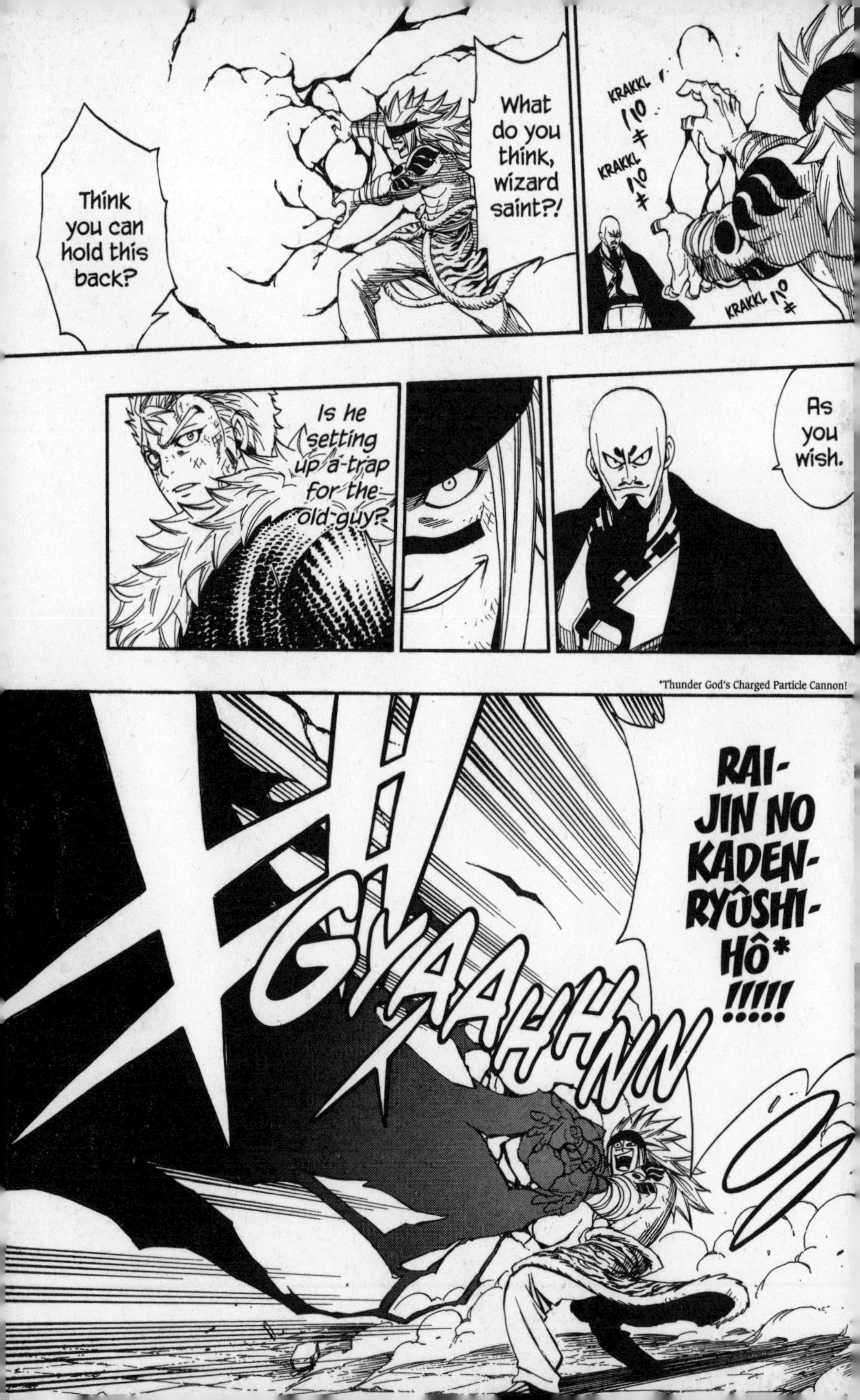
KRAKKL パキ
KRAKKL パキ
KRAKKL パキ
What do you think, wizard saint?!
Think you can hold this back?
As you wish.
Is he setting up a trap for the old guy?
RAI-JIN NO KADEN-RYÛSHI-HÔ* !!!!!
GYAAHHNN

*Thunder God's Charged Particle Cannon!

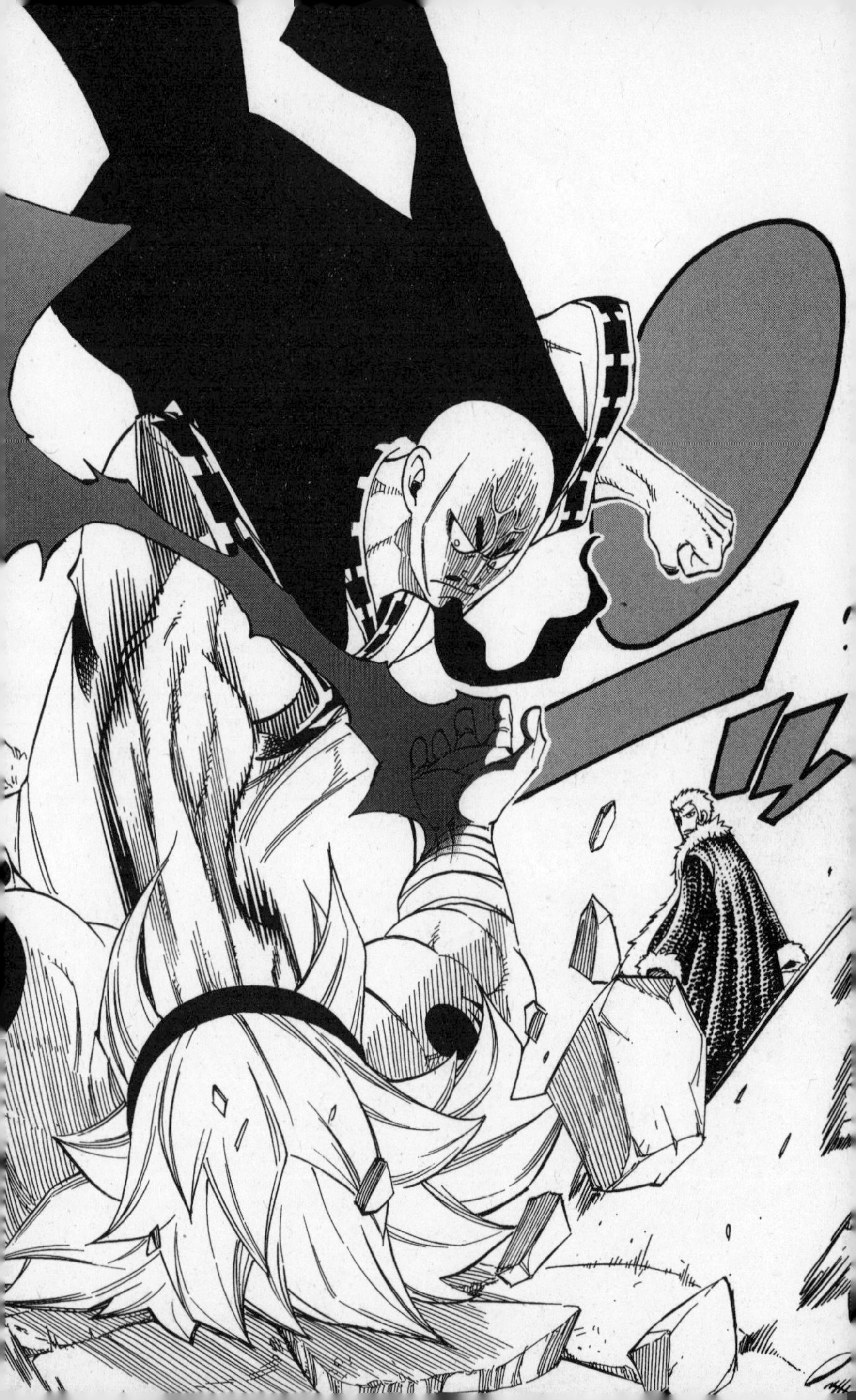

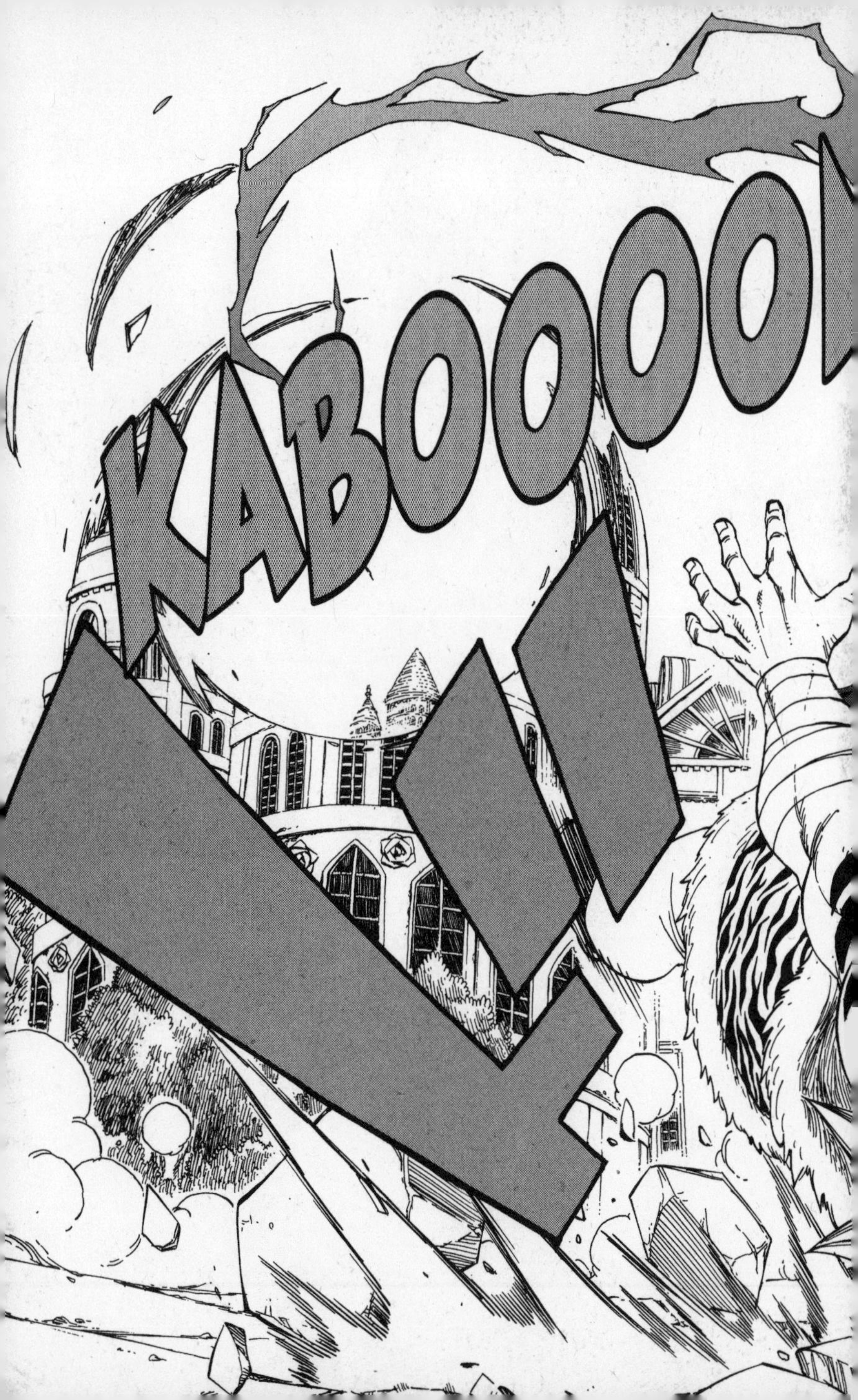
KABOOOOM!!

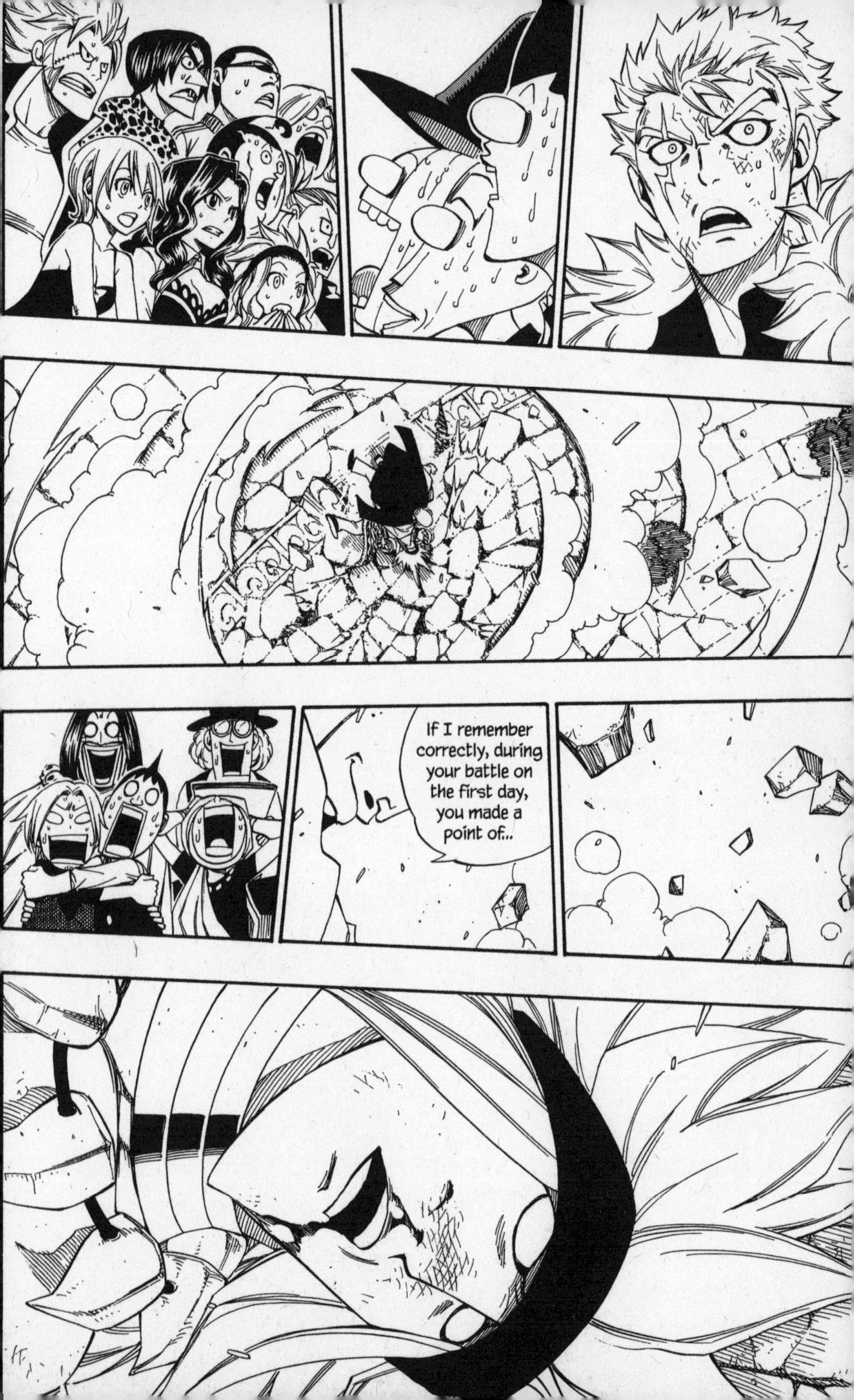
If I remember correctly, during your battle on the first day, you made a point of...

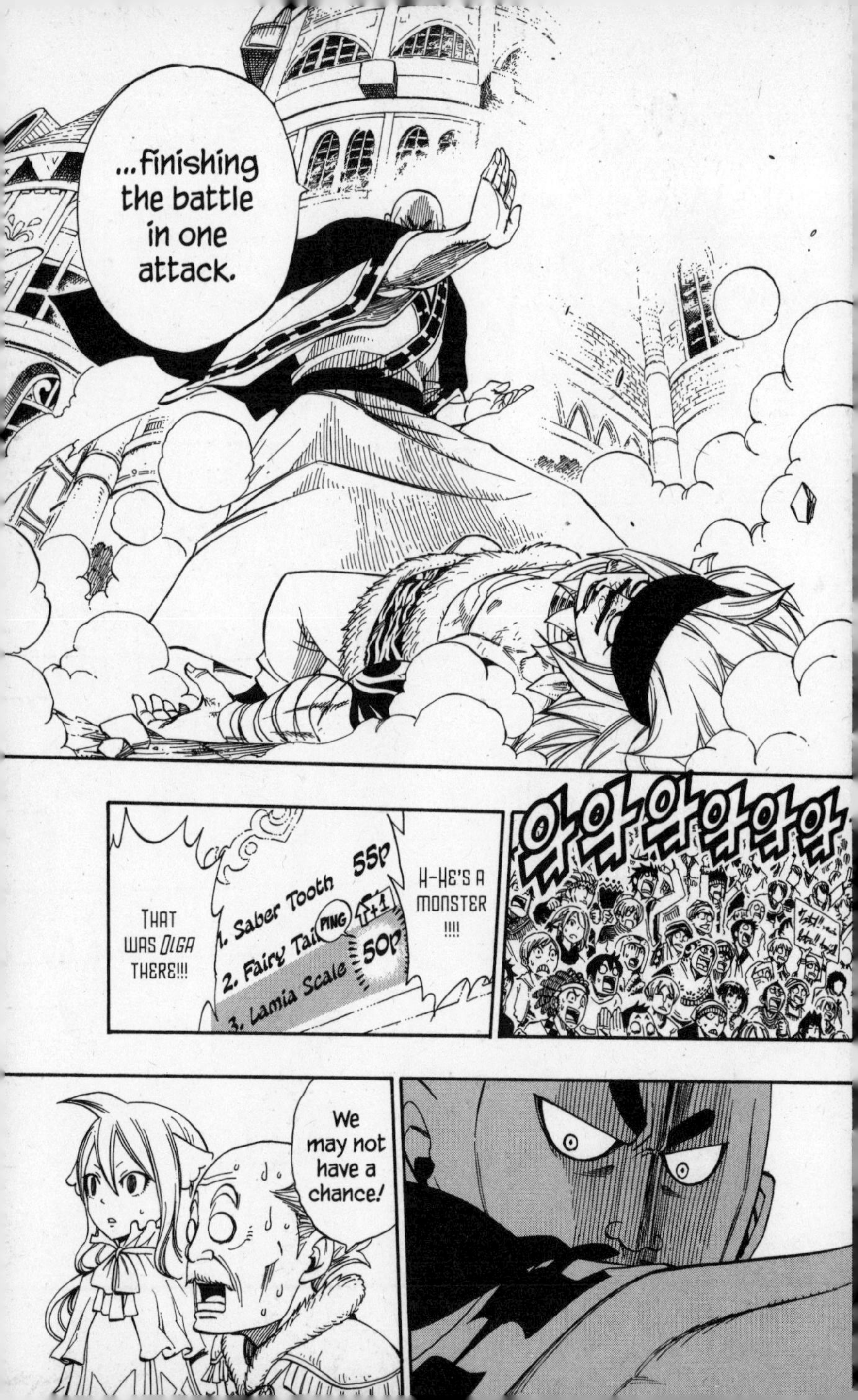
...finishing the battle in one attack.
와와와와와와
H-He's a monster!!!!
1. Saber Tooth 55p
2. Fairy Tail 50p
PING
↑+1
3. Lamia Scale
That was Olga there!!!
We may not have a chance!

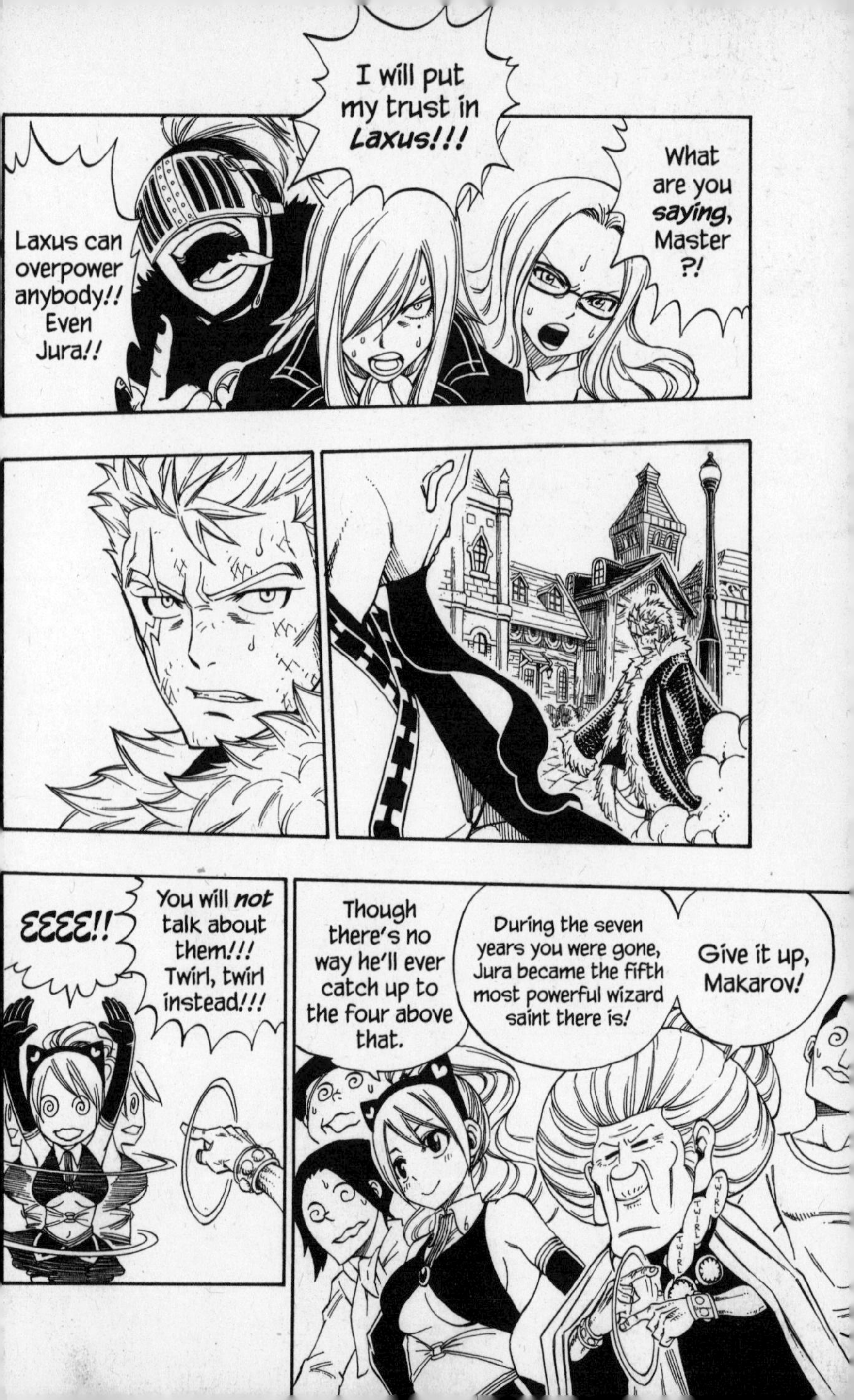
I will put my trust in *Laxus!!!*
What are you *saying,* Master?!
Laxus can overpower anybody!! Even Jura!!
Give it up, Makarov!
During the seven years you were gone, Jura became the fifth most powerful wizard saint there is!
Though there's no way he'll ever catch up to the four above that.
TWIRL
TWIRL
TWIRL
You will *not* talk about them!!! Twirl, twirl instead!!!
EEEE!!

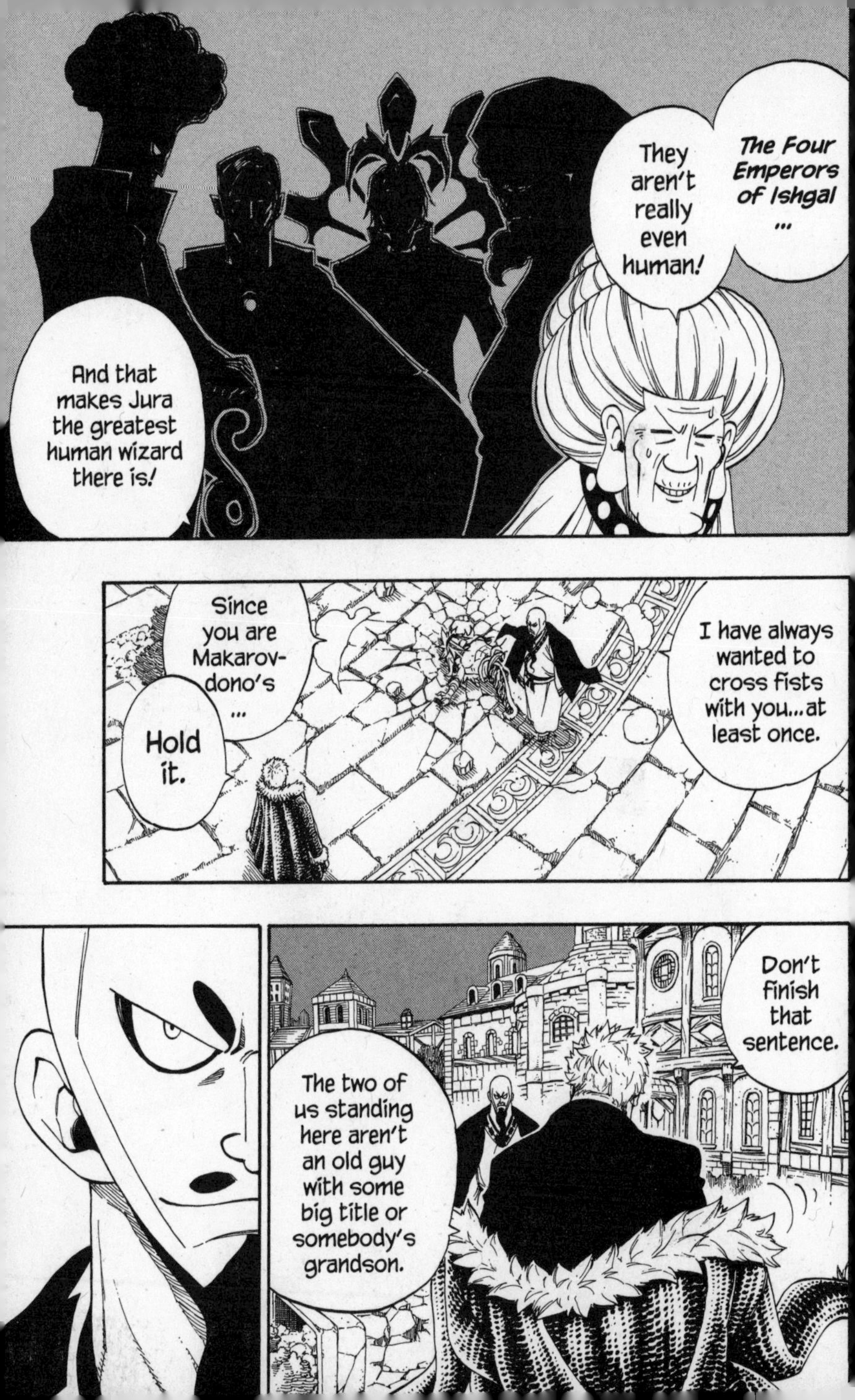
The Four Emperors of Ishgal ...
They aren't really even human!
And that makes Jura the greatest human wizard there is!
I have always wanted to cross fists with you...at least once.
Since you are Makarov-dono's ...
Hold it.
Don't finish that sentence.
The two of us standing here aren't an old guy with some big title or somebody's grandson.

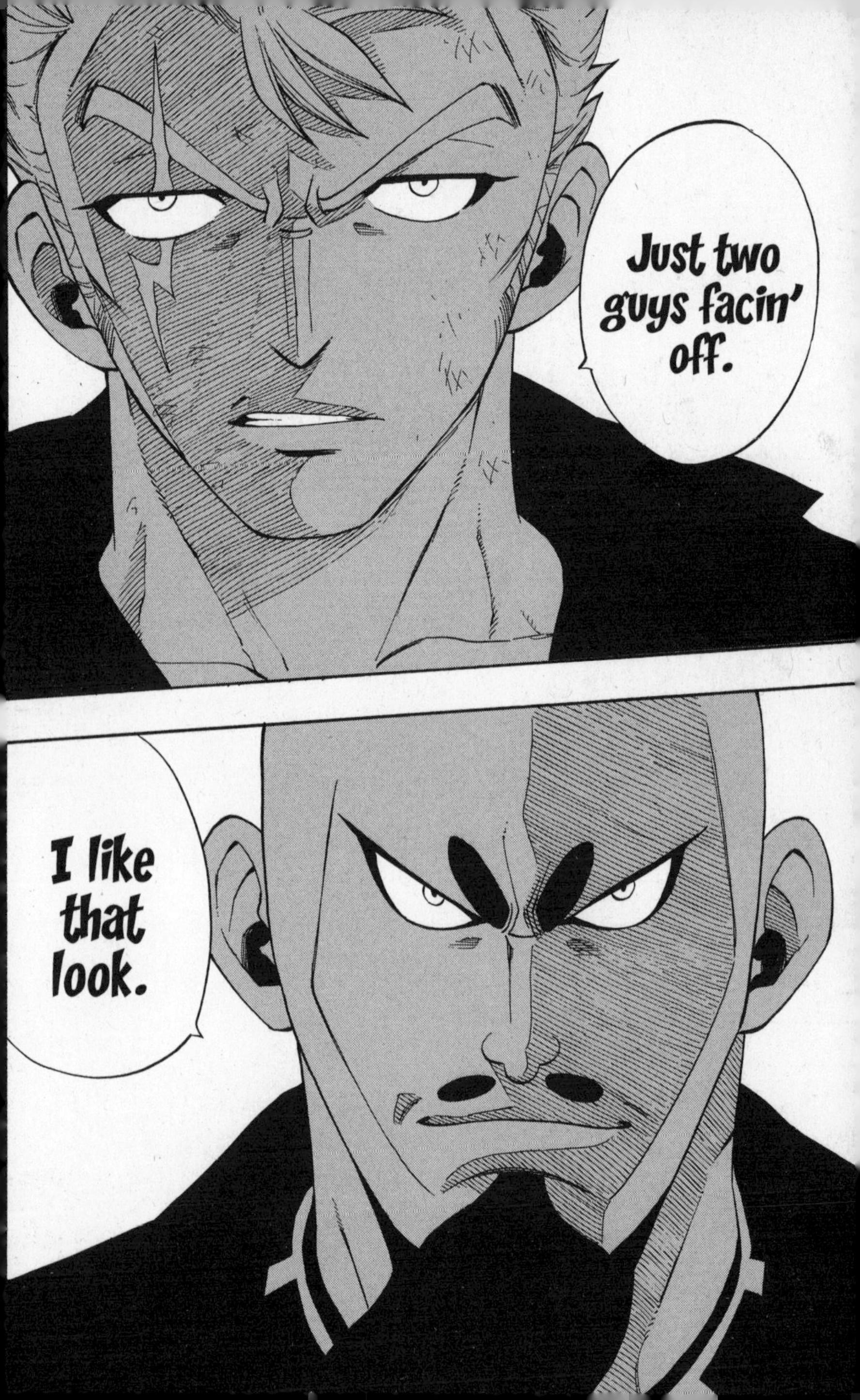
Just two guys facin' off.
I like that look.

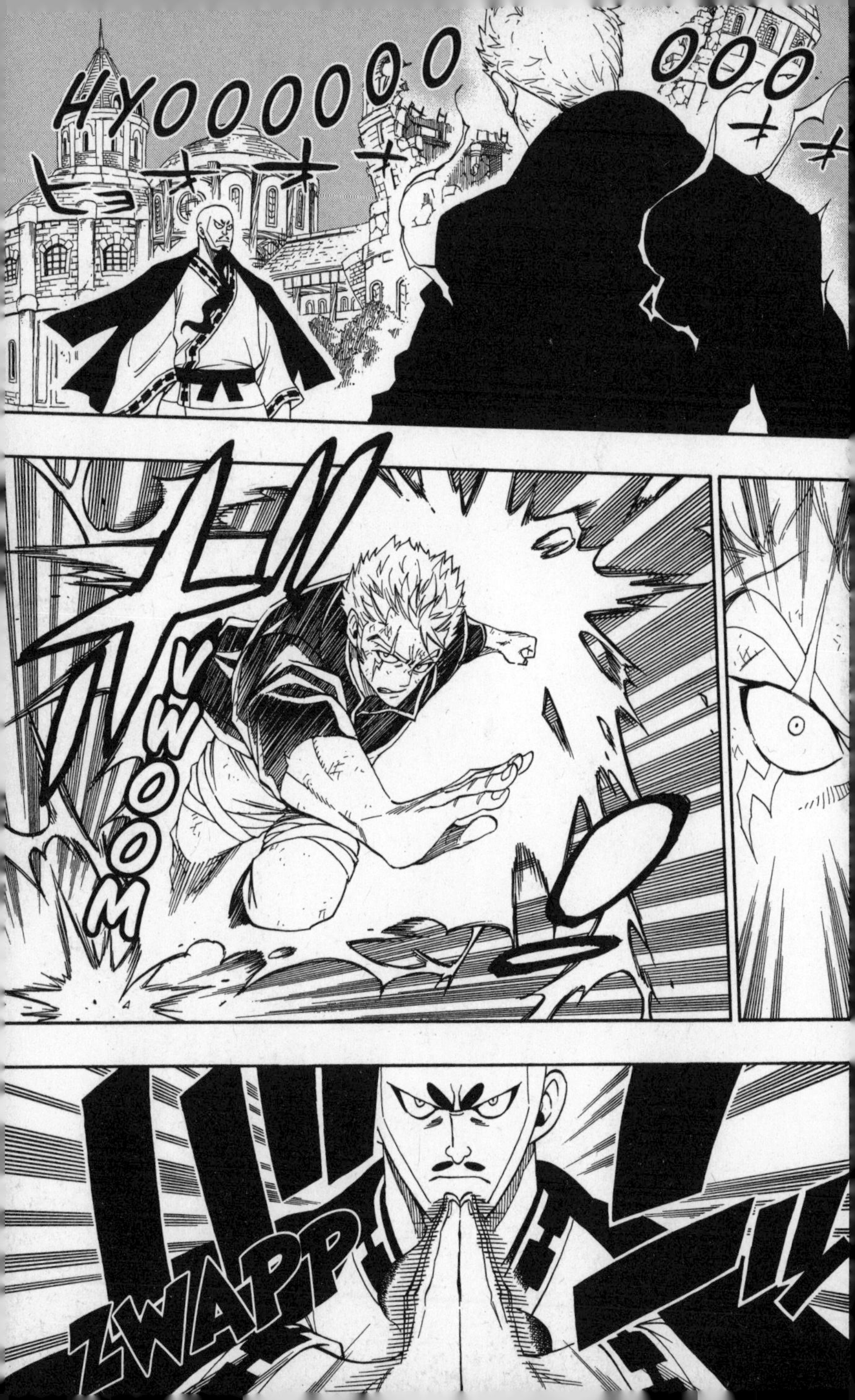
HYOOOOOOO OOO
VWOOOM
ZWAPP

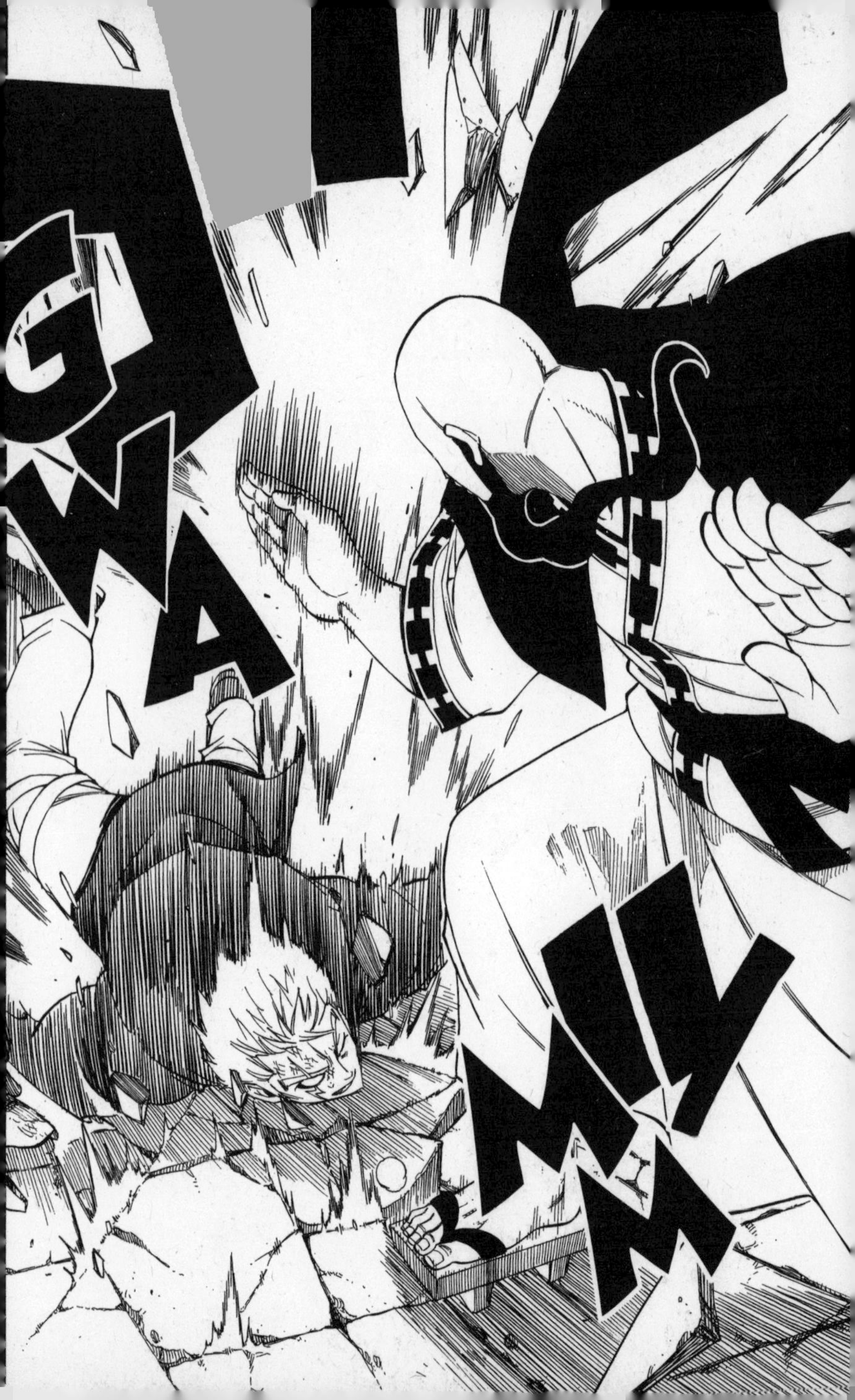
GWA
MM

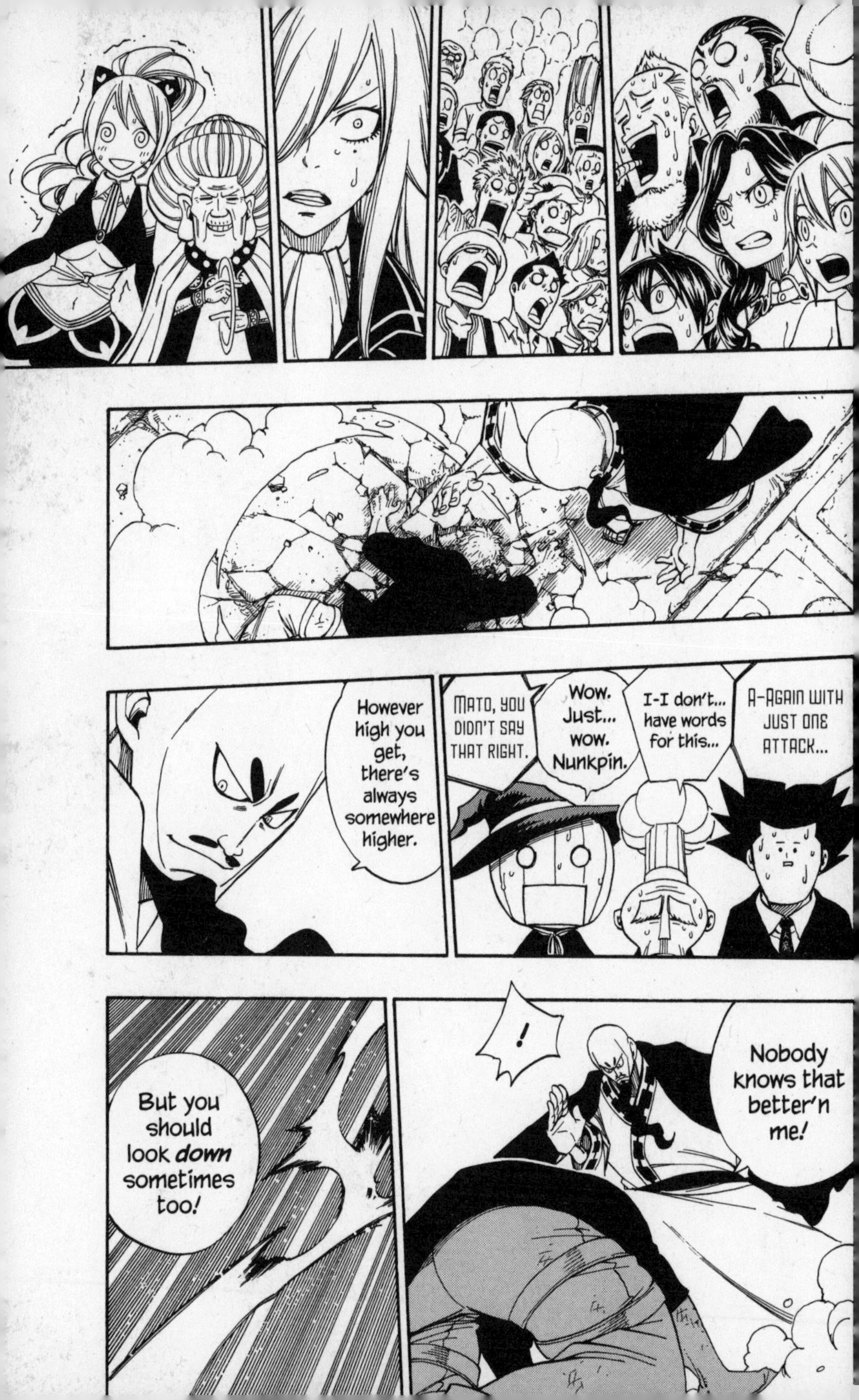
A-Again with just one attack...
I-I don't... have words for this...
Wow. Just... wow. Nunkpin.
Mato, you didn't say that right.
However high you get, there's always somewhere higher.
Nobody knows that better'n me!
!
But you should look *down* sometimes too!

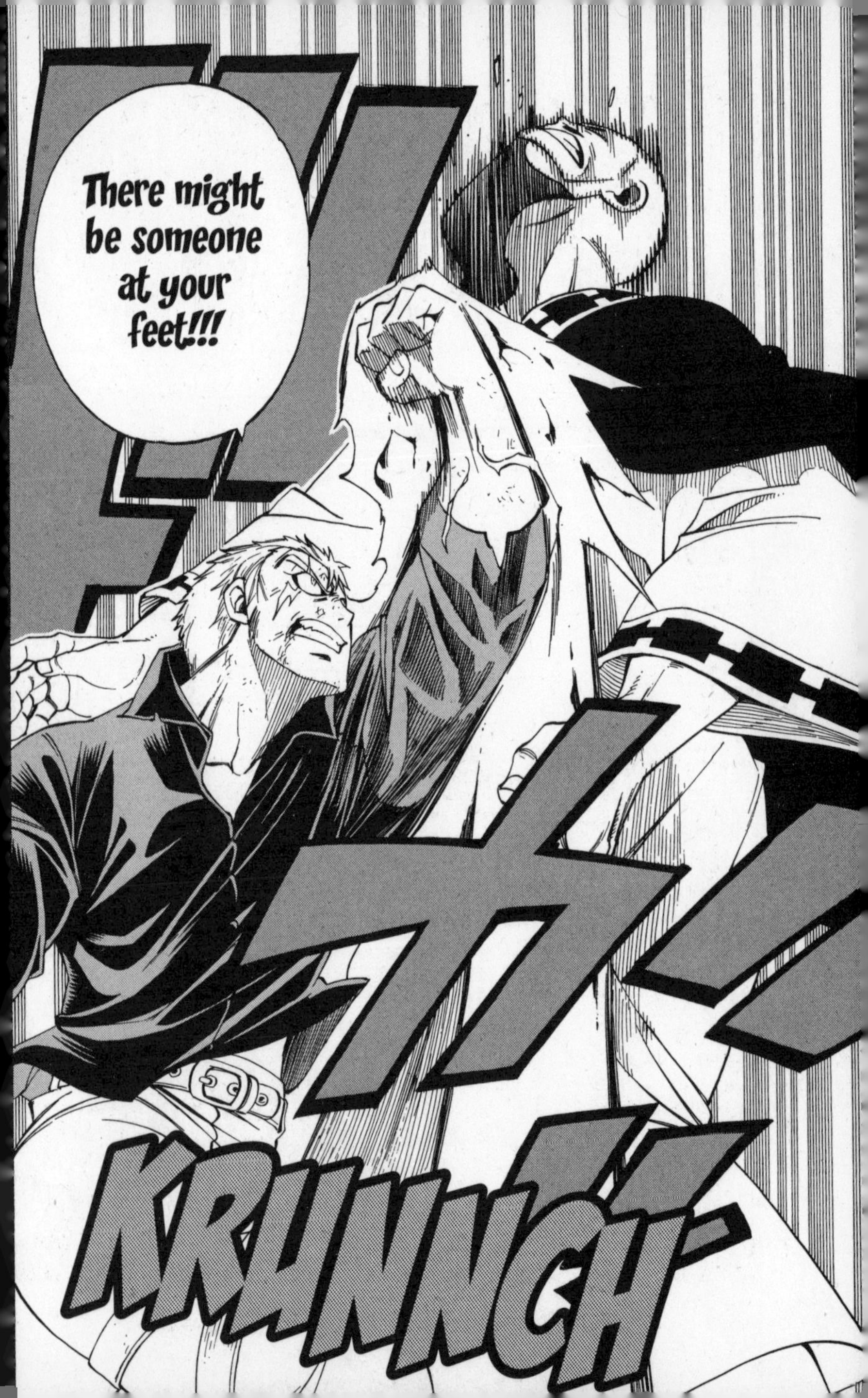
There might be someone at your feet!!!
KRUNNCH

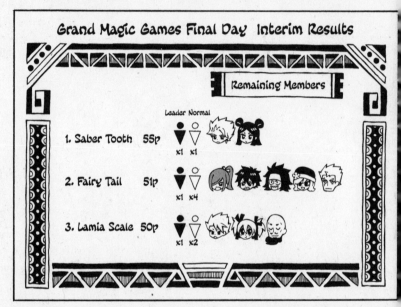

Grand Magic Games Final Day Interim Results

Remaining Members

Leader Normal

1. Saber Tooth 55p ×1 ×1

2. Fairy Tail 51p ×1 ×4

3. Lamia Scale 50p ×1 ×2

I get the feeling something weird is attached to me...

Just my imagination, I guess.

もぞ NUZZLE もぞ NUZZLE もぞ NUZZLE

Chapter 321: Laxus vs. Jura

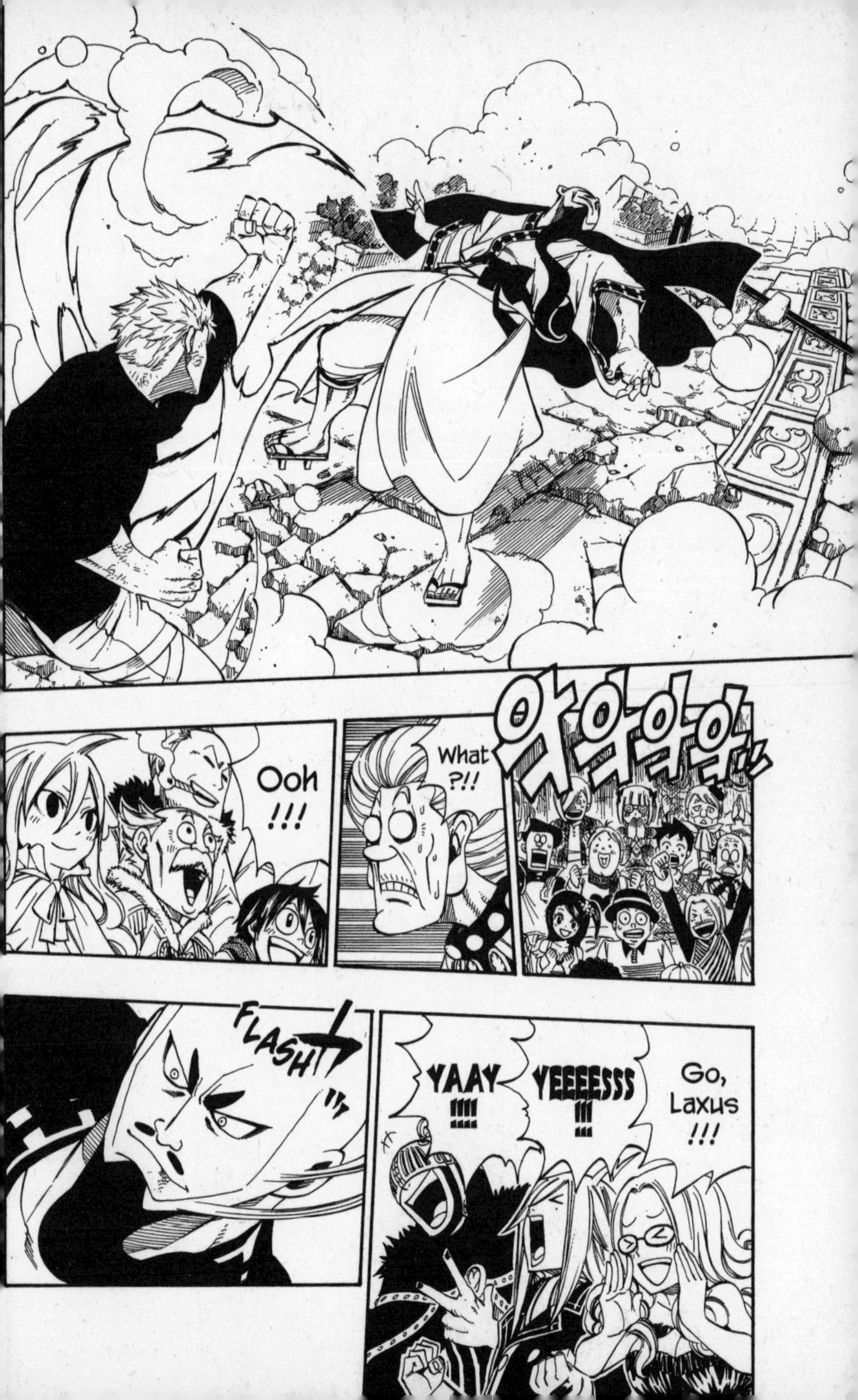
와와와와!!
What ?!!
Ooh !!!
Go, Laxus !!!
YEEEESSS !!!
YAAY !!!!
FLASH

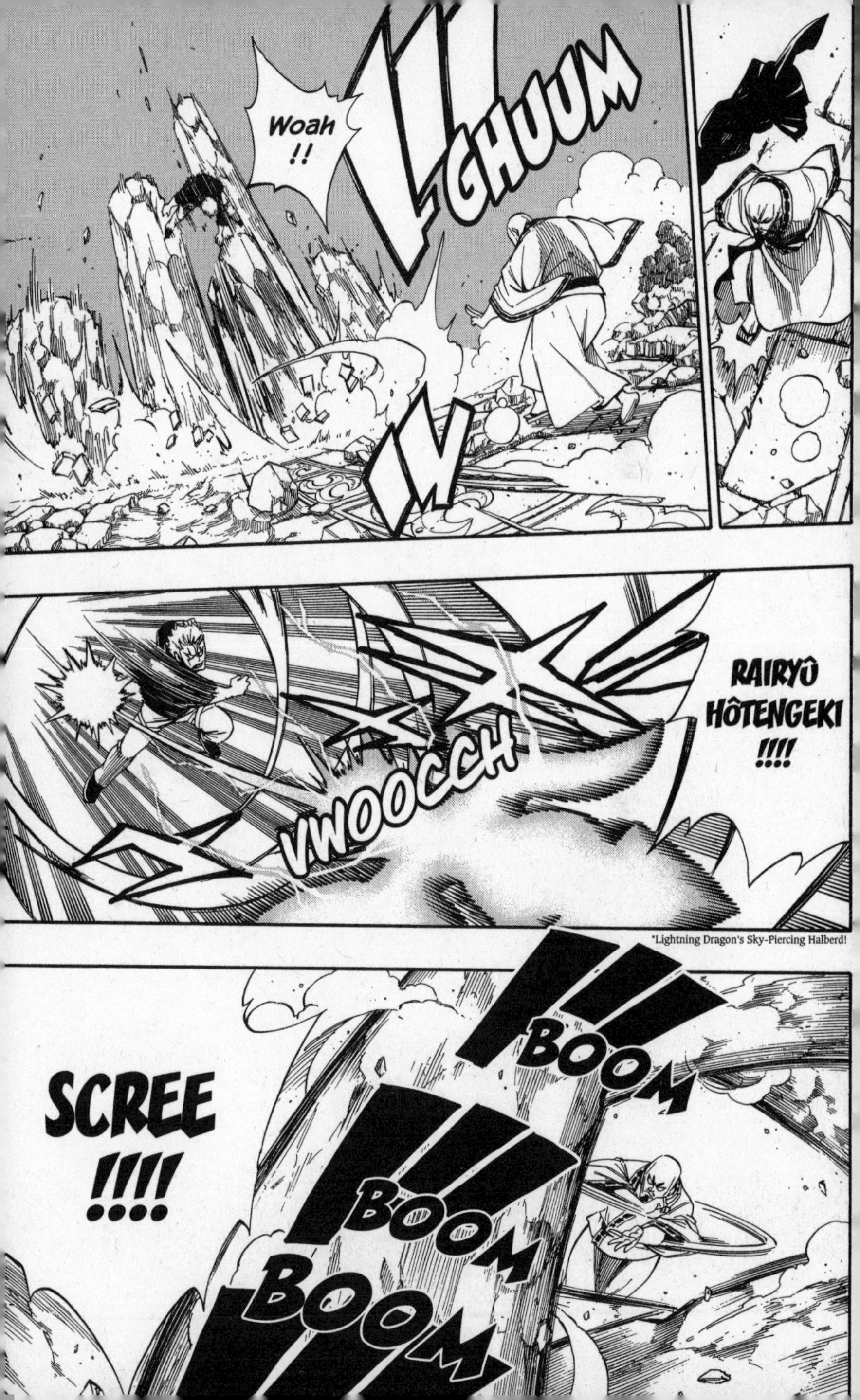
GHUUM
Woah !!
N
RAIRYÛ HÔTENGEKI !!!!
VWOOCCH
BOOM
BOOM
BOOM
SCREE !!!!

*Lightning Dragon's Sky-Piercing Halberd!

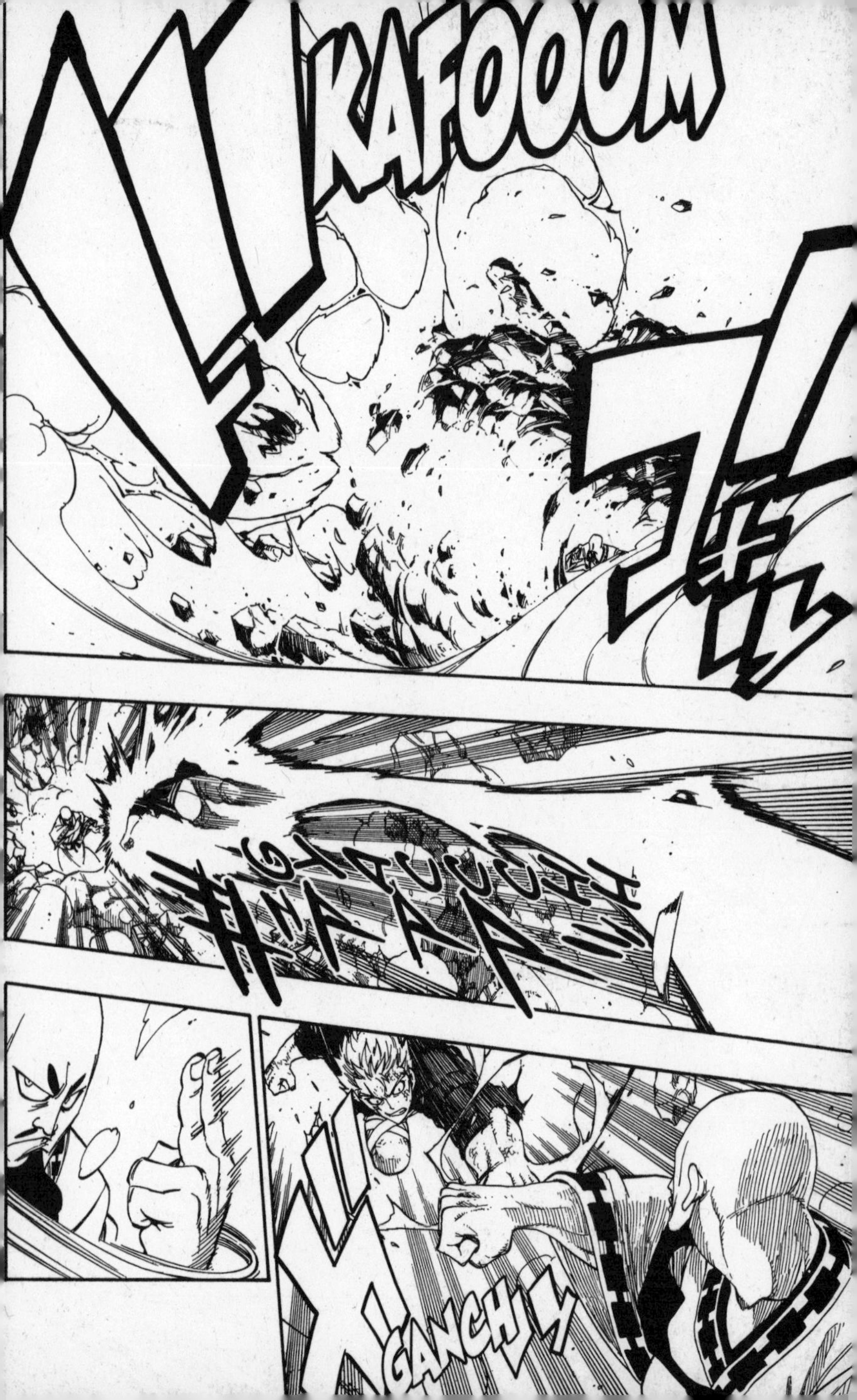
KAFOOOM
GANCH

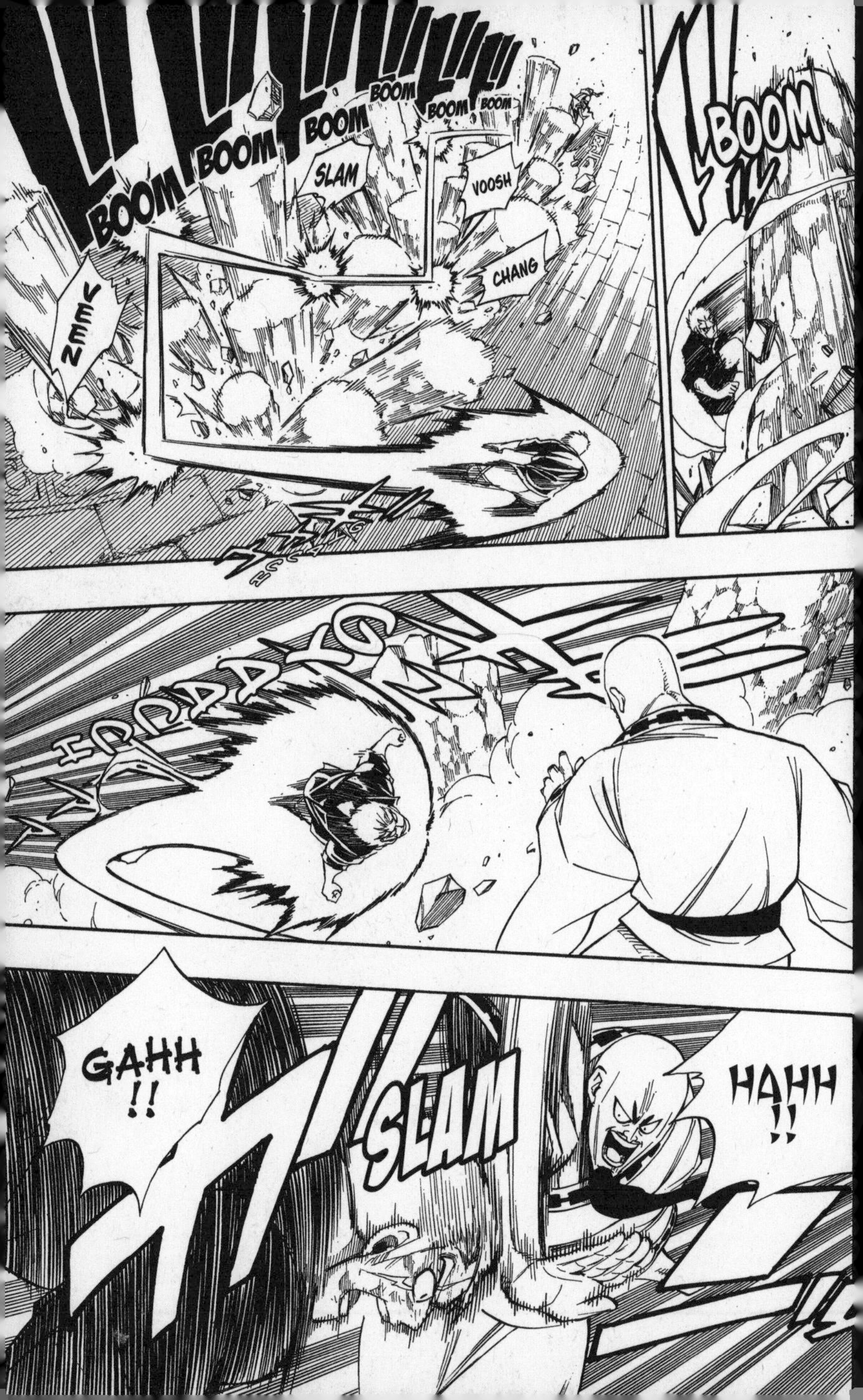
BOOM
BOOM
BOOM
BOOM
BOOM
BOOM
BOOM
VOOSH
SLAM
CHANG
VEEN
HAHH!!
SLAM
GAHH!!

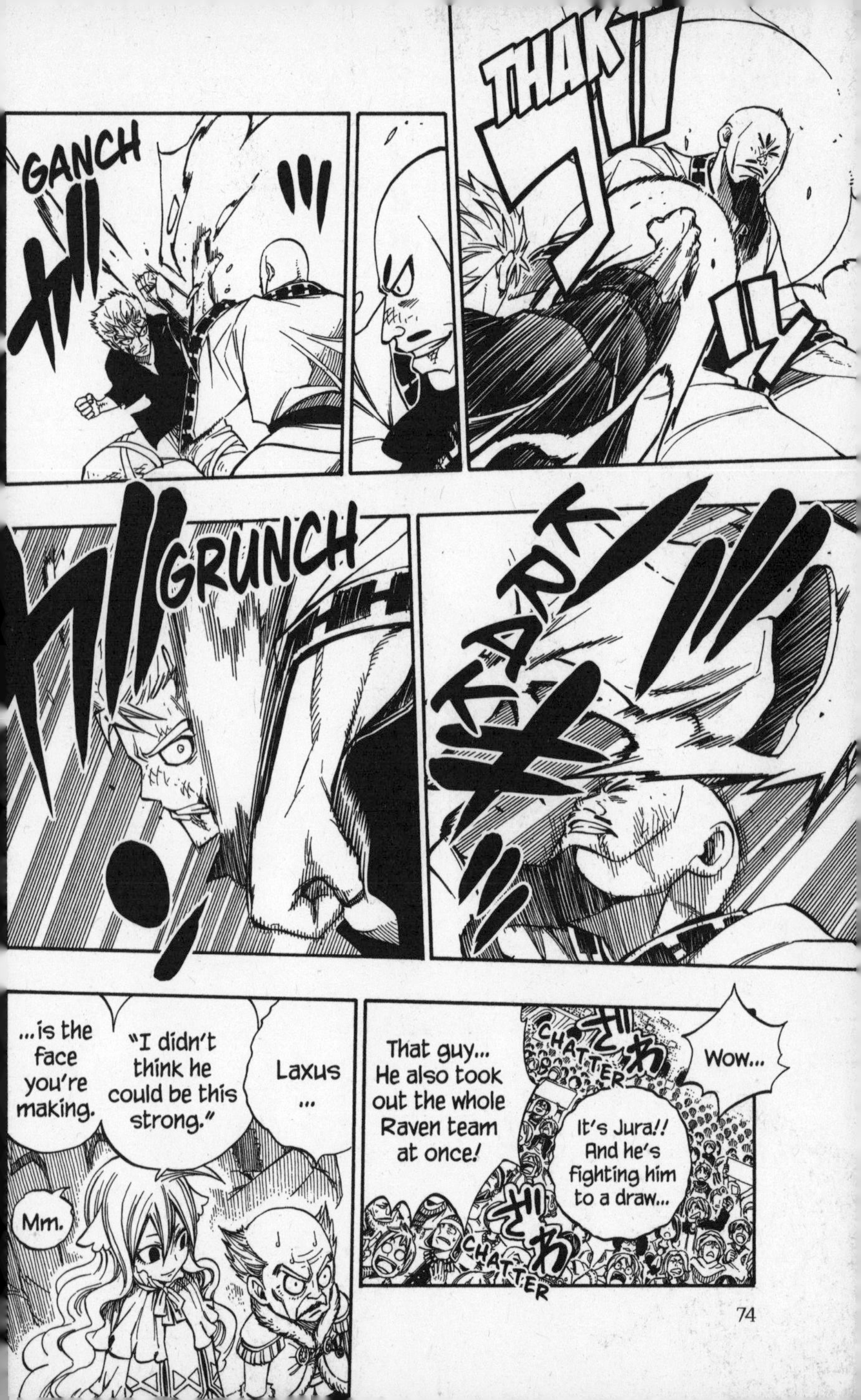
THAK!!
GANCH!!
KARAK!!
GRUNCH!!
CHATTER
Wow...
It's Jura!! And he's fighting him to a draw...
That guy... He also took out the whole Raven team at once!
CHATTER
Laxus ...
"I didn't think he could be this strong."
...is the face you're making.
Mm.

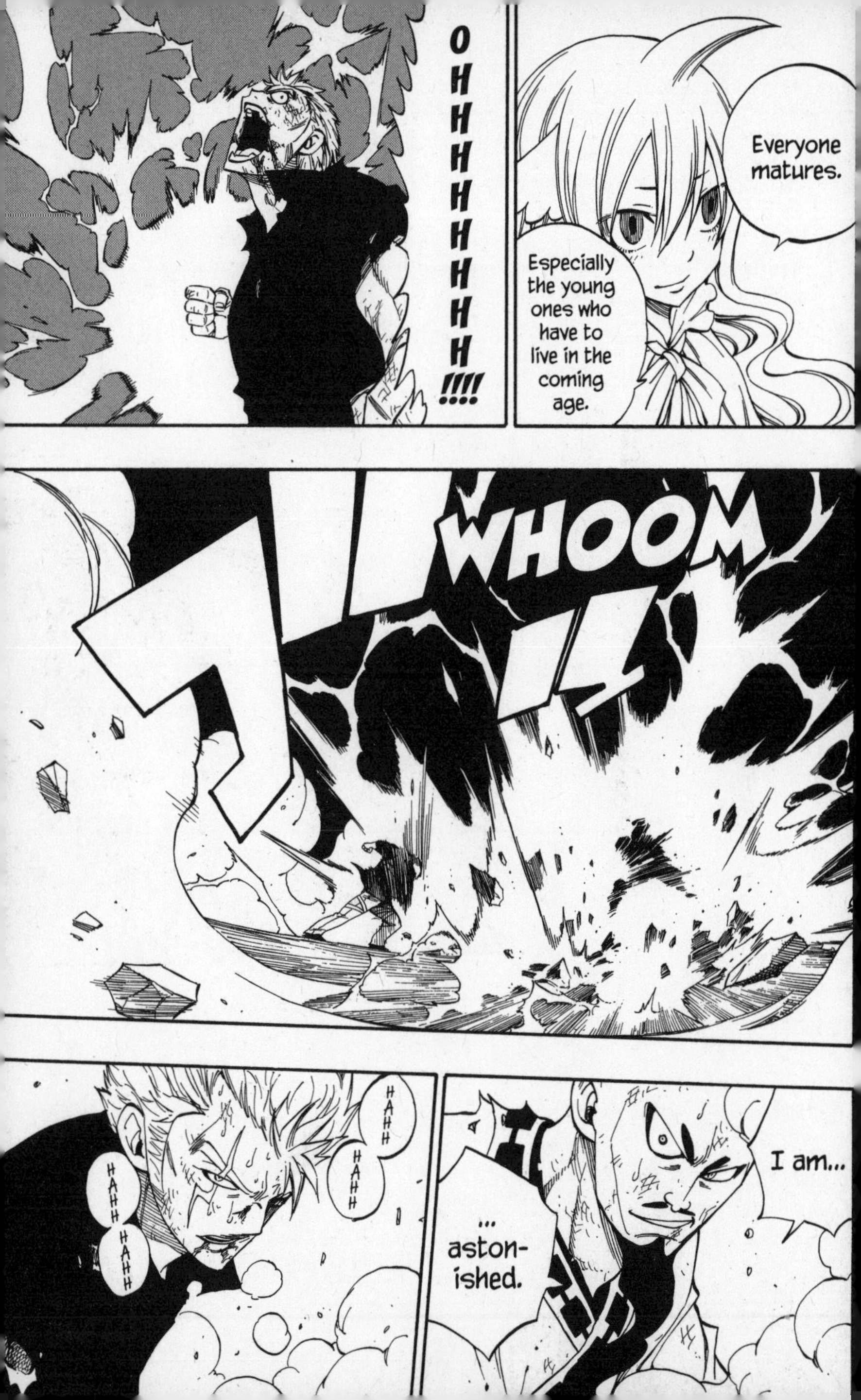
Everyone matures.
Especially the young ones who have to live in the coming age.
OHHHHHHHH!!!!
WHOOM
I am...
...aston-ished.
HAHH HAHH
HAHH HAHH

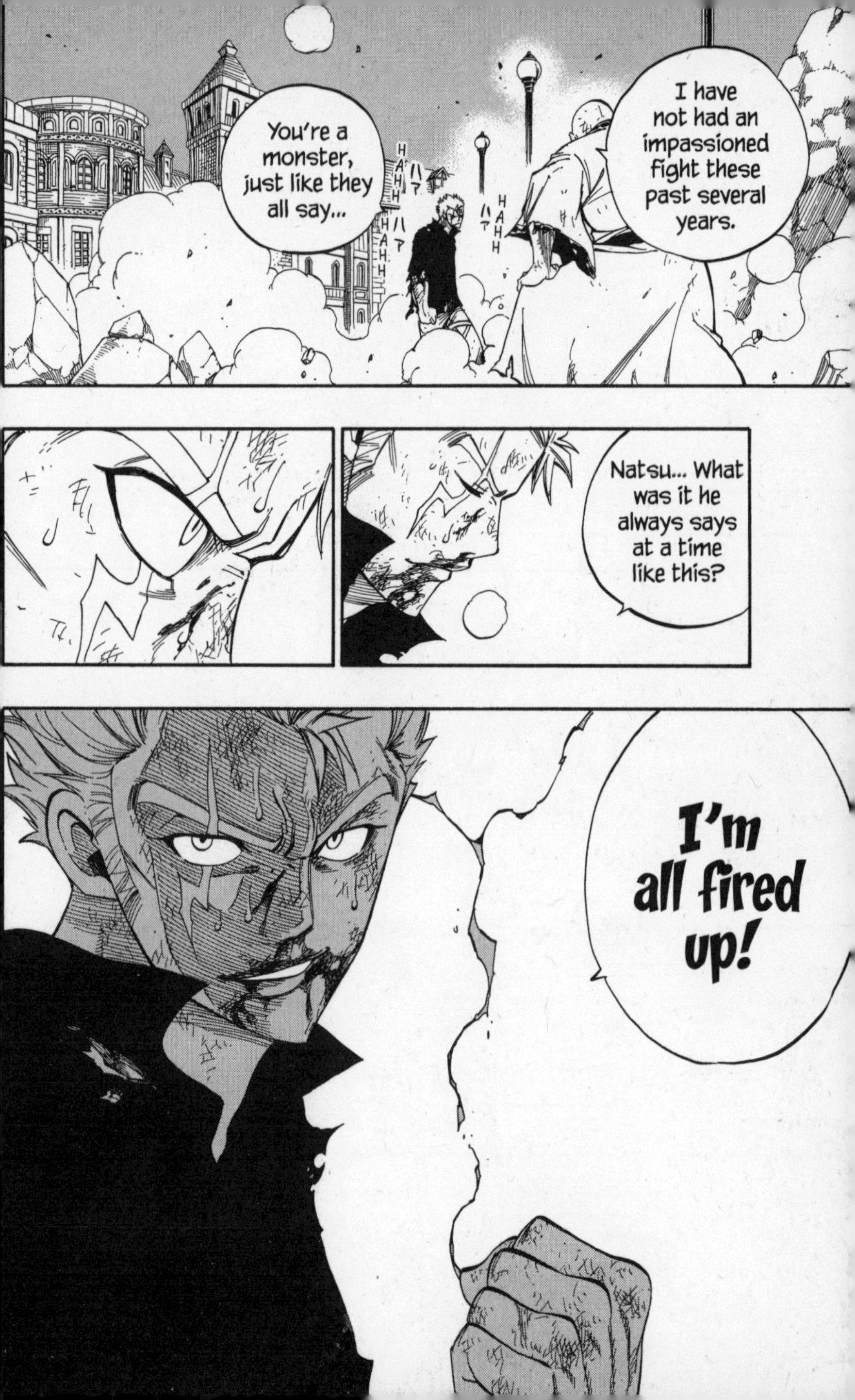
I have not had an impassioned fight these past several years.
HAHH
You're a monster, just like they all say...
HAHH
HAHH
Natsu... What was it he always says at a time like this?
I'm all fired up!

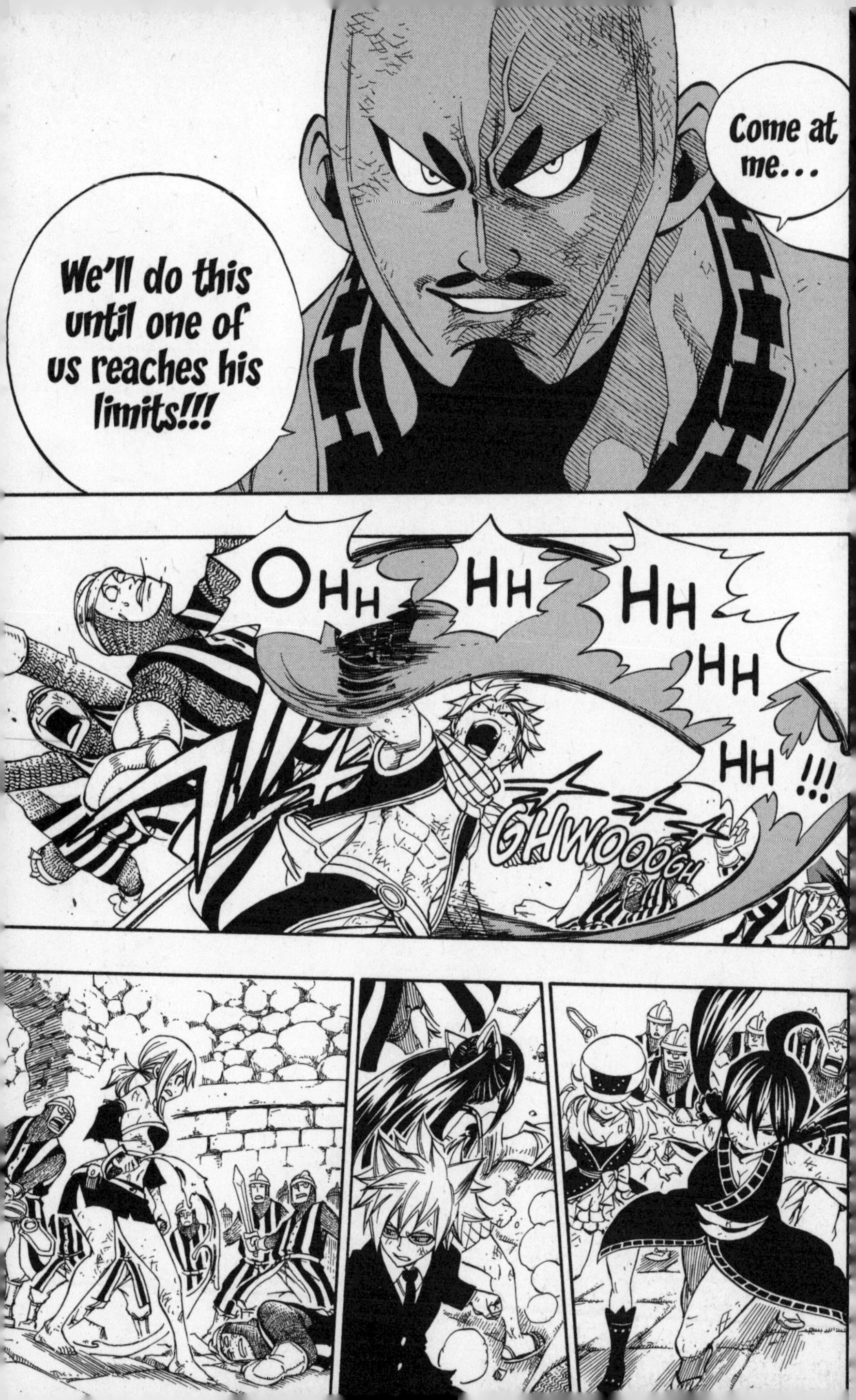
Come at me...
We'll do this until one of us reaches his limits!!!
OHHHHHHHHHH!!!
GHWOOOOGH

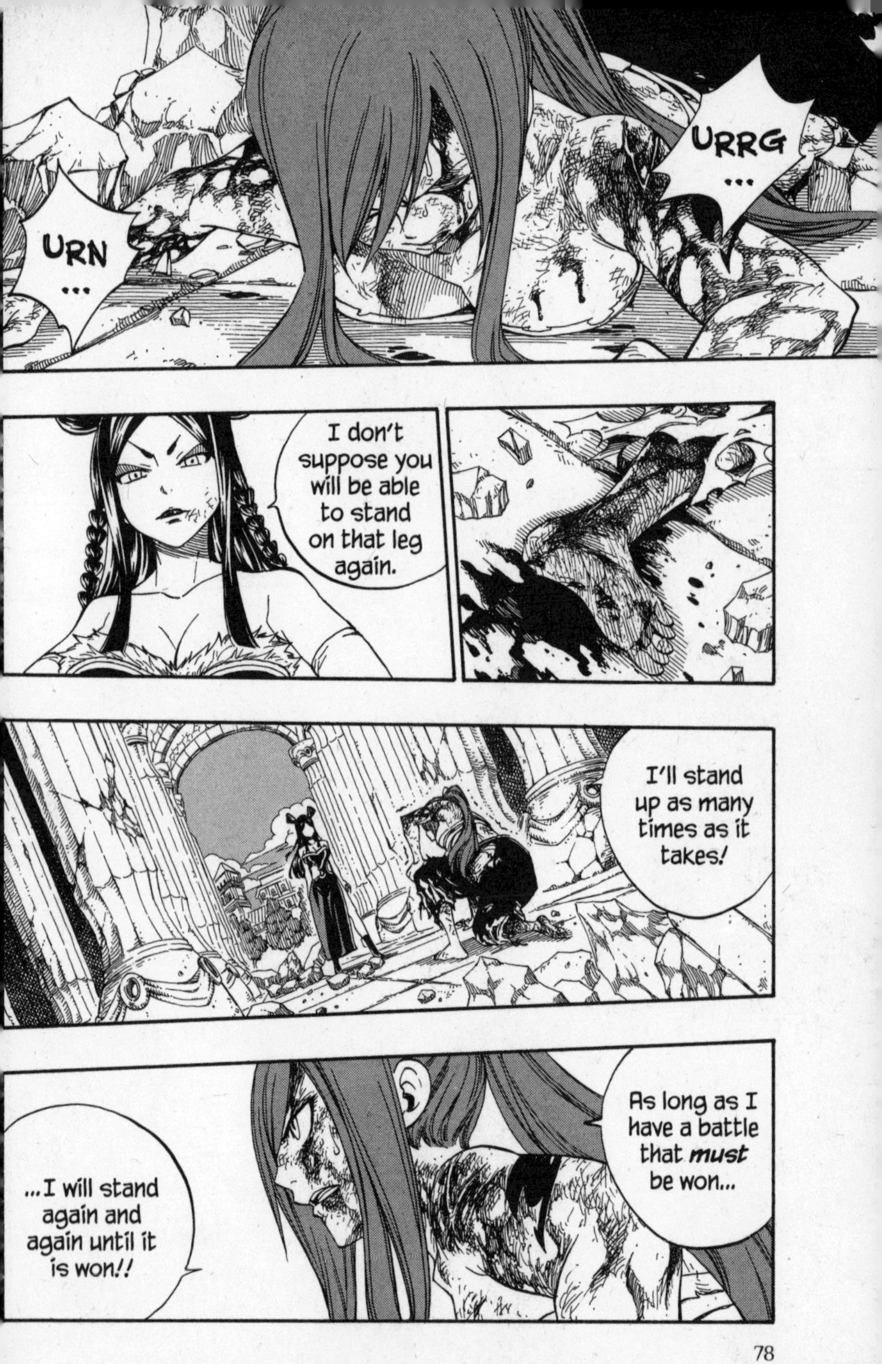
URRG ...
URN ...
I don't suppose you will be able to stand on that leg again.
I'll stand up as many times as it takes!
As long as I have a battle that *must* be won...
...I will stand again and again until it is won!!

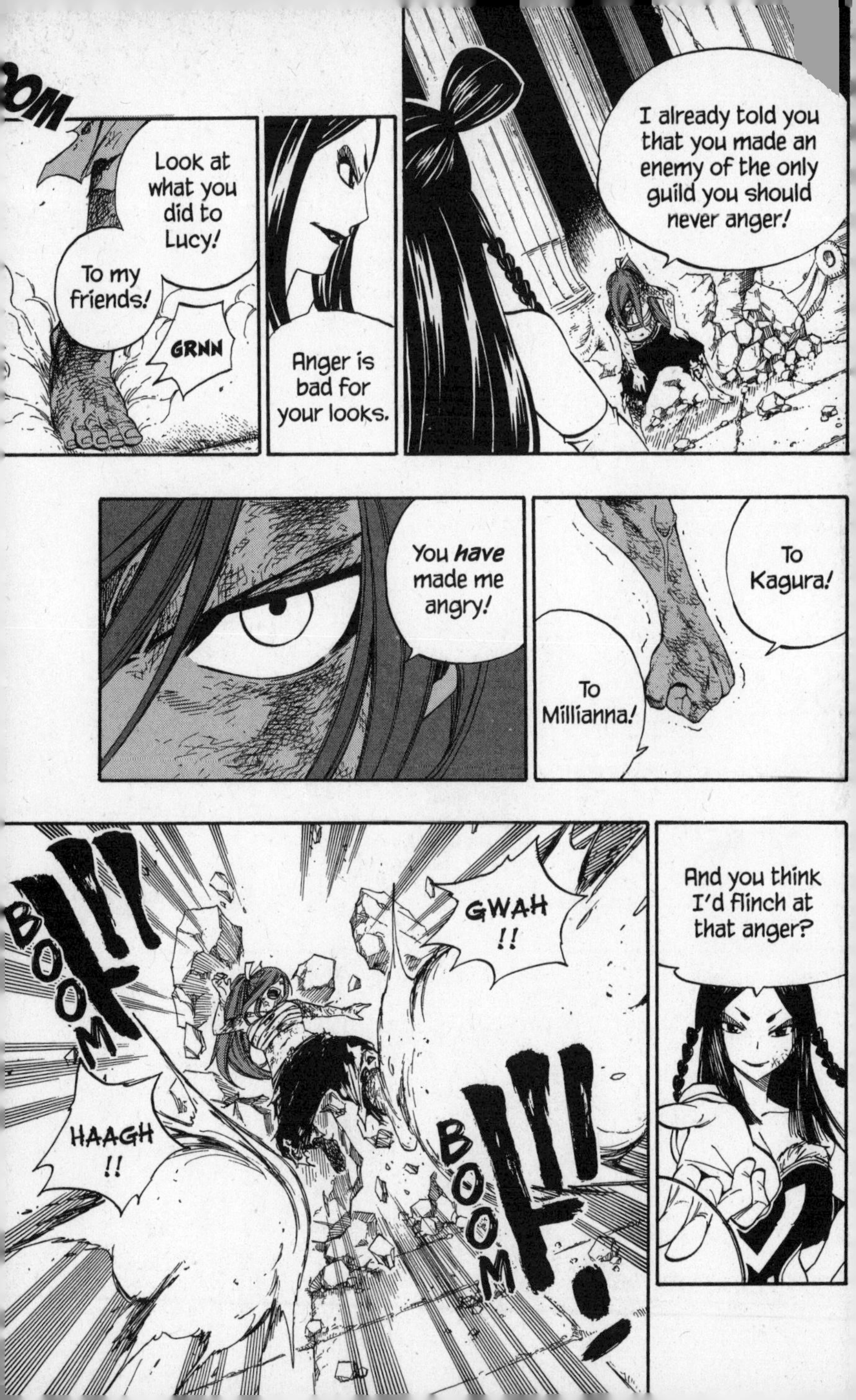
I already told you that you made an enemy of the only guild you should never anger!
Anger is bad for your looks.
Look at what you did to Lucy!
To my friends!
GRNN
To Kagura!
To Millianna!
You *have* made me angry!
And you think I'd flinch at that anger?
GWAH!!
BOOM!!
BOOM!!
HAAGH!!

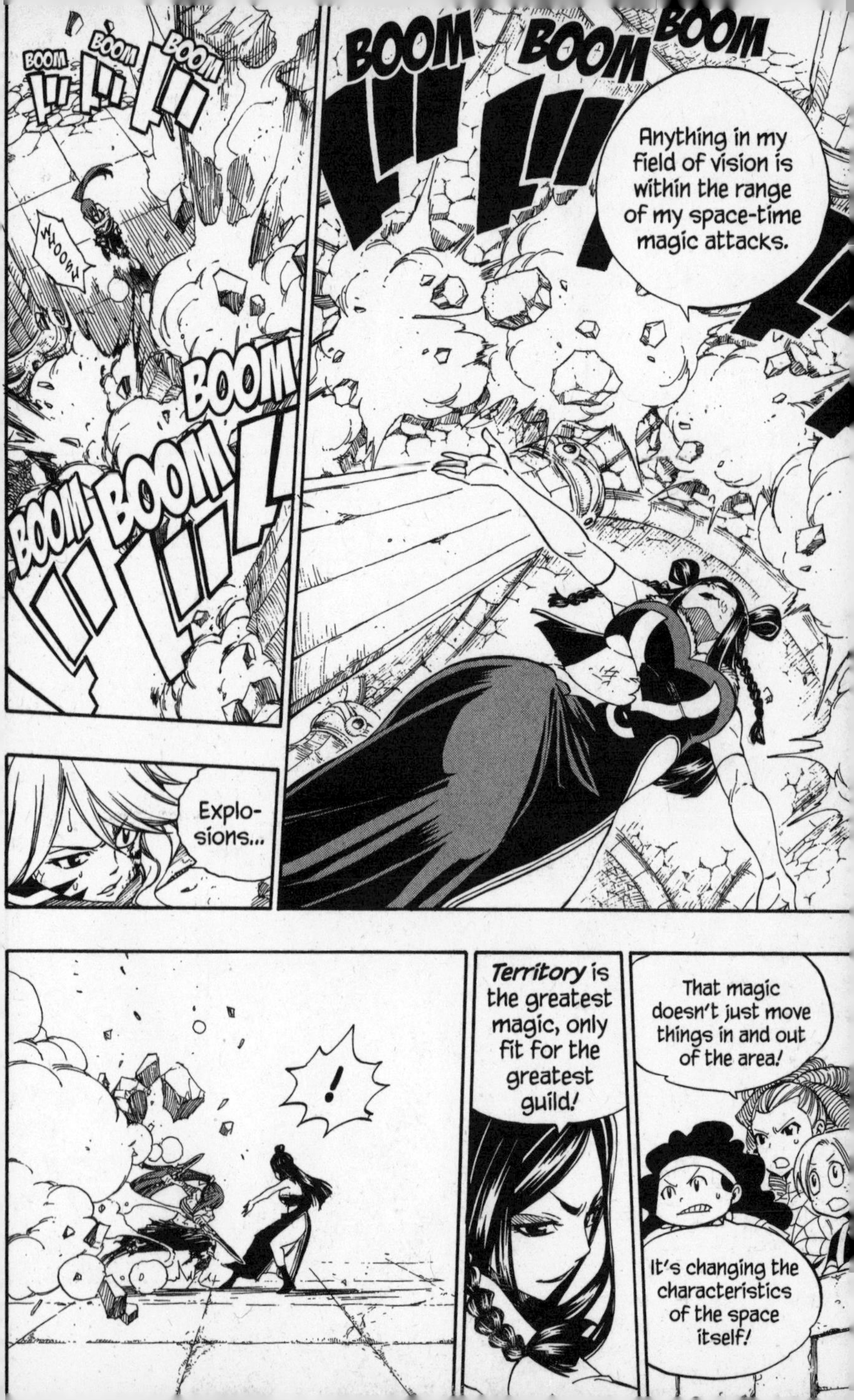
BOOM
BOOM
BOOM
Anything in my field of vision is within the range of my space-time magic attacks.
BOOM
BOOM
BOOM
BOOM
BOOM
BOOM
Explo-sions...
That magic doesn't just move things in and out of the area!
It's changing the characteristics of the space itself!
Territory is the greatest magic, only fit for the greatest guild!
!

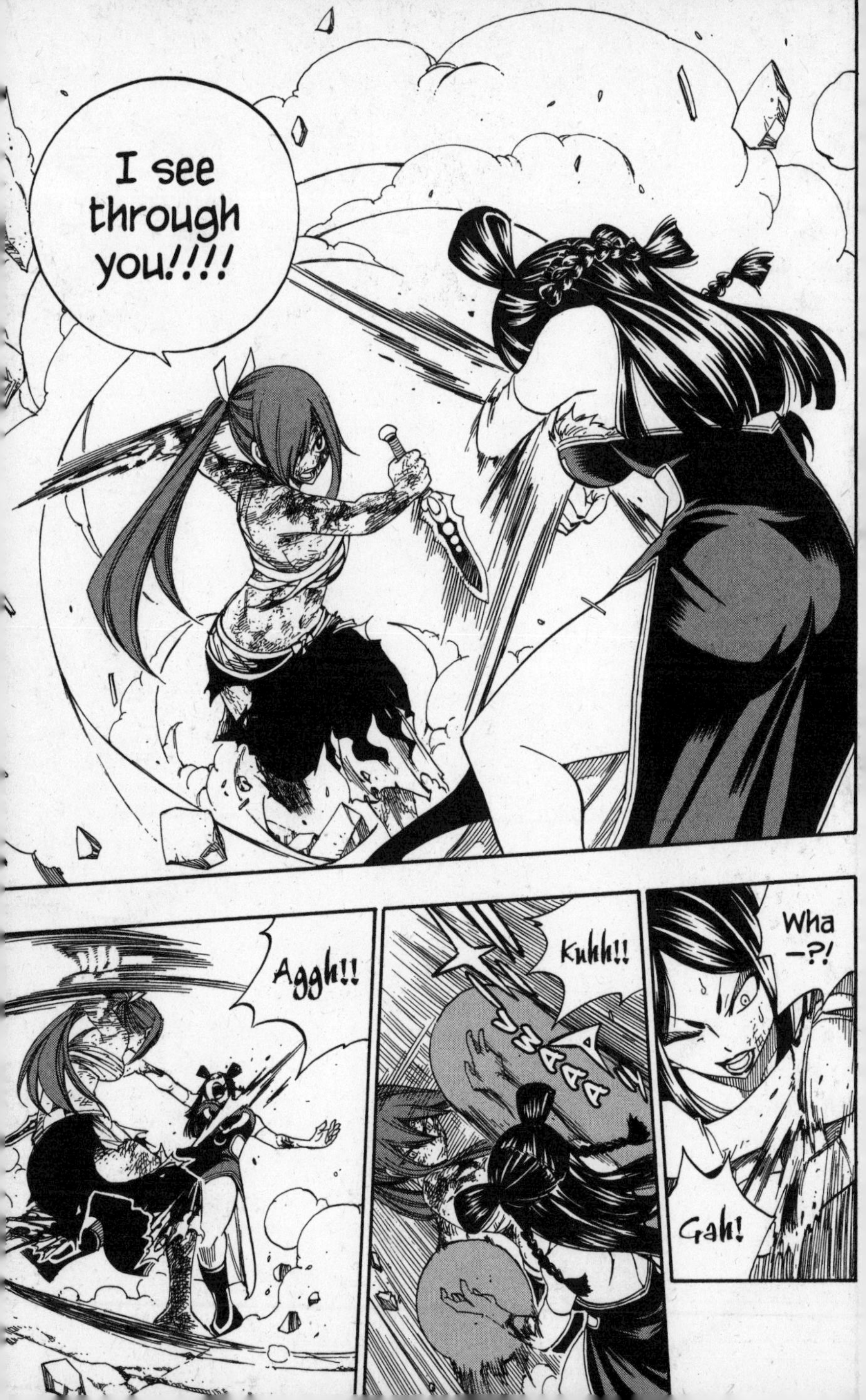
I see through you!!!!
Wha—?!
Gah!
Kuhh!!
Aggh!!

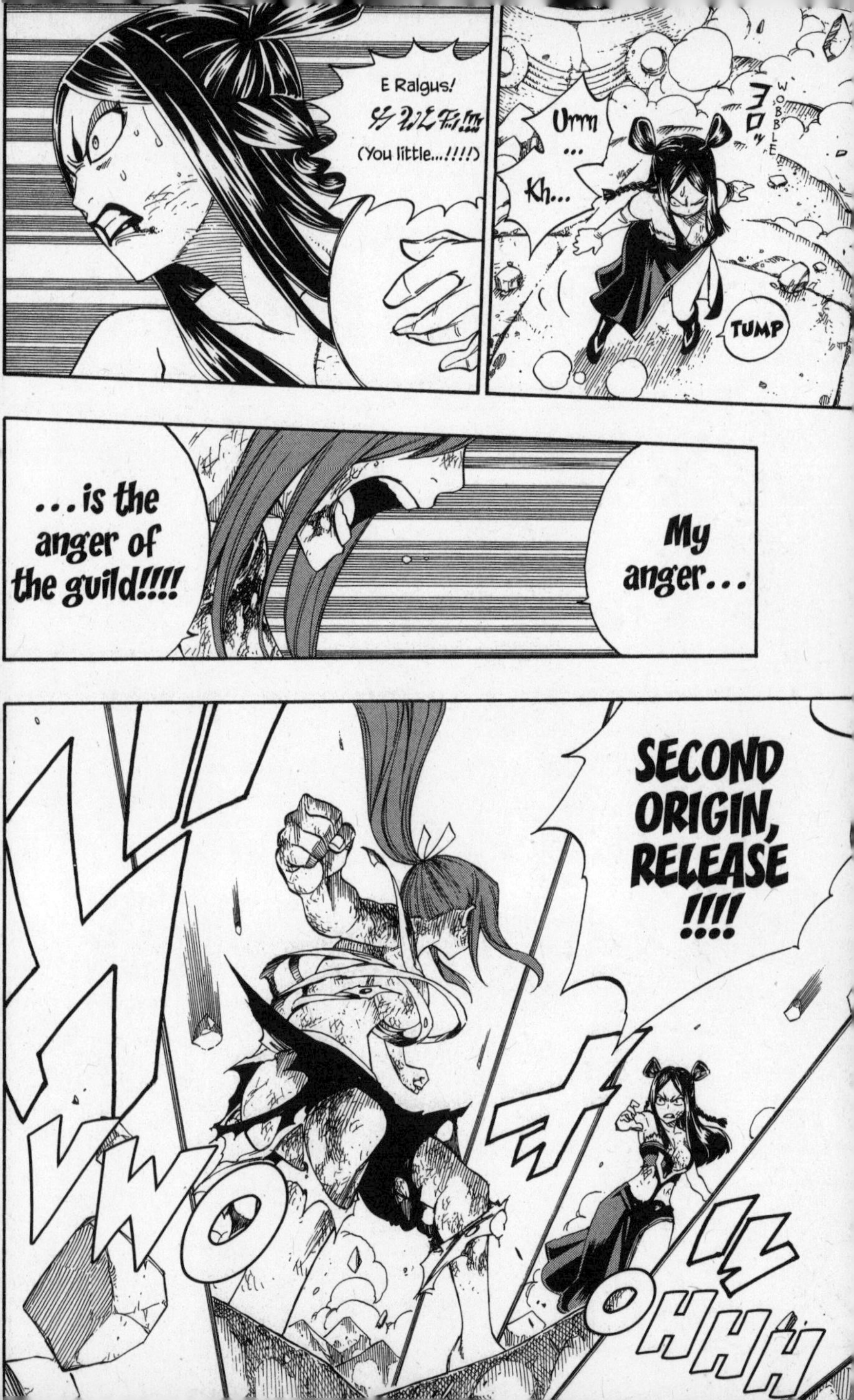
Urrn
...
Kh...
ヨロッ
WOBBLE
TUMP
E Ralgus!
(You little...!!!!)
My anger...
...is the anger of the guild!!!!
SECOND ORIGIN, RELEASE !!!!

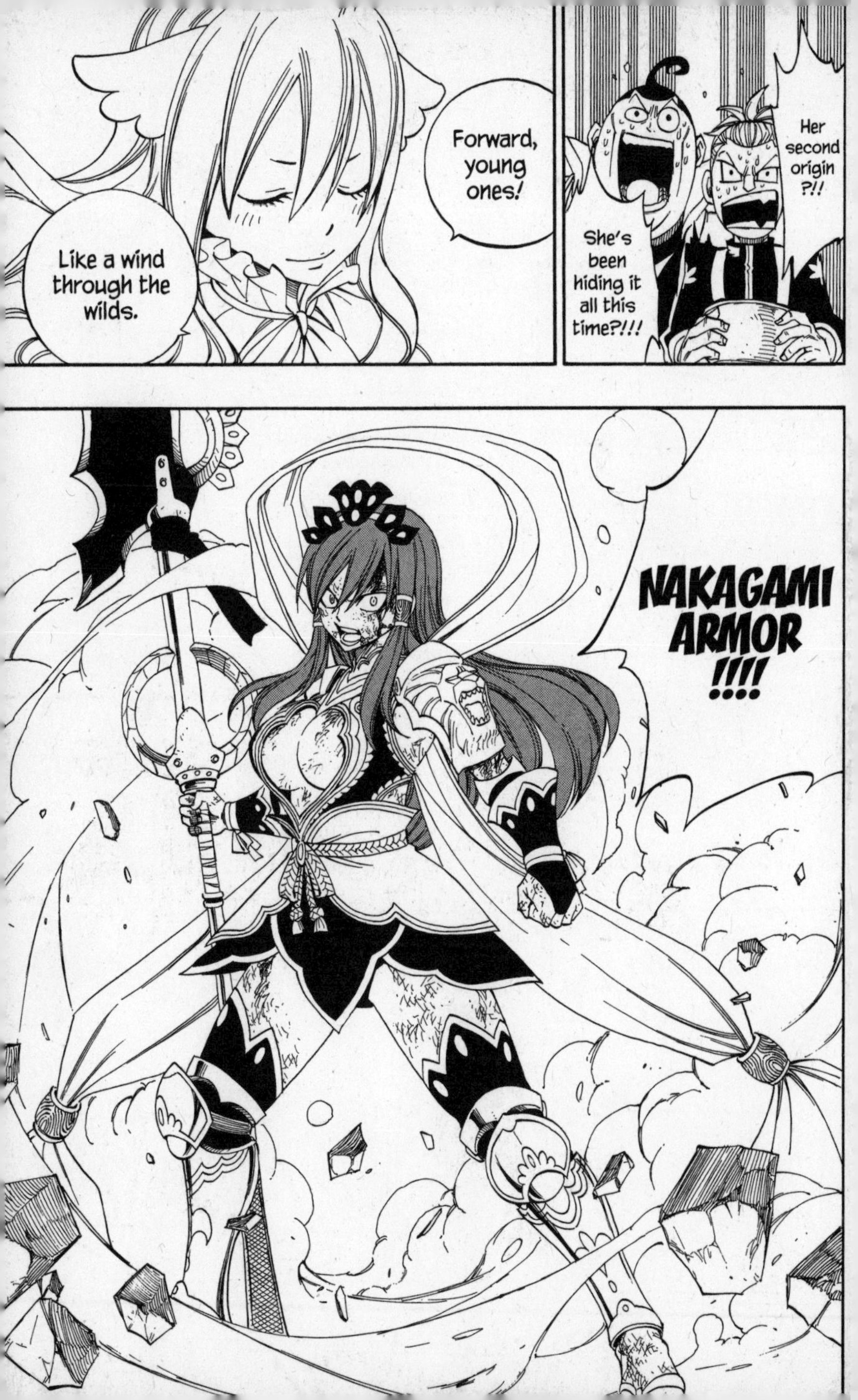
Her second origin ?!!
She's been hiding it all this time?!!!
Forward, young ones!
Like a wind through the wilds.
NAKAGAMI ARMOR !!!!

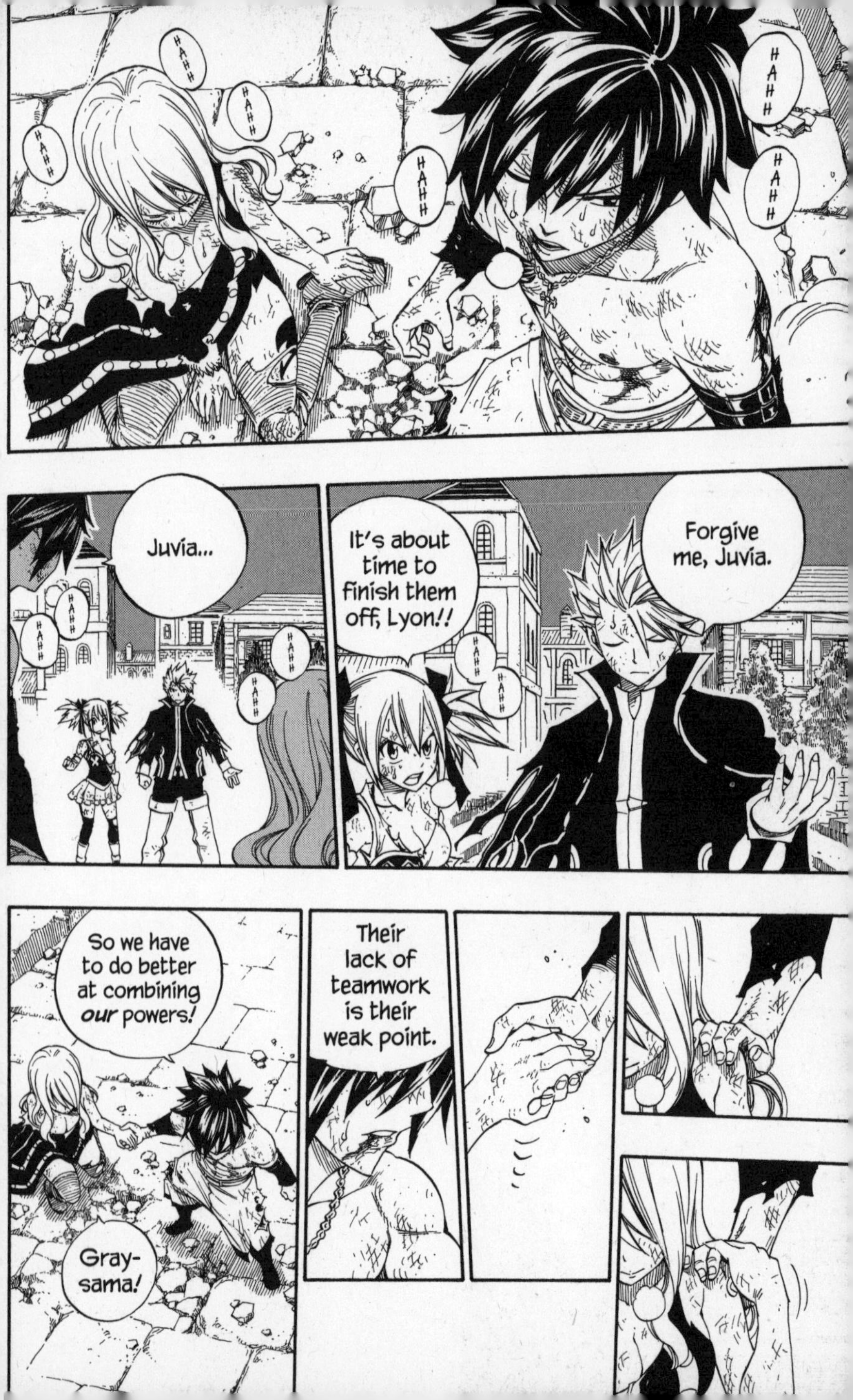
HAHH
HAHH
HAHH
HAHH
HAHH
HAHH
Forgive me, Juvia.
It's about time to finish them off, Lyon!!
HAHH
HAHH
Juvia...
HAHH
HAHH
HAHH
HAHH
Their lack of teamwork is their weak point.
So we have to do better at combining *our* powers!
Gray-sama!

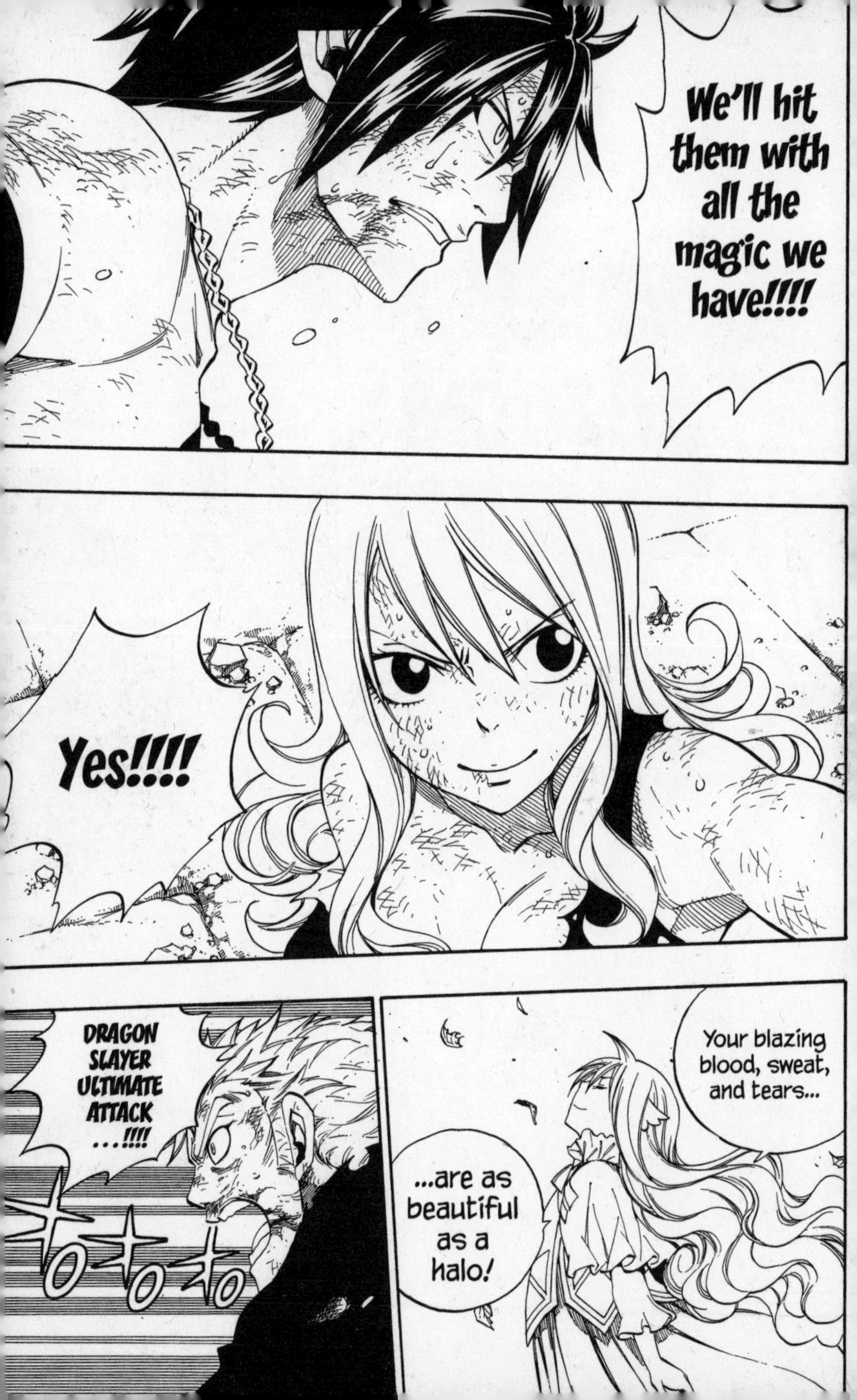
We'll hit them with all the magic we have!!!!
Yes!!!!
Your blazing blood, sweat, and tears...
...are as beautiful as a halo!
DRAGON SLAYER ULTIMATE ATTACK ...!!!!

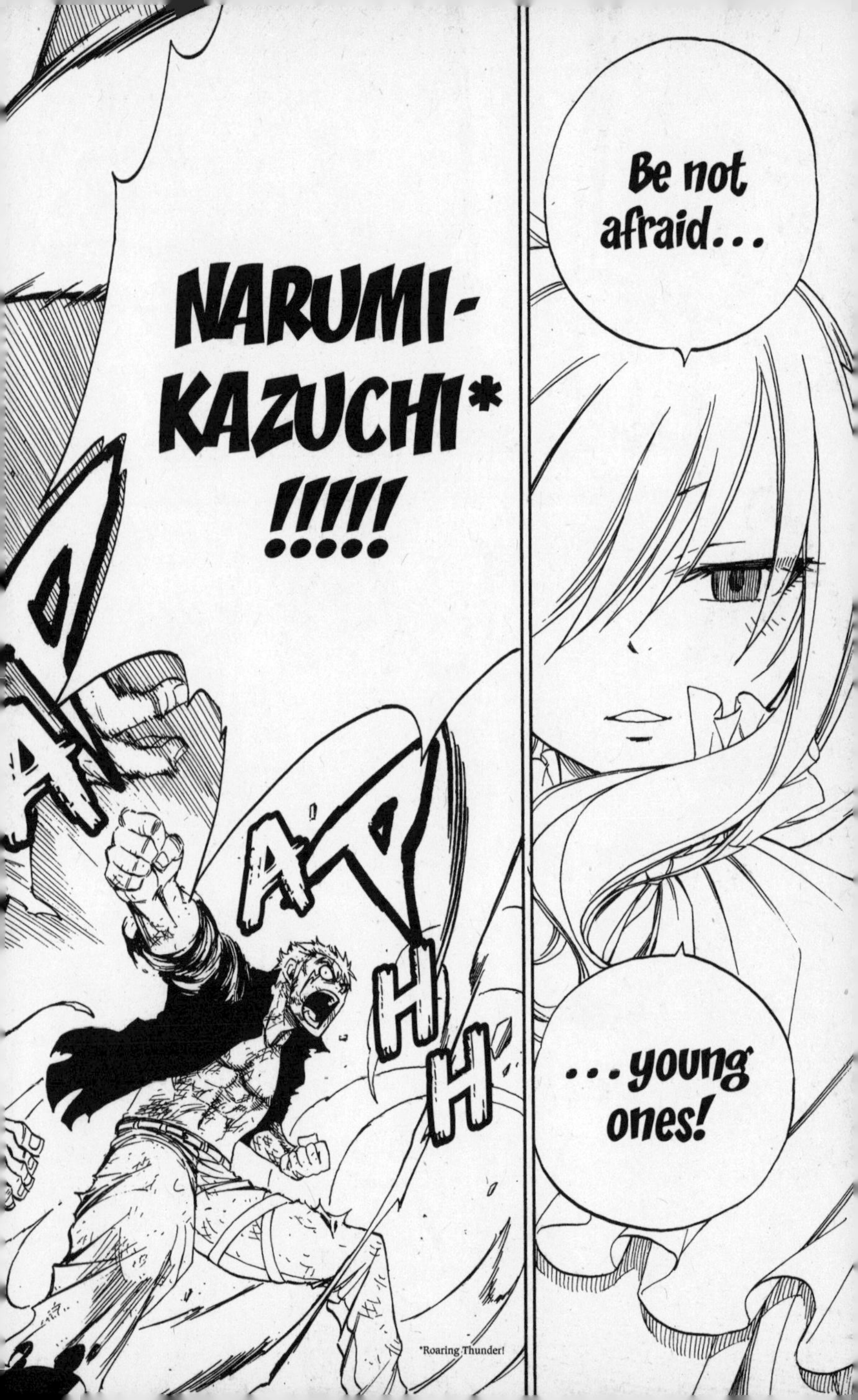
Be not afraid...
...young ones!
NARUMI-KAZUCHI*!!!!!
*Roaring Thunder!

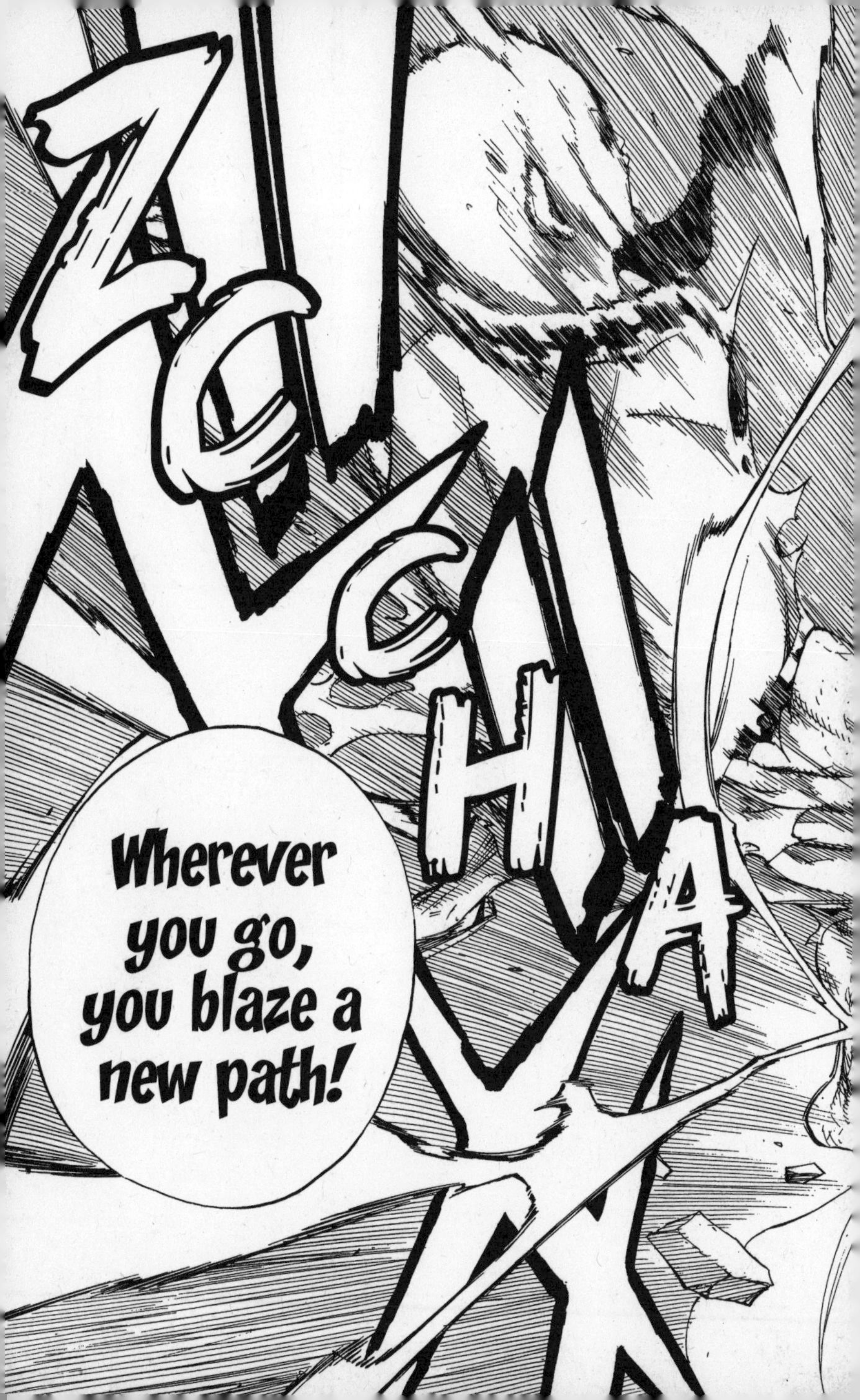
ZGCHA
Wherever you go, you blaze a new path!

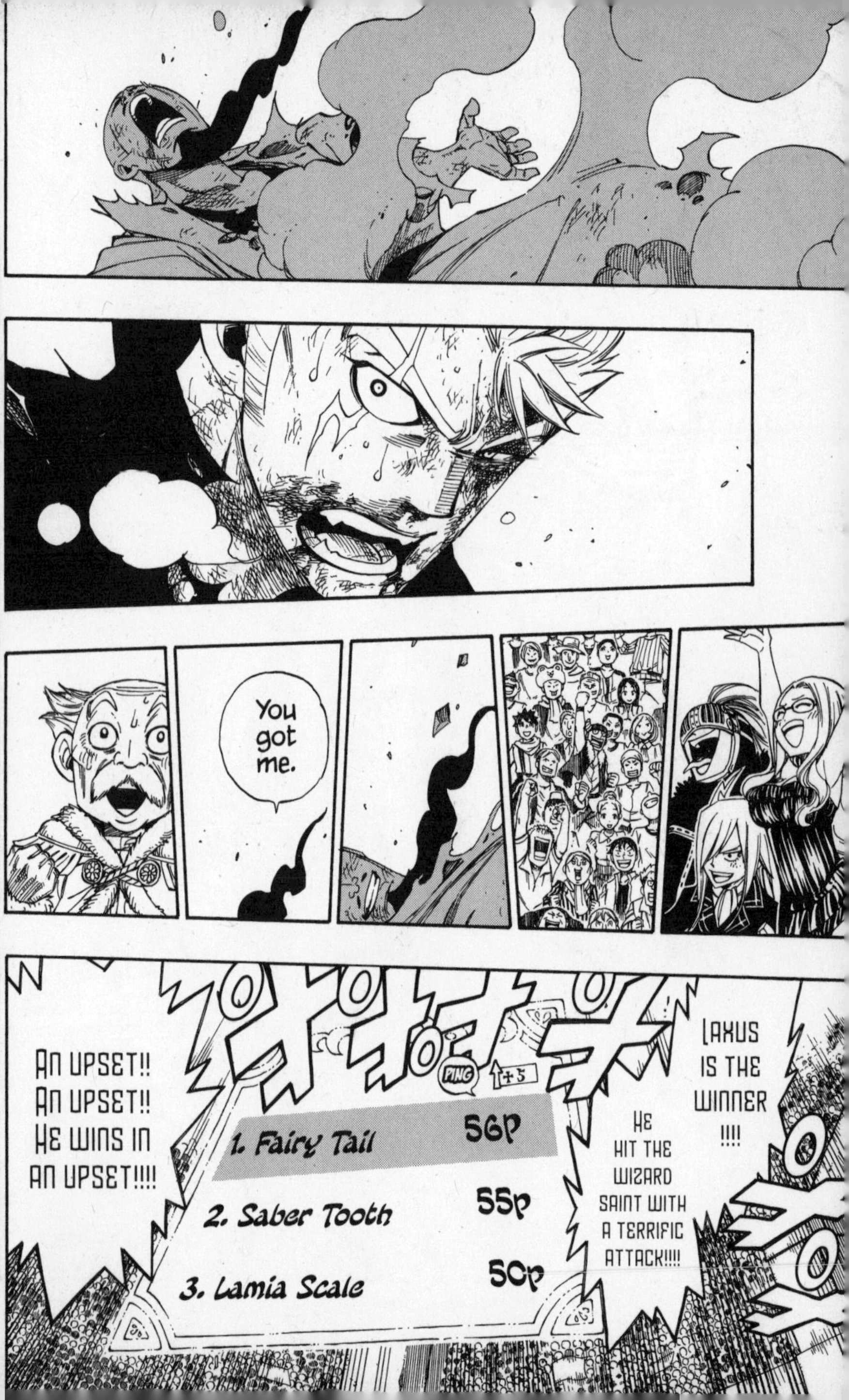
You got me.
LAXUS IS THE WINNER!!!!
HE HIT THE WIZARD SAINT WITH A TERRIFIC ATTACK!!!!
PING
+5
1. Fairy Tail 56p
2. Saber Tooth 55p
3. Lamia Scale 50p
AN UPSET!! AN UPSET!! HE WINS IN AN UPSET!!!!

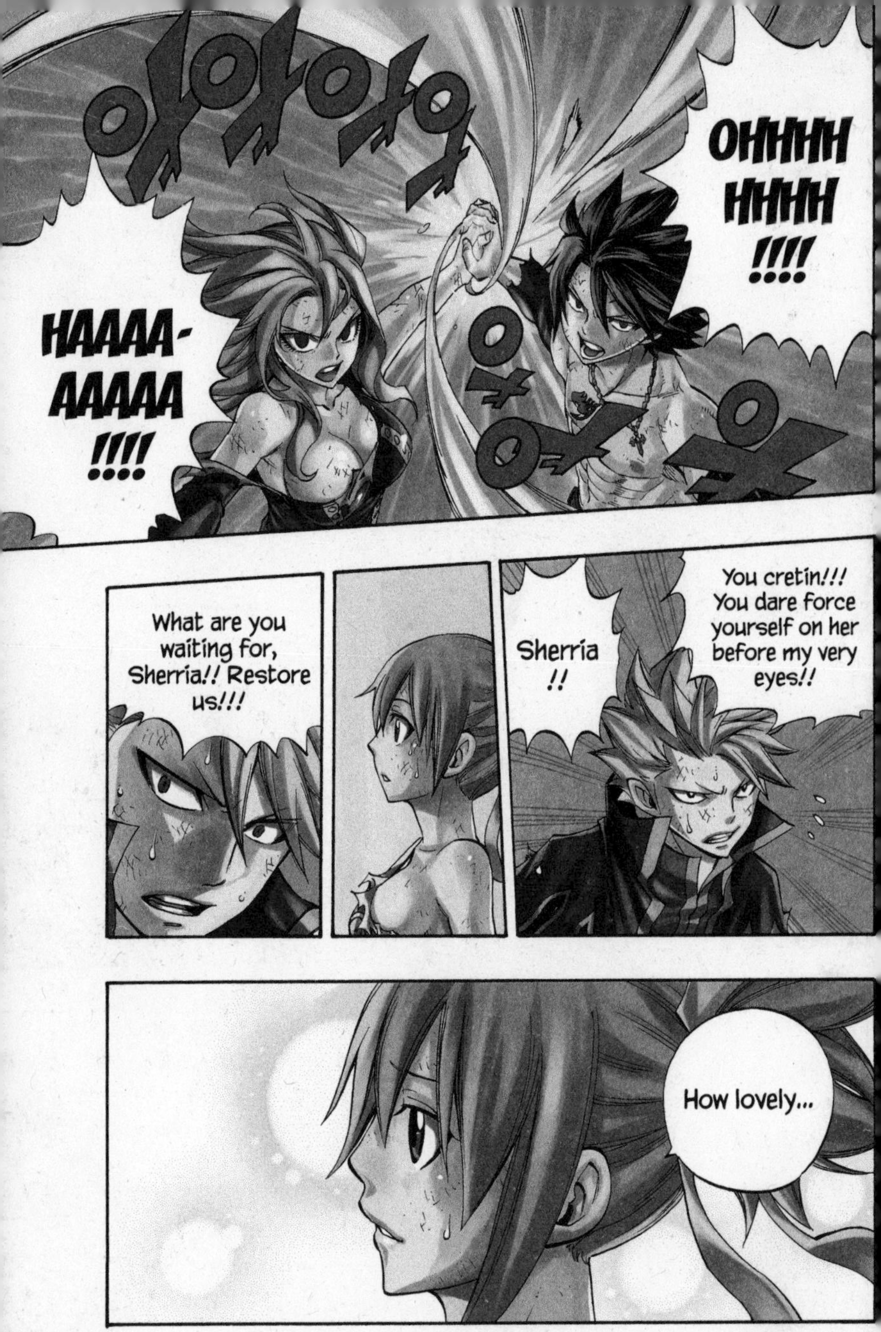
OHHHH HHHHH!!!!
HAAAA-AAAAA!!!!
You cretin!!! You dare force yourself on her before my very eyes!!
Sherria!!
What are you waiting for, Sherria!! Restore us!!!
How lovely...

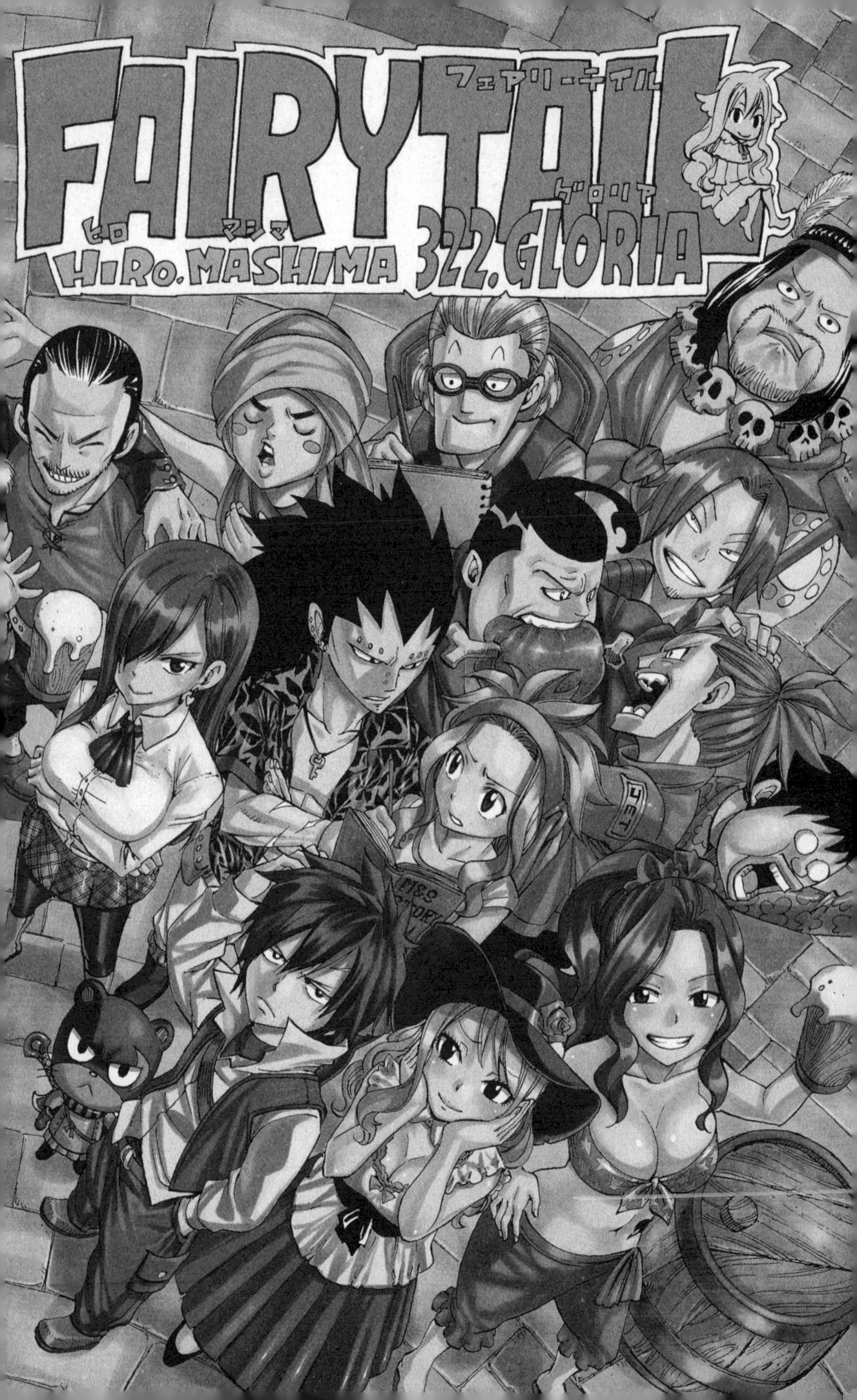
FAIRY TAIL
フェアリーテイル
ヒロ マシマ
H.Ro.MASHIMA
グロリア
322. GLORIA

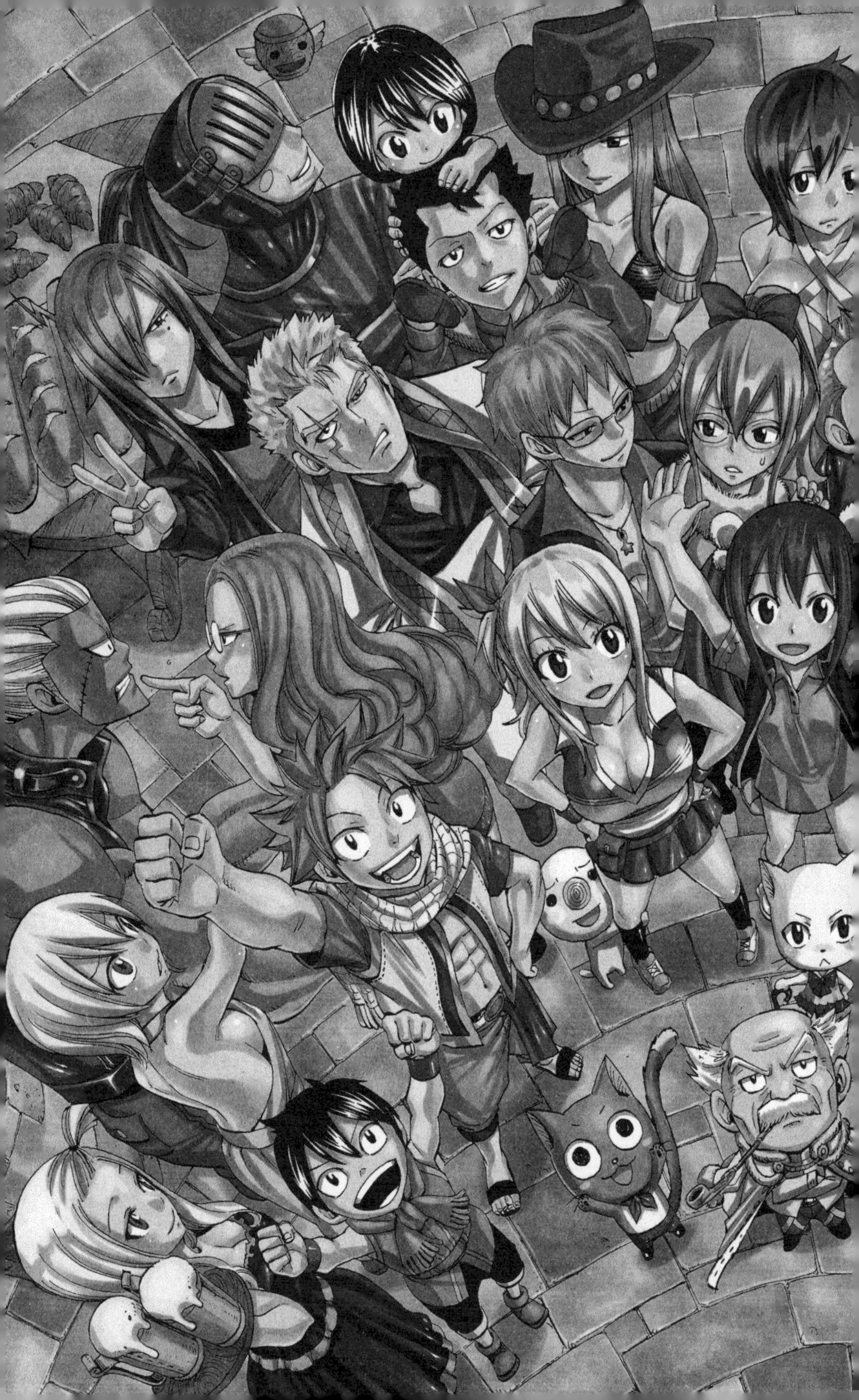

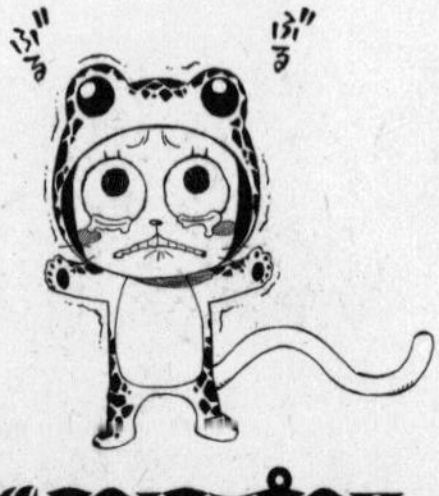
ぶる
ぶる

FAIRY TAIL

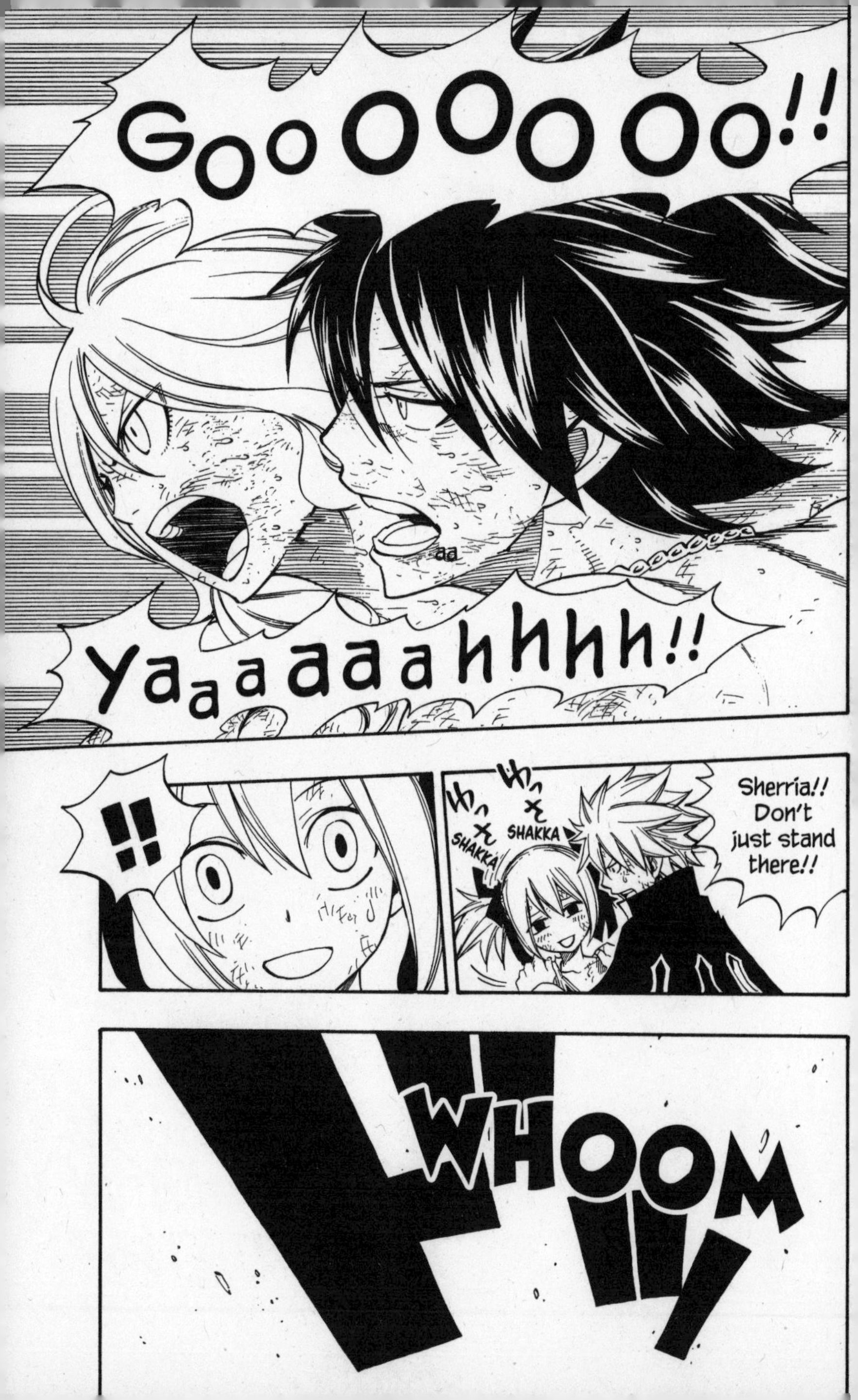
Goooooooo!!
aa
Yaaaaaahhhh!!
SHAKKA
SHAKKA
Sherria!! Don't just stand there!!
!!
WHOOM!!

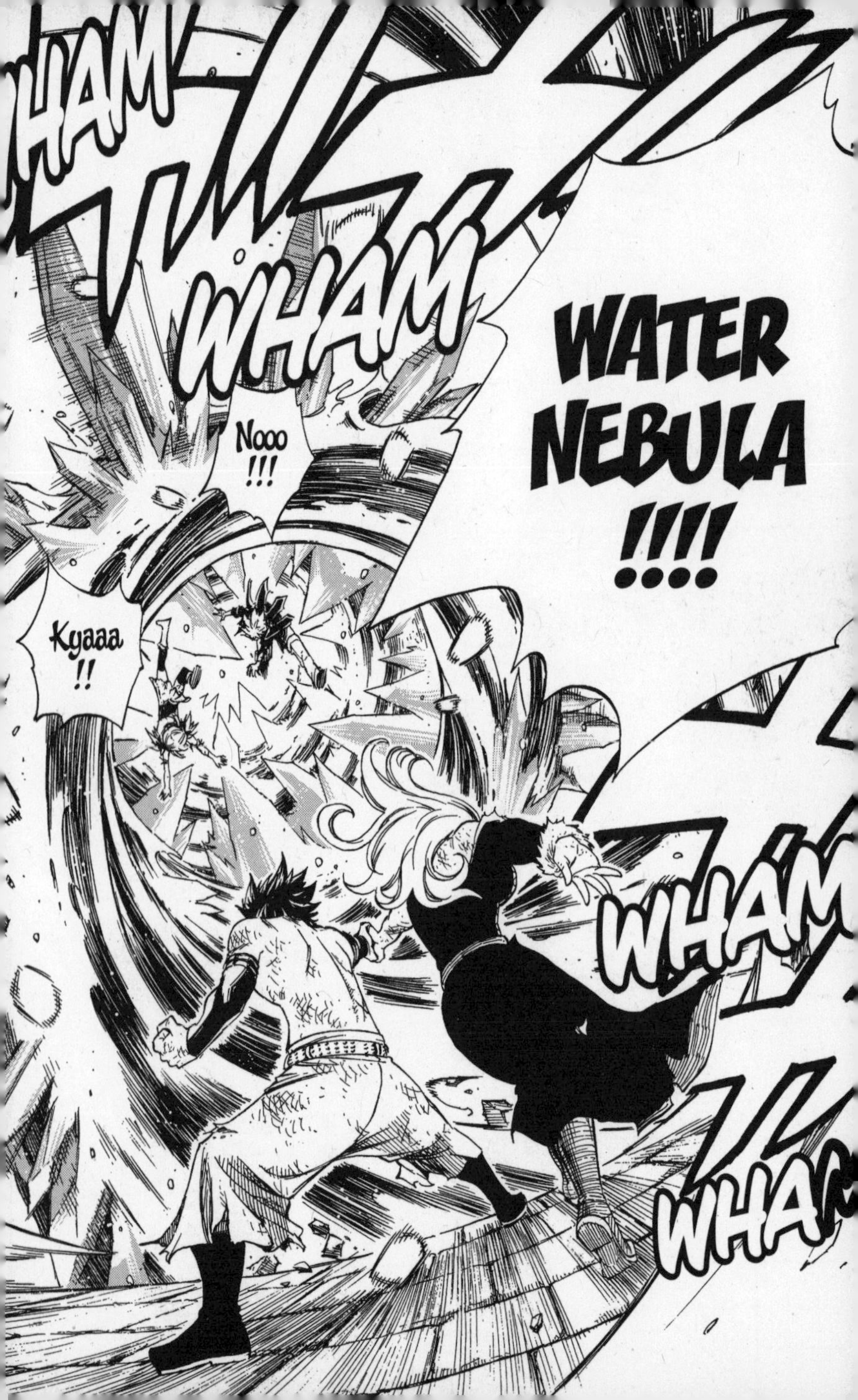
WHAM
WHAM
WATER NEBULA !!!!
Nooo !!!
Kyaaa !!
WHAM
WHAM

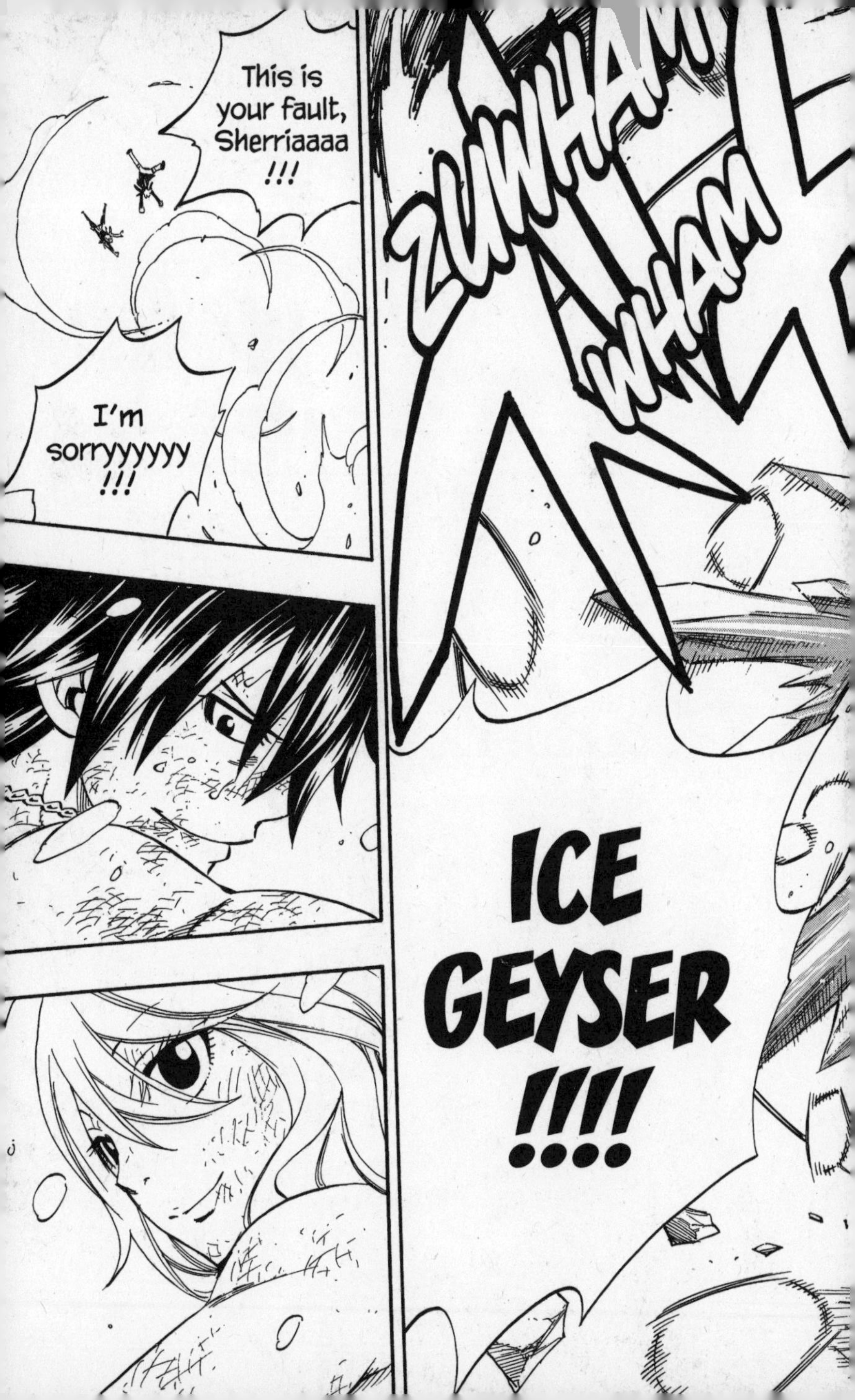
ZUWHAM
WHAM
ICE GEYSER!!!!
This is your fault, Sherriaaaa!!!
I'm sorryyyyyy!!!

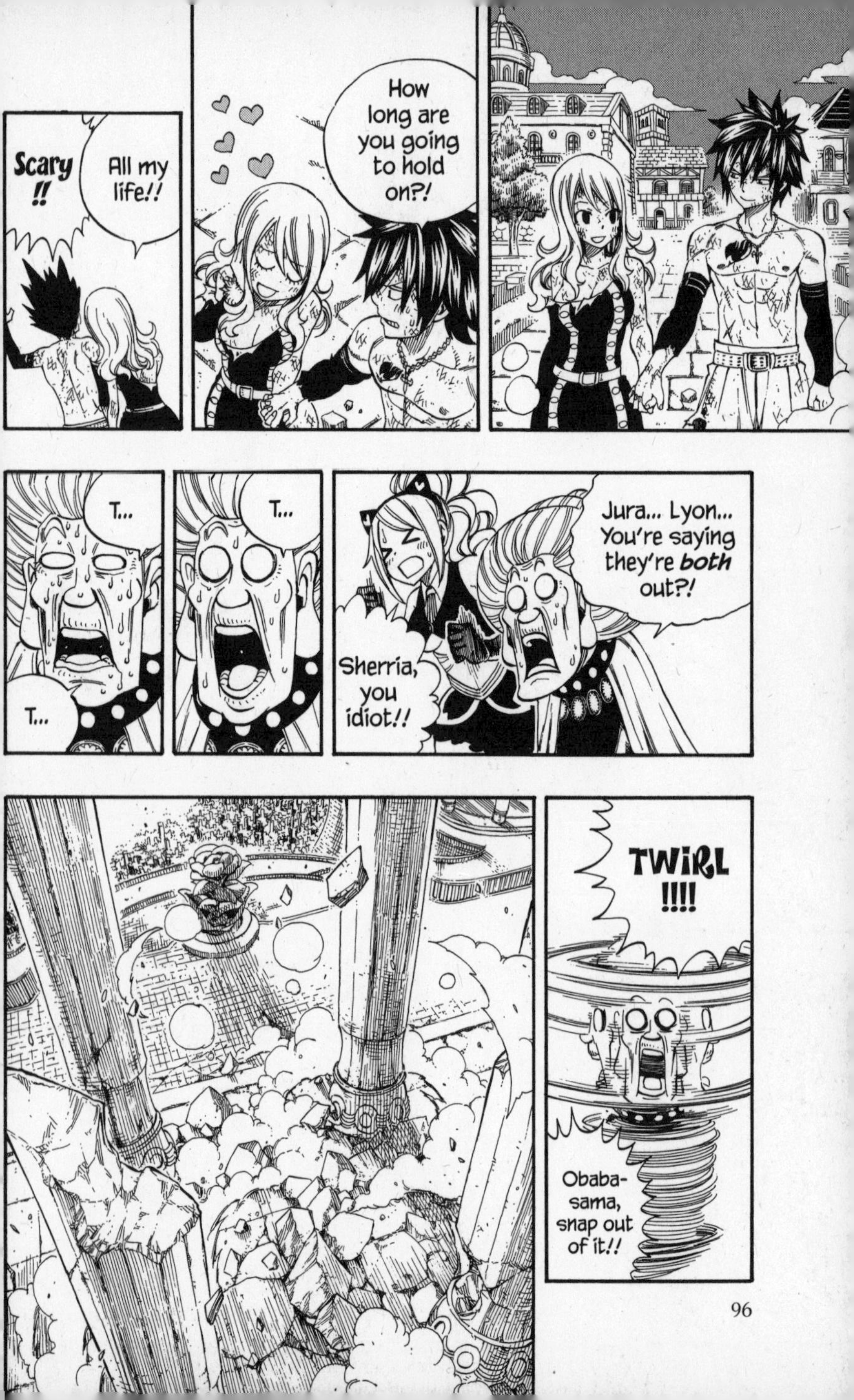
How long are you going to hold on?!
All my life!!
Scary!!
Jura... Lyon... You're saying they're *both* out?!
Sherria, you idiot!!
T...
T...
T...
TWIRL!!!!
Obaba-sama, snap out of it!!

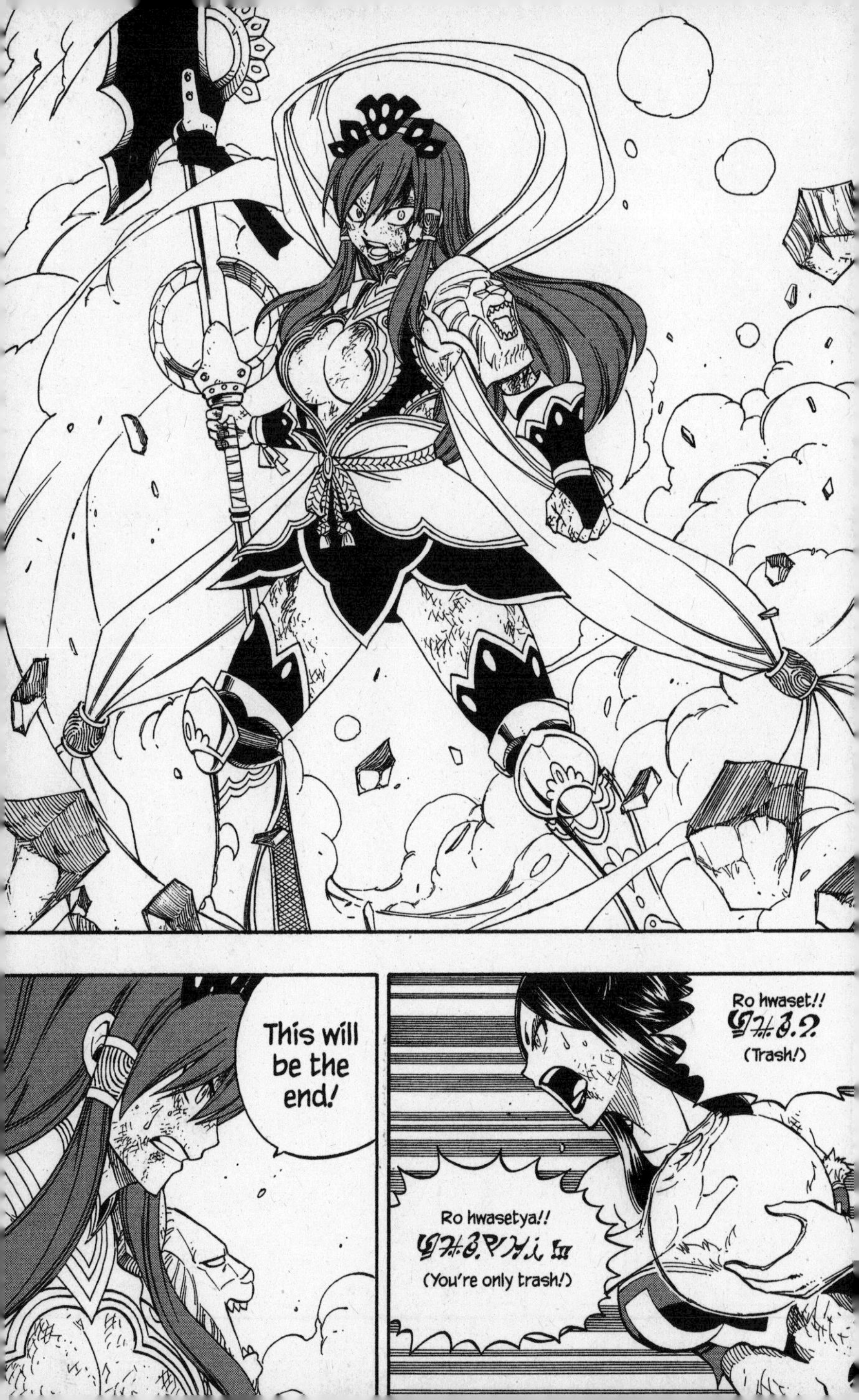
Ro hwaset!!
(Trash!)
Ro hwasetya!!
(You're only trash!)
This will be the end!

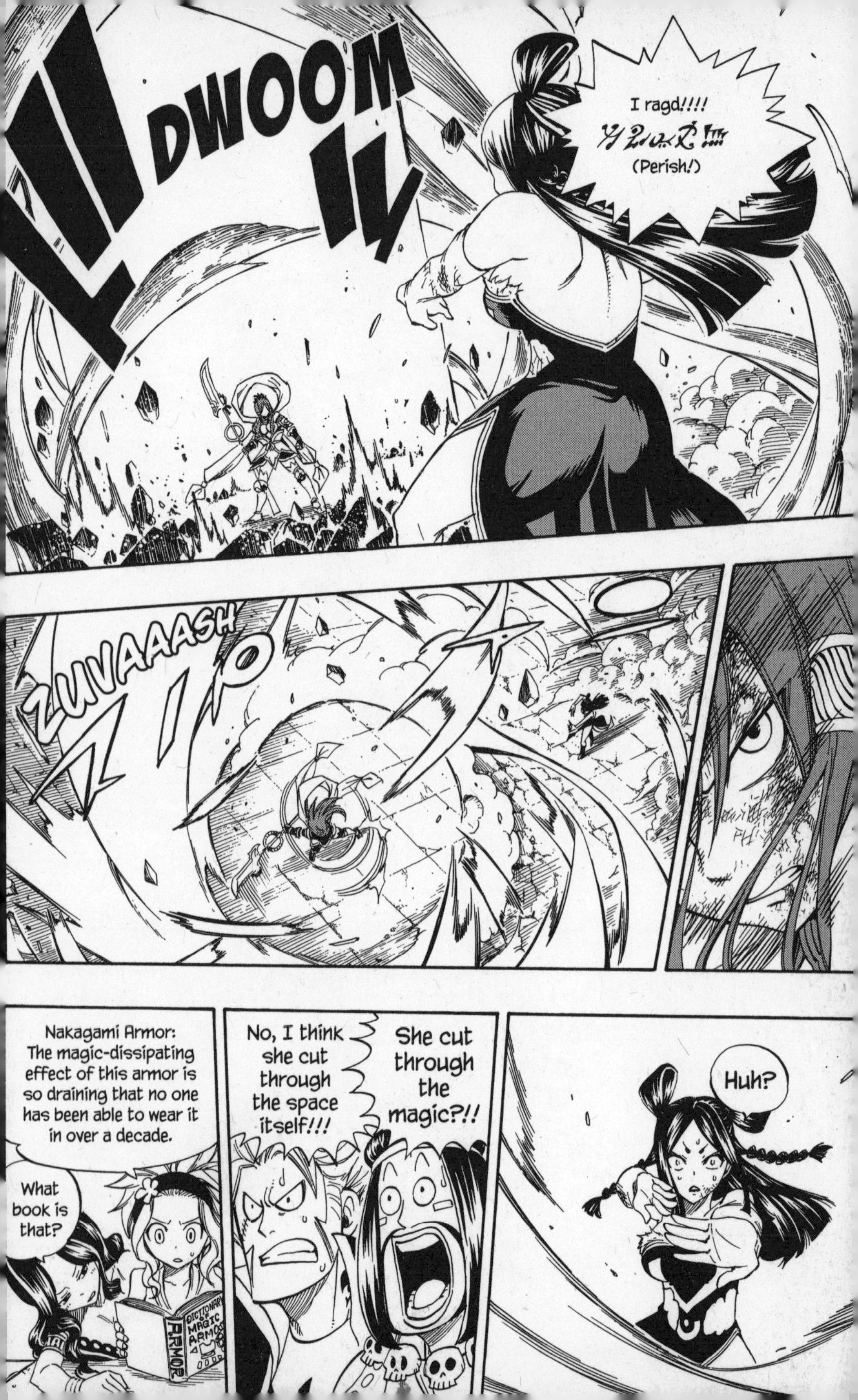
I ragd!!!!
(Perish!)
DWOOM
ZUVAASH
Huh?
She cut through the magic?!!
No, I think she cut through the space itself!!!
Nakagami Armor: The magic-dissipating effect of this armor is so draining that no one has been able to wear it in over a decade.
What book is that?
DICTIONARY OF MAGIC ARMOR

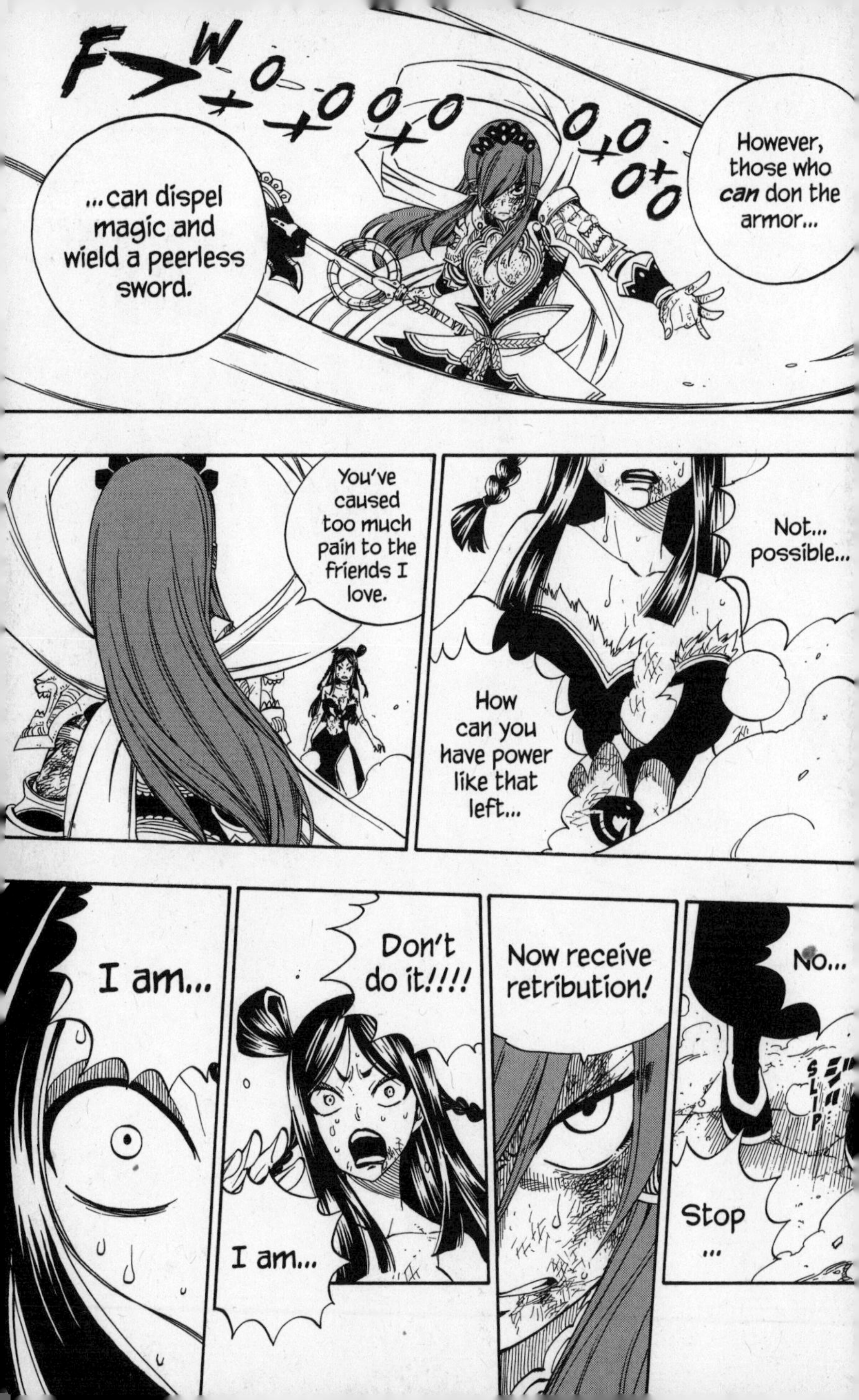

However, those who *can* don the armor...
FWOOOOOOOO
...can dispel magic and wield a peerless sword.
Not... possible...
How can you have power like that left...
You've caused too much pain to the friends I love.
No...
SLIP
Stop...
Now receive retribution!
Don't do it!!!!
I am...
I am...

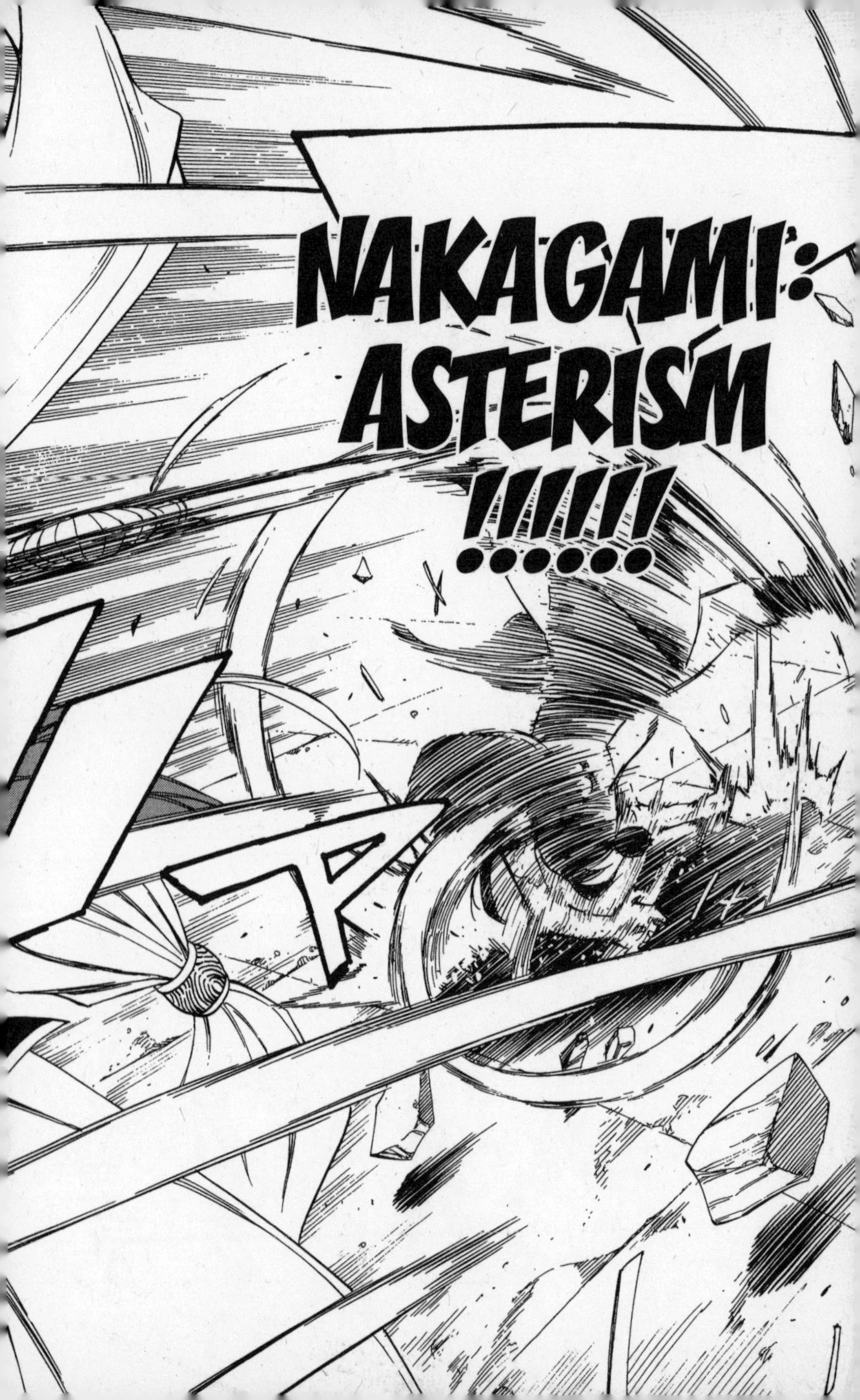
NAKAGAMI: ASTERISM!!!!!!......

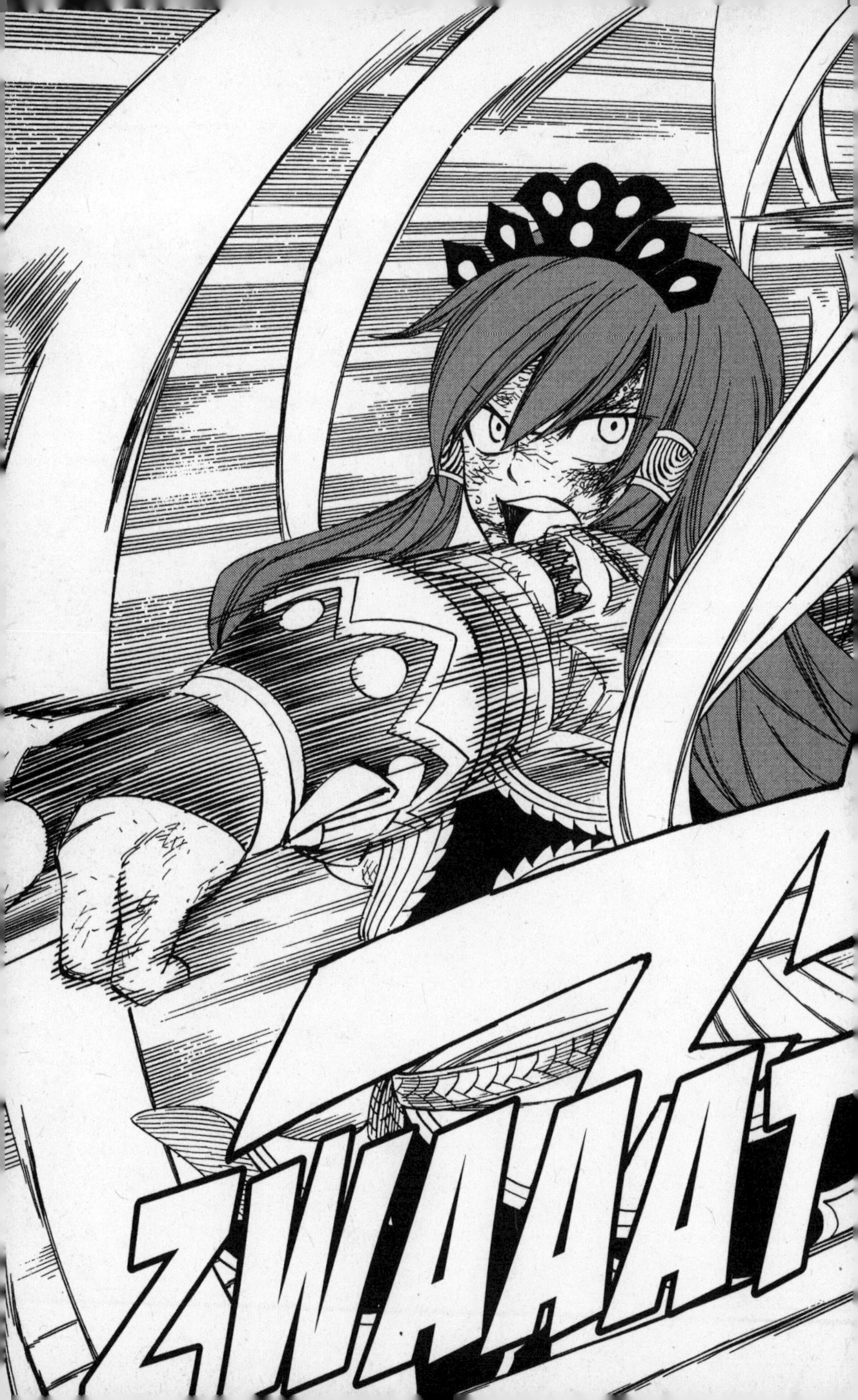
ZWAAAT

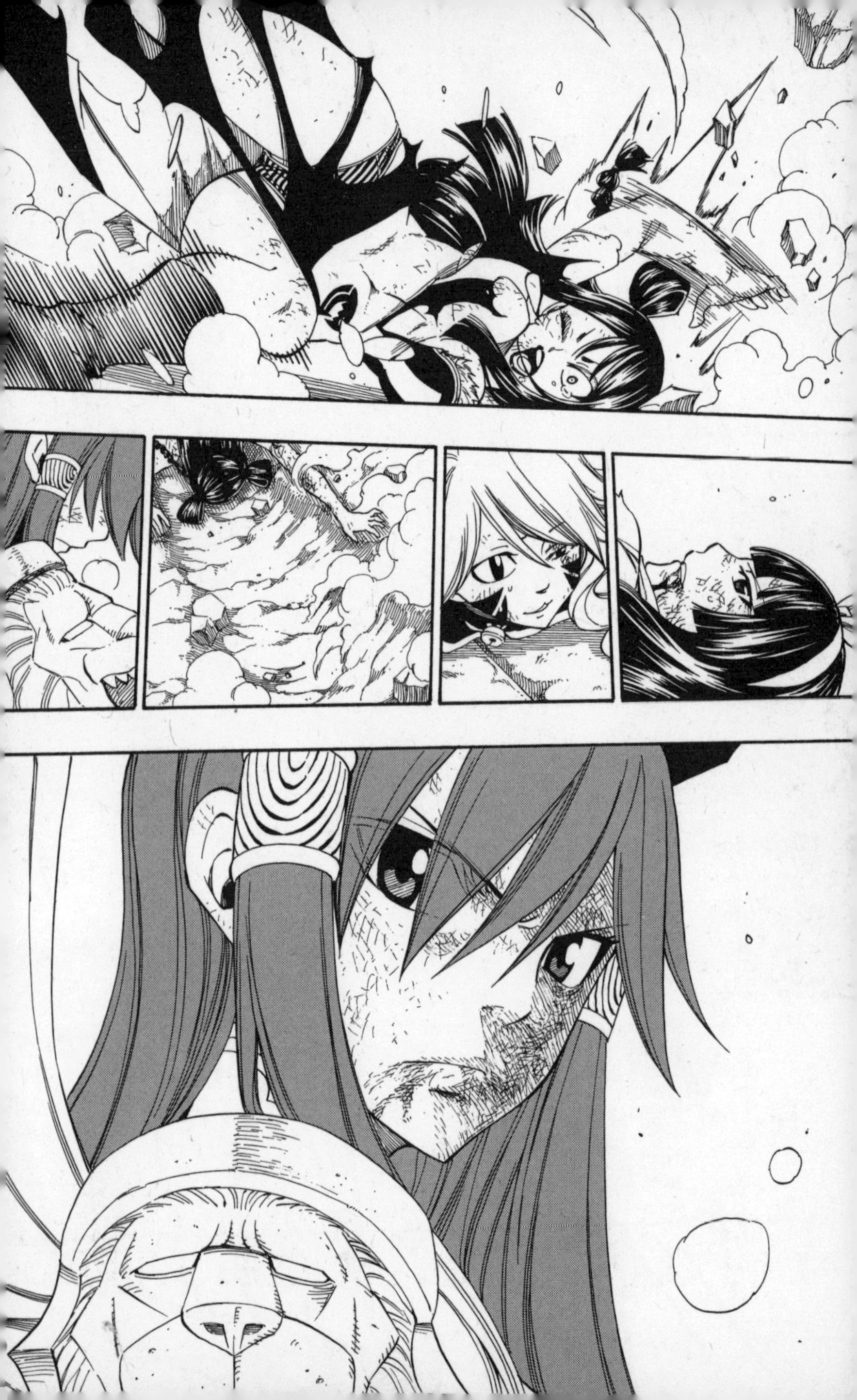

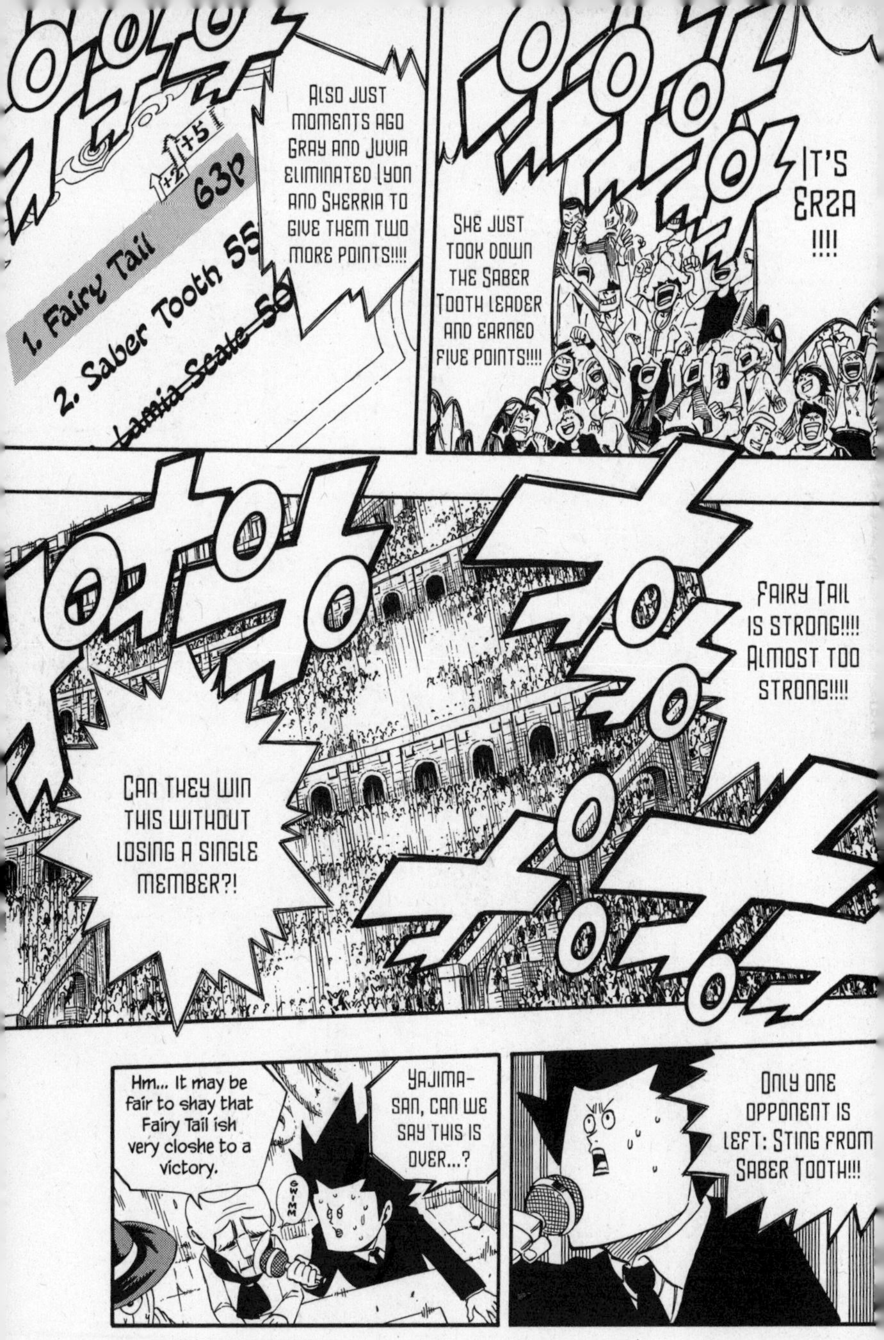
It's Erza!!!!
She just took down the Saber Tooth leader and earned five points!!!!
Also just moments ago Gray and Juvia eliminated Lyon and Sherria to give them two more points!!!!
1. Fairy Tail 63p
+2
+5
2. Saber Tooth 55
~~Lamia Scale 58~~
Fairy Tail is strong!!!! Almost too strong!!!!
Can they win this without losing a single member?!
Only one opponent is left: Sting from Saber Tooth!!!
Yajima-san, can we say this is over...?
Hm... It may be fair to shay that Fairy Tail ish very closhe to a victory.
GWIMM

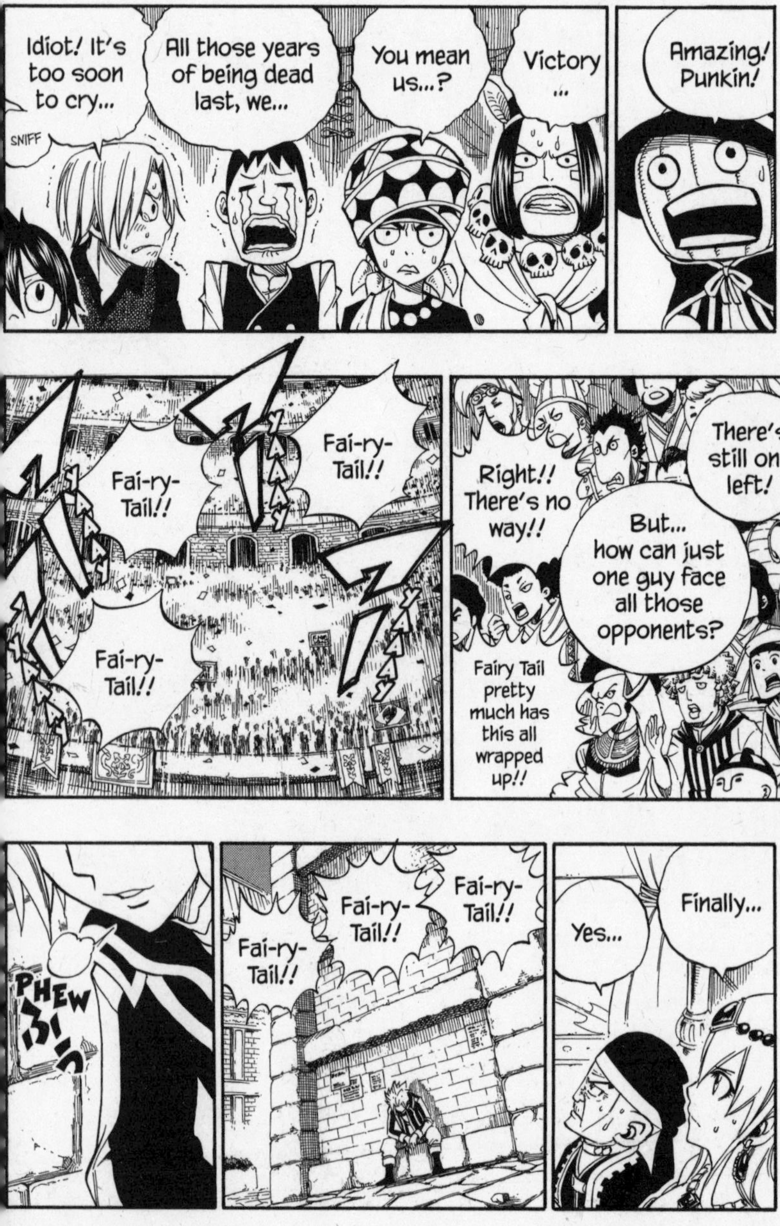
Amazing! Punkin!
Victory ...
You mean us...?
All those years of being dead last, we...
Idiot! It's too soon to cry...
SNIFF
There's still one left!
But... how can just one guy face all those opponents?
Right!! There's no way!!
Fairy Tail pretty much has this all wrapped up!!
Fai-ry-Tail!!
Fai-ry-Tail!!
Fai-ry-Tail!!
Finally...
Yes...
Fai-ry-Tail!!
Fai-ry-Tail!!
Fai-ry-Tail!!
PHEW

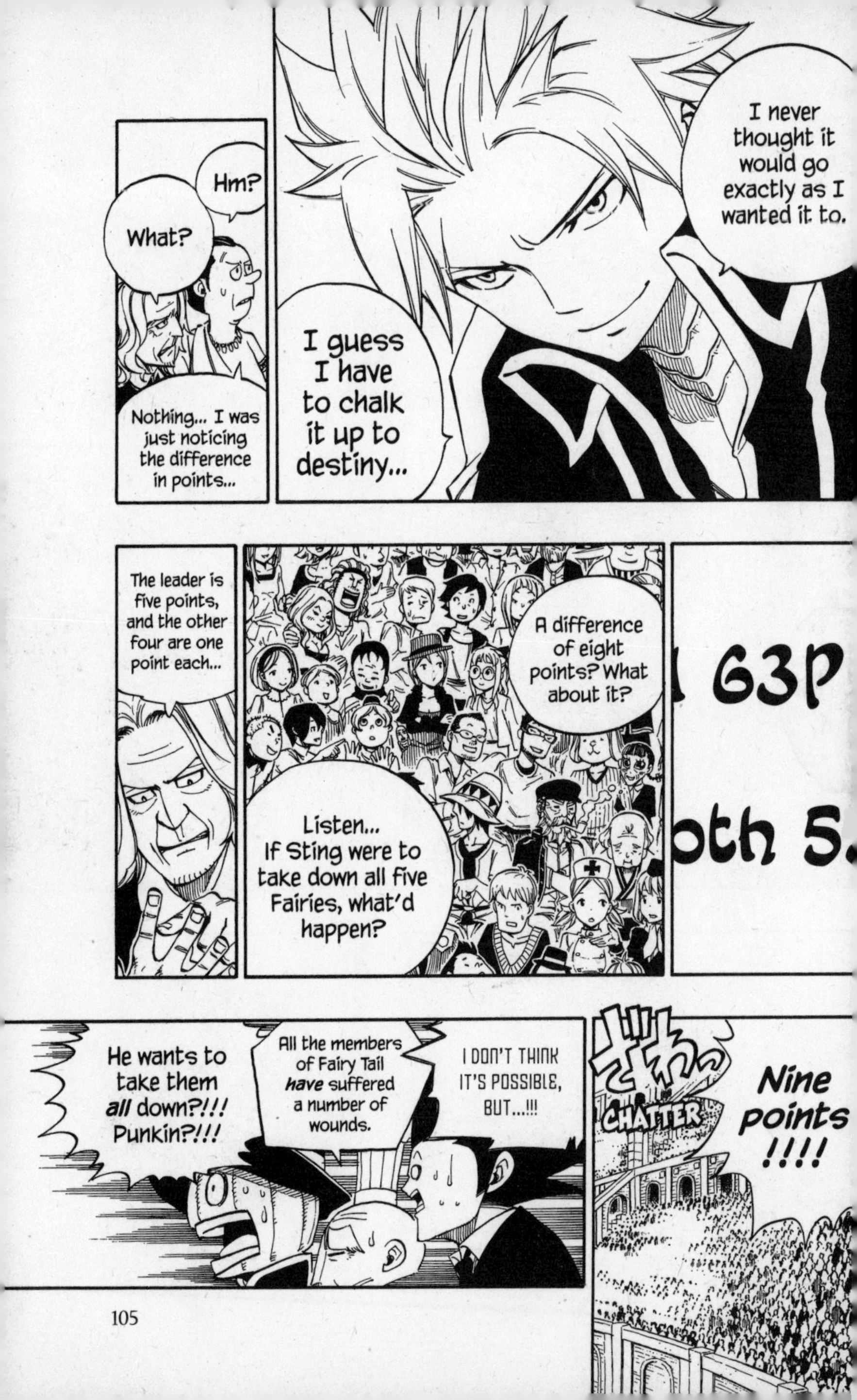
I never thought it would go exactly as I wanted it to.
I guess I have to chalk it up to destiny...
Hm?
What?
Nothing... I was just noticing the difference in points...
63P
oth 5.
A difference of eight points? What about it?
Listen... If Sting were to take down all five Fairies, what'd happen?
The leader is five points, and the other four are one point each...
CHATTER
Nine points!!!!
I DON'T THINK IT'S POSSIBLE, BUT...!!!
All the members of Fairy Tail *have* suffered a number of wounds.
He wants to take them *all* down?!!! Punkin?!!!

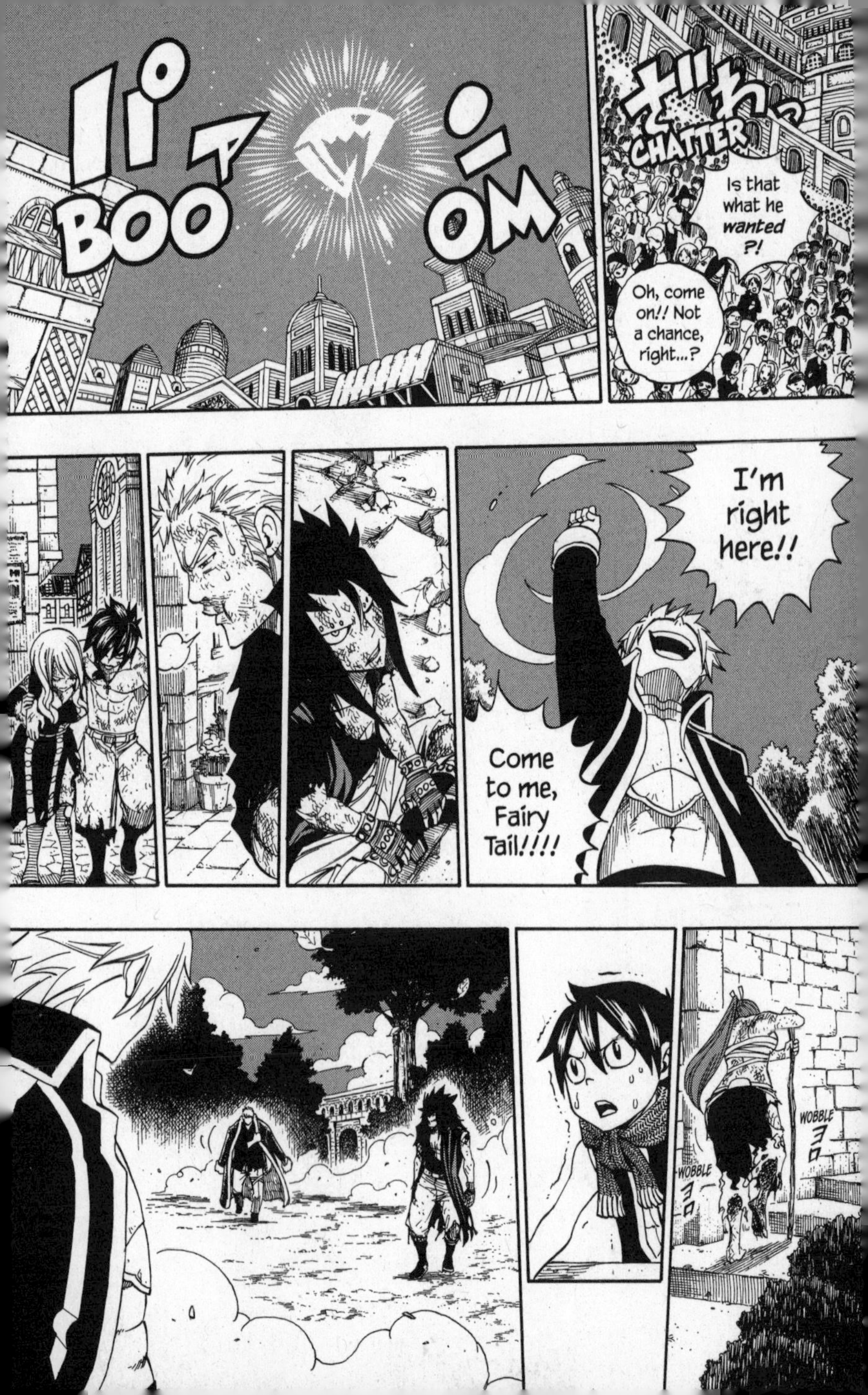
CHATTER
Is that what he *wanted* ?!
Oh, come on!! Not a chance, right...?
BOOOM
I'm right here!!
Come to me, Fairy Tail!!!!
WOBBLE
WOBBLE

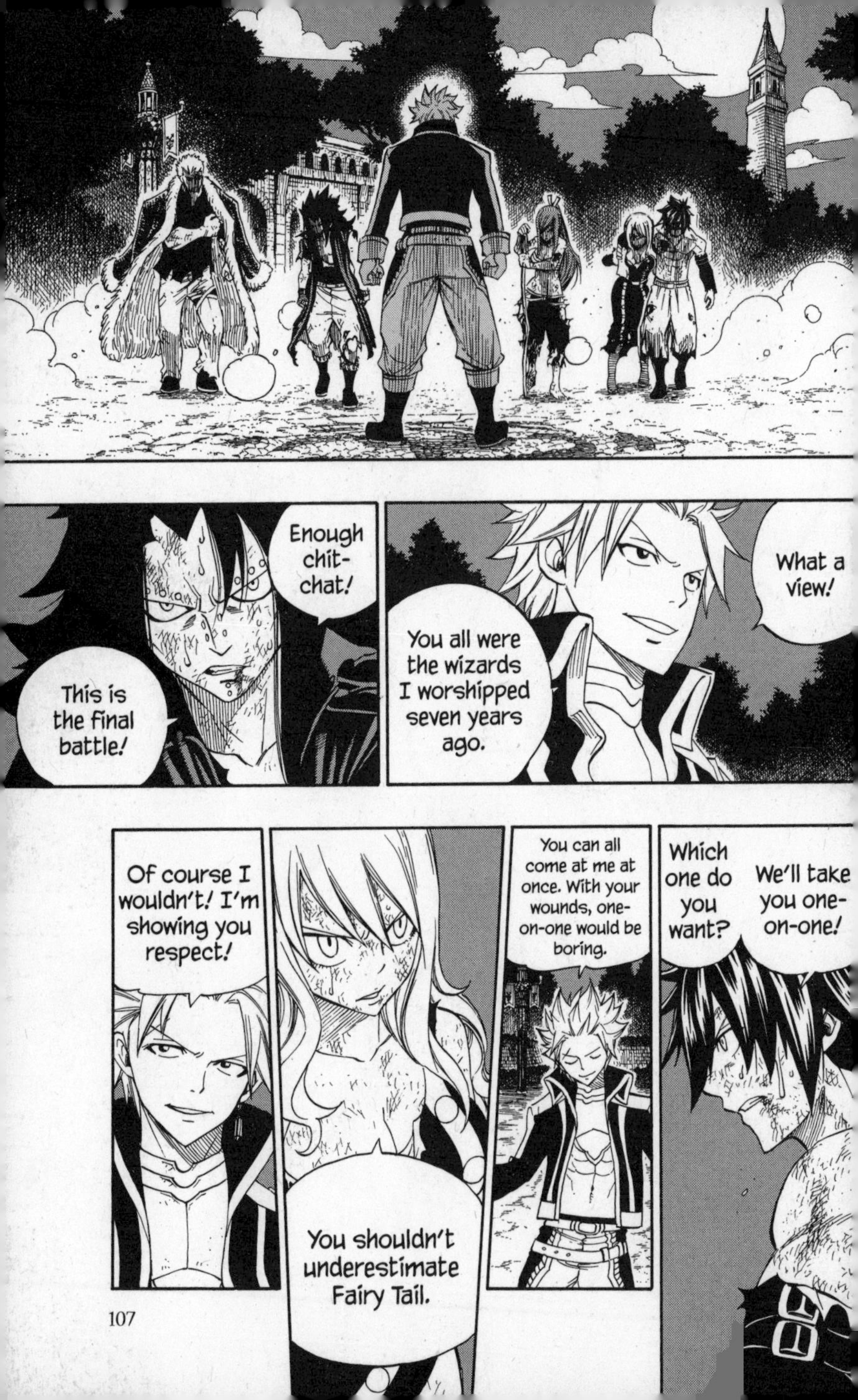
What a view!
You all were the wizards I worshipped seven years ago.
Enough chit-chat!
This is the final battle!
We'll take you one-on-one!
Which one do you want?
You can all come at me at once. With your wounds, one-on-one would be boring.
You shouldn't underestimate Fairy Tail.
Of course I wouldn't! I'm showing you respect!

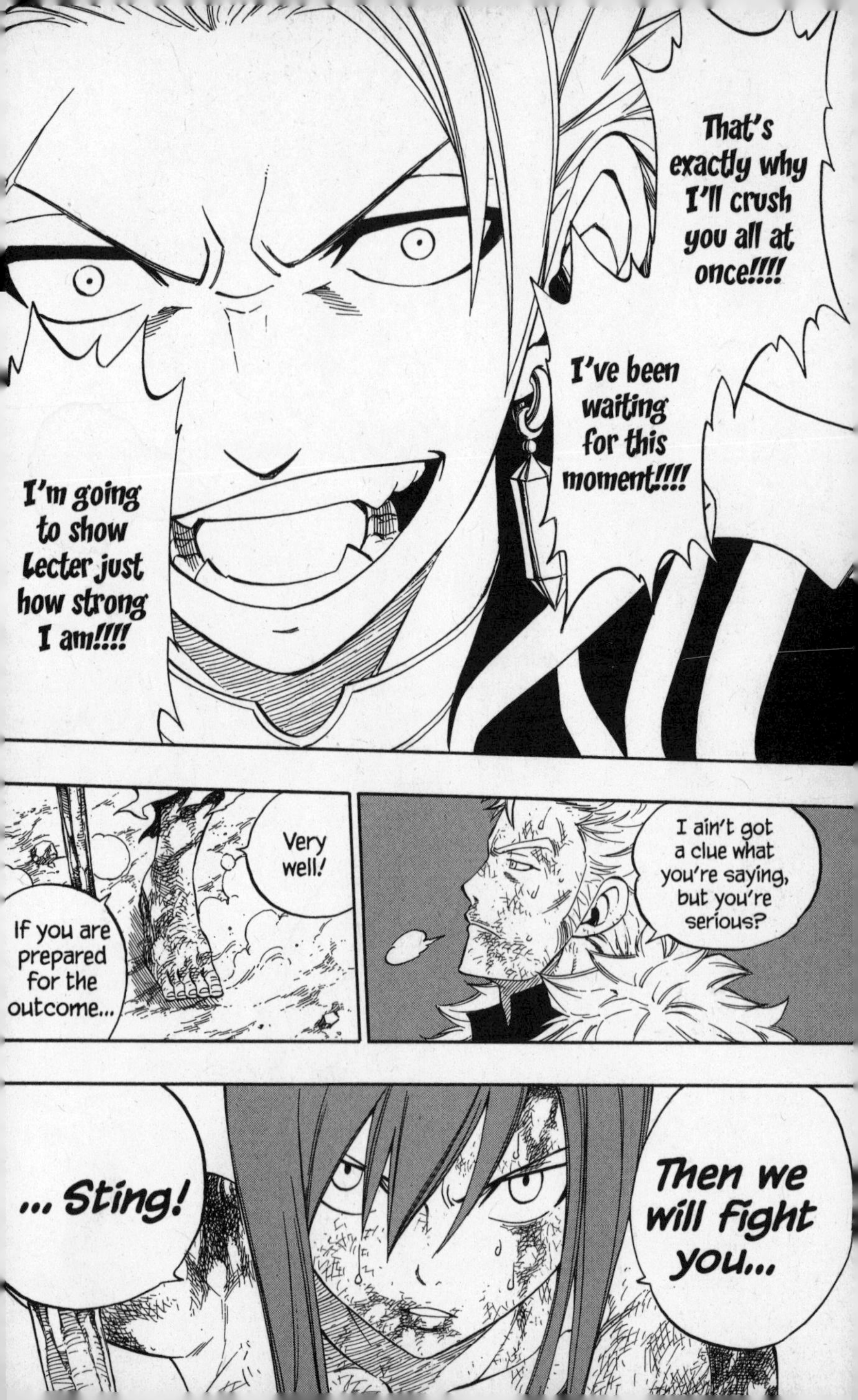
That's exactly why I'll crush you all at once!!!!
I've been waiting for this moment!!!!
I'm going to show Lecter just how strong I am!!!!
I ain't got a clue what you're saying, but you're serious?
Very well!
If you are prepared for the outcome...
Then we will fight you...
... Sting!

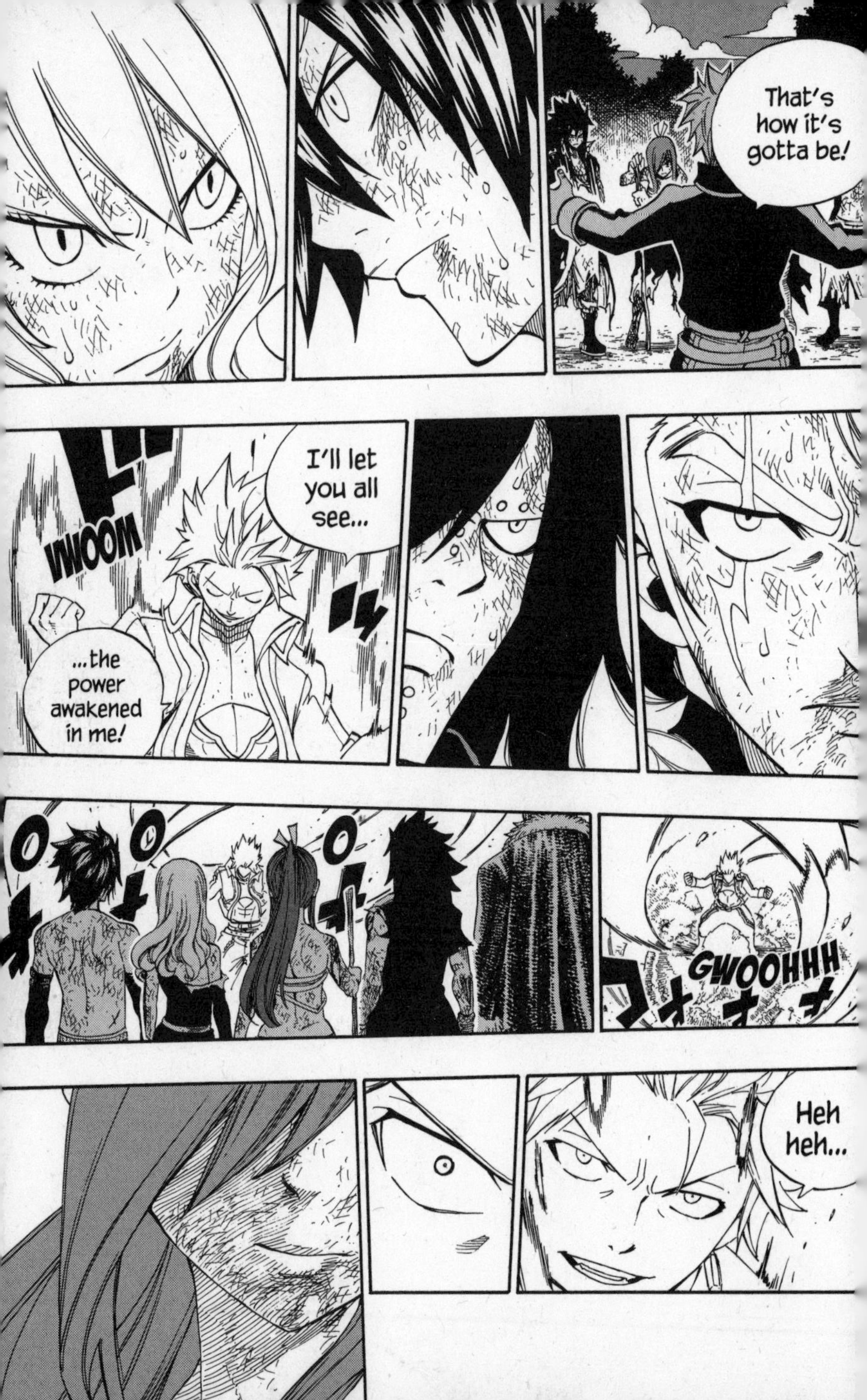
That's how it's gotta be!
VWOOM
I'll let you all see...
...the power awakened in me!
GWOOHHH
Heh heh...

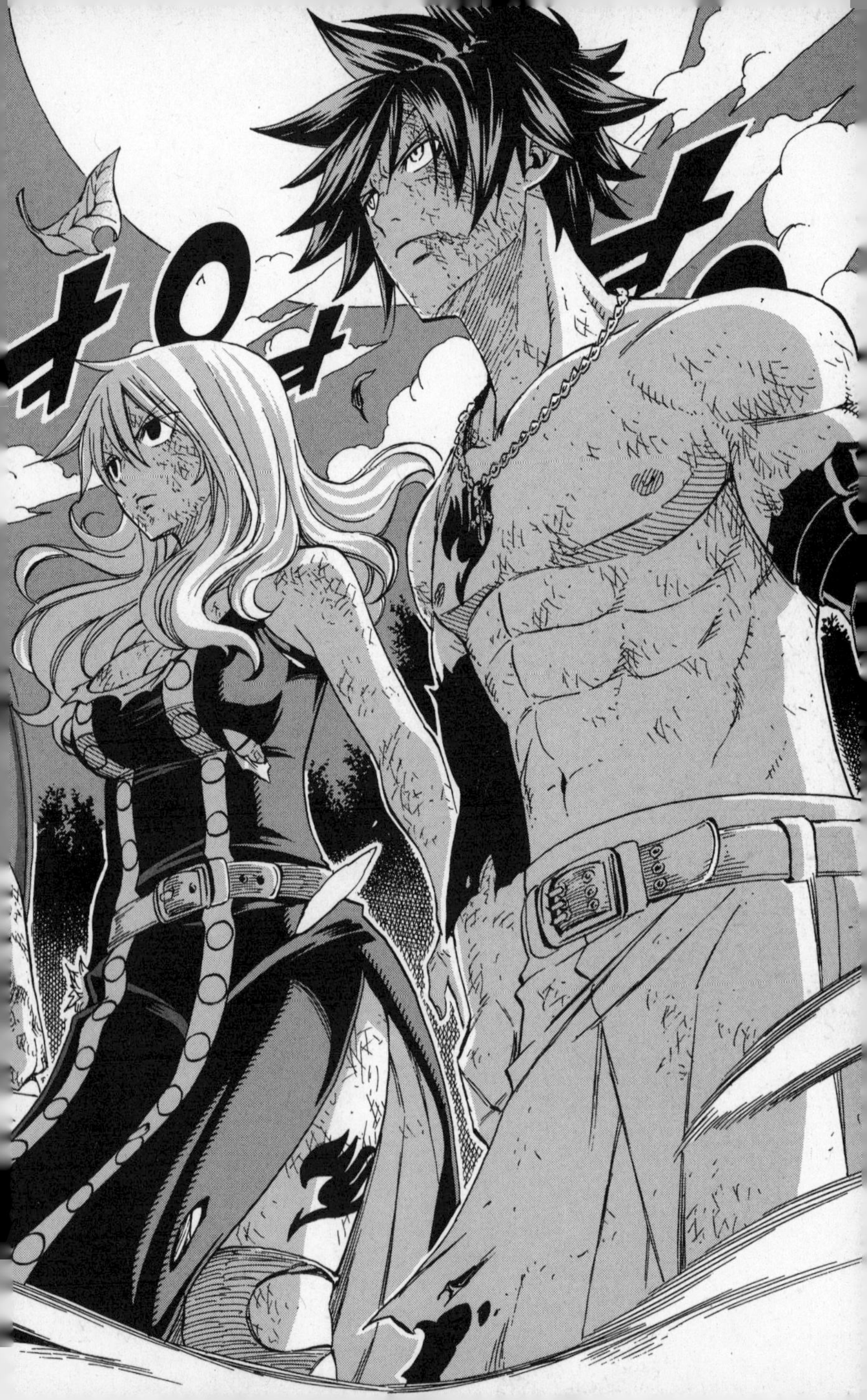

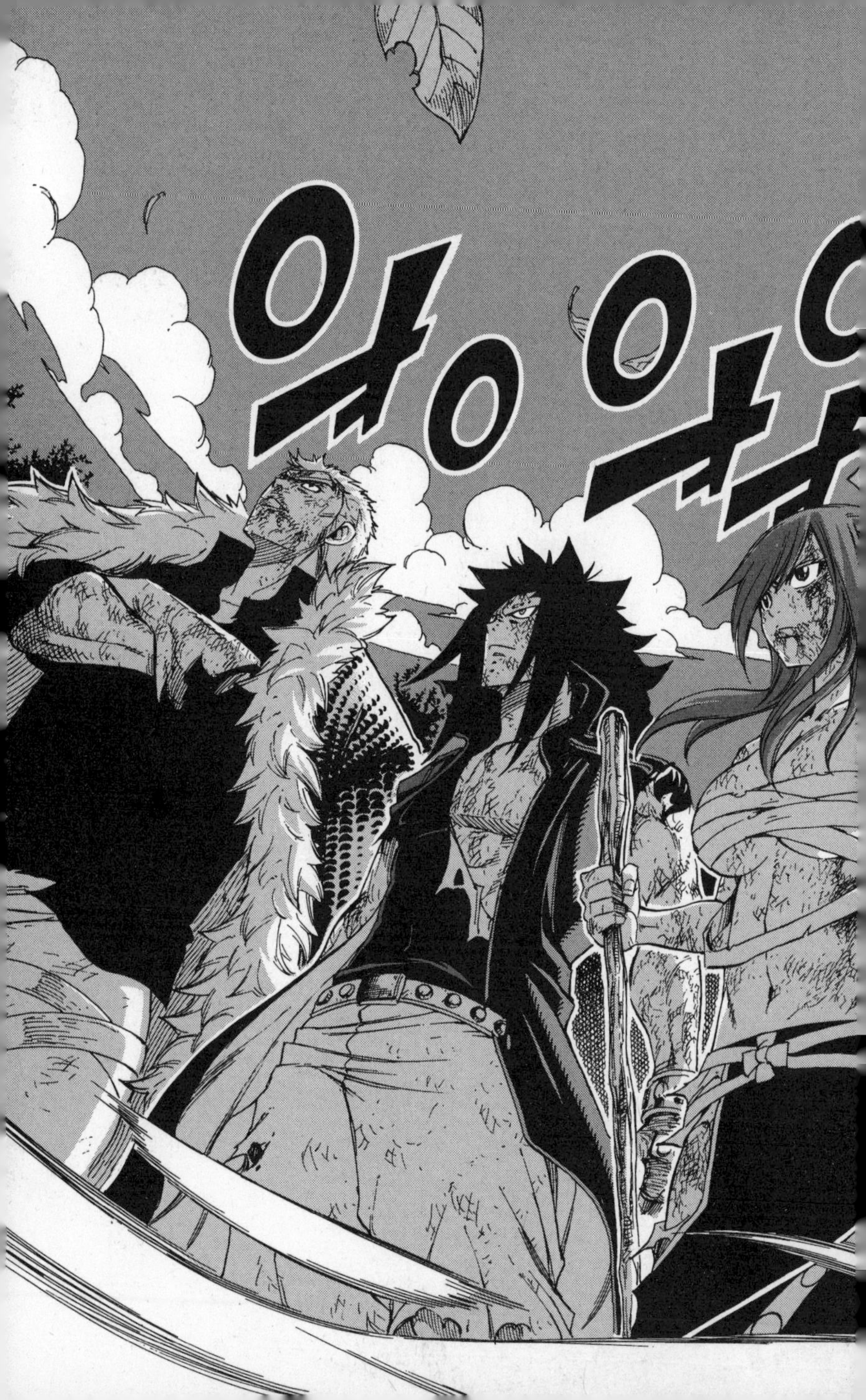
와아와

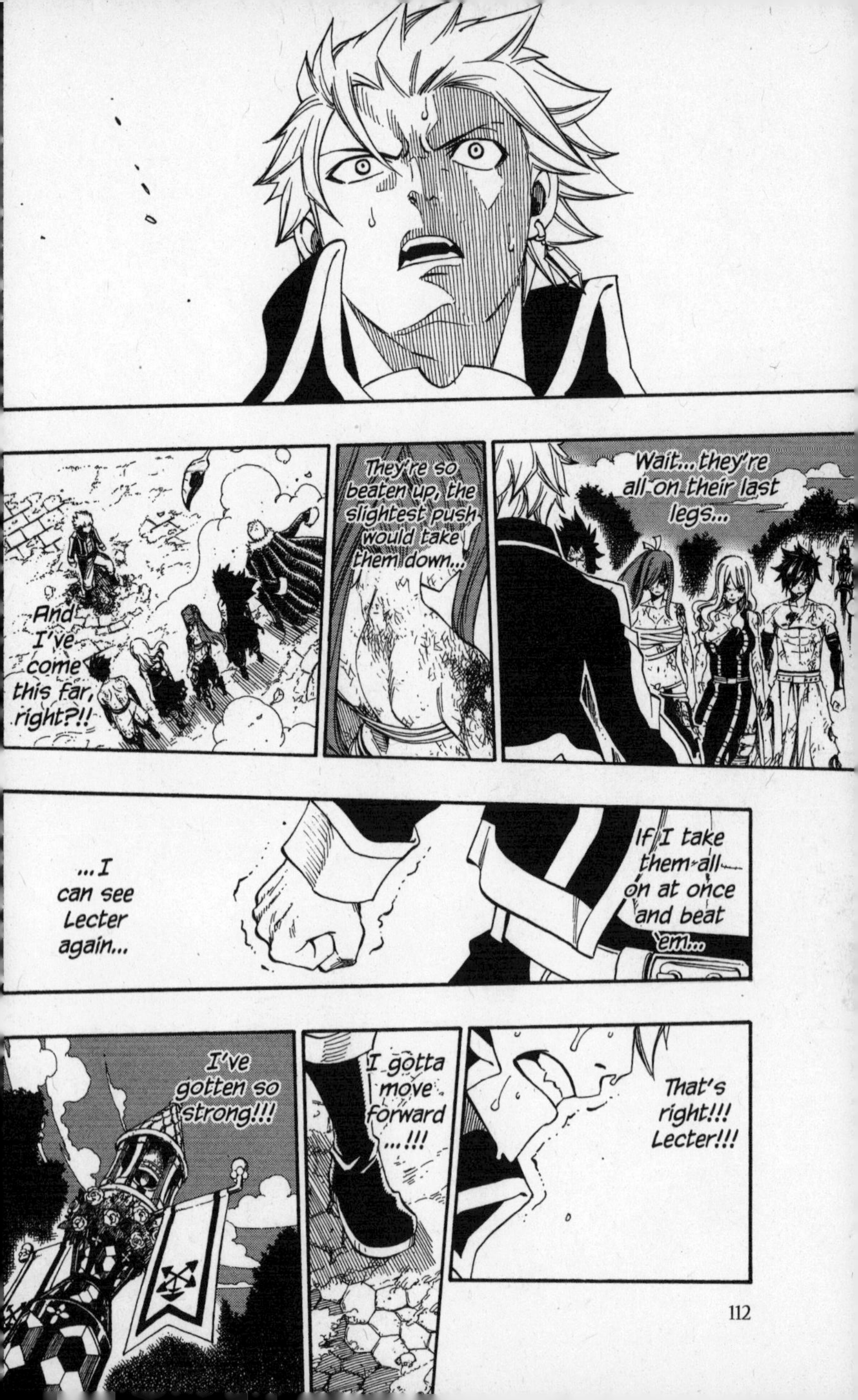
Wait... they're all on their last legs...
They're so beaten up, the slightest push would take them down...
And I've come this far, right?!!
If I take them all on at once and beat 'em...
...I can see Lecter again...
That's right!!! Lecter!!!
I gotta move forward ...!!!
I've gotten so strong!!!

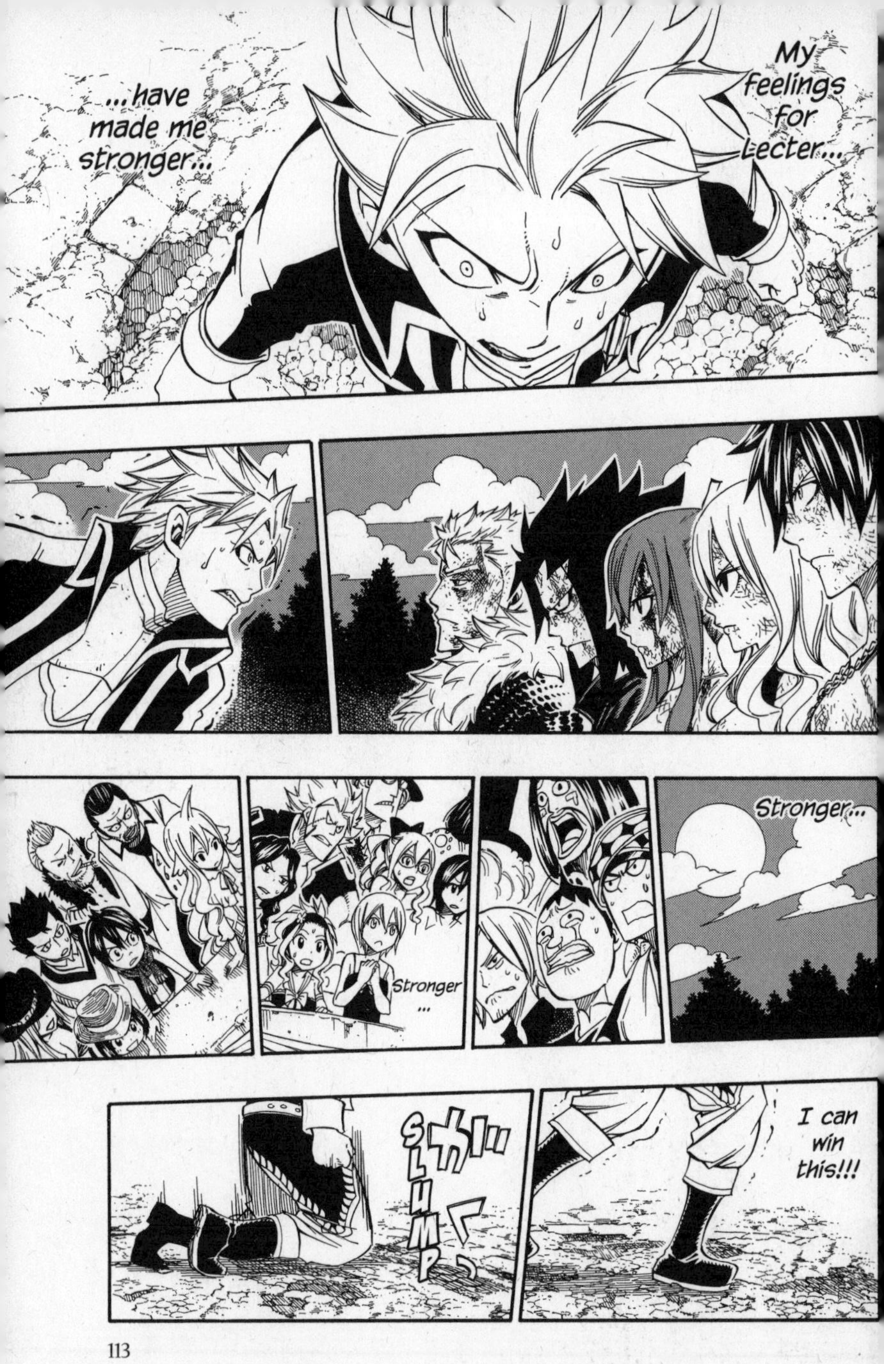
My feelings for Lecter...
...have made me stronger...
Stronger...
Stronger ...
I can win this!!!
SLUMP

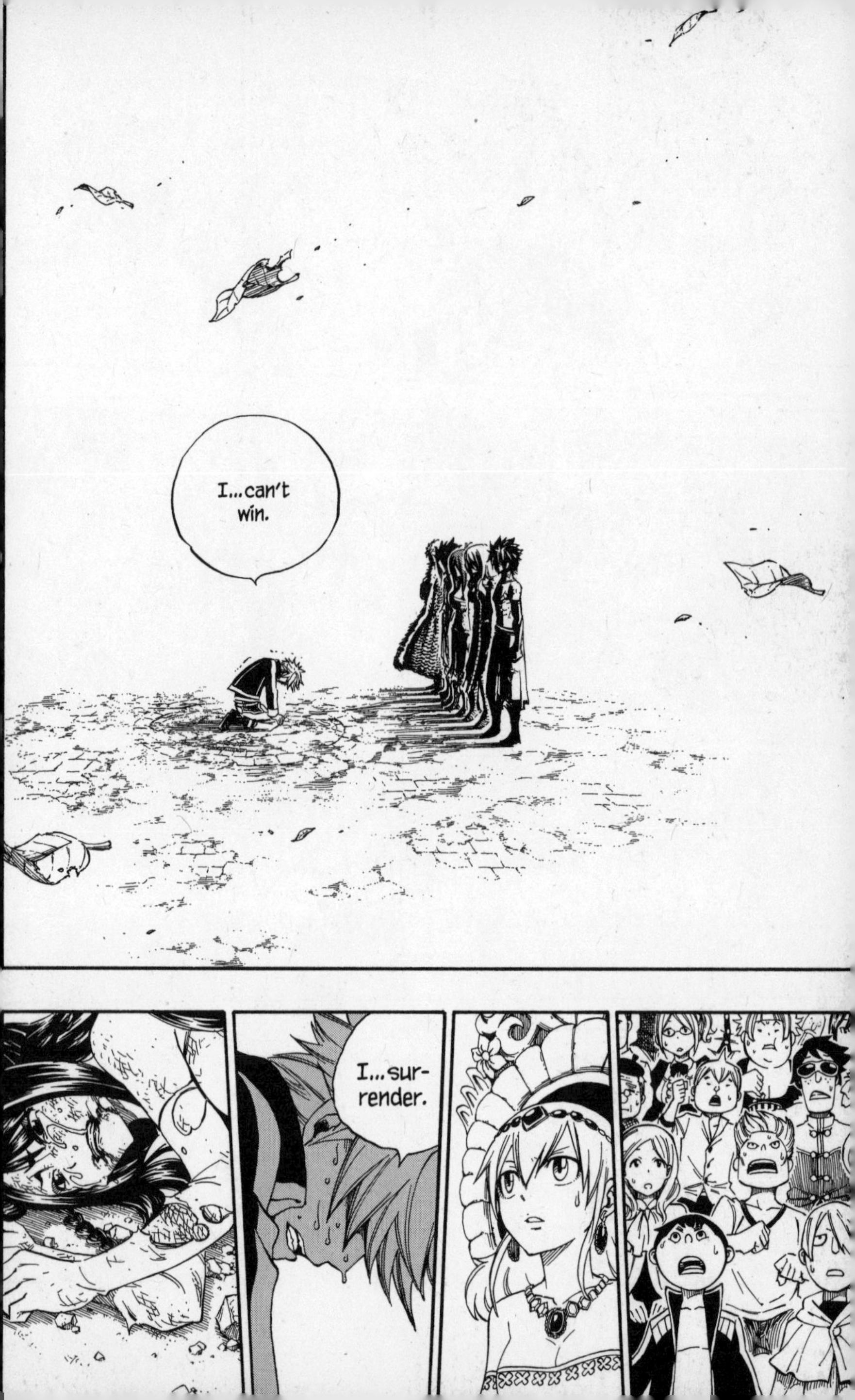
I...can't win.
I...surrender.

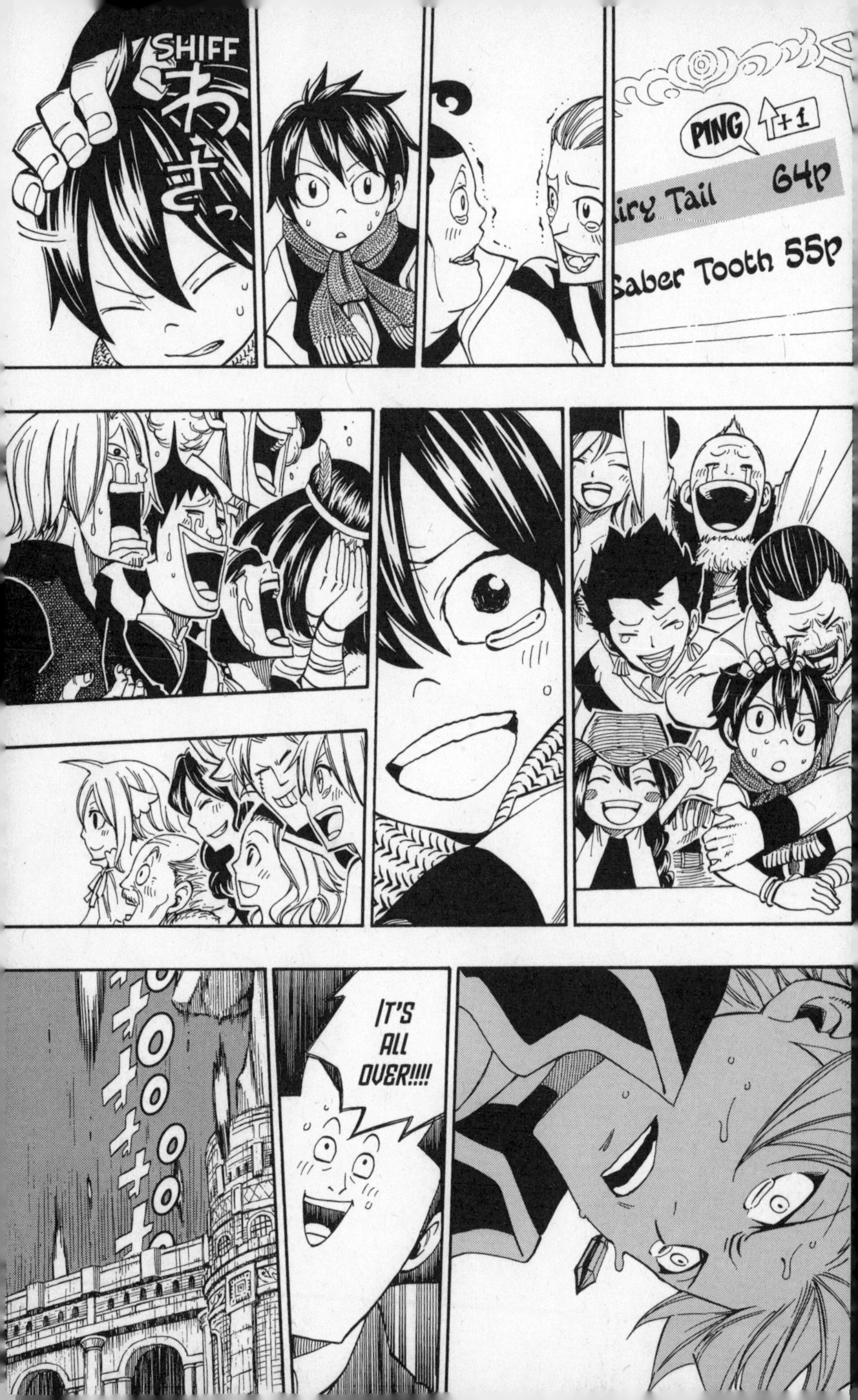
PING
+1
iry Tail 64p
Saber Tooth 55p
SHIFF
わさっ
IT'S ALL OVER!!!!

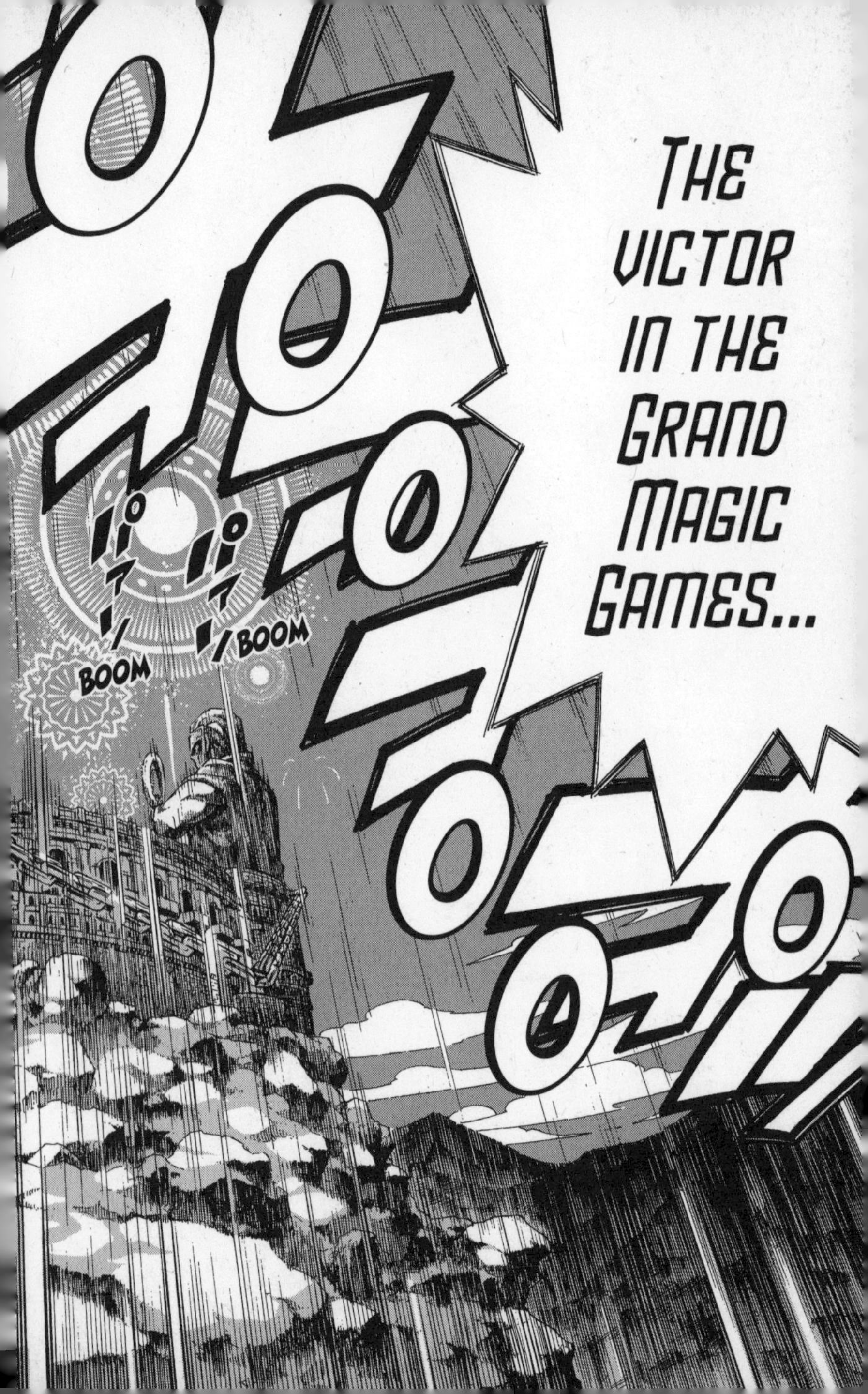

THE VICTOR IN THE GRAND MAGIC GAMES...
BOOM
BOOM

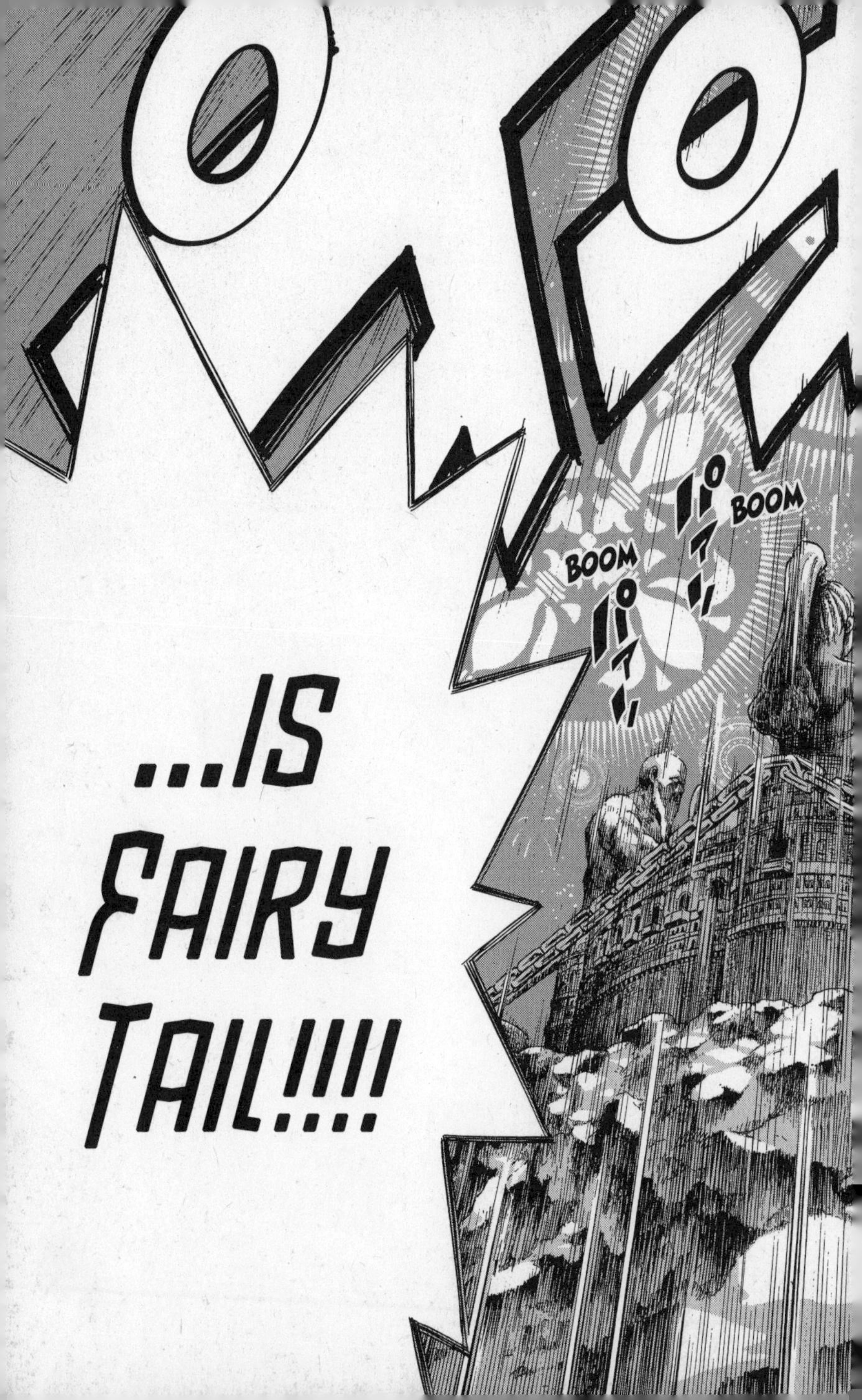
BOOM
BOOM
...IS FAIRY TAIL!!!!

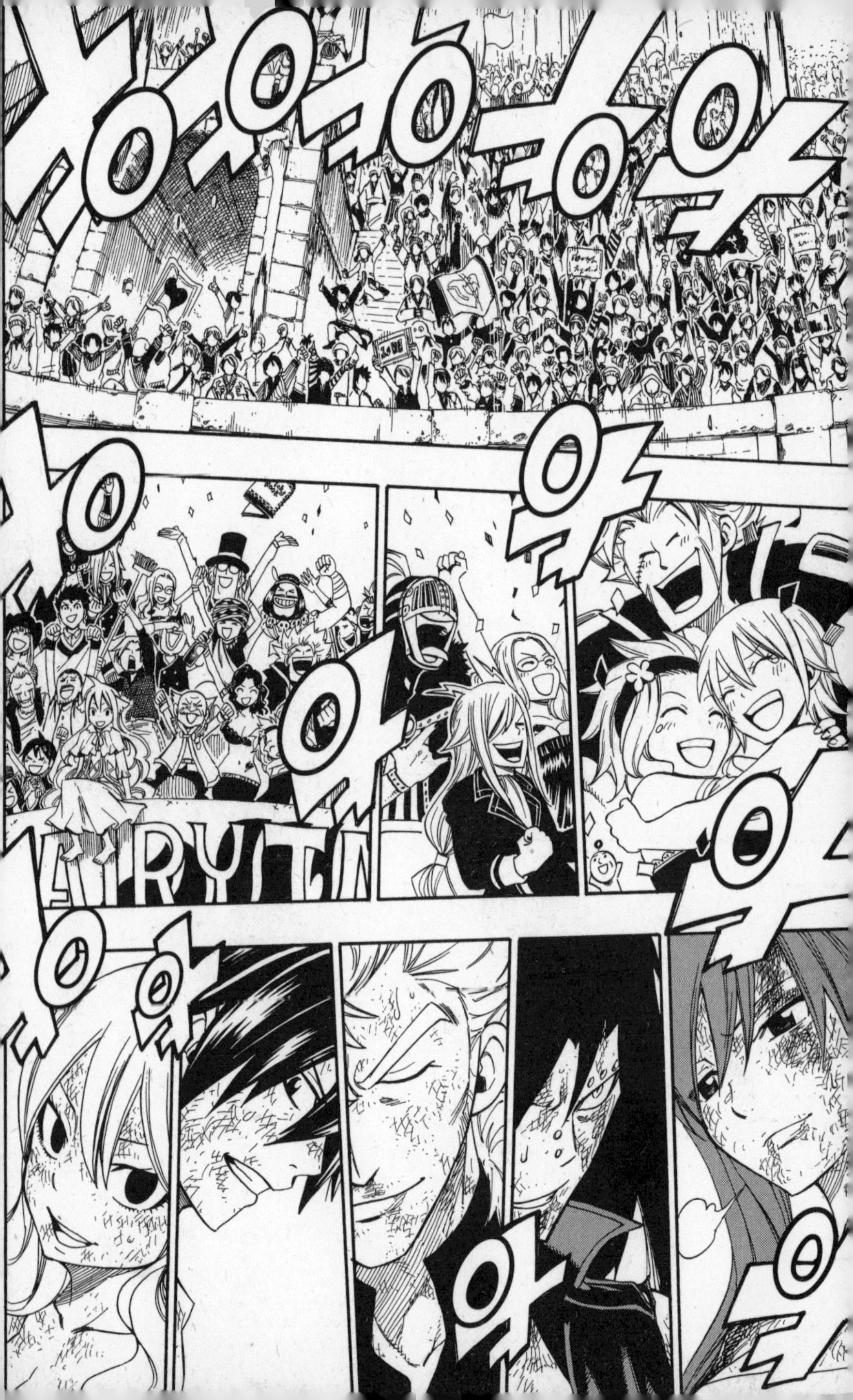

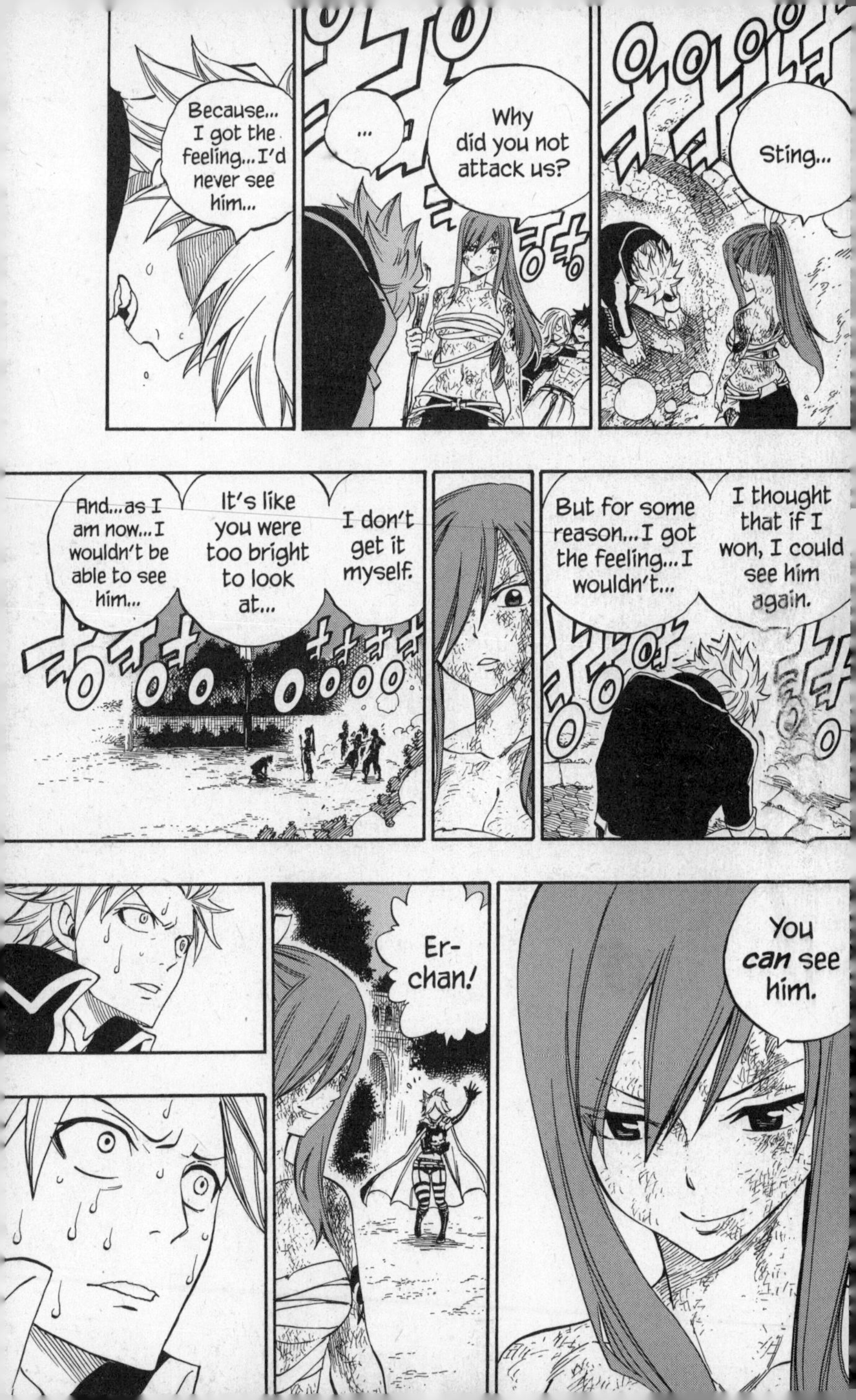

Sting...
Why did you not attack us?
...
Because... I got the feeling...I'd never see him...
I thought that if I won, I could see him again.
But for some reason...I got the feeling...I wouldn't...
I don't get it myself.
It's like you were too bright to look at...
And...as I am now...I wouldn't be able to see him...
You *can* see him.
Er-chan!

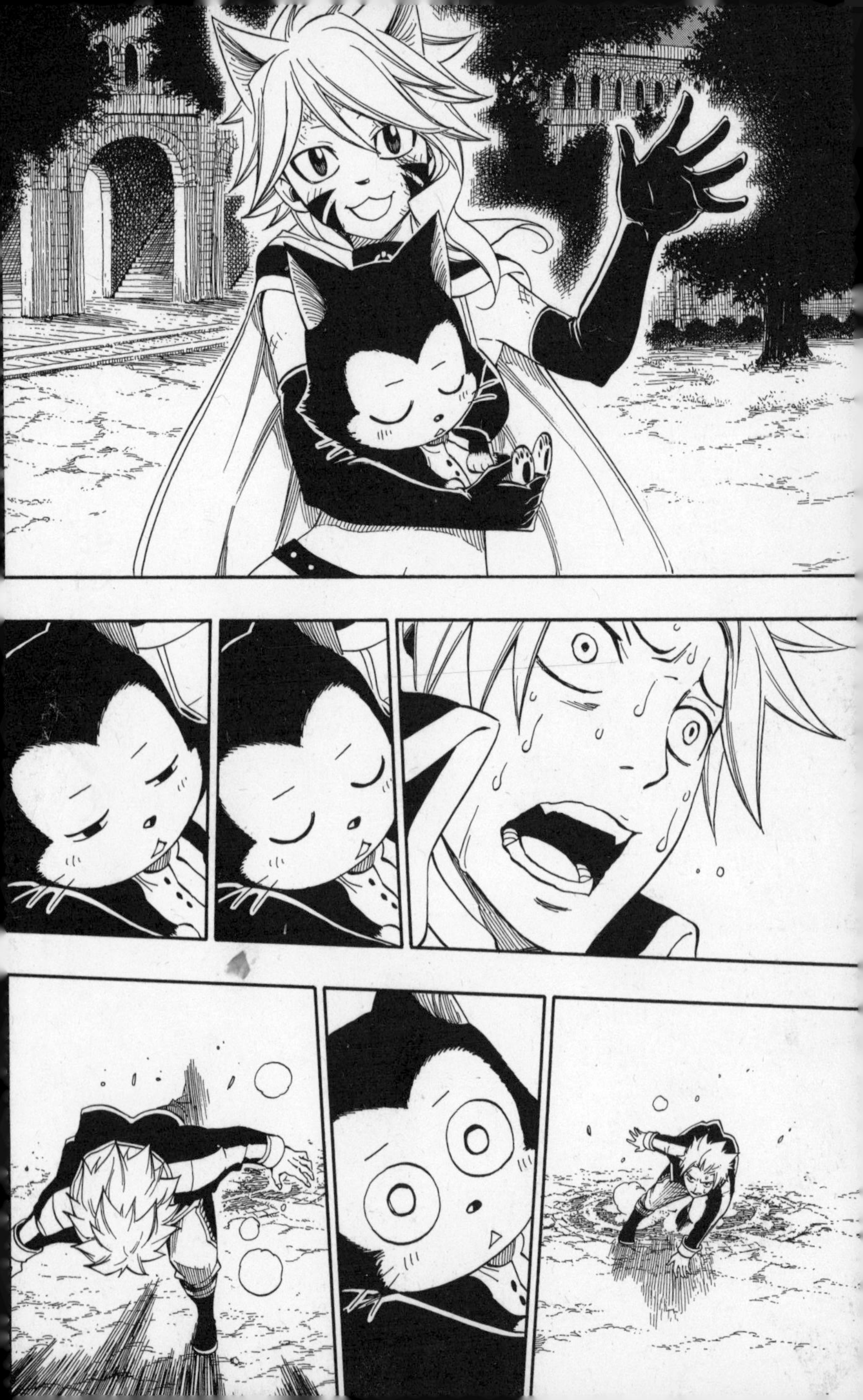

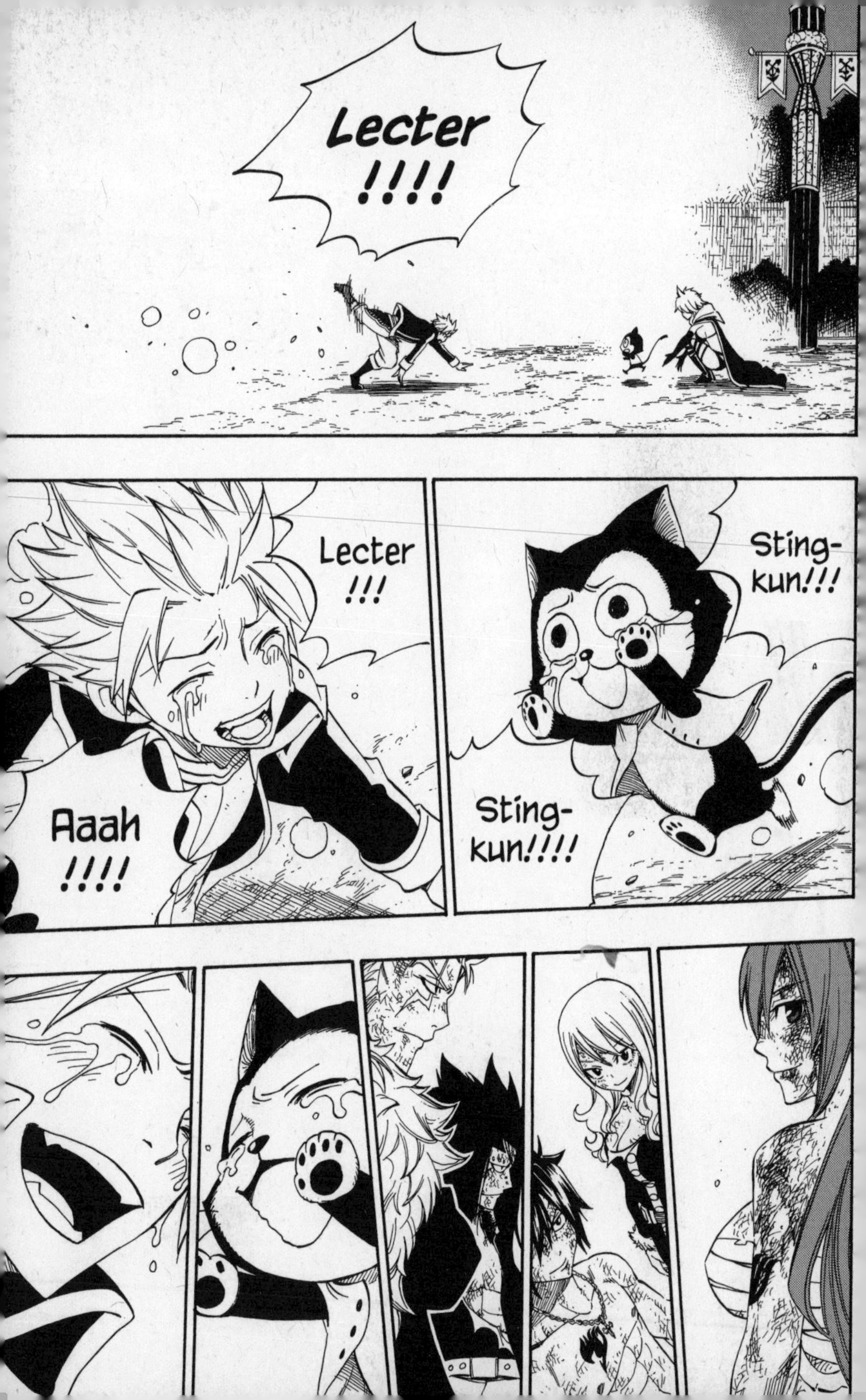
Lecter !!!!
Sting-kun!!!
Sting-kun!!!!
Lecter !!!
Aaah !!!!

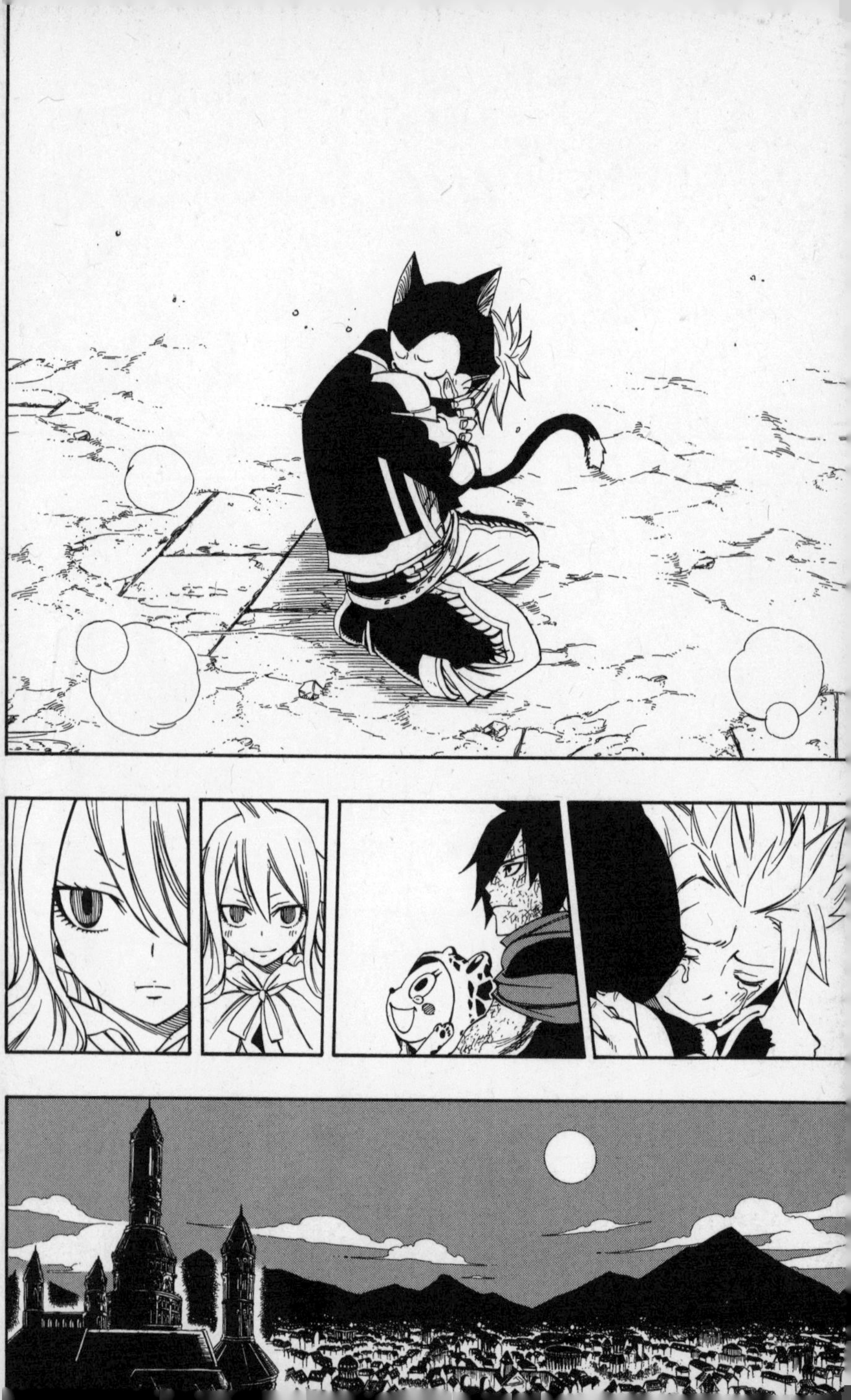

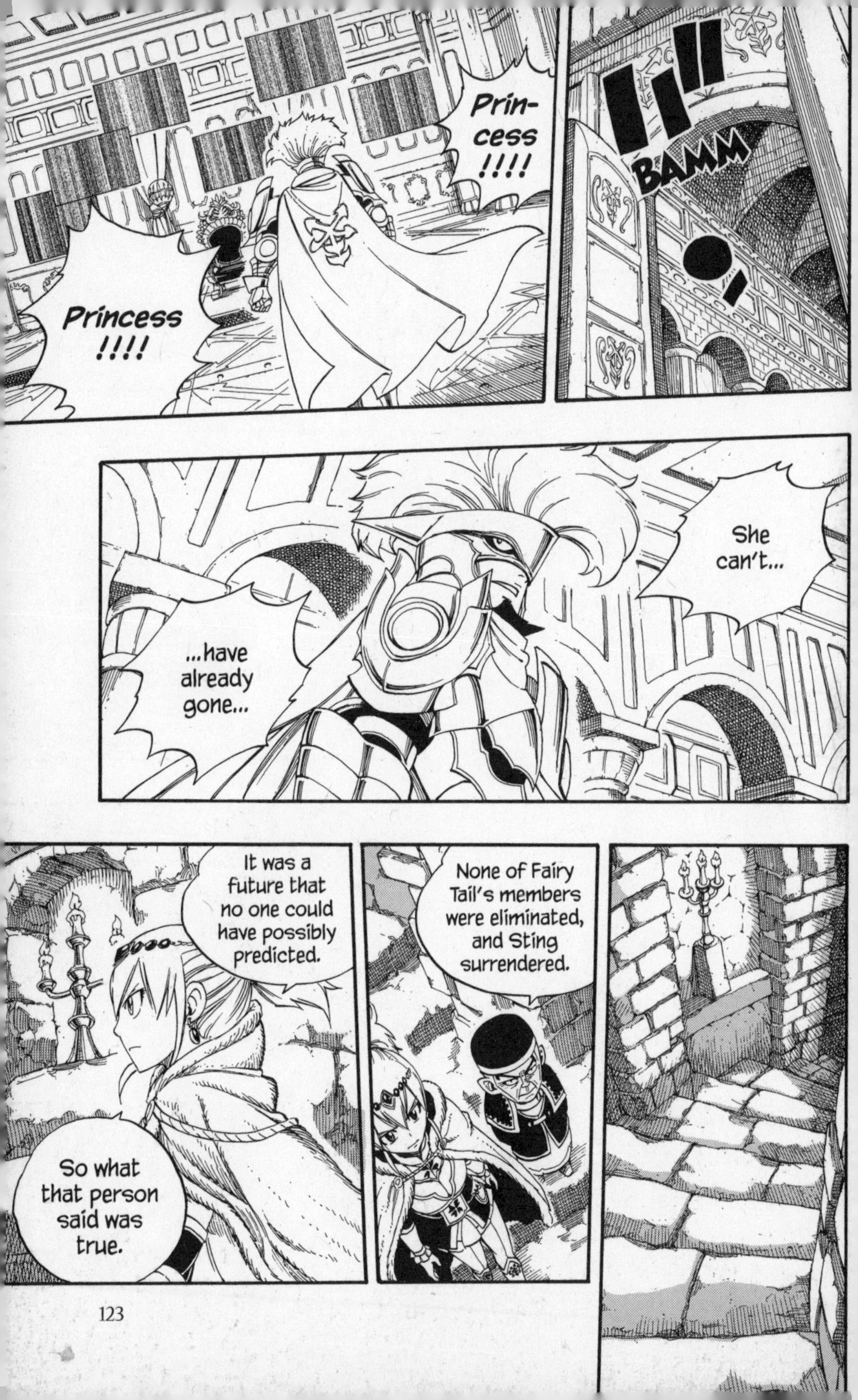
BAMM
Prin-cess!!!!
Princess!!!!
She can't...
...have already gone...
None of Fairy Tail's members were eliminated, and Sting surrendered.
It was a future that no one could have possibly predicted.
So what that person said was true.

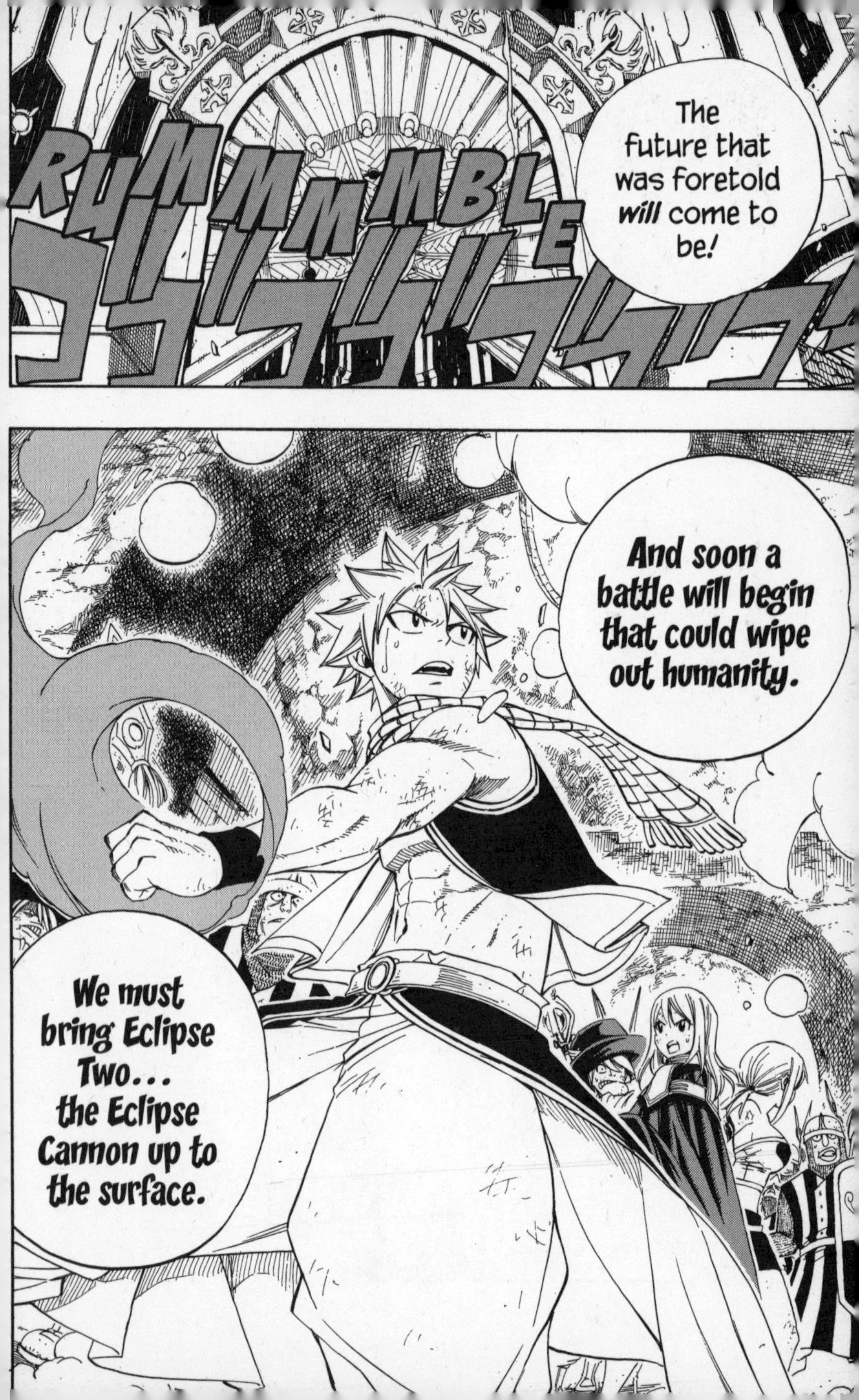
The future that was foretold *will* come to be!
RUMMMMBLE
And soon a battle will begin that could wipe out humanity.
We must bring Eclipse Two... the Eclipse Cannon up to the surface.

FAIRY TAIL
フェアリーテイル

Chapter 323: The Shadow: There and Back Again

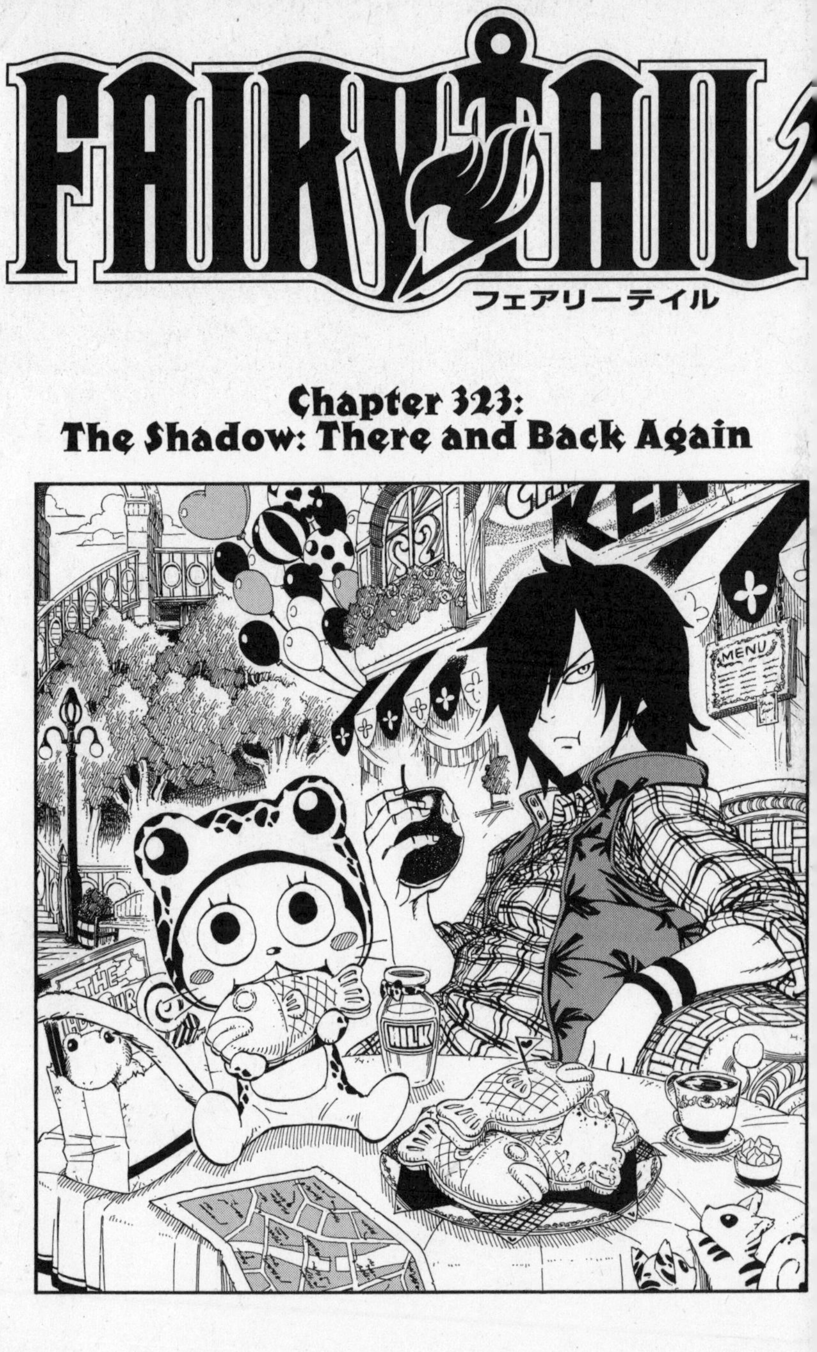
MENU
MILK

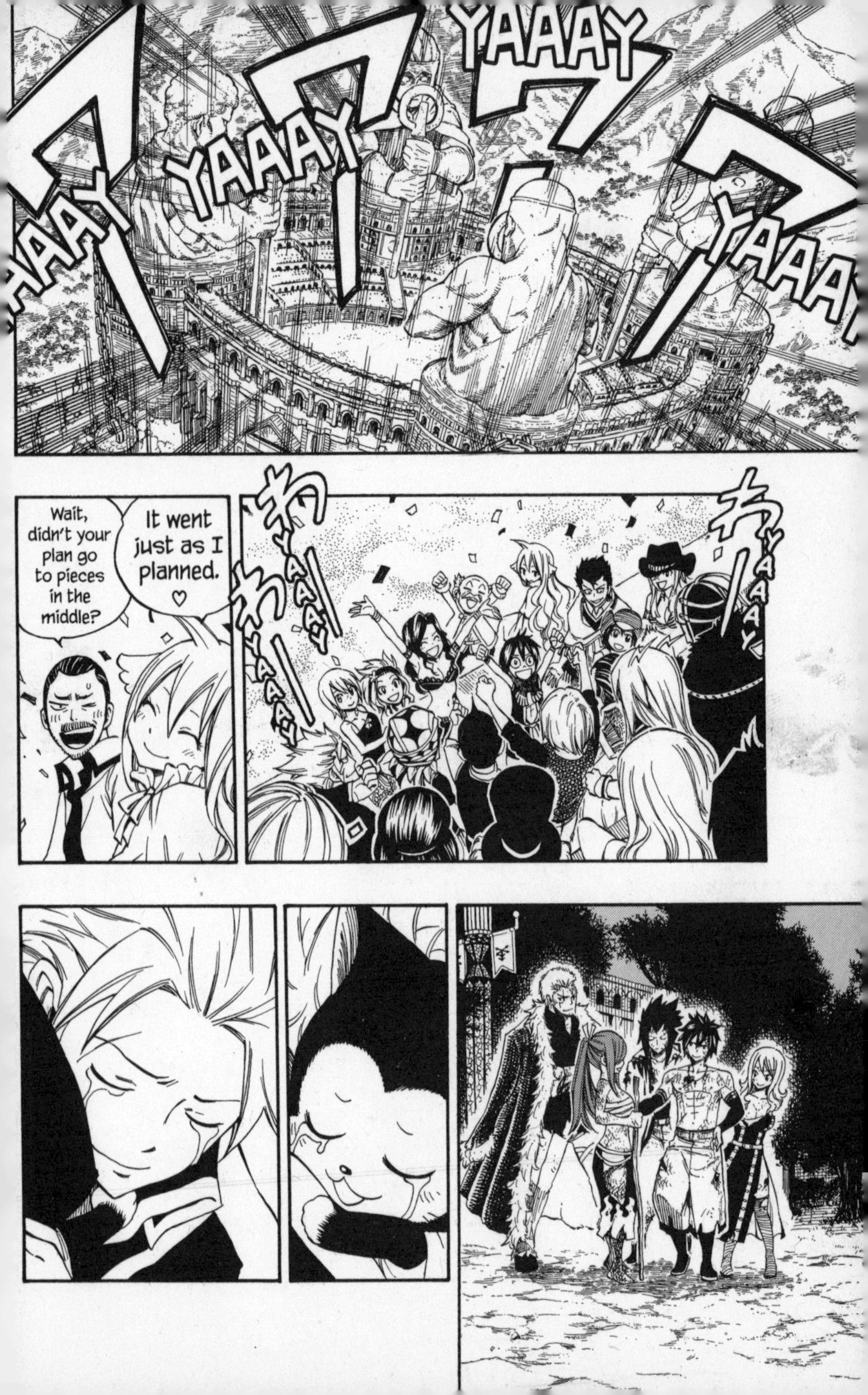
YAAAY
YAAAY
YAAAY
YAAAY
YAAAY
わ
YAAAY
わ
YAAAY
わ
YAAAY
It went just as I planned. ♡
Wait, didn't your plan go to pieces in the middle?

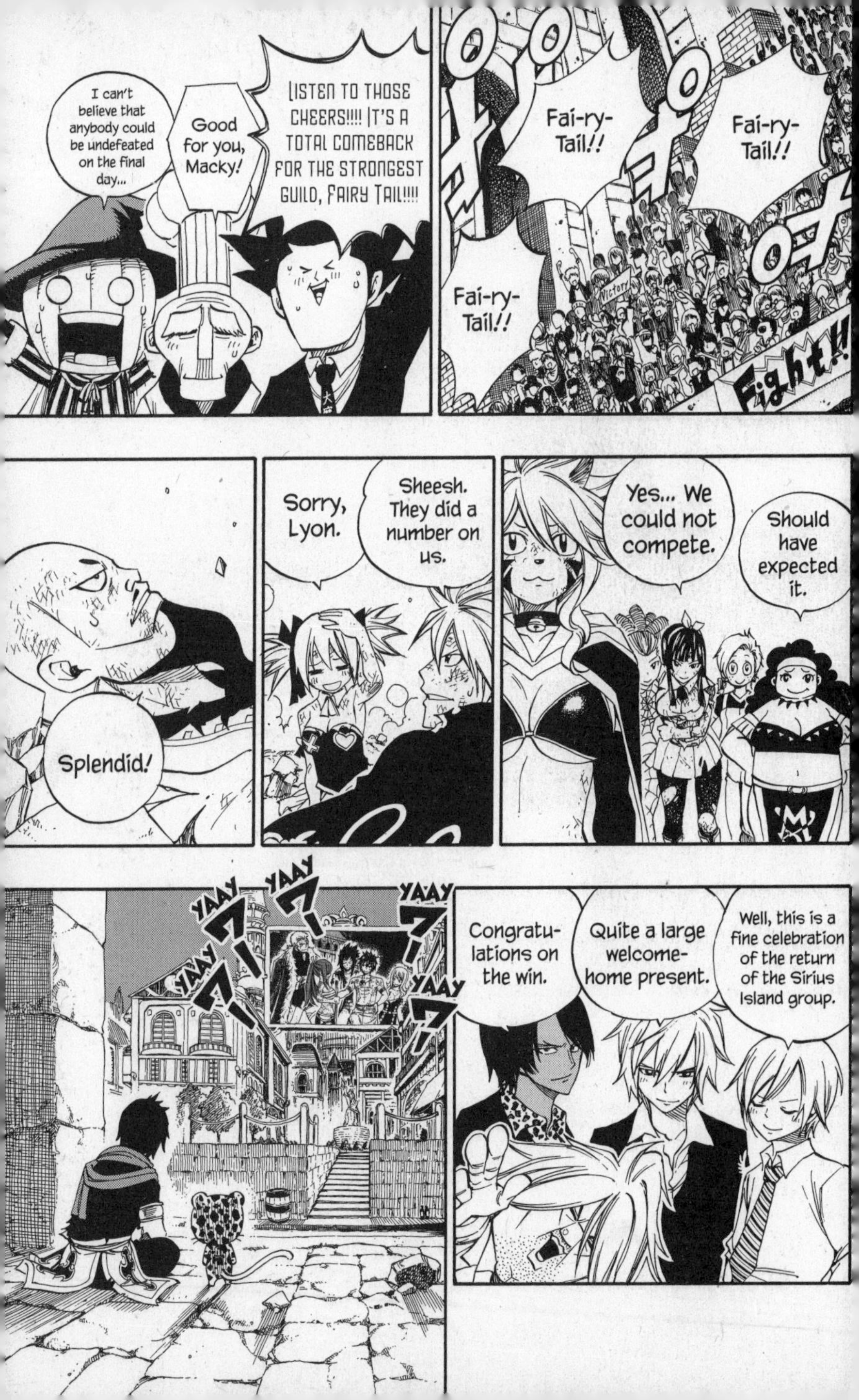

Fai-ry-Tail!!
Fai-ry-Tail!!
Fai-ry-Tail!!
Victory
Fight!!
LISTEN TO THOSE CHEERS!!!! IT'S A TOTAL COMEBACK FOR THE STRONGEST GUILD, FAIRY TAIL!!!!
Good for you, Macky!
I can't believe that anybody could be undefeated on the final day...
Should have expected it.
Yes... We could not compete.
Sheesh. They did a number on us.
Sorry, Lyon.
Splendid!
Well, this is a fine celebration of the return of the Sirius Island group.
Quite a large welcome-home present.
Congratulations on the win.
YAAY
YAAY
YAAY
YAAY
YAAY

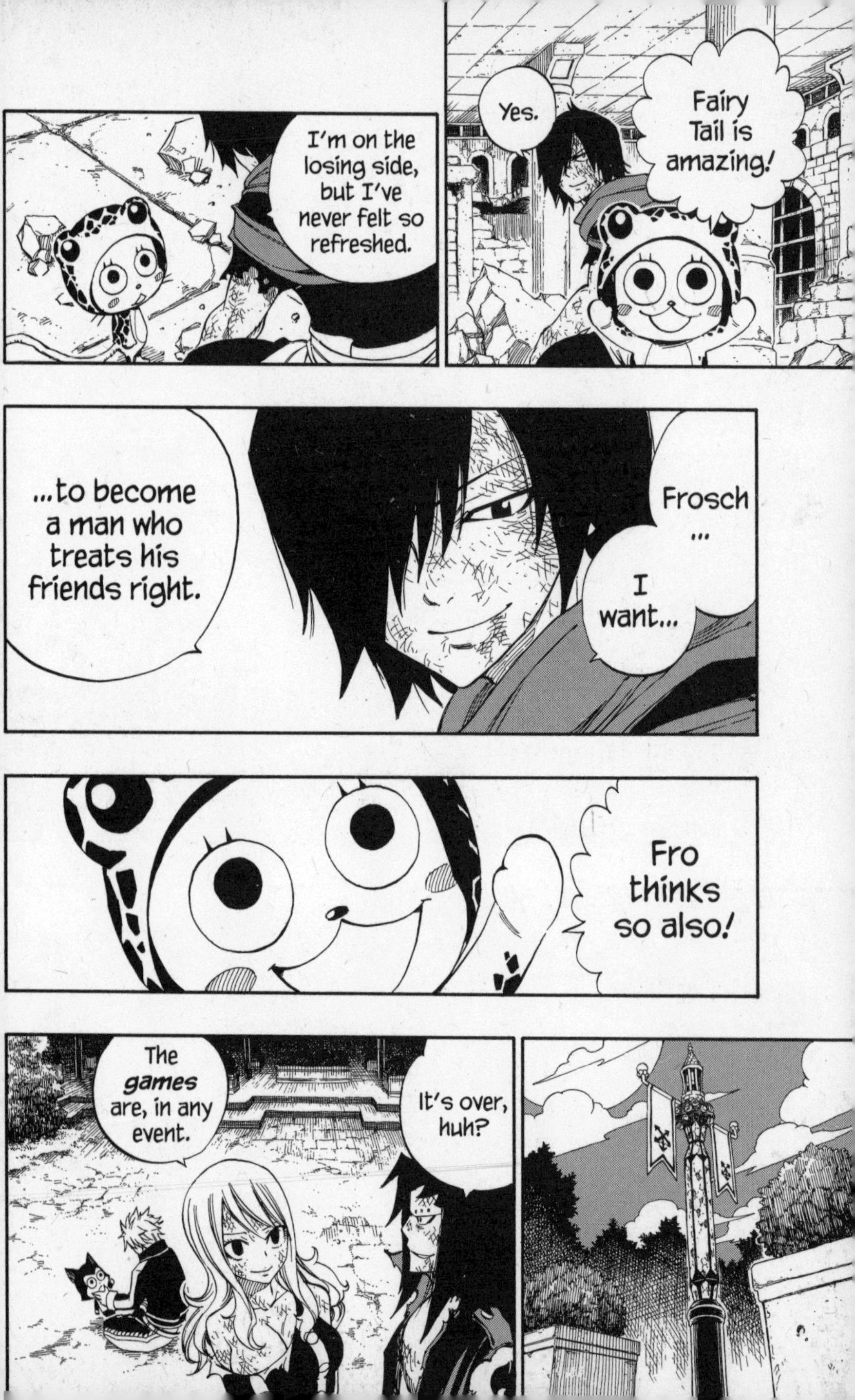
Fairy Tail is amazing!
Yes.
I'm on the losing side, but I've never felt so refreshed.
Frosch...
I want...
...to become a man who treats his friends right.
Fro thinks so also!
It's over, huh?
The *games* are, in any event.

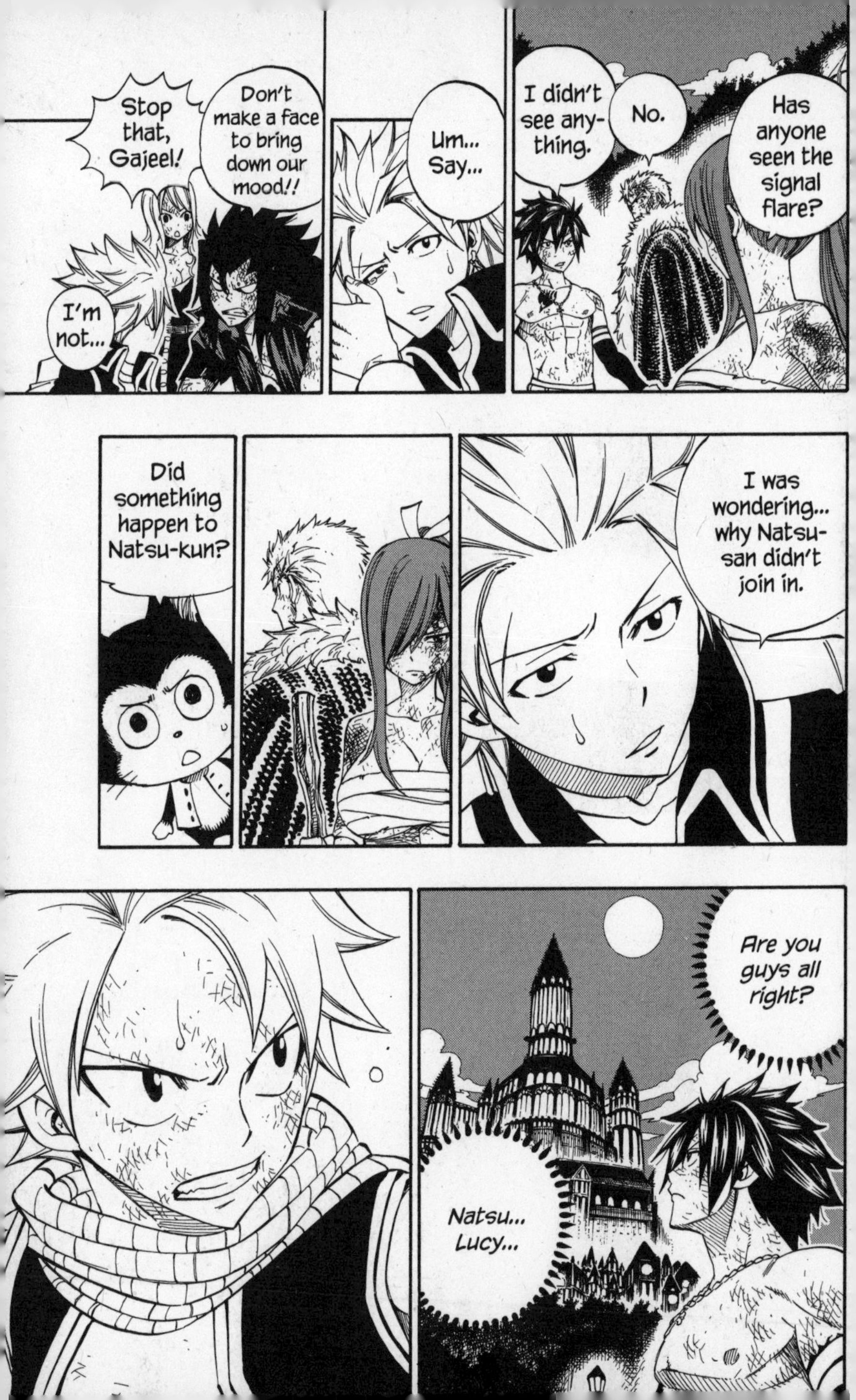
Has anyone seen the signal flare?
No.
I didn't see anything.
Um... Say...
Don't make a face to bring down our mood!!
Stop that, Gajeel!
I'm not...
I was wondering... why Natsu-san didn't join in.
Did something happen to Natsu-kun?
Are you guys all right?
Natsu... Lucy...

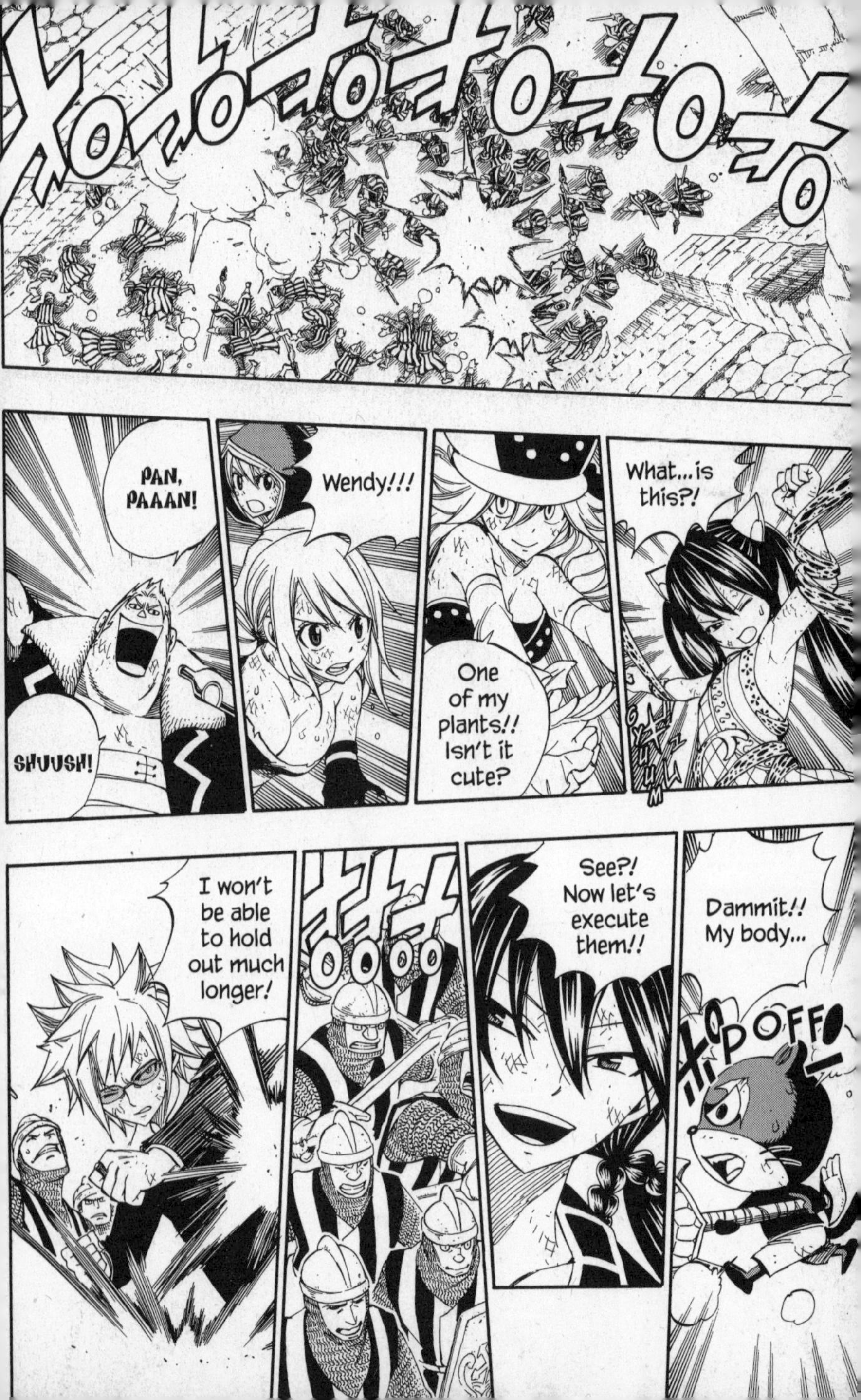
What...is this?!
One of my plants!! Isn't it cute?
Wendy!!!
PAN, PAAAN!
SHUUSH!
Dammit!! My body...
POFF
See?! Now let's execute them!!
I won't be able to hold out much longer!

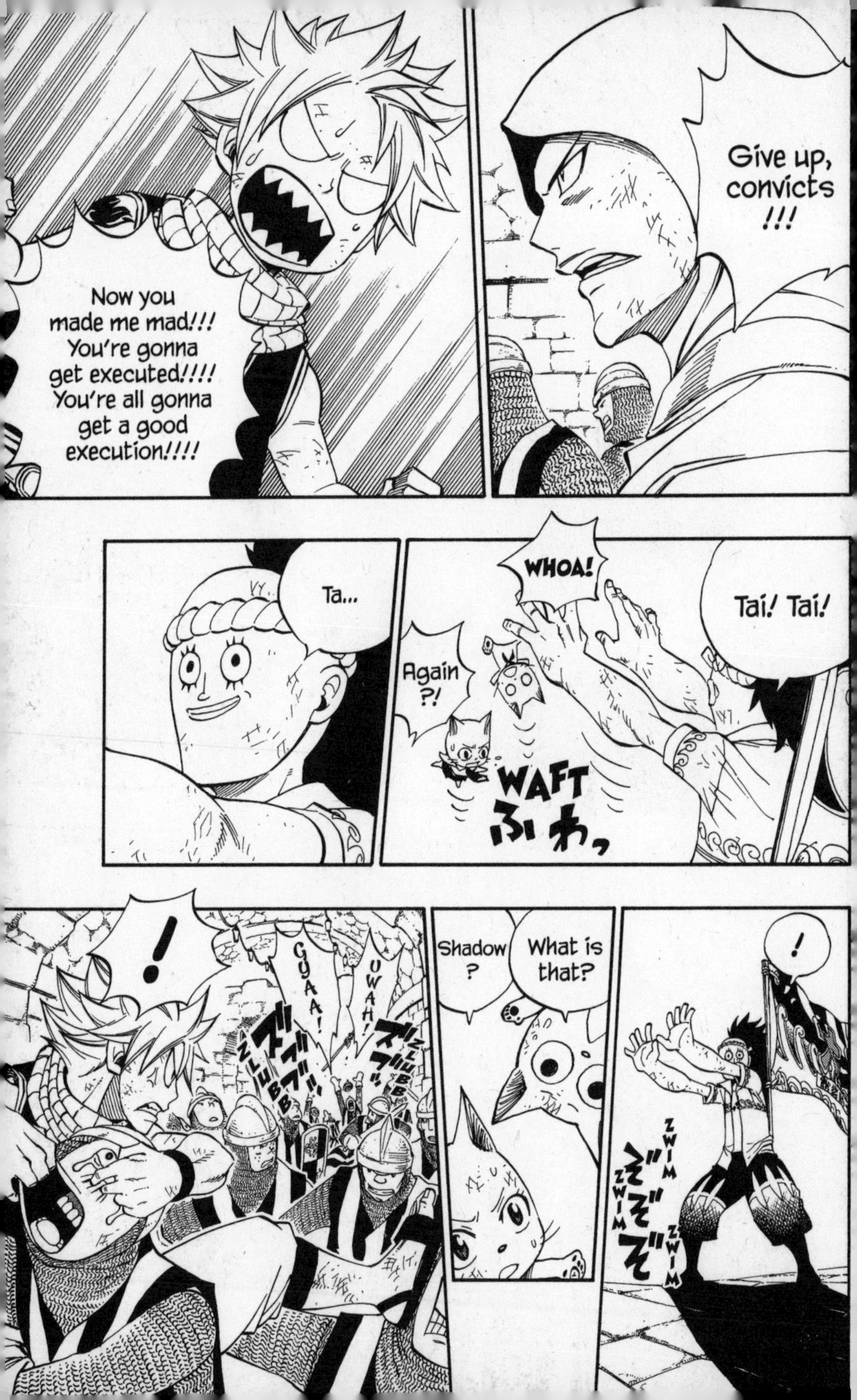
Give up, convicts!!!
Now you made me mad!!! You're gonna get executed!!!! You're all gonna get a good execution!!!!
Tai! Tai!
WHOA!
Again?!
WAFT
ふわっ
Ta...
!
ZWIM
ZWIM
ZWIM
ZWIM
What is that?
Shadow?
!
GYAAA!
UWAH!
ZLUBB
ZLUBB

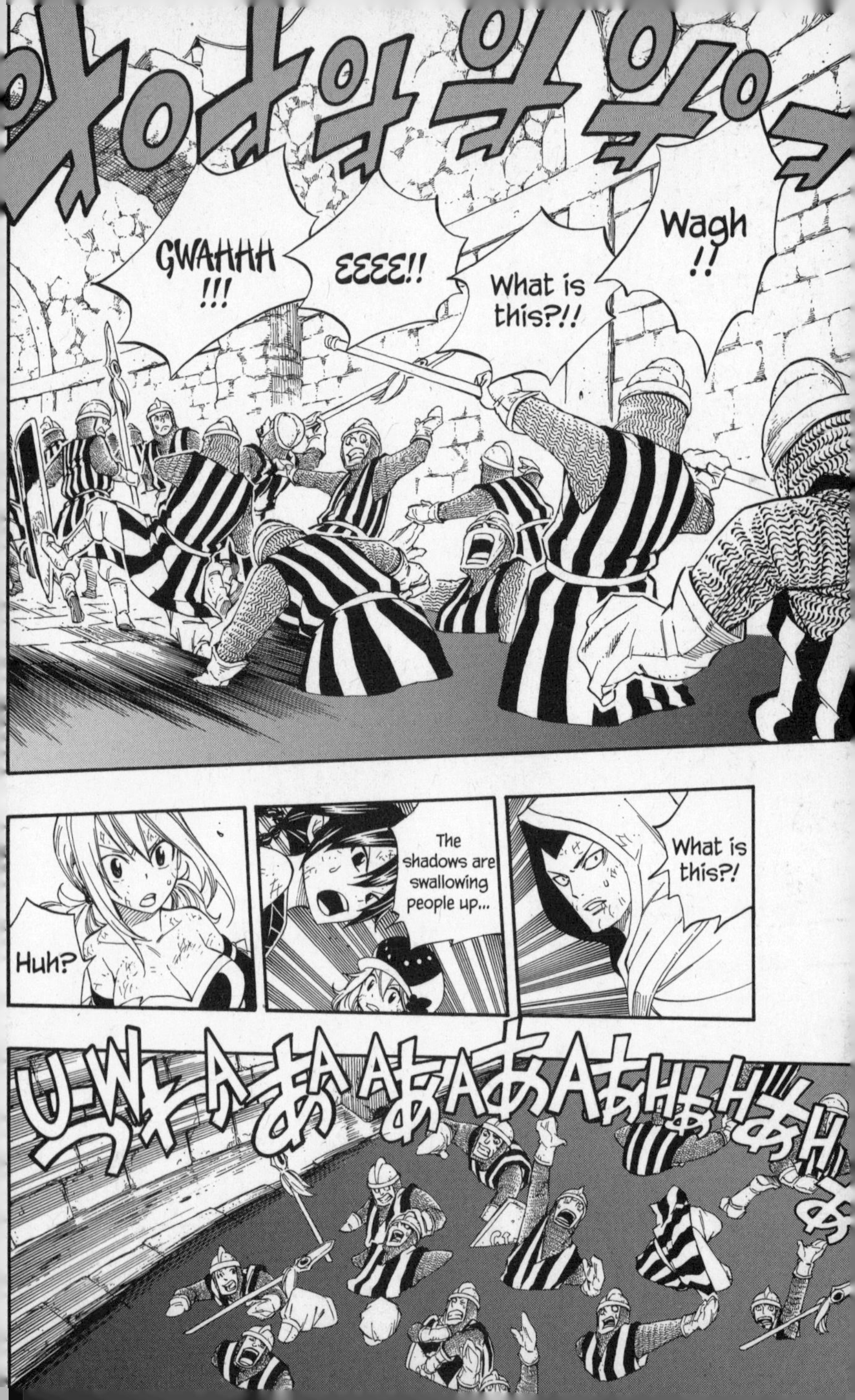

Wagh !!
What is this?!!
ƐƐƐƐ!!
GWAHHH !!!
What is this?!
The shadows are swallowing people up...
Huh?
U-WAAAAHHH

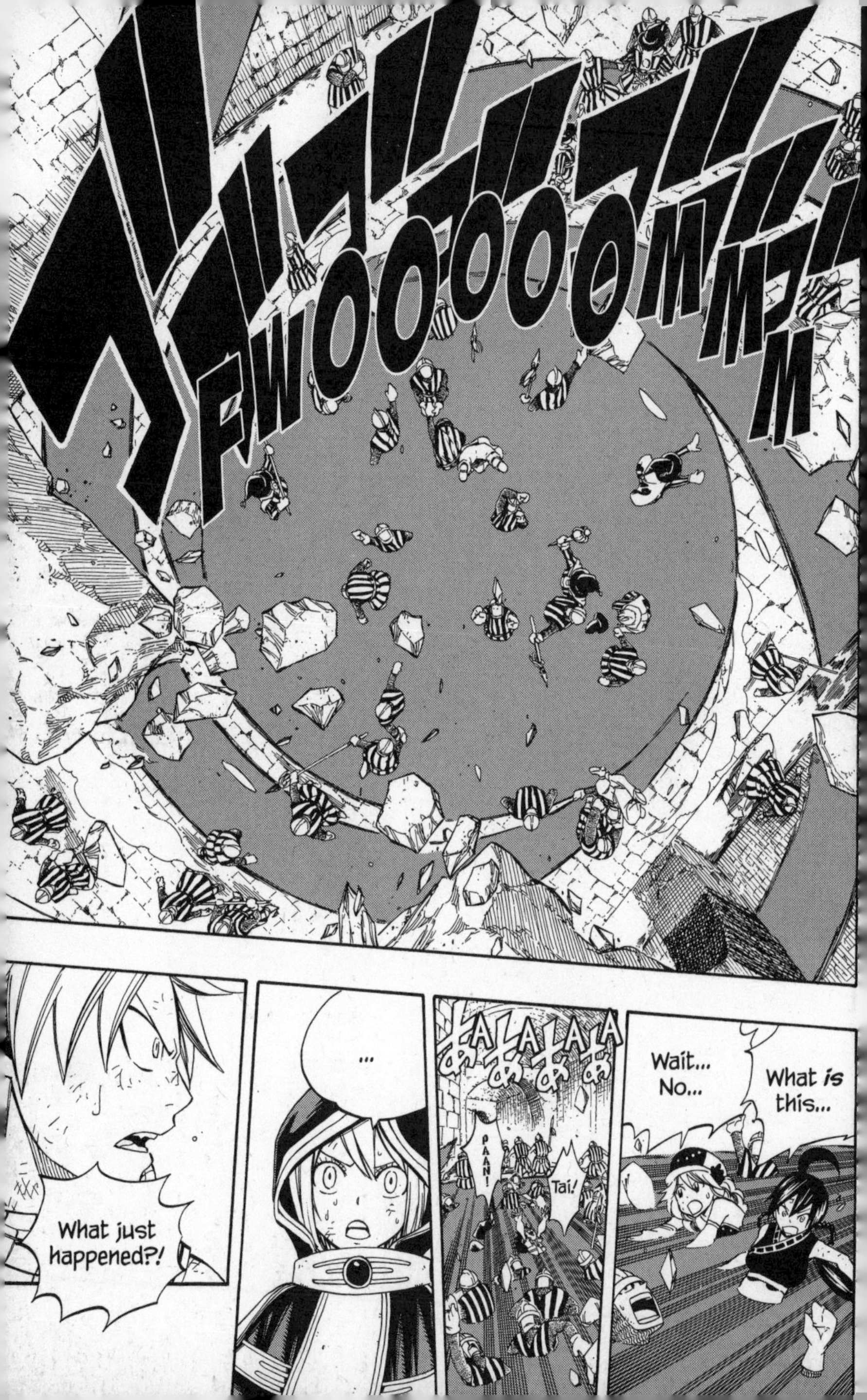
FWOOOOOMMM
Wait... No...
What is this...
AAAA
PAAN!
Tai!
...
What just happened?!

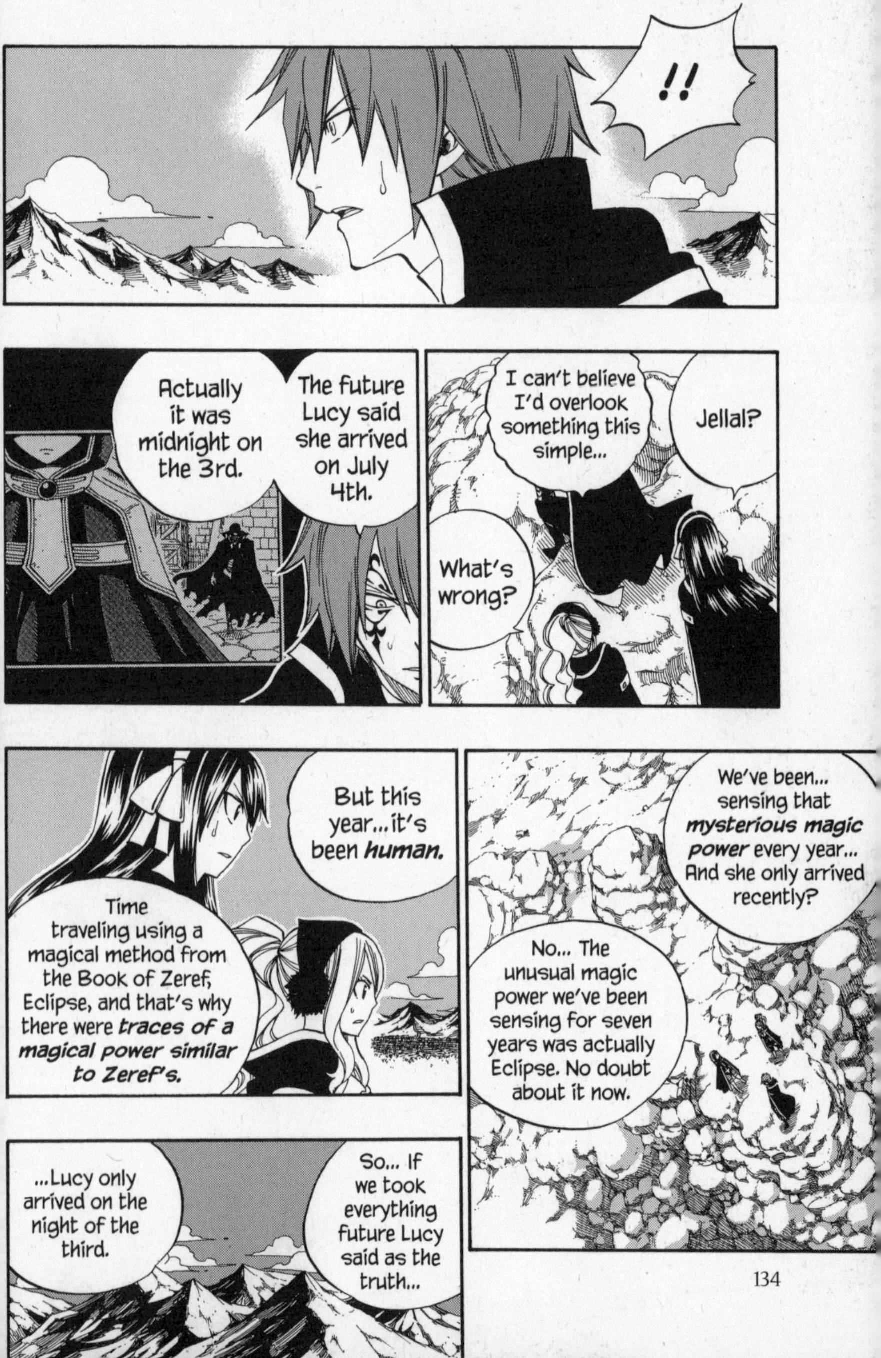
!!
Jellal?
I can't believe I'd overlook something this simple...
What's wrong?
The future Lucy said she arrived on July 4th.
Actually it was midnight on the 3rd.
We've been... sensing that ***mysterious magic power*** every year... And she only arrived recently?
No... The unusual magic power we've been sensing for seven years was actually Eclipse. No doubt about it now.
But this year...it's been ***human.***
Time traveling using a magical method from the Book of Zeref, Eclipse, and that's why there were ***traces of a magical power similar to Zeref's.***
So... If we took everything future Lucy said as the truth...
...Lucy only arrived on the night of the third.

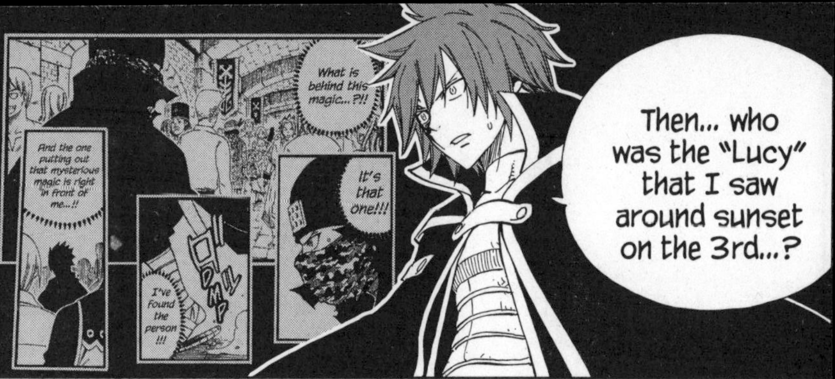
Then... who was the "Lucy" that I saw around sunset on the 3rd...?
What is behind this magic...?!!
It's that one!!!
I've found the person!!!
And the one putting out that mysterious magic is right in front of me...!!

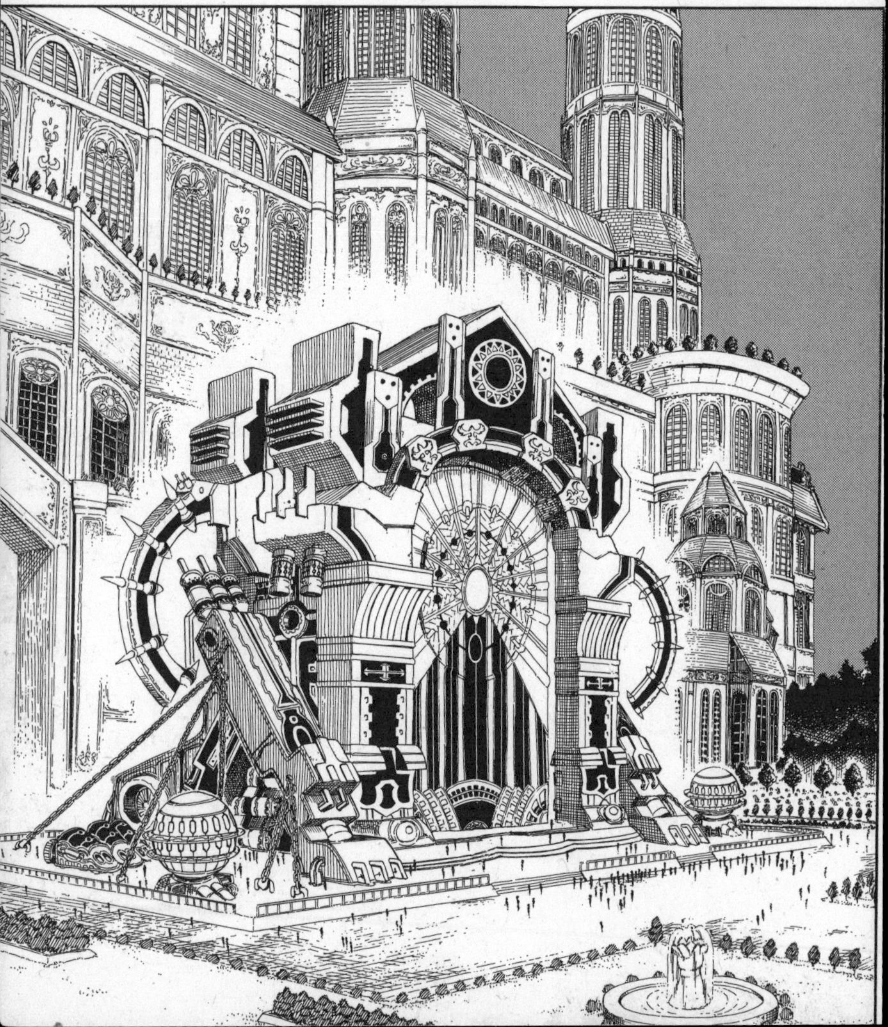

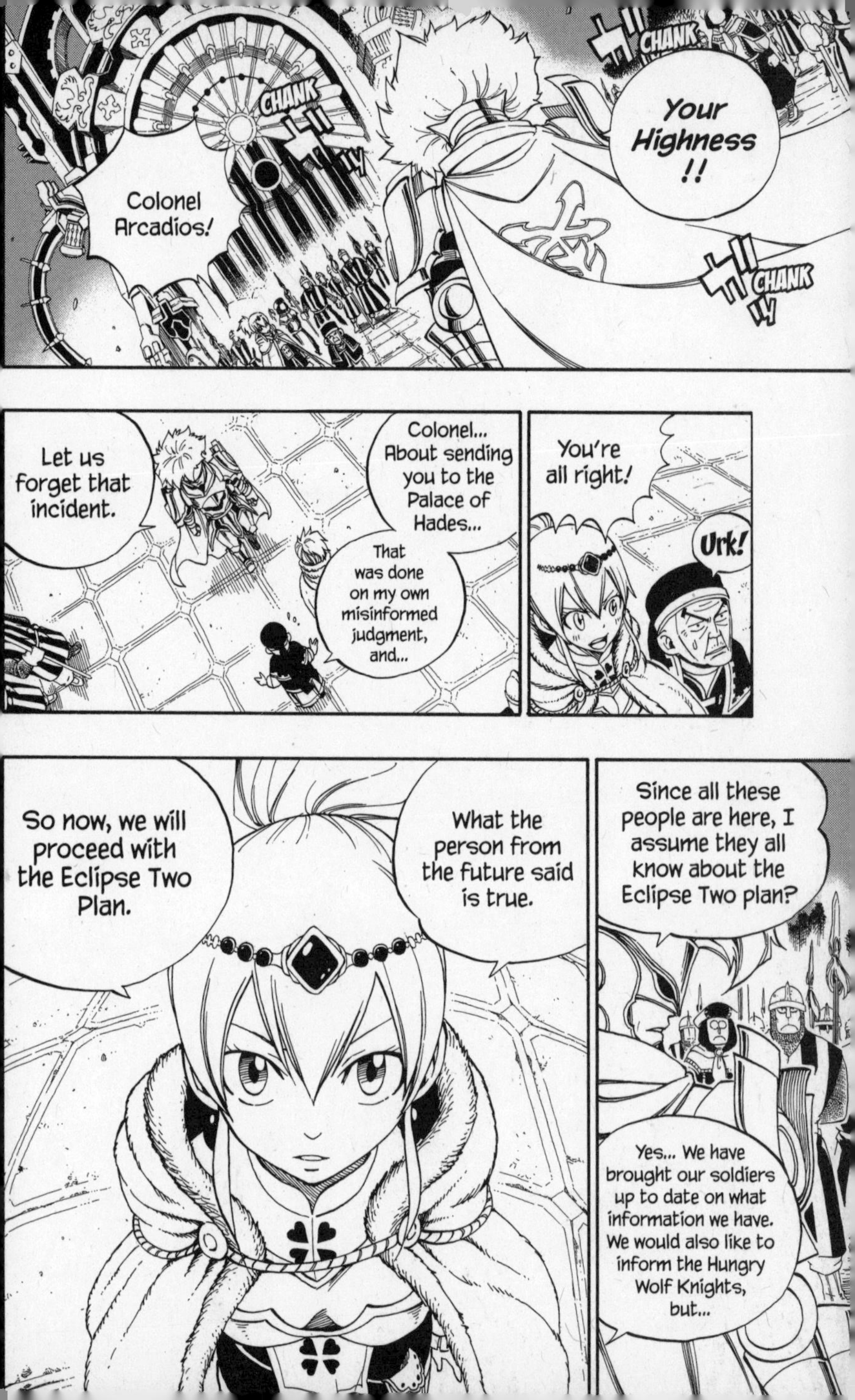
CHANK
Your Highness!!
CHANK
CHANK
Colonel Arcadios!
You're all right!
Urk!
Colonel... About sending you to the Palace of Hades...
That was done on my own misinformed judgment, and...
Let us forget that incident.
Since all these people are here, I assume they all know about the Eclipse Two plan?
Yes... We have brought our soldiers up to date on what information we have. We would also like to inform the Hungry Wolf Knights, but...
What the person from the future said is true.
So now, we will proceed with the Eclipse Two Plan.

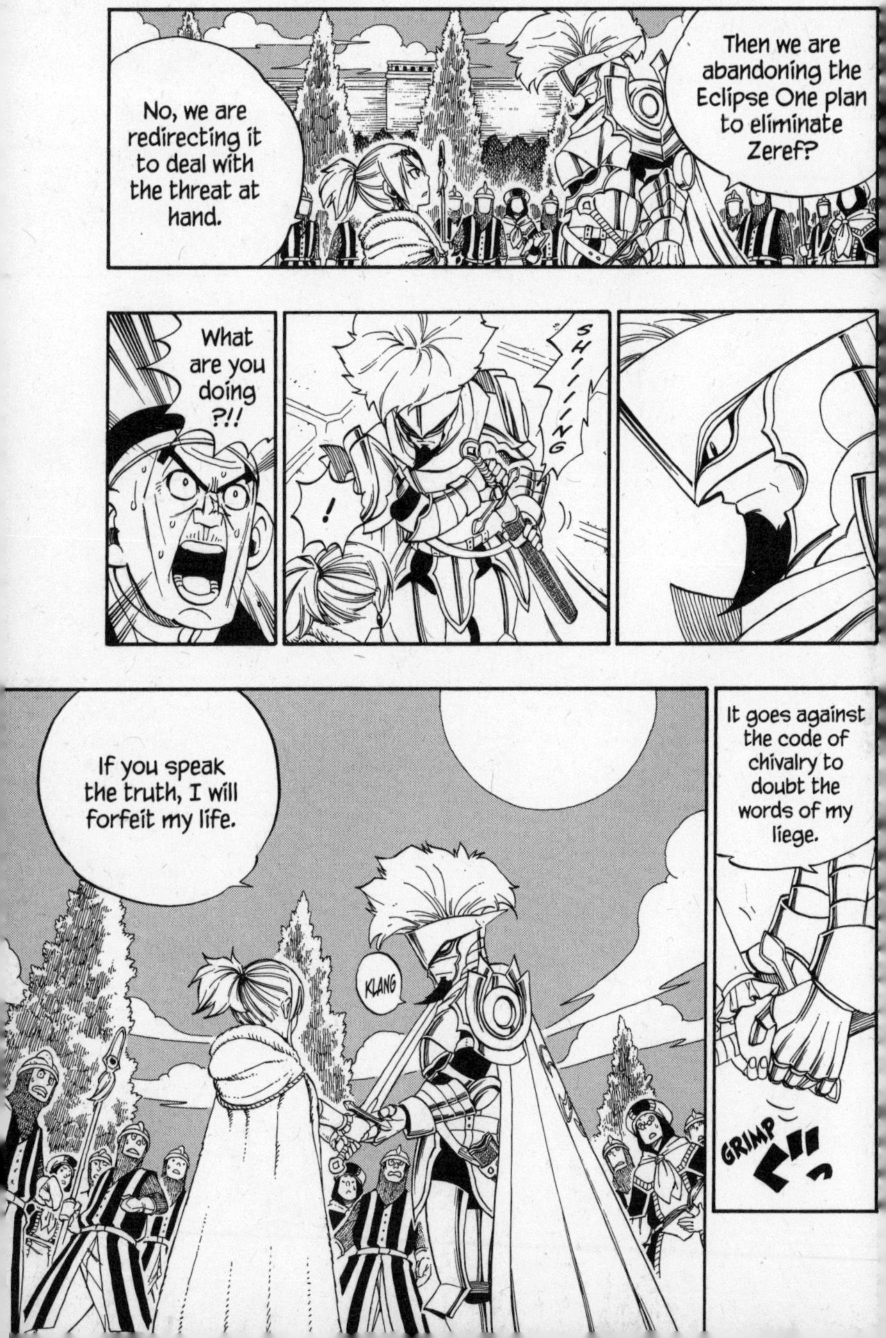
Then we are abandoning the Eclipse One plan to eliminate Zeref?
No, we are redirecting it to deal with the threat at hand.
SHIIIIING
!
What are you doing ?!!
It goes against the code of chivalry to doubt the words of my liege.
GRIMP
If you speak the truth, I will forfeit my life.
KLANG

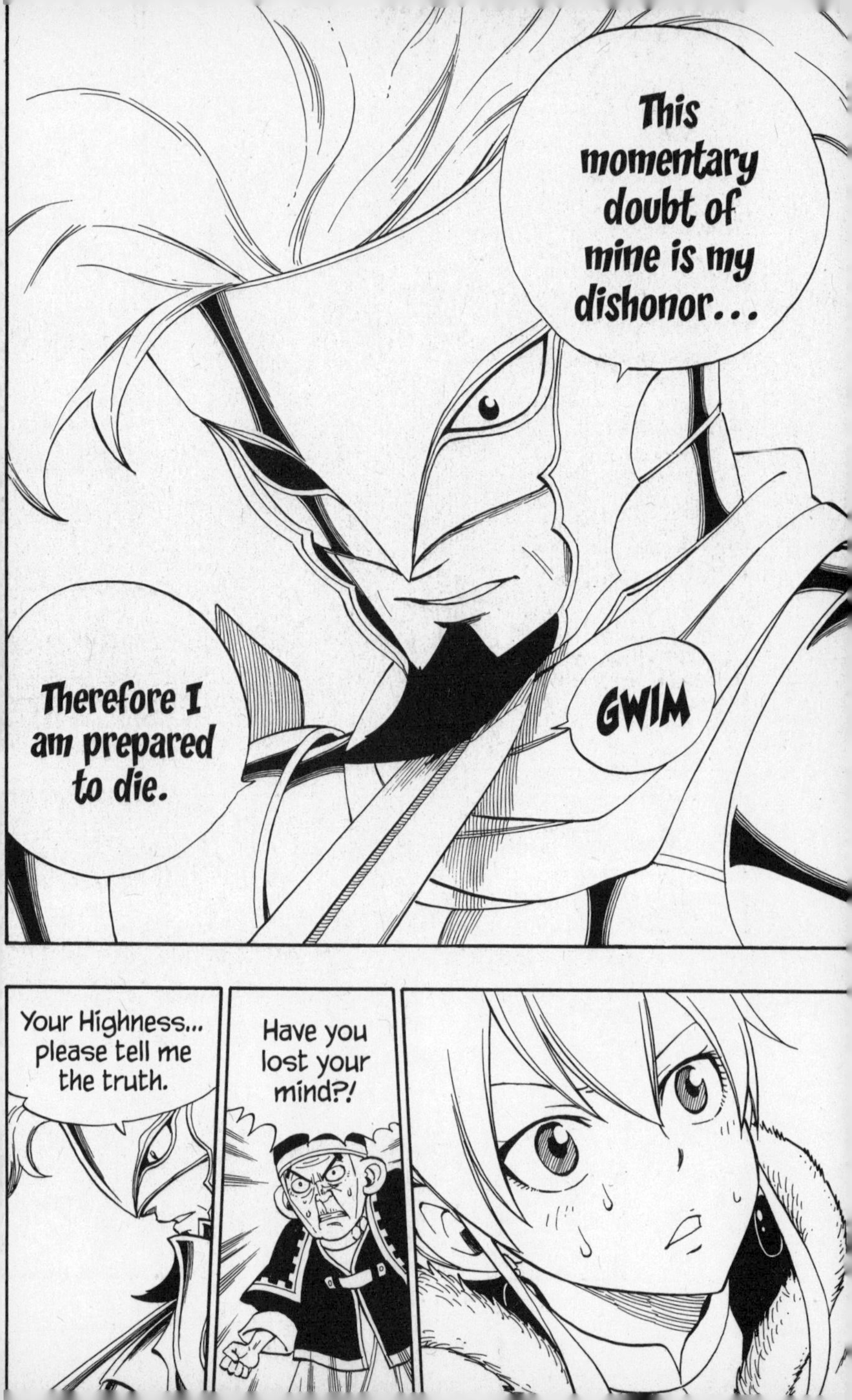
This momentary doubt of mine is my dishonor...
GWIM
Therefore I am prepared to die.
Have you lost your mind?!
Your Highness... please tell me the truth.

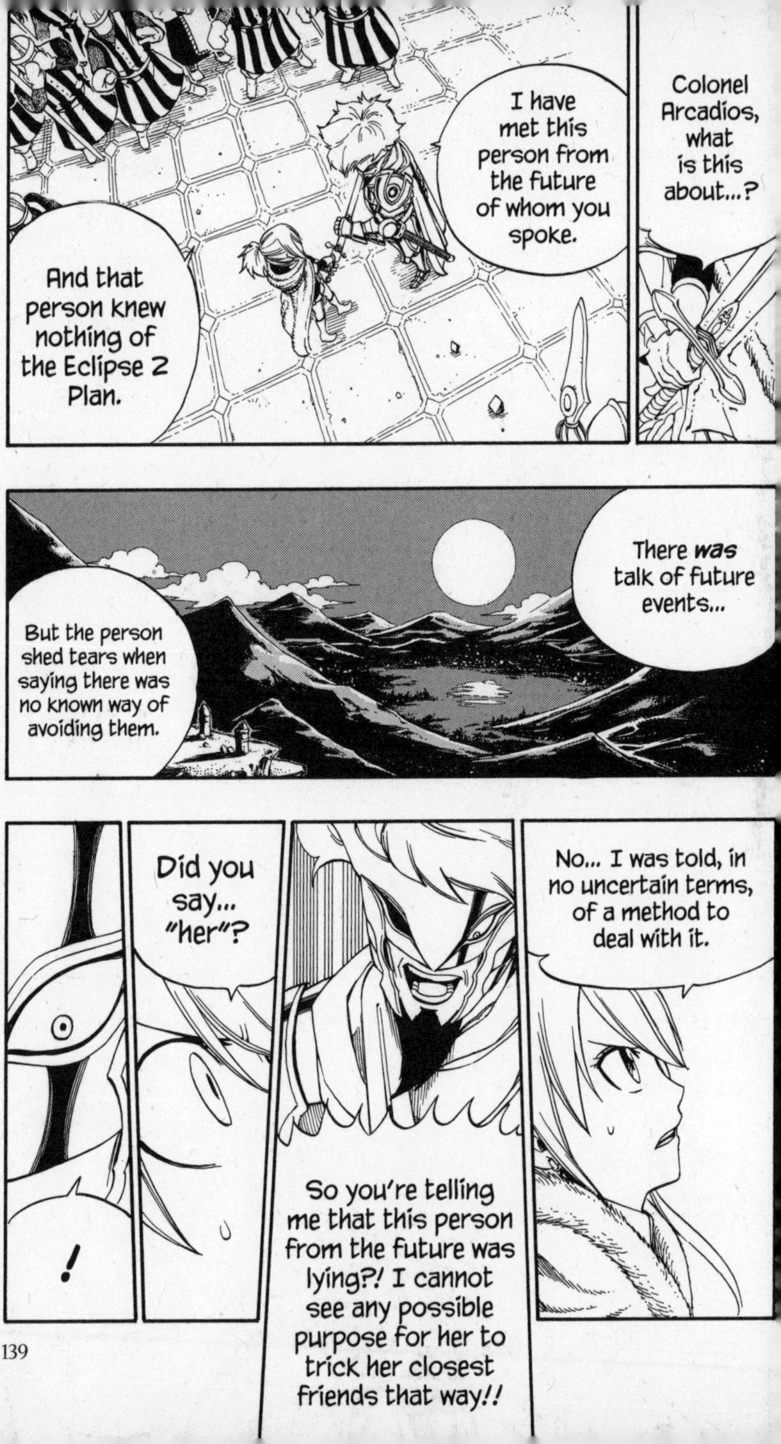
Colonel Arcadios, what is this about...?
I have met this person from the future of whom you spoke.
And that person knew nothing of the Eclipse 2 Plan.
There *was* talk of future events...
But the person shed tears when saying there was no known way of avoiding them.
No... I was told, in no uncertain terms, of a method to deal with it.
So you're telling me that this person from the future was lying?! I cannot see any possible purpose for her to trick her closest friends that way!!
Did you say... "her"?
!

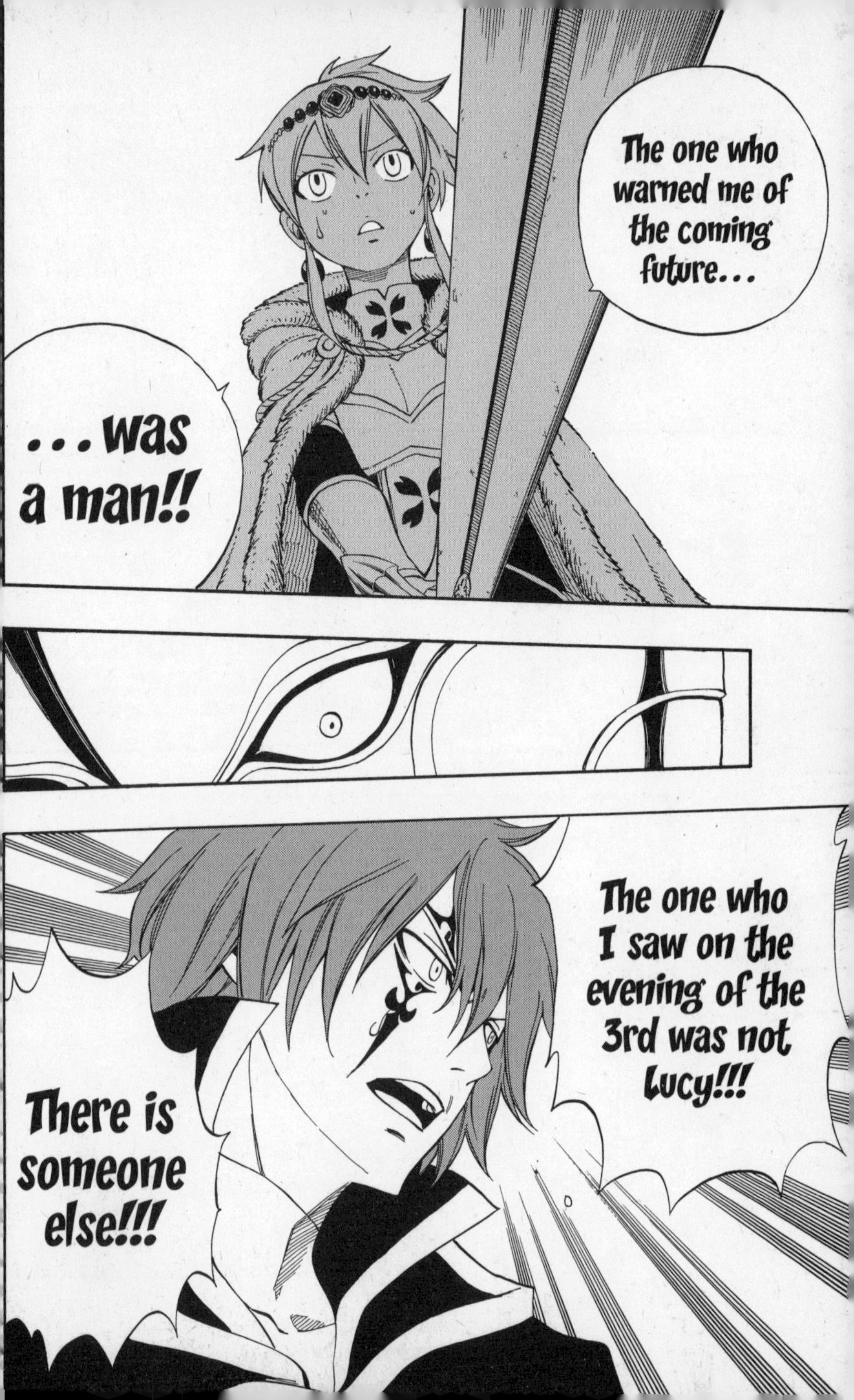
The one who warned me of the coming future...
...was a man!!
The one who I saw on the evening of the 3rd was not Lucy!!!
There is someone else!!!

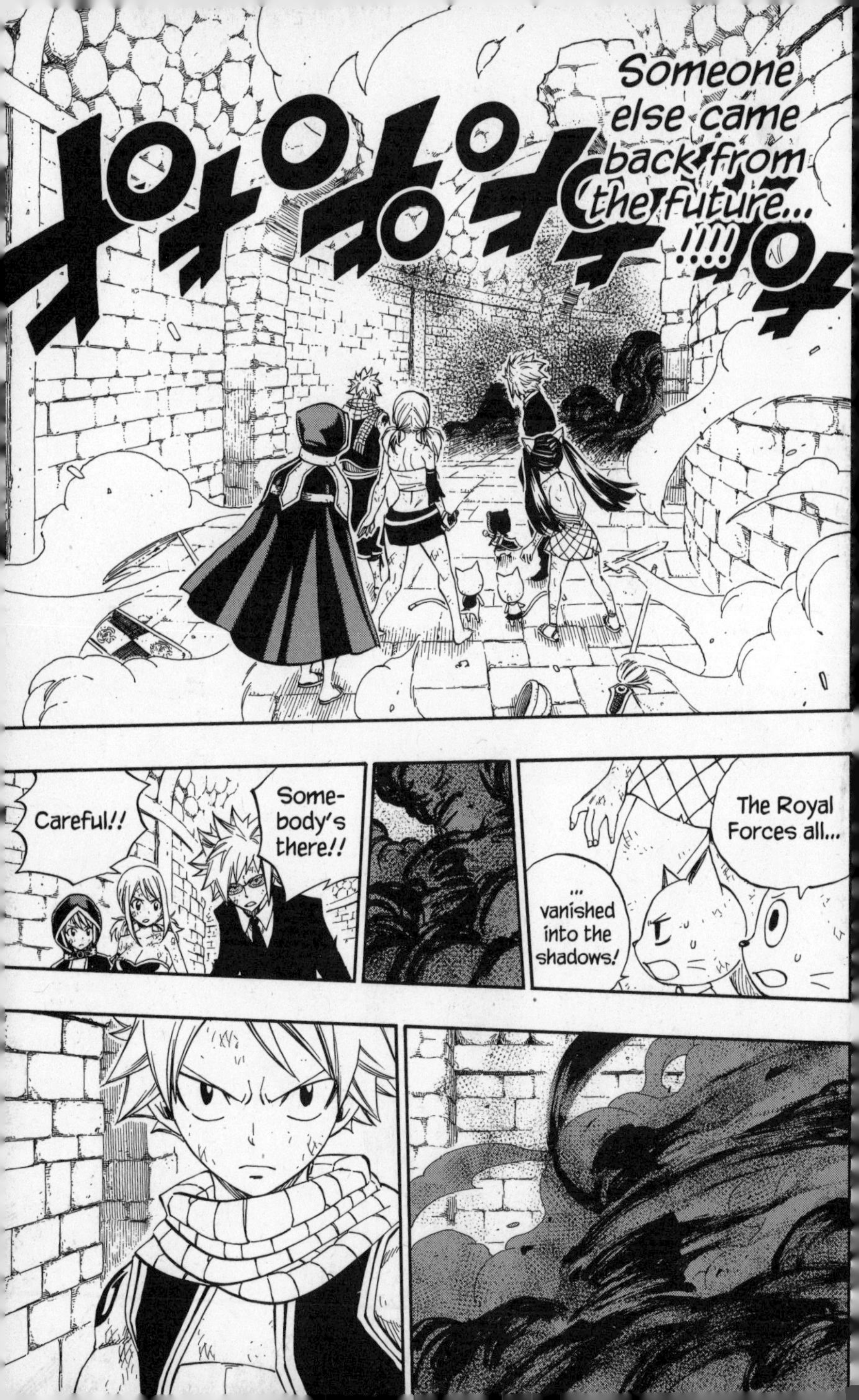

Someone else came back from the future...!!!!
The Royal Forces all...
... vanished into the shadows!
Some-body's there!!
Careful!!

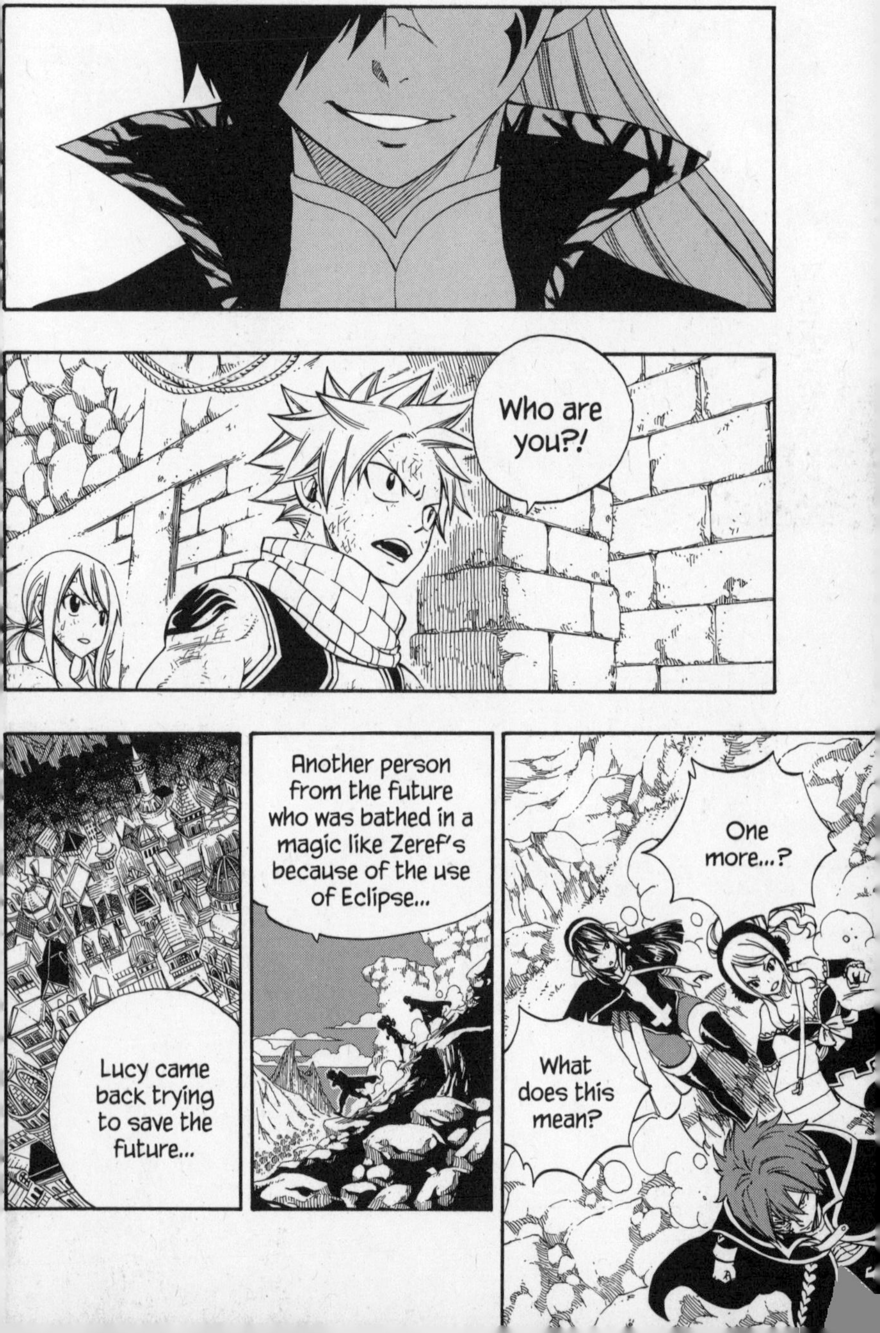
Who are you?!
One more...?
What does this mean?
Another person from the future who was bathed in a magic like Zeref's because of the use of Eclipse...
Lucy came back trying to save the future...

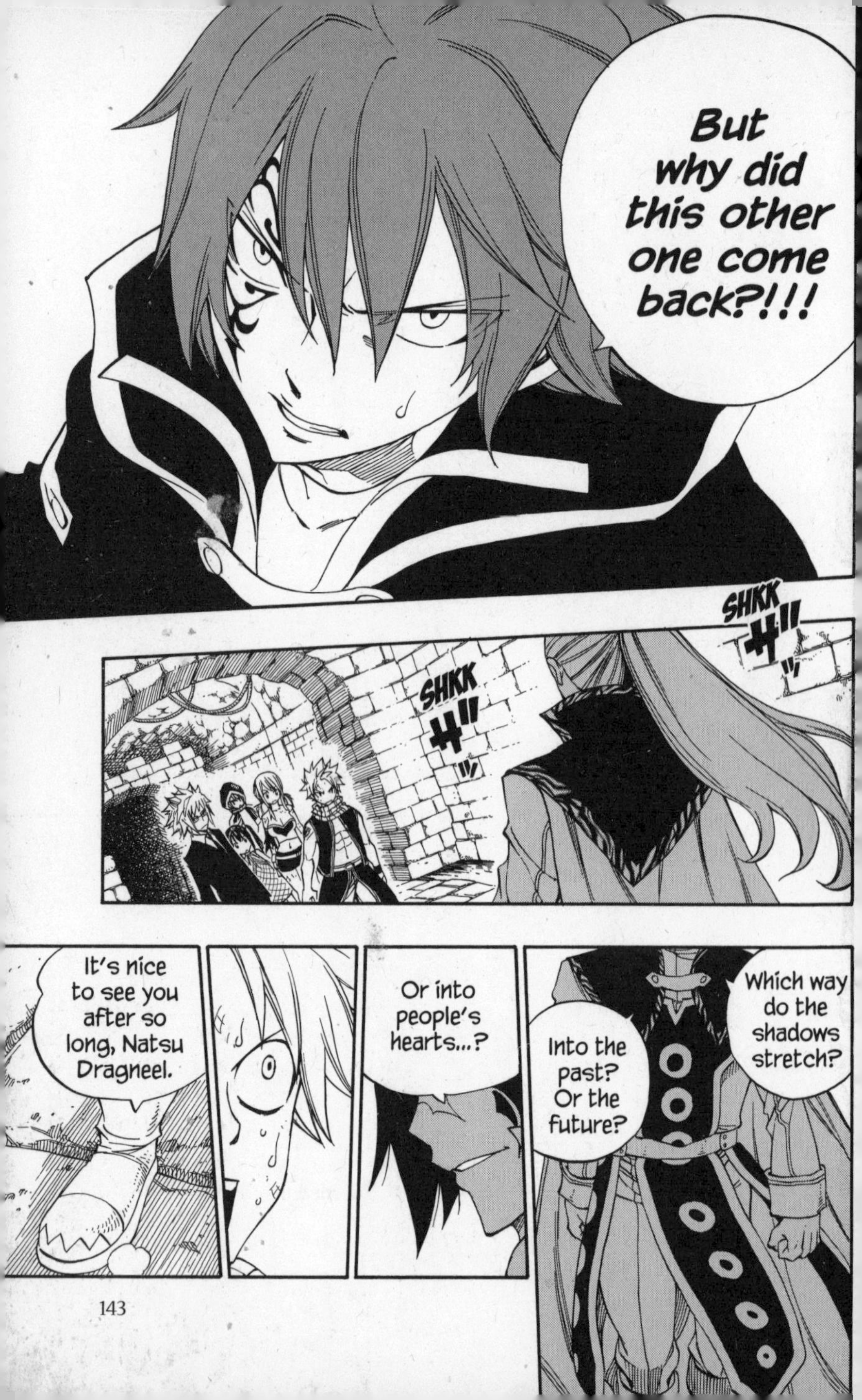
But why did this other one come back?!!!
SHKK
SHKK
Which way do the shadows stretch?
Into the past? Or the future?
Or into people's hearts...?
It's nice to see you after so long, Natsu Dragneel.

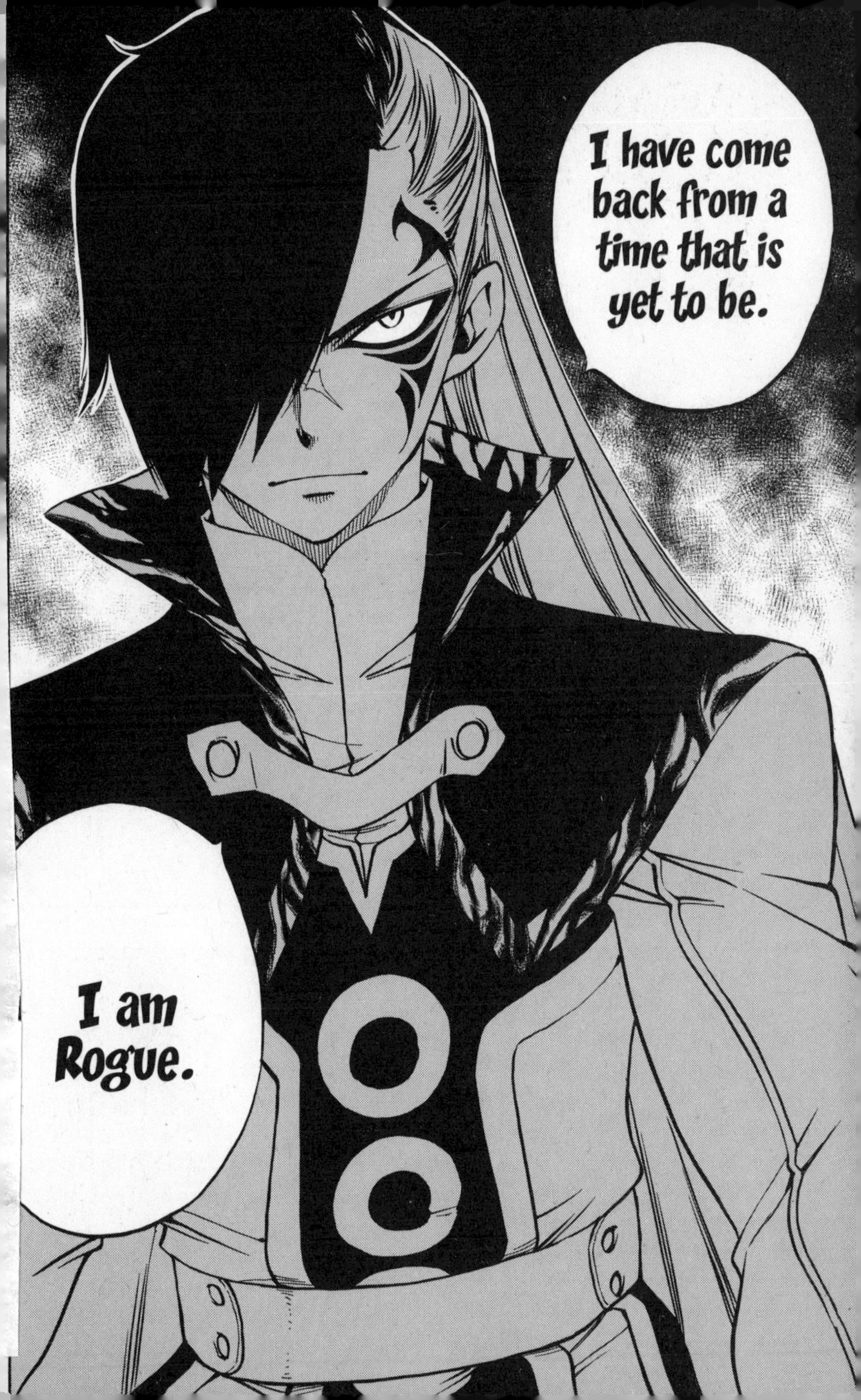
I have come back from a time that is yet to be.
I am Rogue.

FAIRY TAIL

フェアリーテイル

Chapter 324: One Who Would Close the Doo

SOAP

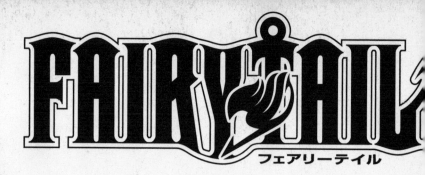

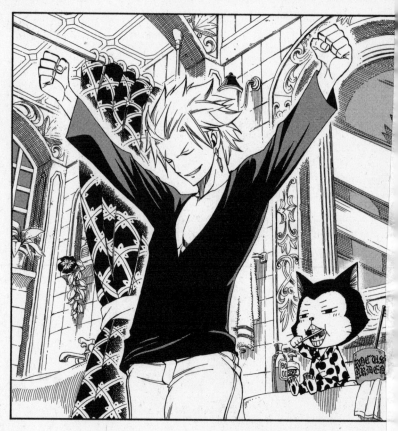

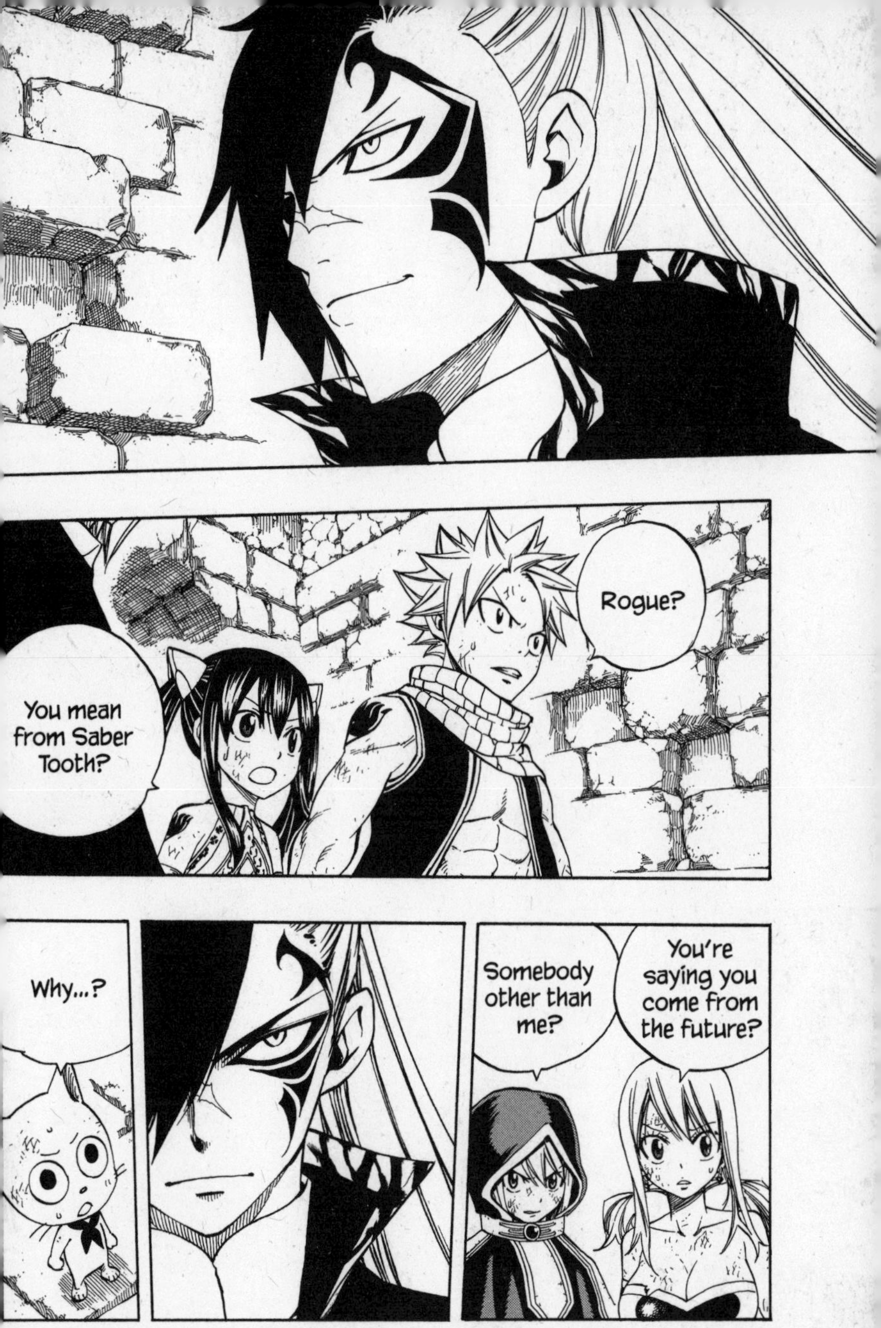

Rogue?
You mean from Saber Tooth?
You're saying you come from the future?
Somebody other than me?
Why...?

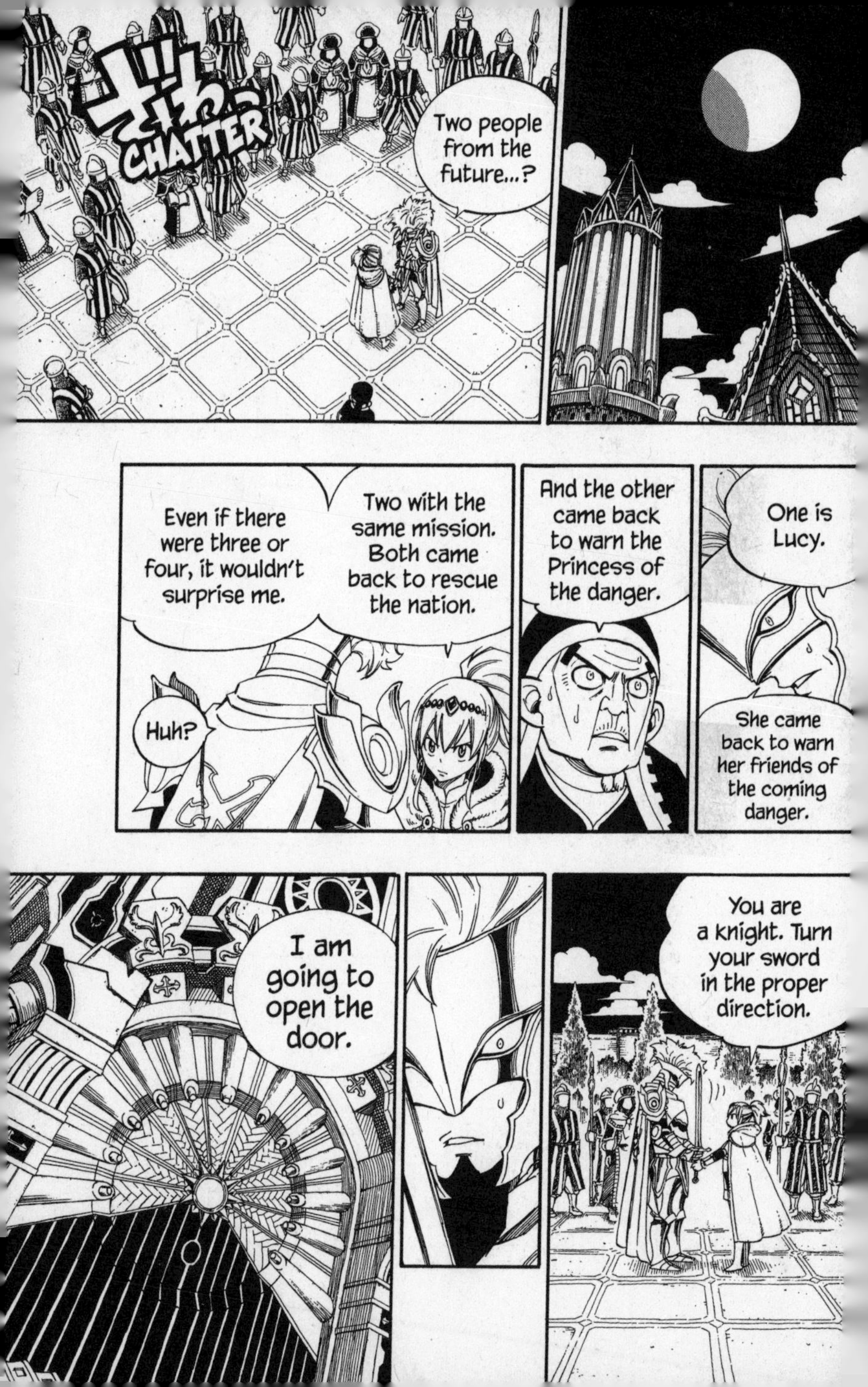
Two people from the future...?
CHATTER
One is Lucy.
She came back to warn her friends of the coming danger.
And the other came back to warn the Princess of the danger.
Two with the same mission. Both came back to rescue the nation.
Even if there were three or four, it wouldn't surprise me.
Huh?
You are a knight. Turn your sword in the proper direction.
I am going to open the door.

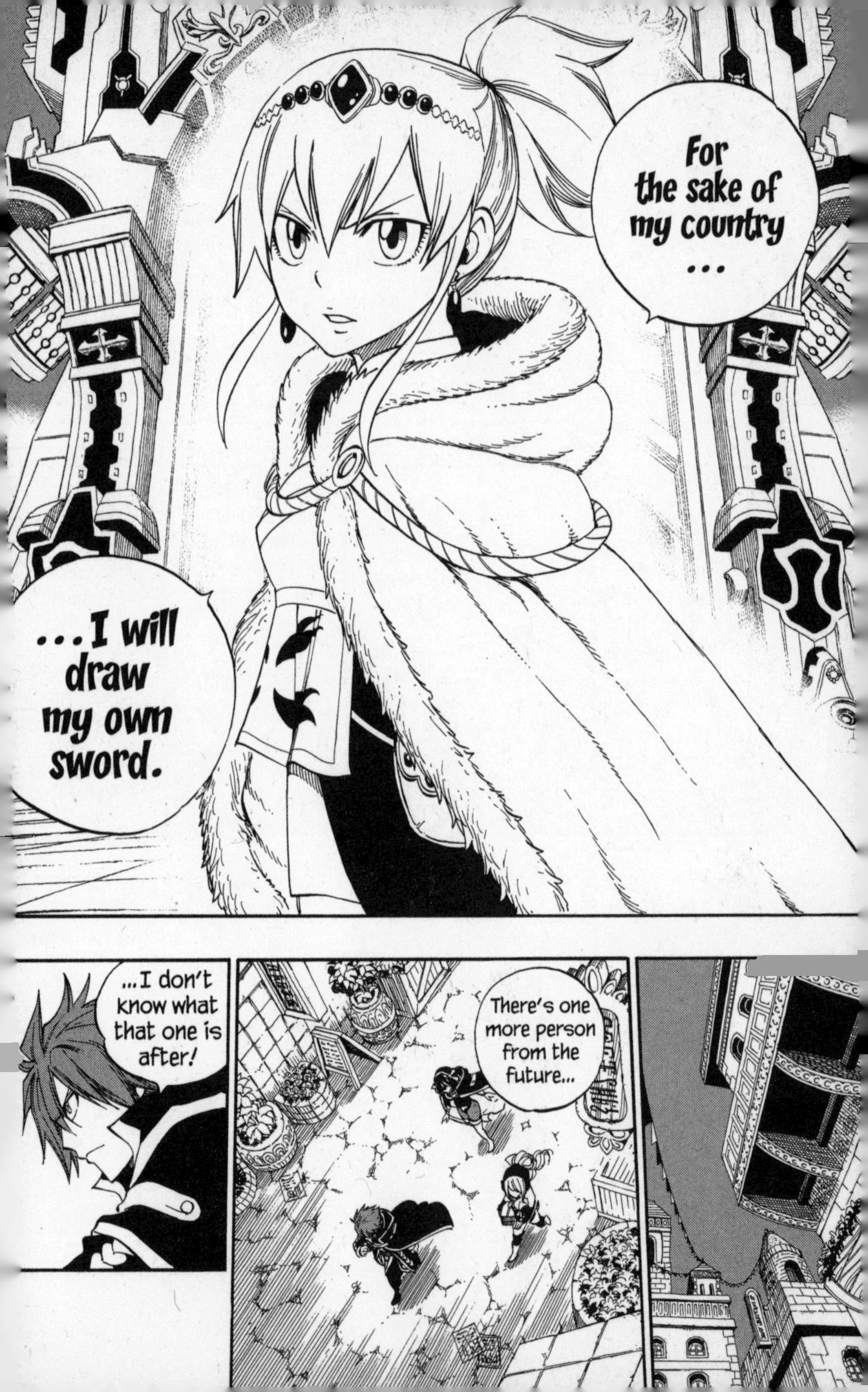
For the sake of my country ...
...I will draw my own sword.
There's one more person from the future...
...I don't know what that one is after!

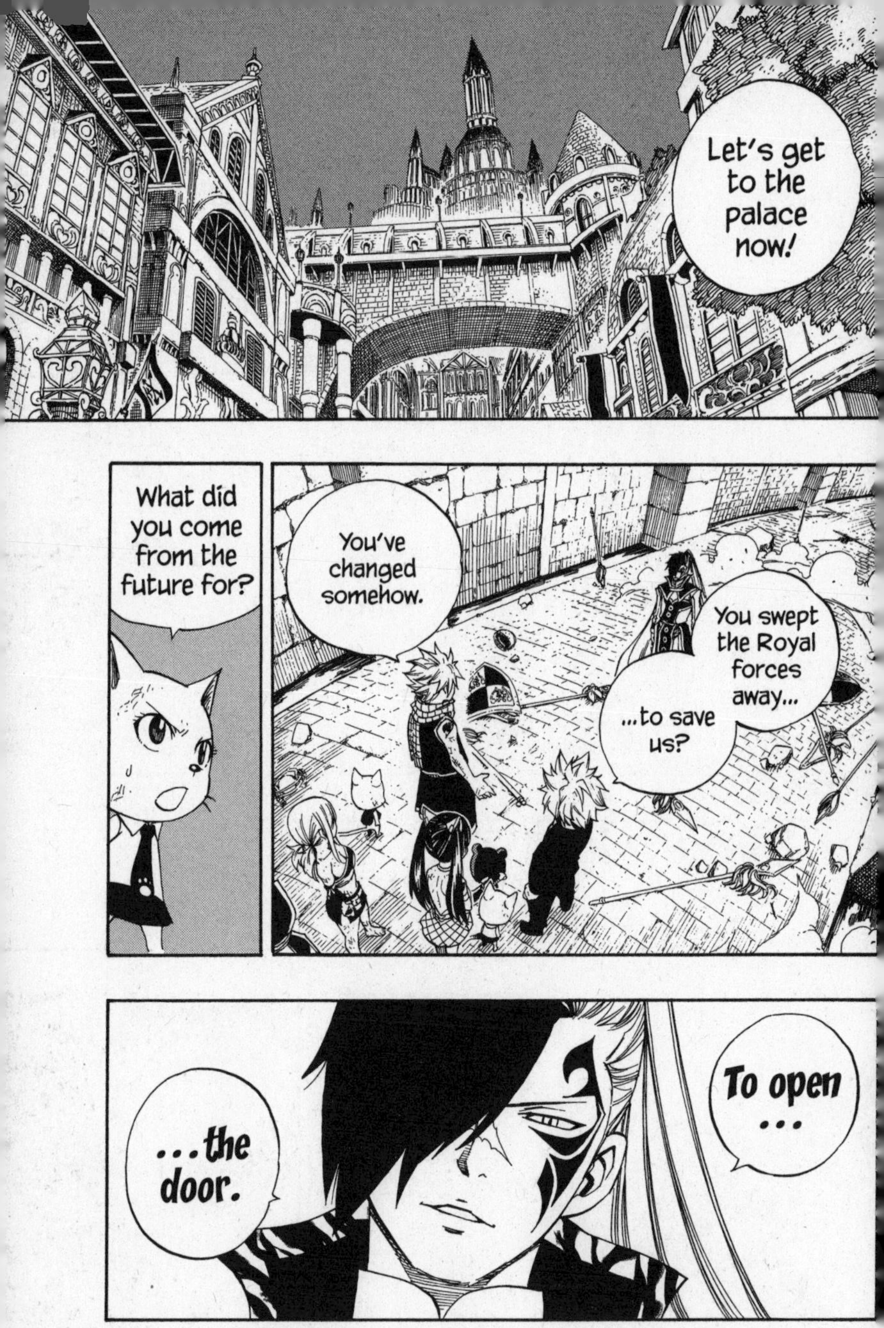

Let's get to the palace now!
You've changed somehow.
You swept the Royal forces away...
...to save us?
What did you come from the future for?
To open...
...the door.

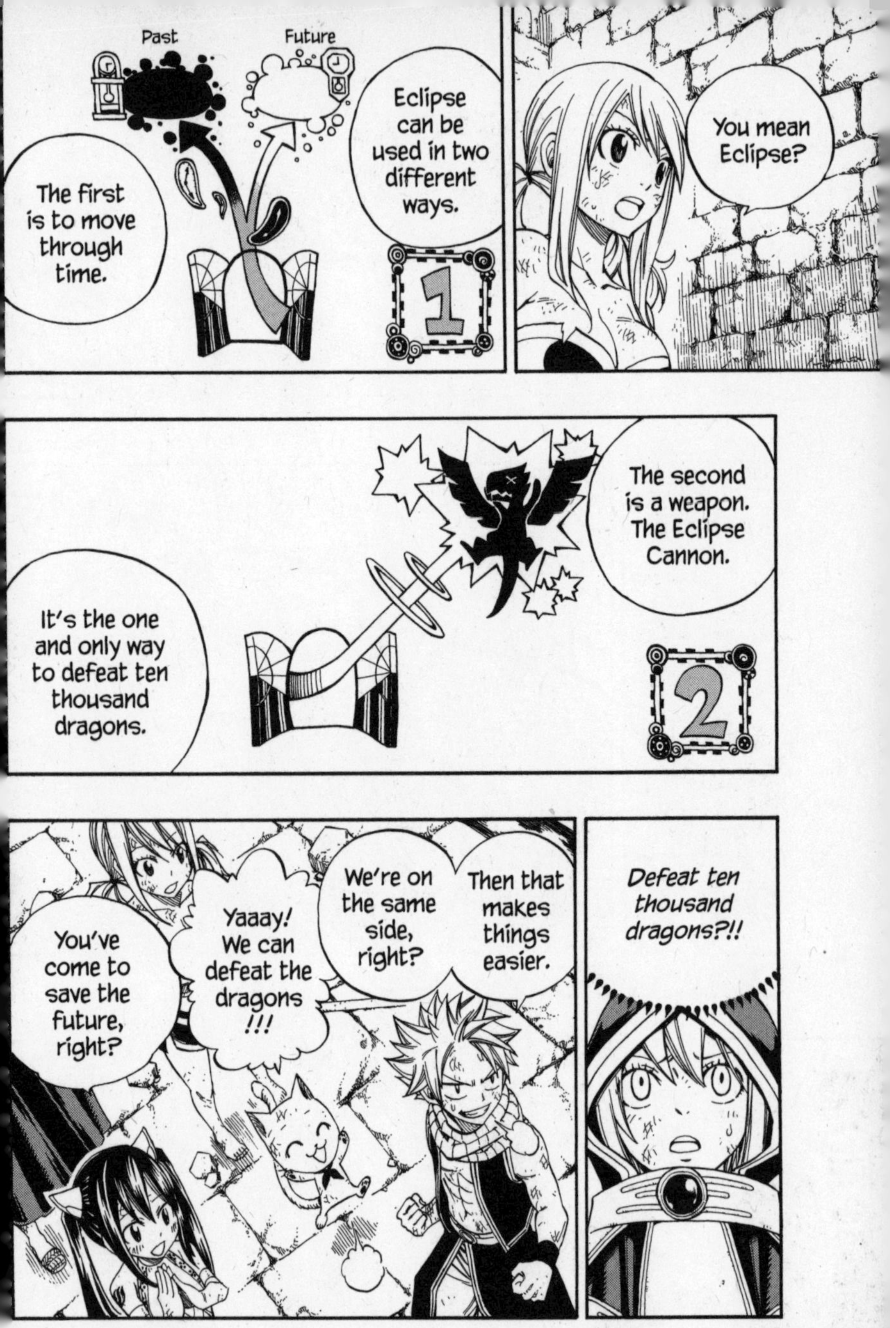
You mean Eclipse?
Eclipse can be used in two different ways.
1
Future
Past
The first is to move through time.
The second is a weapon. The Eclipse Cannon.
2
It's the one and only way to defeat ten thousand dragons.
Defeat ten thousand dragons?!!
Then that makes things easier.
We're on the same side, right?
Yaaay! We can defeat the dragons !!!
You've come to save the future, right?

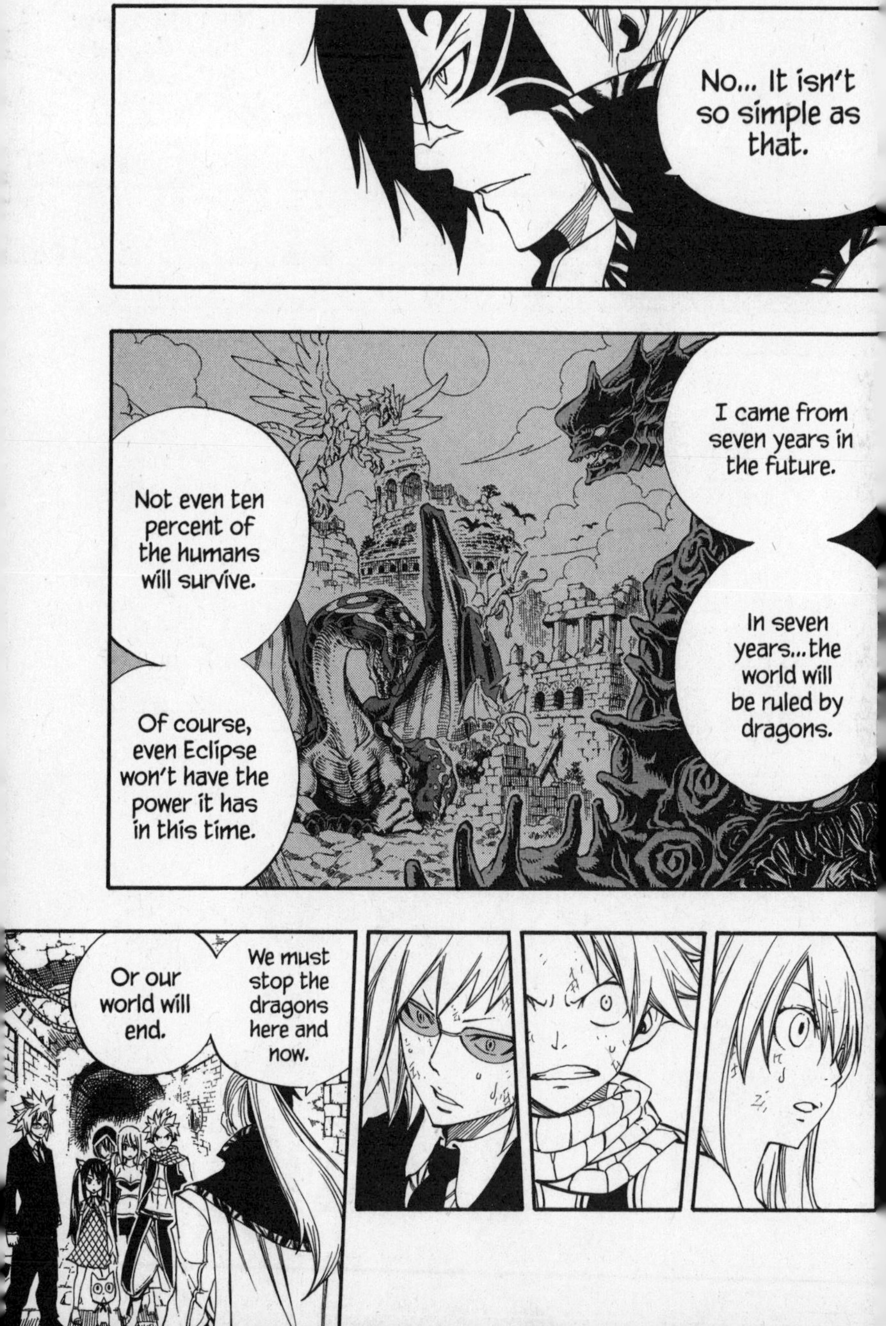
No... It isn't so simple as that.
I came from seven years in the future.
In seven years...the world will be ruled by dragons.
Not even ten percent of the humans will survive.
Of course, even Eclipse won't have the power it has in this time.
We must stop the dragons here and now.
Or our world will end.

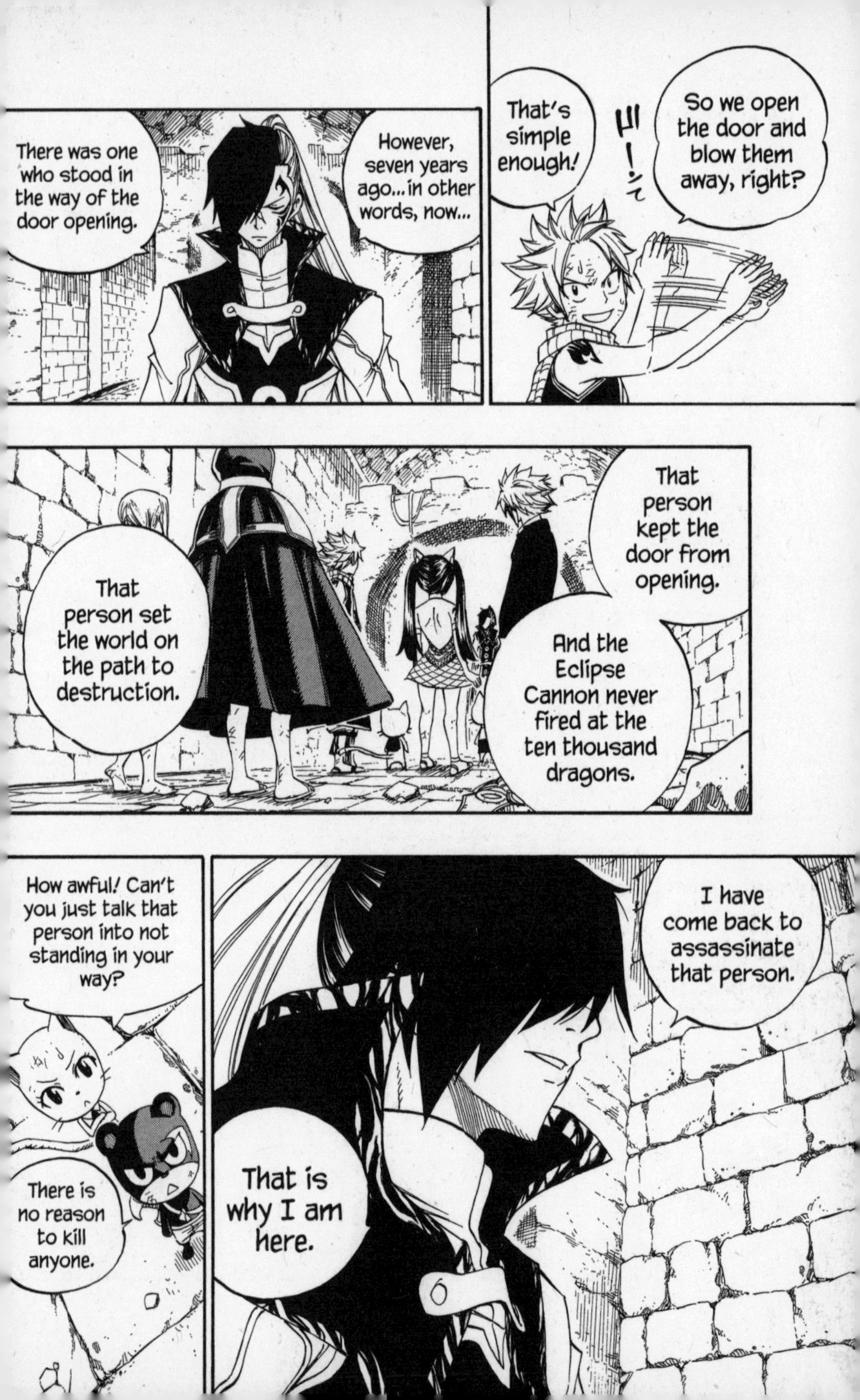
So we open the door and blow them away, right?
That's simple enough!
However, seven years ago...in other words, now...
There was one who stood in the way of the door opening.
That person kept the door from opening.
And the Eclipse Cannon never fired at the ten thousand dragons.
That person set the world on the path to destruction.
I have come back to assassinate that person.
That is why I am here.
How awful! Can't you just talk that person into not standing in your way?
There is no reason to kill anyone.

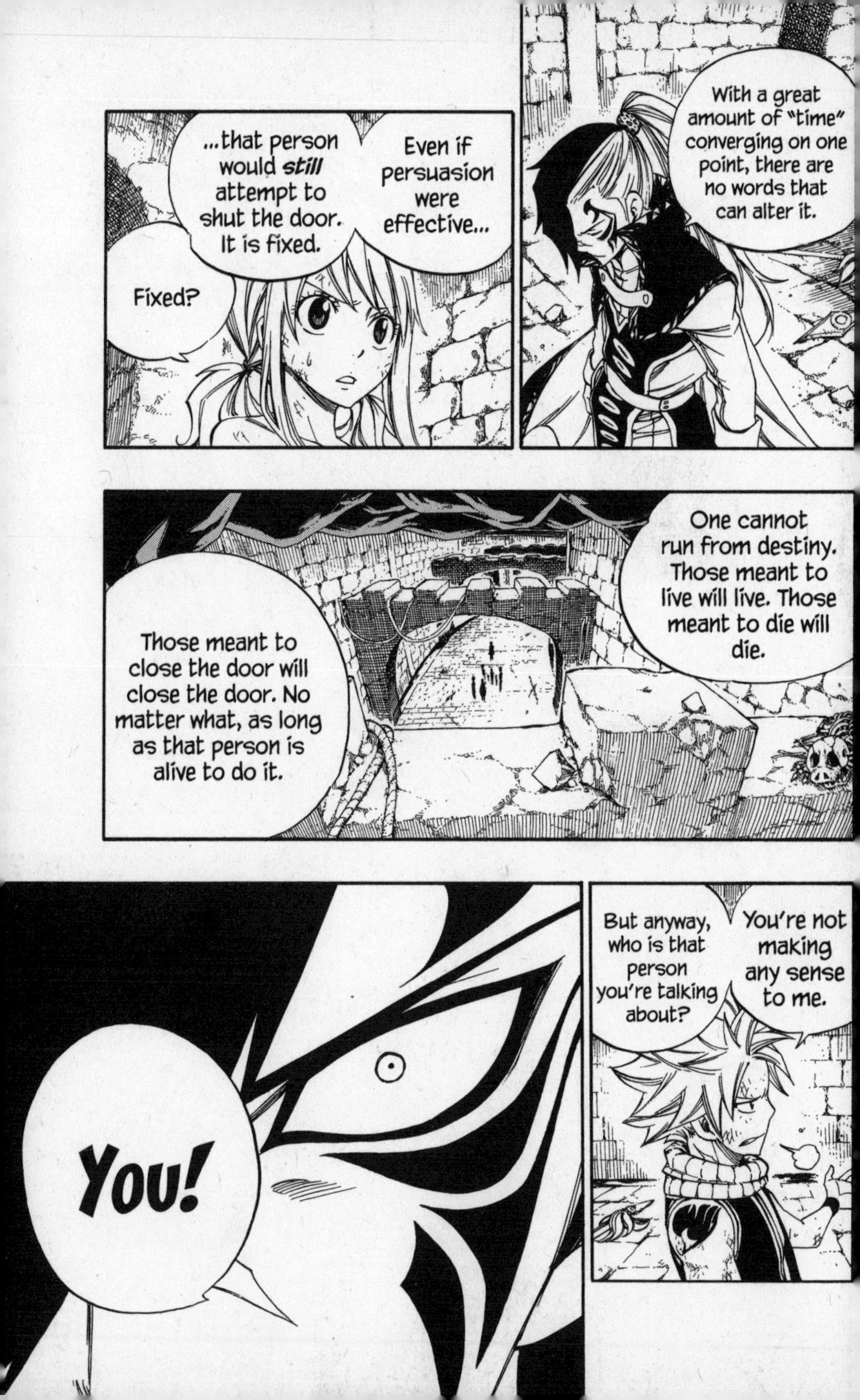
With a great amount of "time" converging on one point, there are no words that can alter it.
Even if persuasion were effective...
...that person would *still* attempt to shut the door. It is fixed.
Fixed?
One cannot run from destiny. Those meant to live will live. Those meant to die will die.
Those meant to close the door will close the door. No matter what, as long as that person is alive to do it.
You're not making any sense to me.
But anyway, who is that person you're talking about?
YOU!

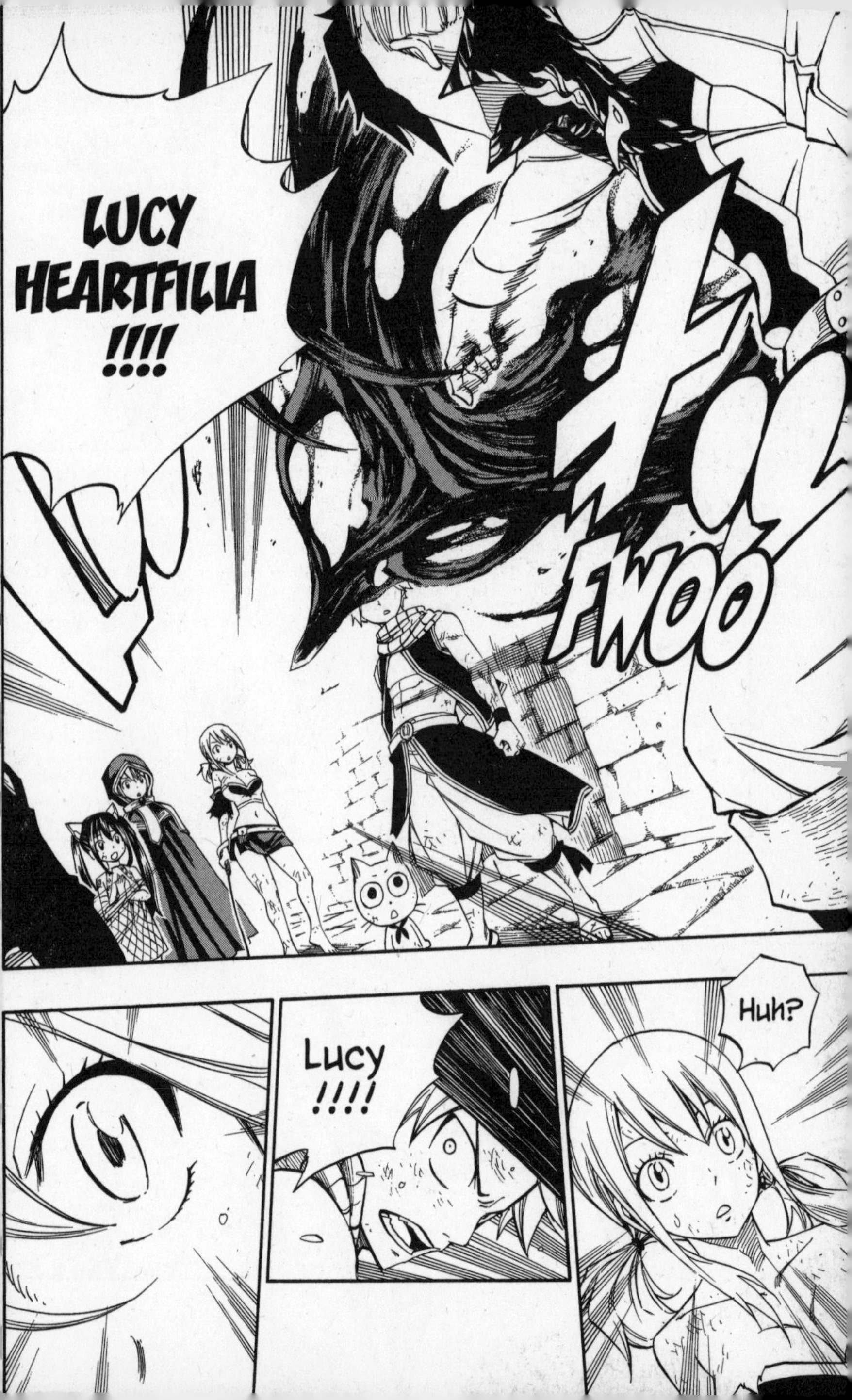
FWOO
LUCY HEARTFILIA !!!!
Huh?
Lucy !!!!

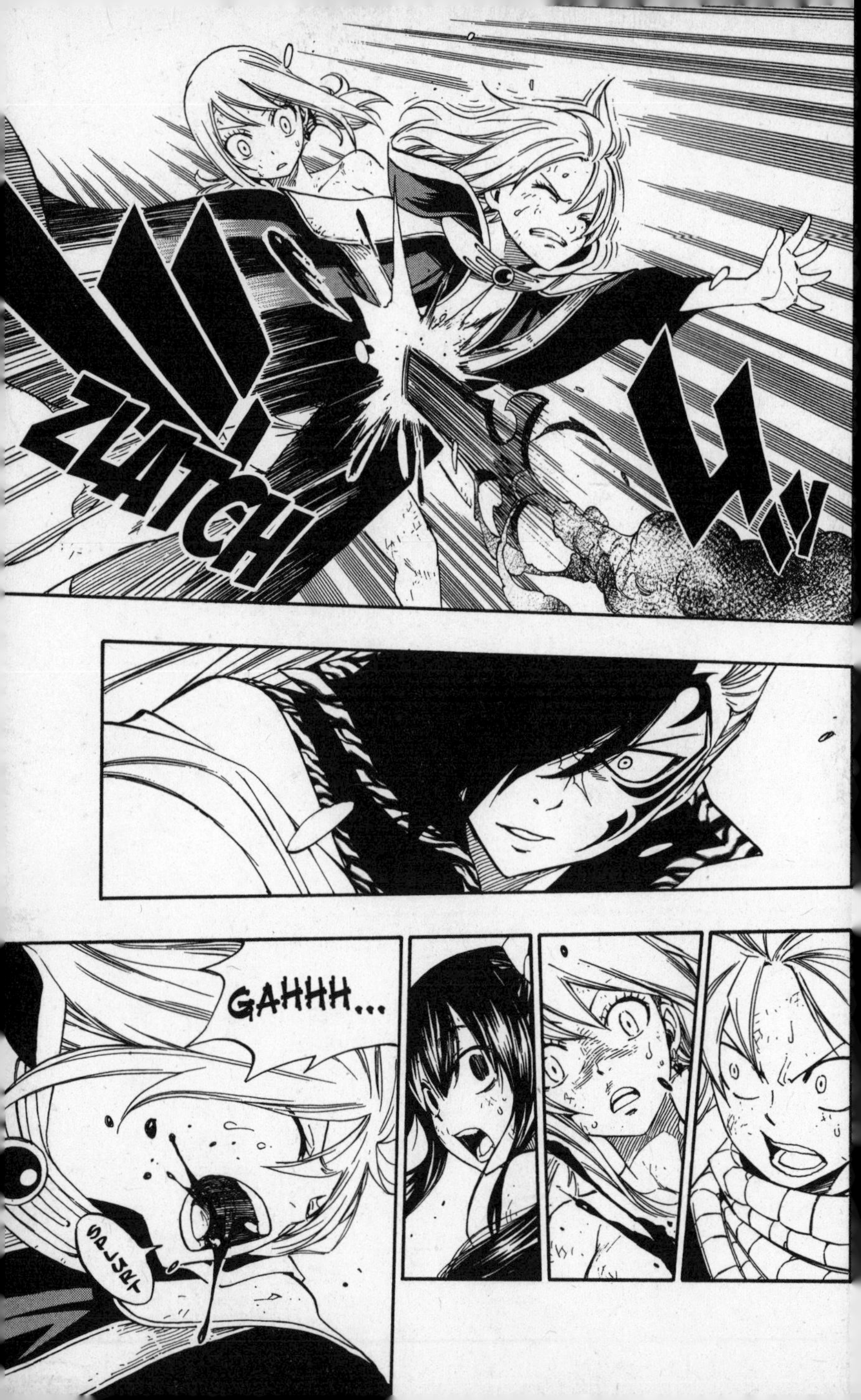
ZLITCH
GAHHH...

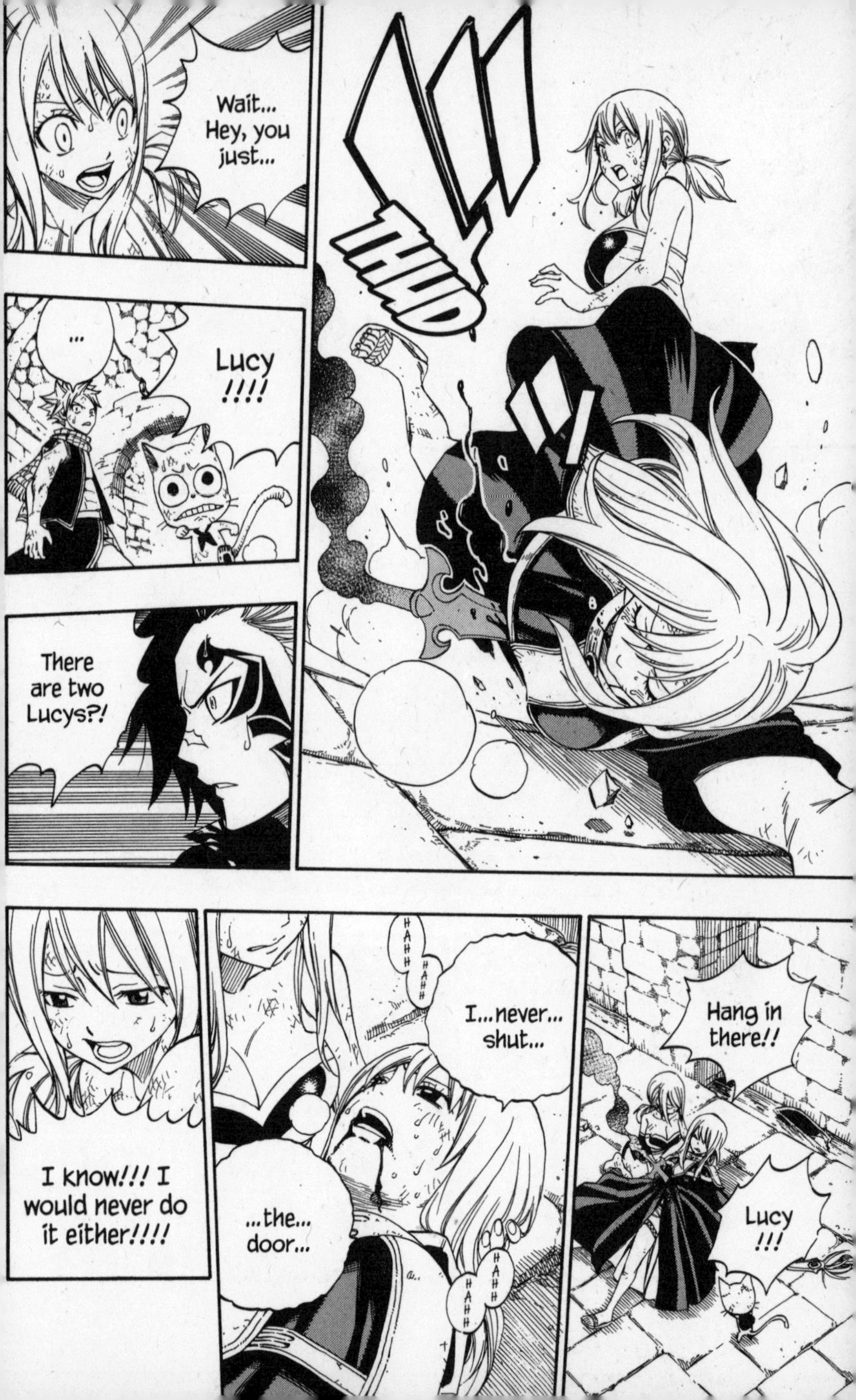
THUD
Wait... Hey, you just...
...
Lucy!!!!
There are two Lucys?!
Hang in there!!
Lucy!!!
I...never... shut...
HAHH HAHH
...the... door...
HAHH HAHH
I know!!! I would never do it either!!!!

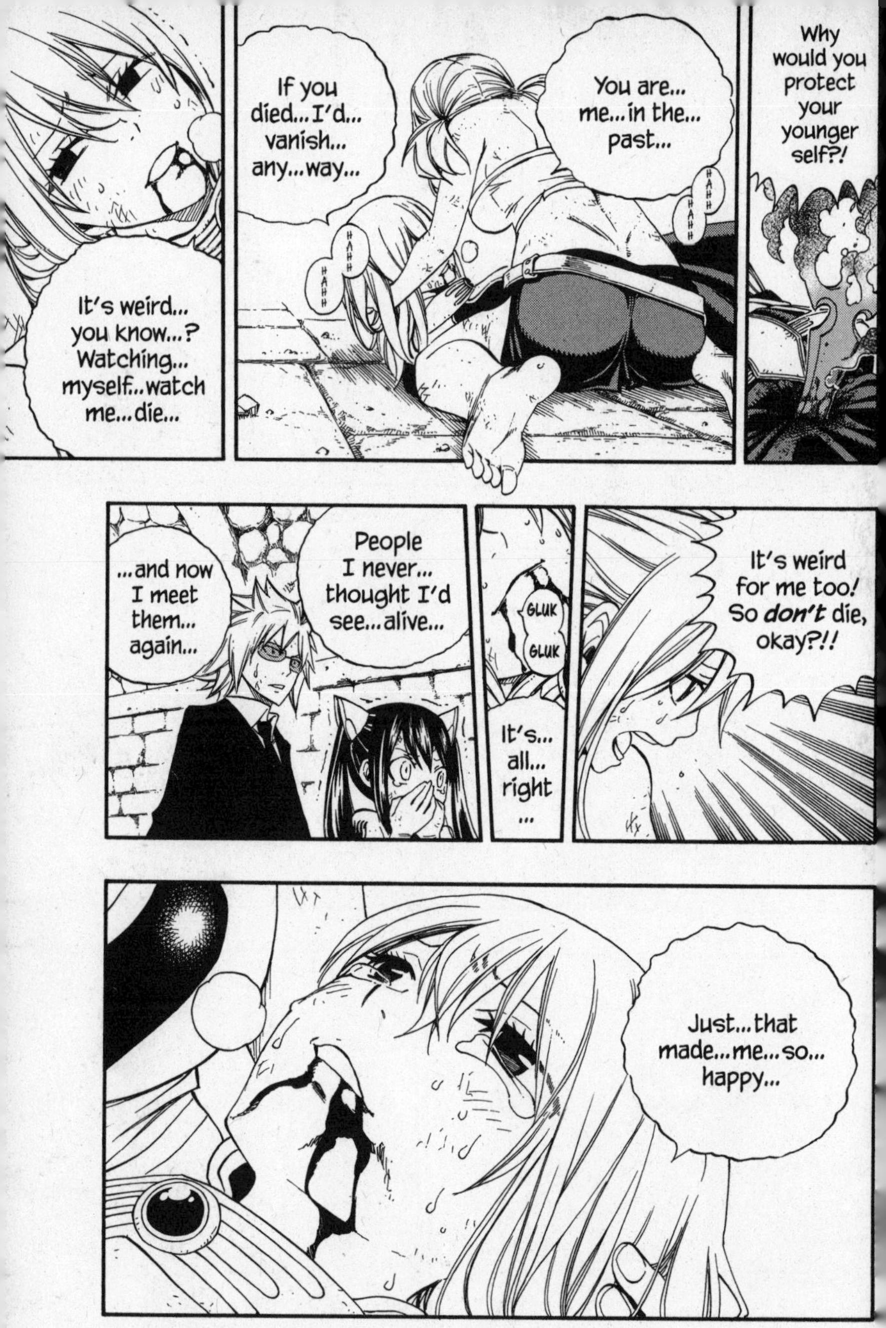
Why would you protect your younger self?!
You are... me...in the... past...
HAHH
HAHH
HAHH
HAHH
If you died...I'd... vanish... any...way...
It's weird... you know...? Watching... myself...watch me...die...
It's weird for me too! So don't die, okay?!!
GLUK
GLUK
It's... all... right ...
People I never... thought I'd see...alive...
...and now I meet them... again...
Just...that made...me...so... happy...

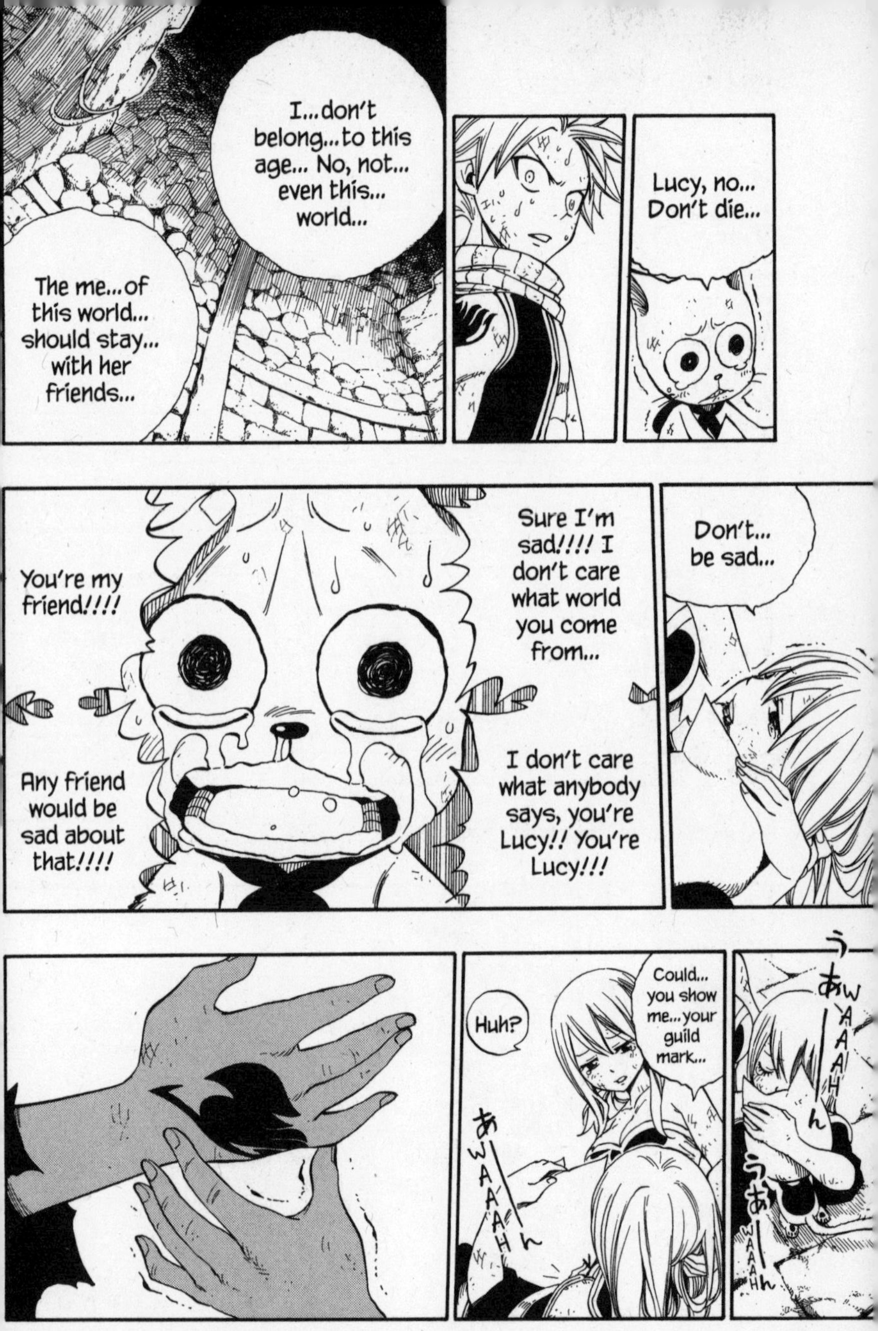

Lucy, no... Don't die...
I...don't belong...to this age... No, not... even this... world...
The me...of this world... should stay... with her friends...
Don't... be sad...
Sure I'm sad!!!! I don't care what world you come from...
You're my friend!!!!
I don't care what anybody says, you're Lucy!! You're Lucy!!!
Any friend would be sad about that!!!!
うあWAAAAHh
うあWAAAHh
Could... you show me...your guild mark...
Huh?
あWAAAAHh

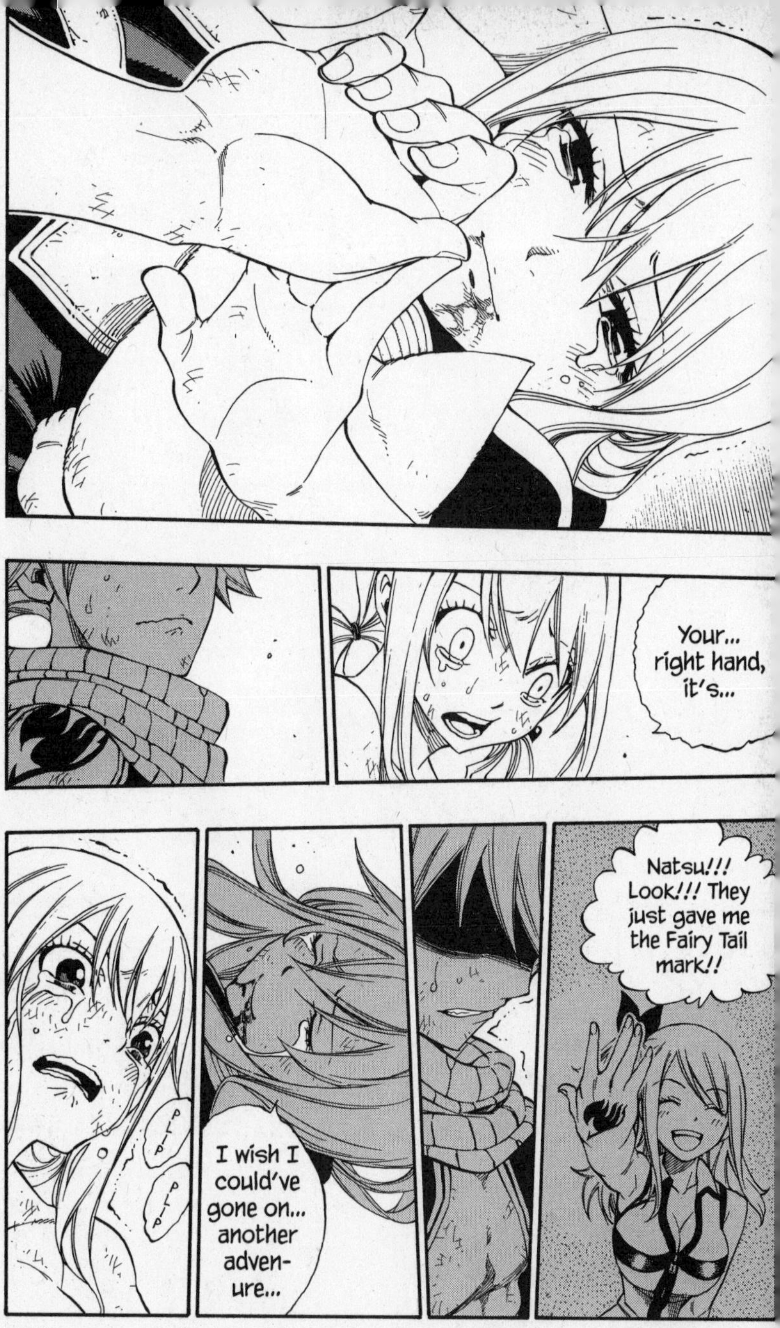
Your... right hand, it's...
Natsu!!! Look!!! They just gave me the Fairy Tail mark!!
I wish I could've gone on... another adven-ure...
PLIP
PLIP

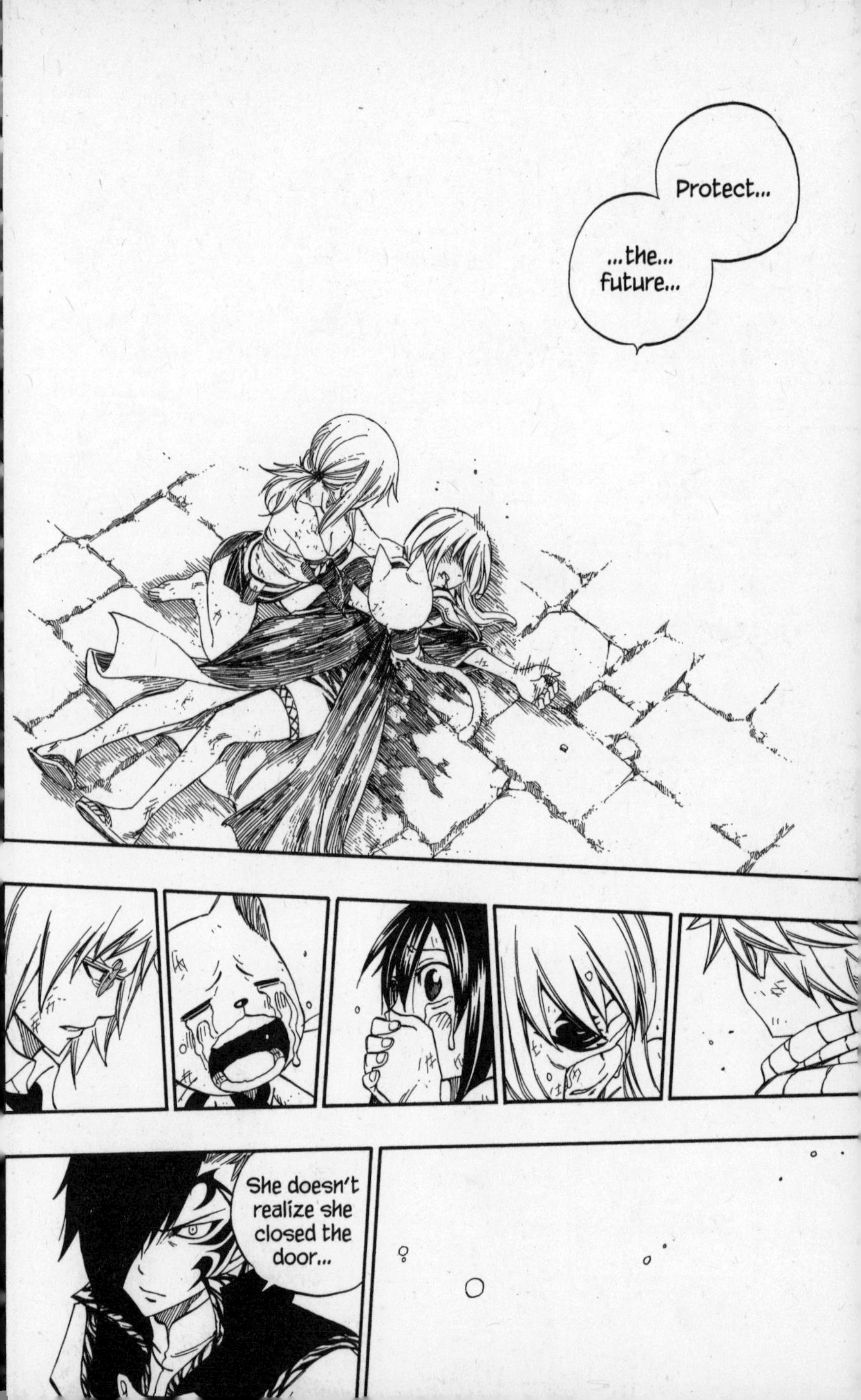
Protect...
...the... future...
She doesn't realize she closed the door...

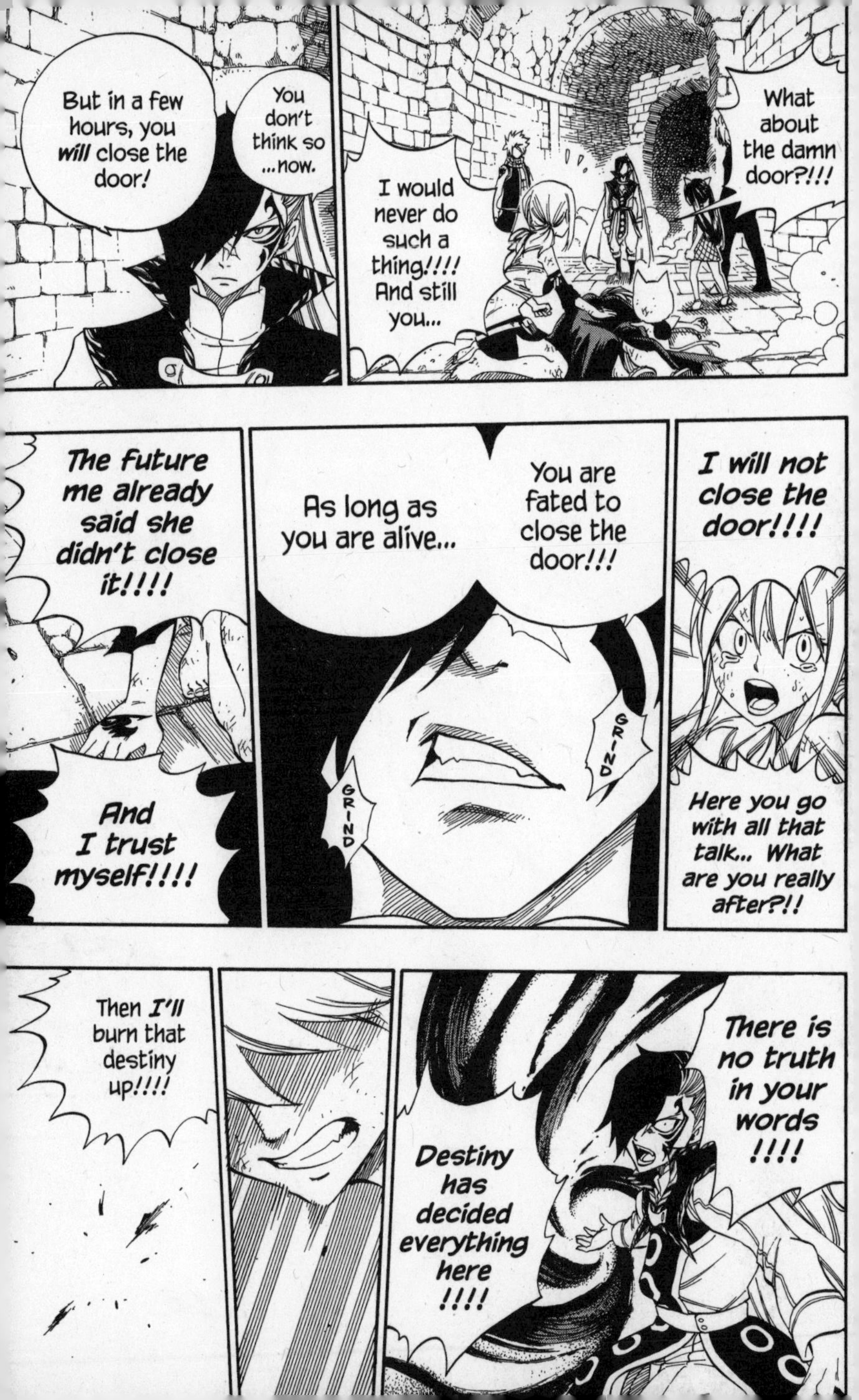

What about the damn door?!!!
I would never do such a thing!!!! And still you...
You don't think so ...now.
But in a few hours, you *will* close the door!
I will not close the door!!!!
Here you go with all that talk... What are you really after?!!
You are fated to close the door!!!
As long as you are alive...
GRIND
GRIND
The future me already said she didn't close it!!!!
And I trust myself!!!!
There is no truth in your words!!!!
Destiny has decided everything here!!!!
Then *I'll* burn that destiny up!!!!

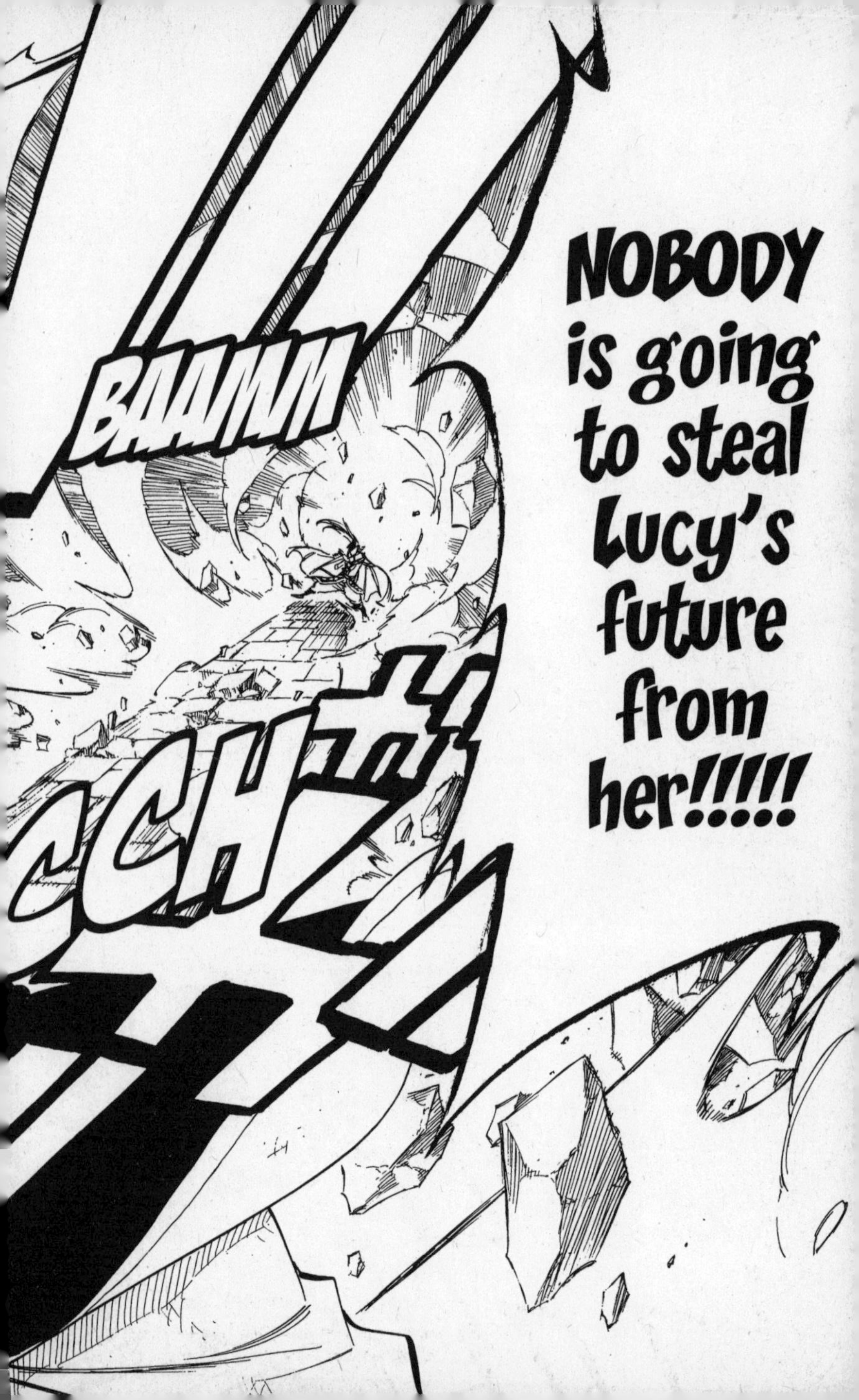
NOBODY is going to steal Lucy's future from her!!!!!
BAAMM
CHZZ

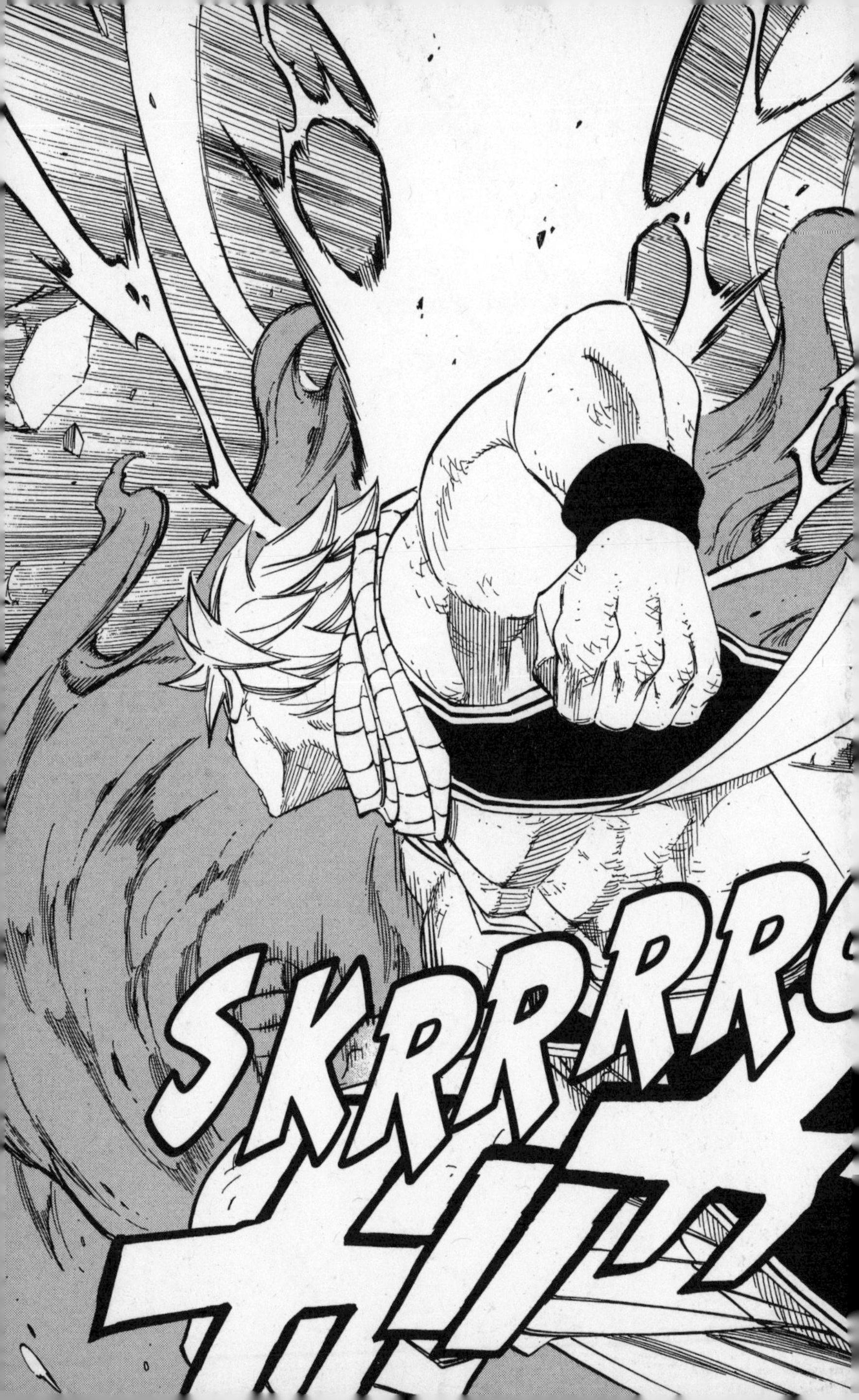
SKRRR

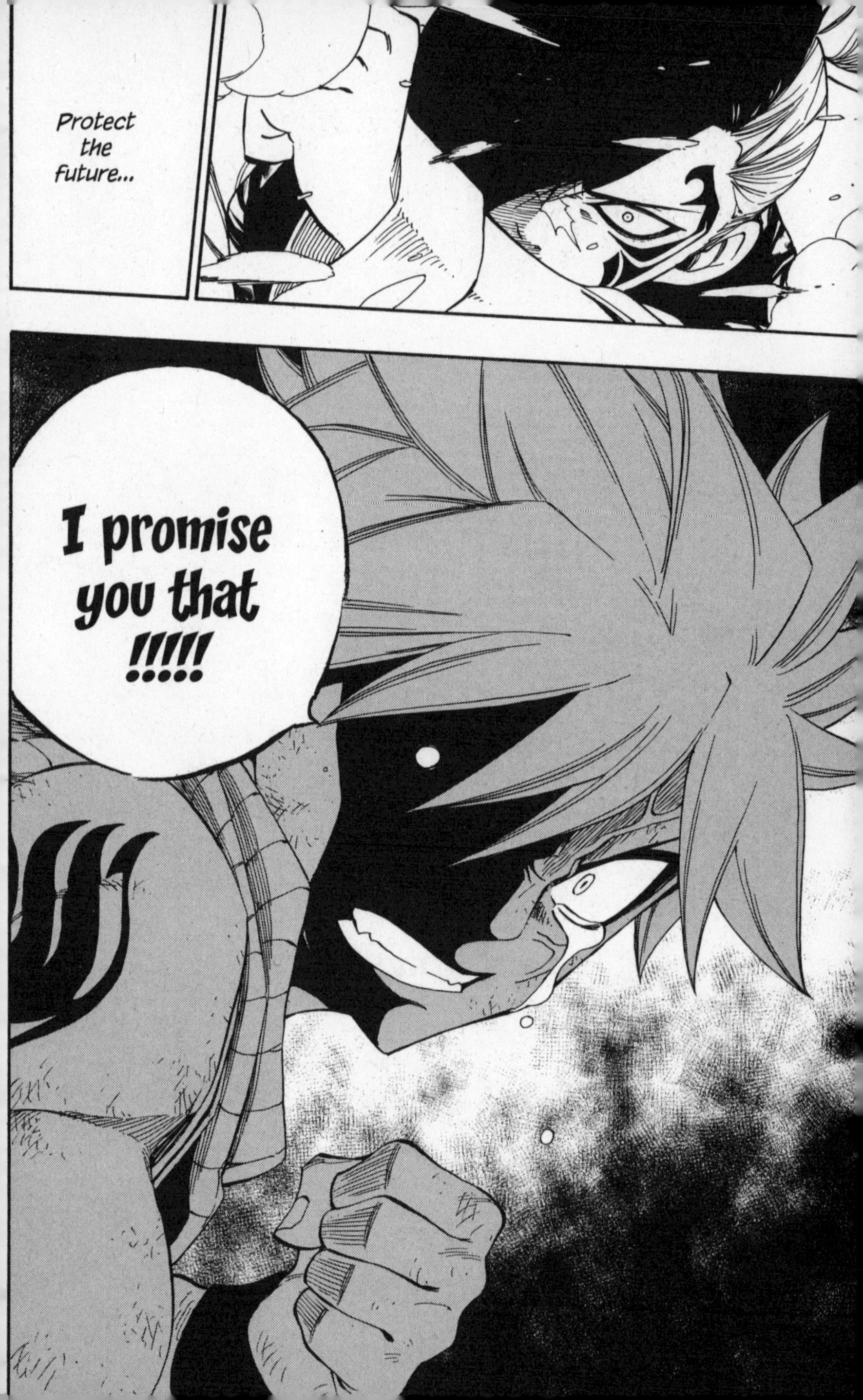
Protect the future...
I promise you that !!!!!

FAIRY TAIL

フェアリーテイル

Chapter 325: Solidarity!!!!

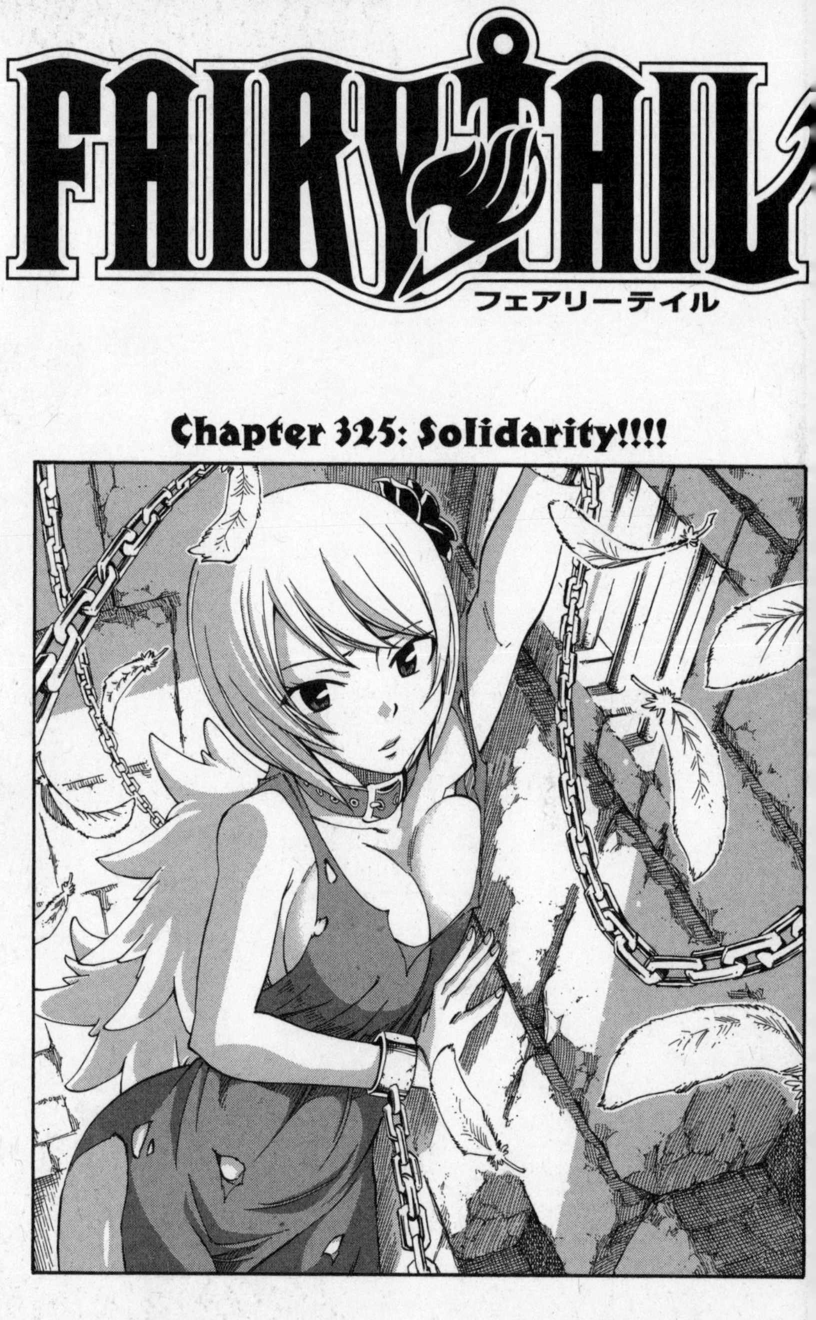

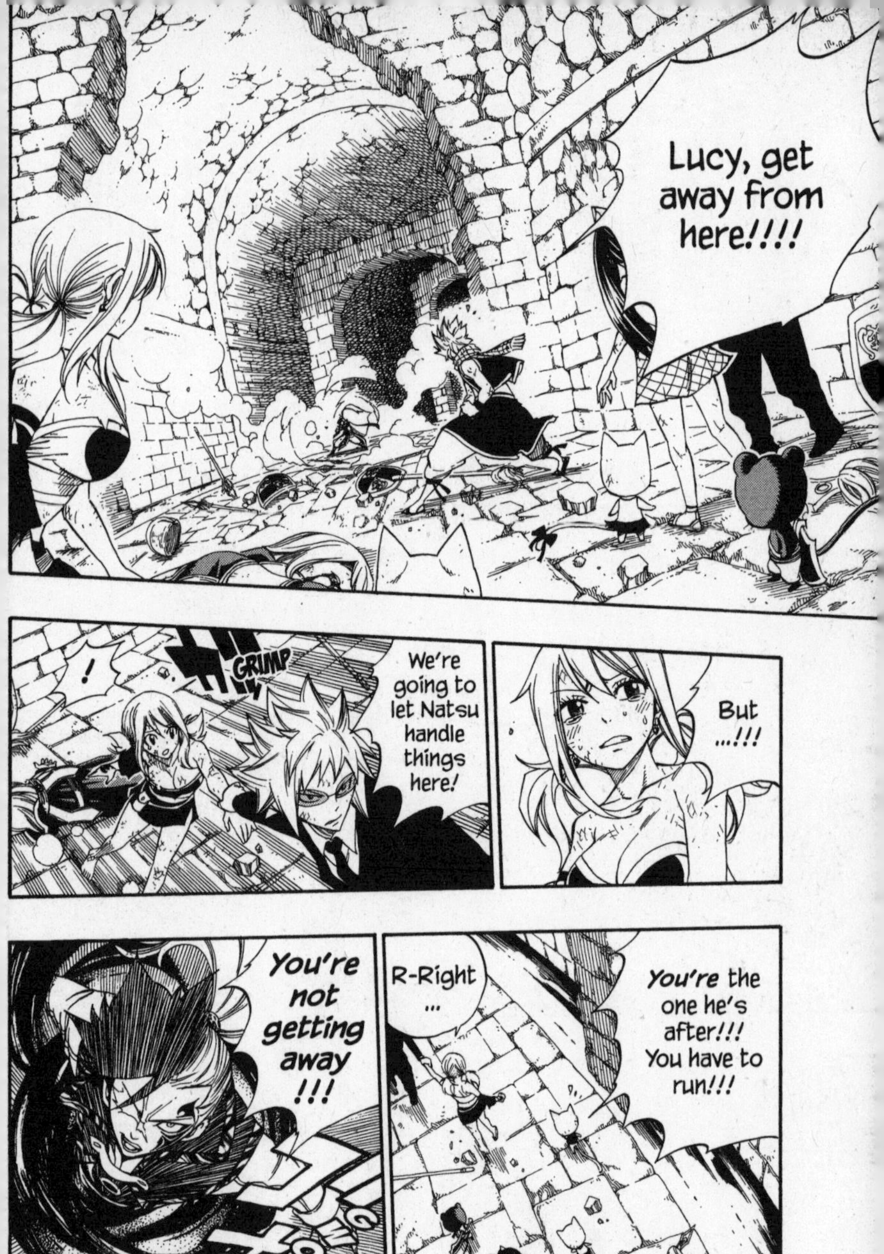
Lucy, get away from here!!!!
But ...!!!
We're going to let Natsu handle things here!
GRIMP
!
You're the one he's after!!! You have to run!!!
R-Right ...
You're not getting away !!!
GWOOOH

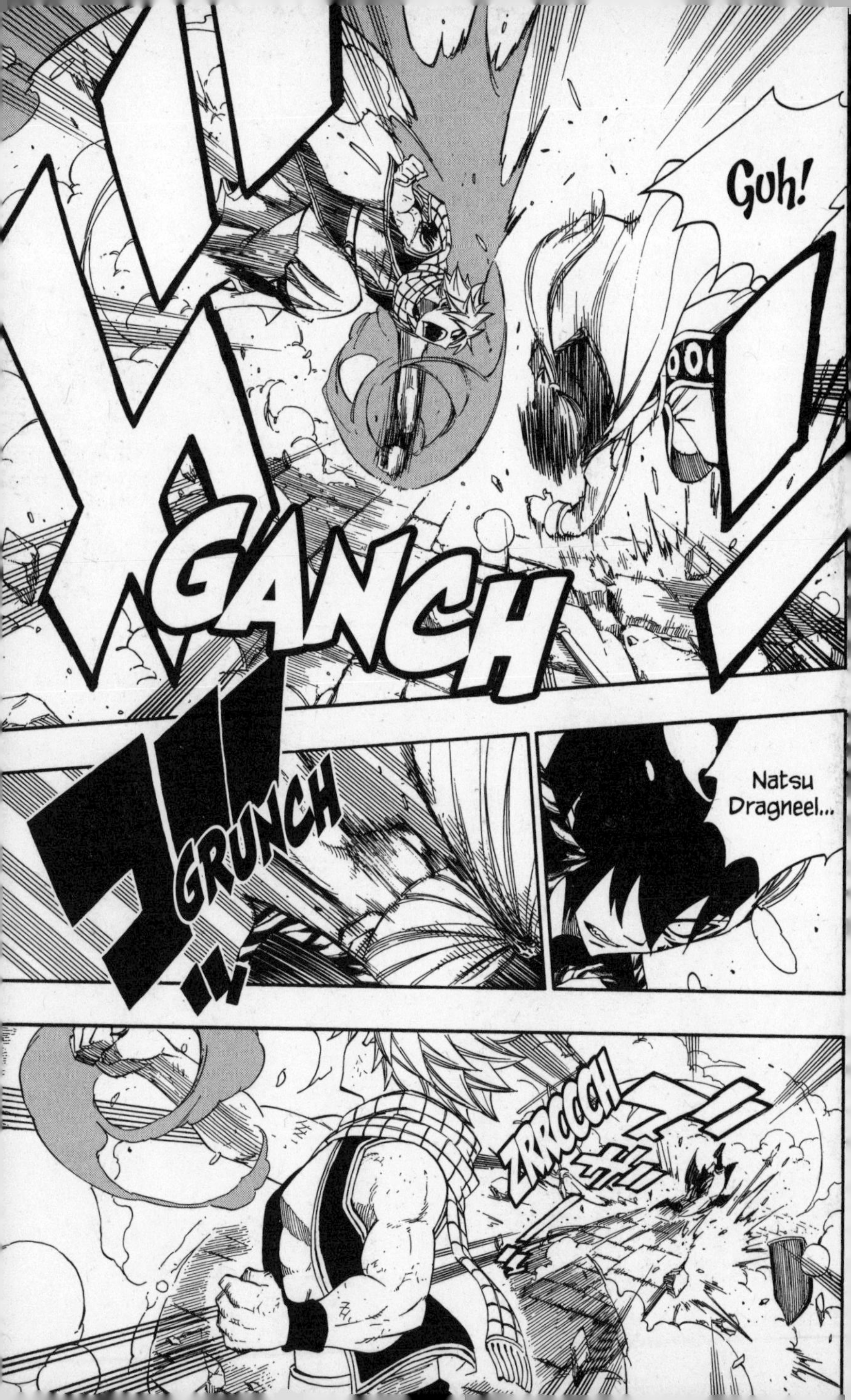
Guh!
GANCH
Natsu Dragneel...
GRUNCH
ZRRCCCH

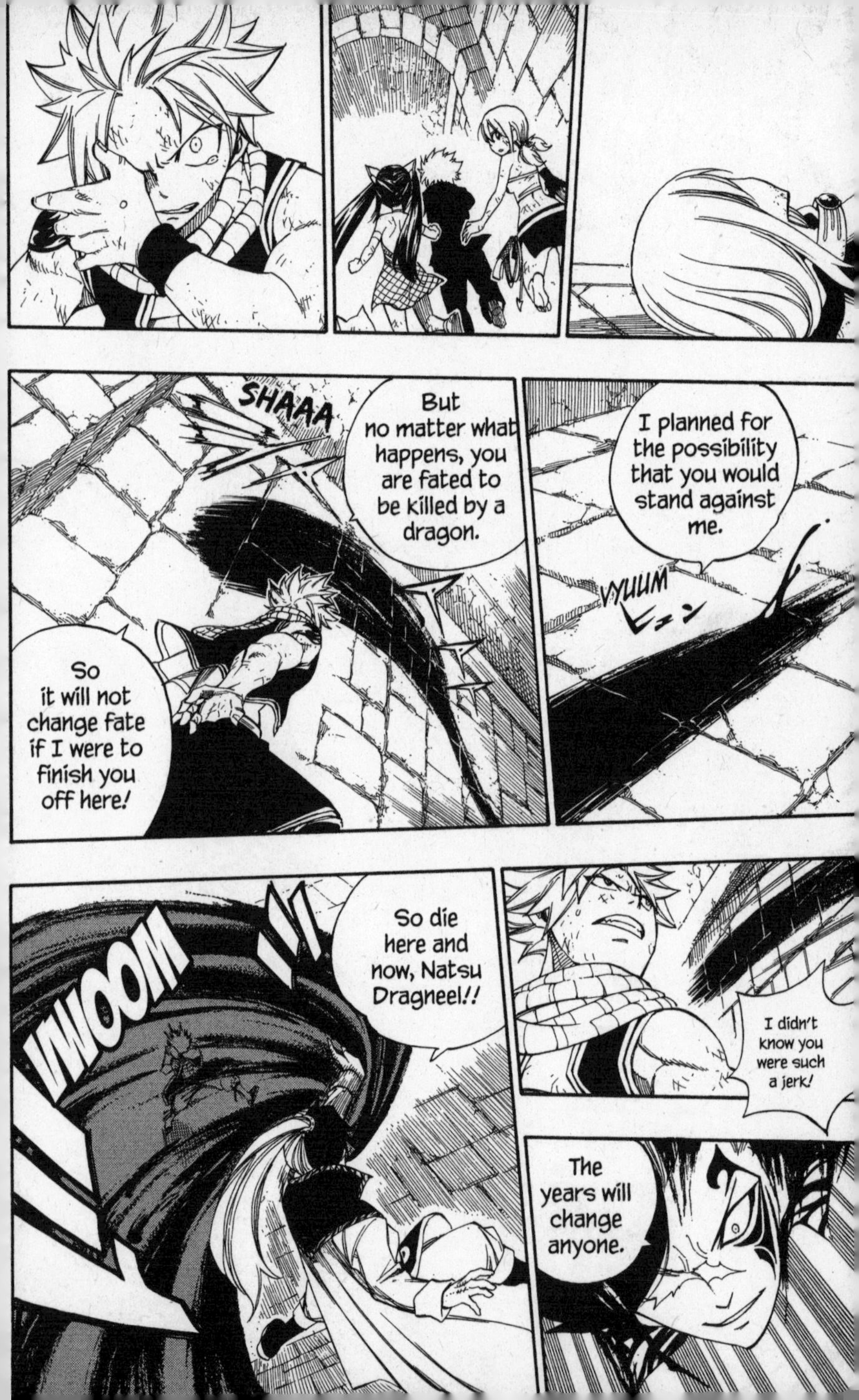
I planned for the possibility that you would stand against me.
VYUUM
ヒュン
But no matter what happens, you are fated to be killed by a dragon.
SHAAA
So it will not change fate if I were to finish you off here!
I didn't know you were such a jerk!
The years will change anyone.
So die here and now, Natsu Dragneel!!
WWOOM!!

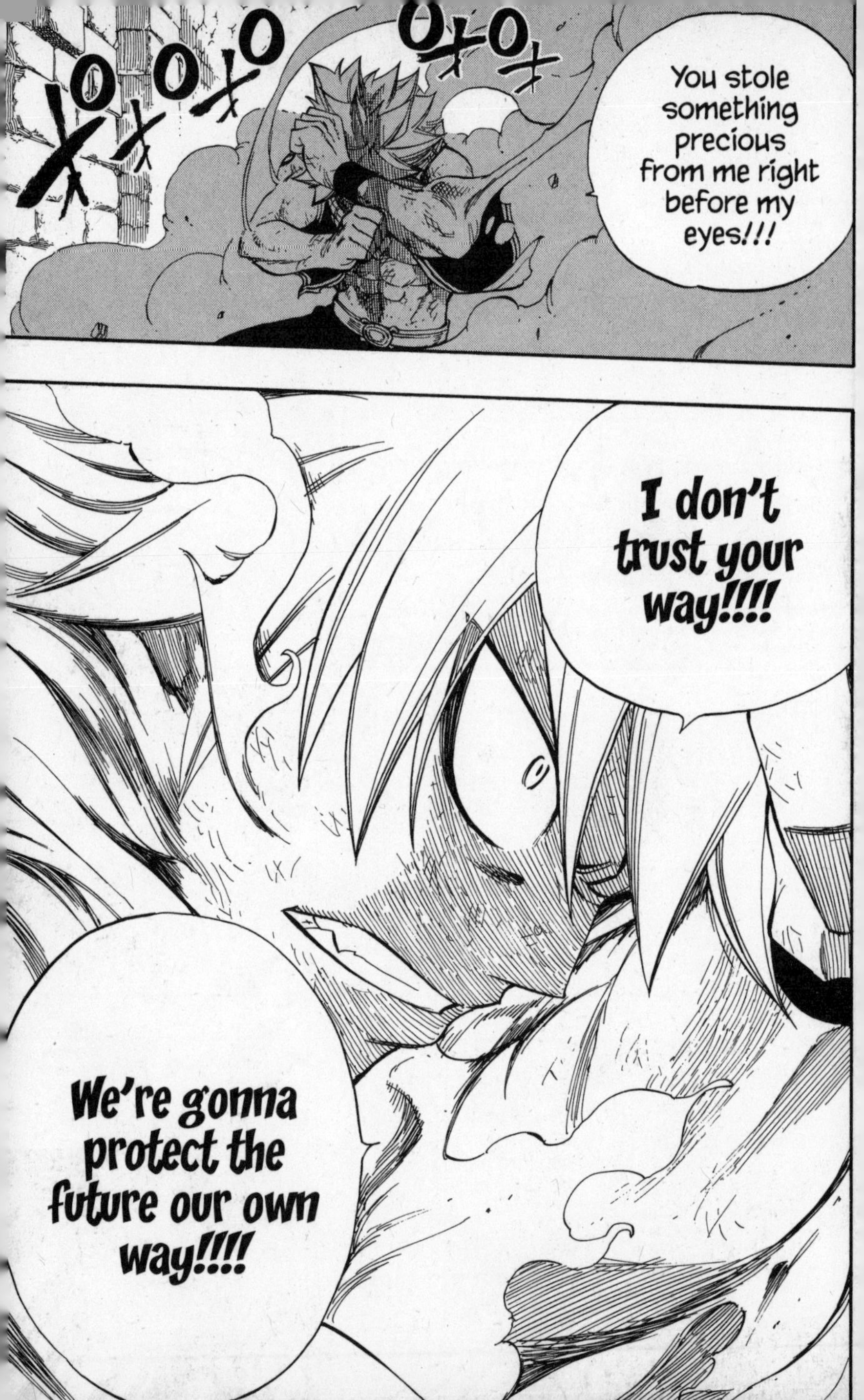
You stole something precious from me right before my eyes!!!
I don't trust your way!!!!
We're gonna protect the future our own way!!!!

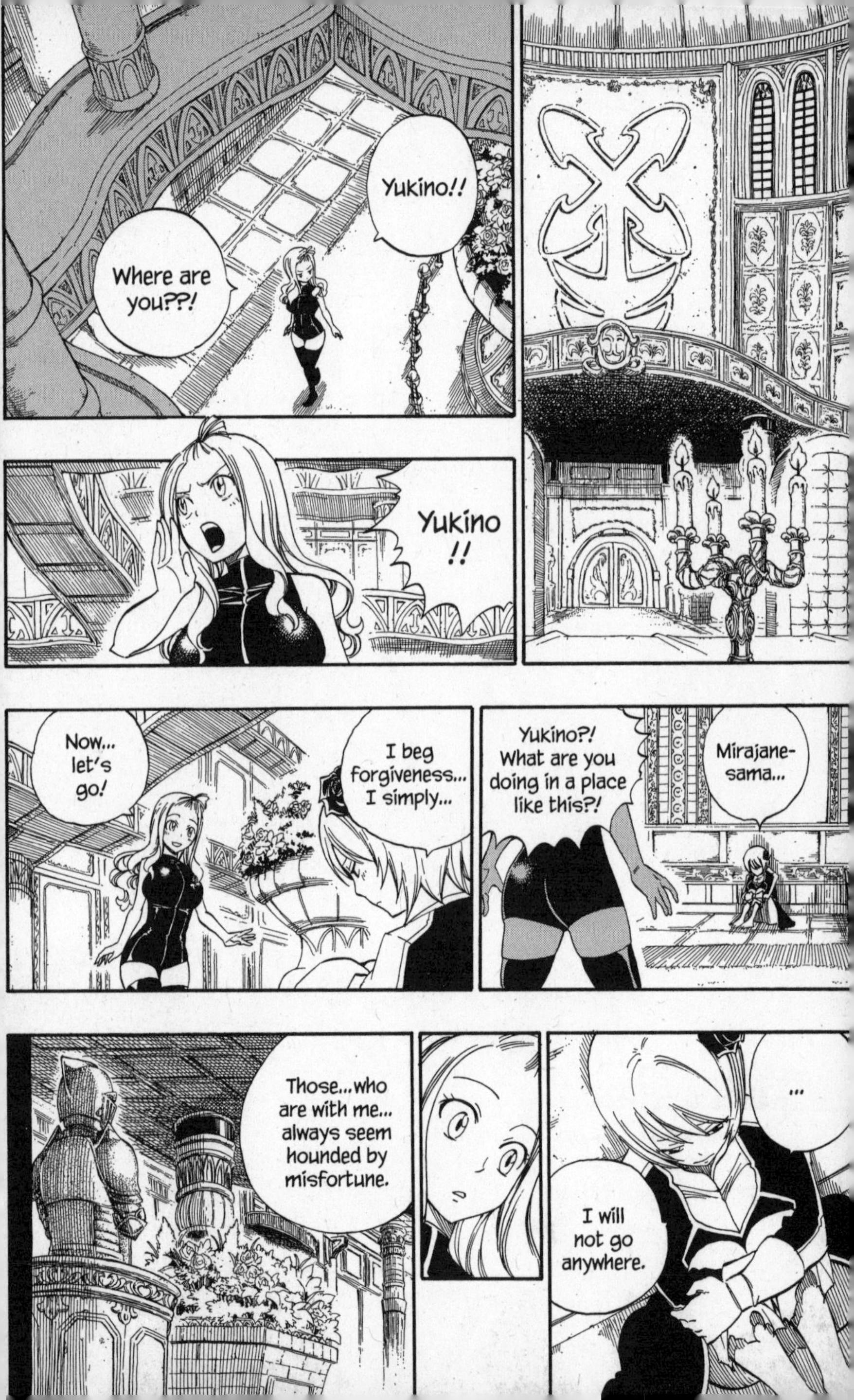
Yukino!!
Where are you??!
Yukino !!
Mirajane-sama...
Yukino?! What are you doing in a place like this?!
I beg forgiveness... I simply...
Now... let's go!
...
I will not go anywhere.
Those...who are with me... always seem hounded by misfortune.

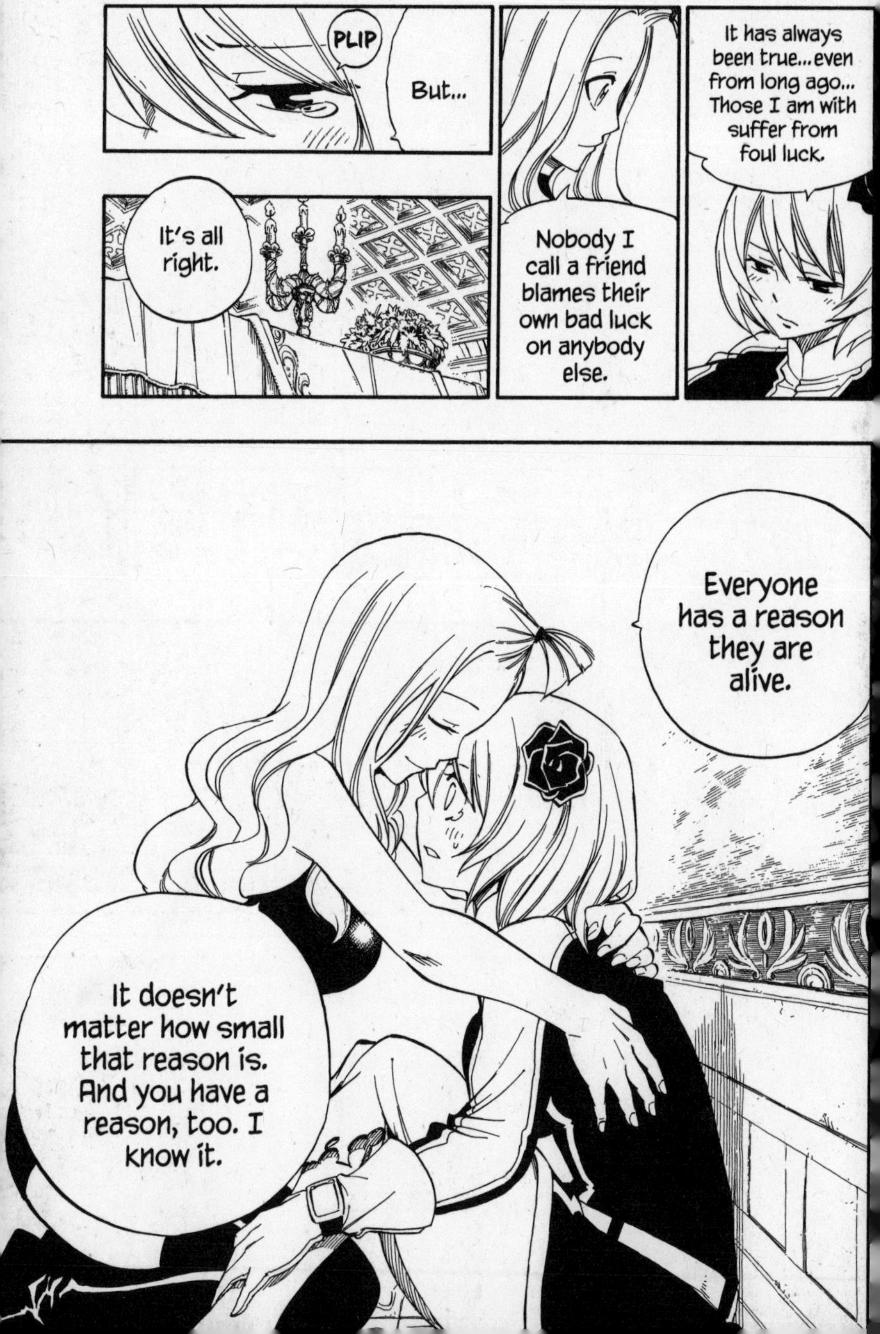
It has always been true...even from long ago... Those I am with suffer from foul luck.
Nobody I call a friend blames their own bad luck on anybody else.
PLIP
But...
It's all right.
Everyone has a reason they are alive.
It doesn't matter how small that reason is. And you have a reason, too. I know it.

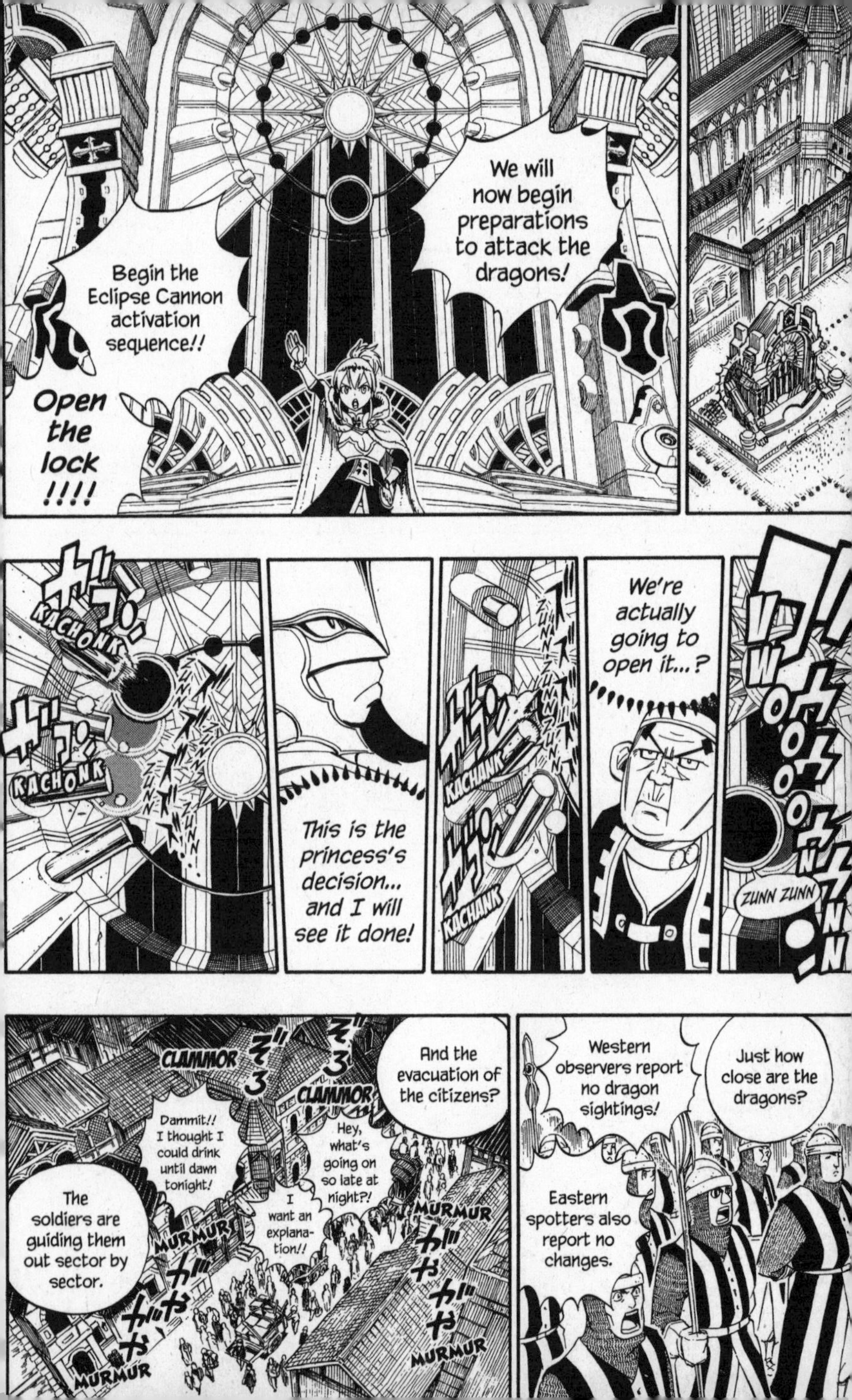
We will now begin preparations to attack the dragons!
Begin the Eclipse Cannon activation sequence!!
Open the lock!!!!
ZUNN ZUNN
We're actually going to open it...?
KACHANK
KACHANK
This is the princess's decision... and I will see it done!
KACHONK
KACHONK
Just how close are the dragons?
Western observers report no dragon sightings!
Eastern spotters also report no changes.
And the evacuation of the citizens?
CLAMMOR
CLAMMOR
Hey, what's going on so late at night?!
Dammit!! I thought I could drink until dawn tonight!
I want an explanation!!
The soldiers are guiding them out sector by sector.
MURMUR
MURMUR
MURMUR
MURMUR

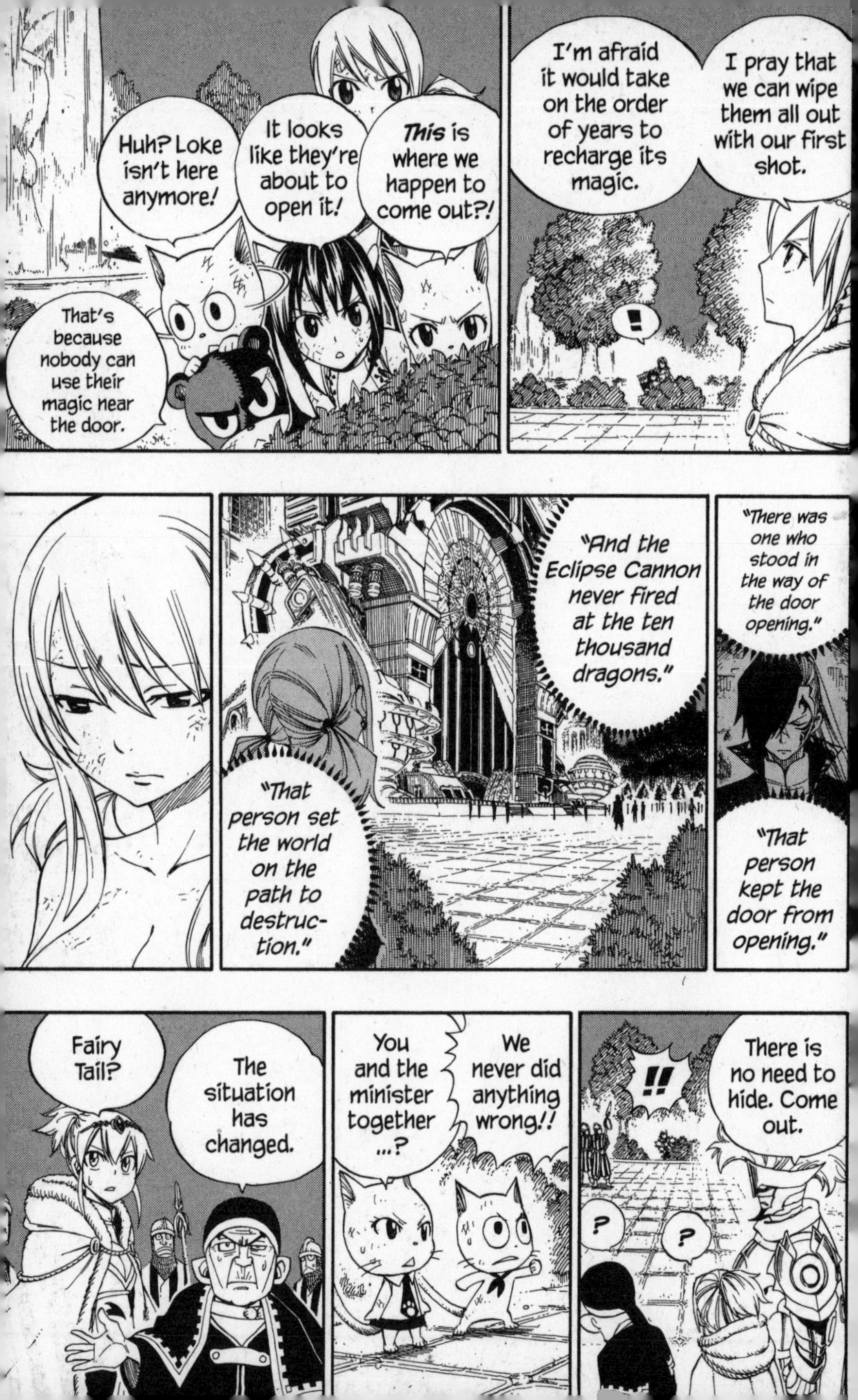
I pray that we can wipe them all out with our first shot.
I'm afraid it would take on the order of years to recharge its magic.
!
This is where we happen to come out?!
It looks like they're about to open it!
Huh? Loke isn't here anymore!
That's because nobody can use their magic near the door.
"There was one who stood in the way of the door opening."
"That person kept the door from opening."
"And the Eclipse Cannon never fired at the ten thousand dragons."
"That person set the world on the path to destruction."
There is no need to hide. Come out.
!!
?
?
We never did anything wrong!!
You and the minister together...?
The situation has changed.
Fairy Tail?

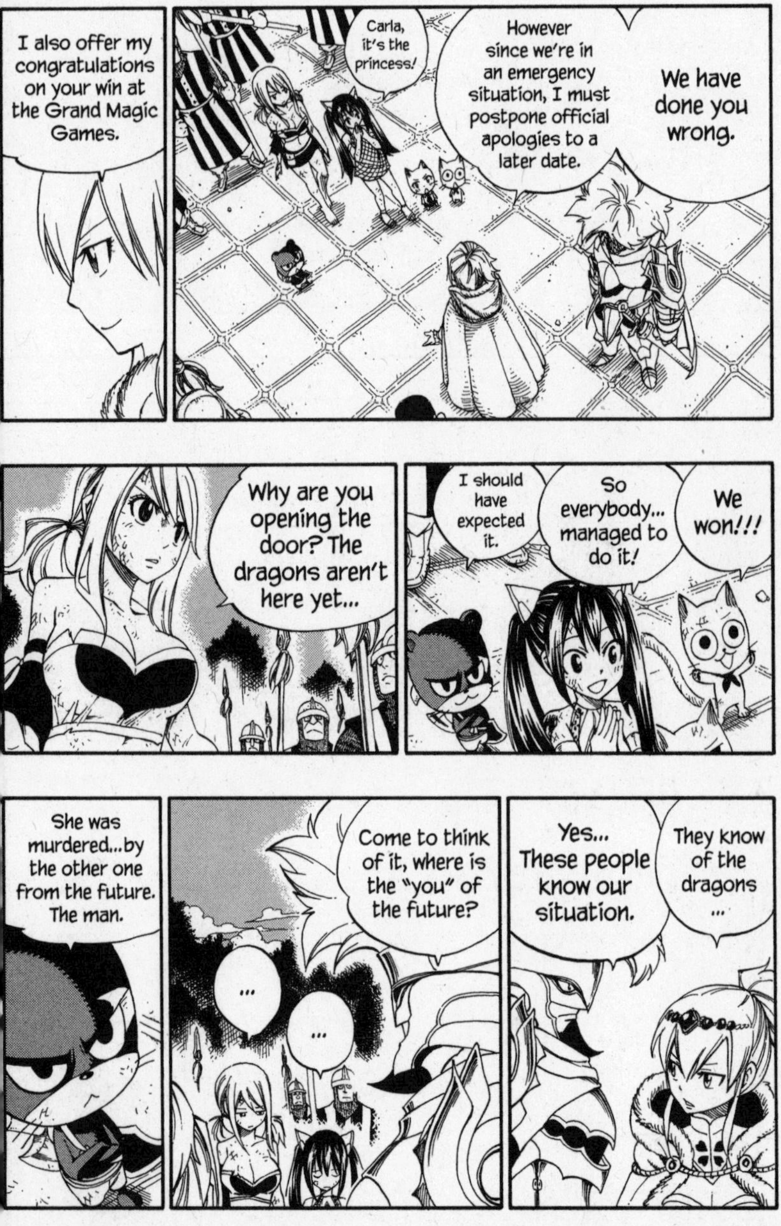
We have done you wrong.
However since we're in an emergency situation, I must postpone official apologies to a later date.
Carla, it's the princess!
I also offer my congratulations on your win at the Grand Magic Games.
We won!!!
So everybody... managed to do it!
I should have expected it.
Why are you opening the door? The dragons aren't here yet...
They know of the dragons ...
Yes... These people know our situation.
Come to think of it, where is the "you" of the future?
...
...
She was murdered...by the other one from the future. The man.

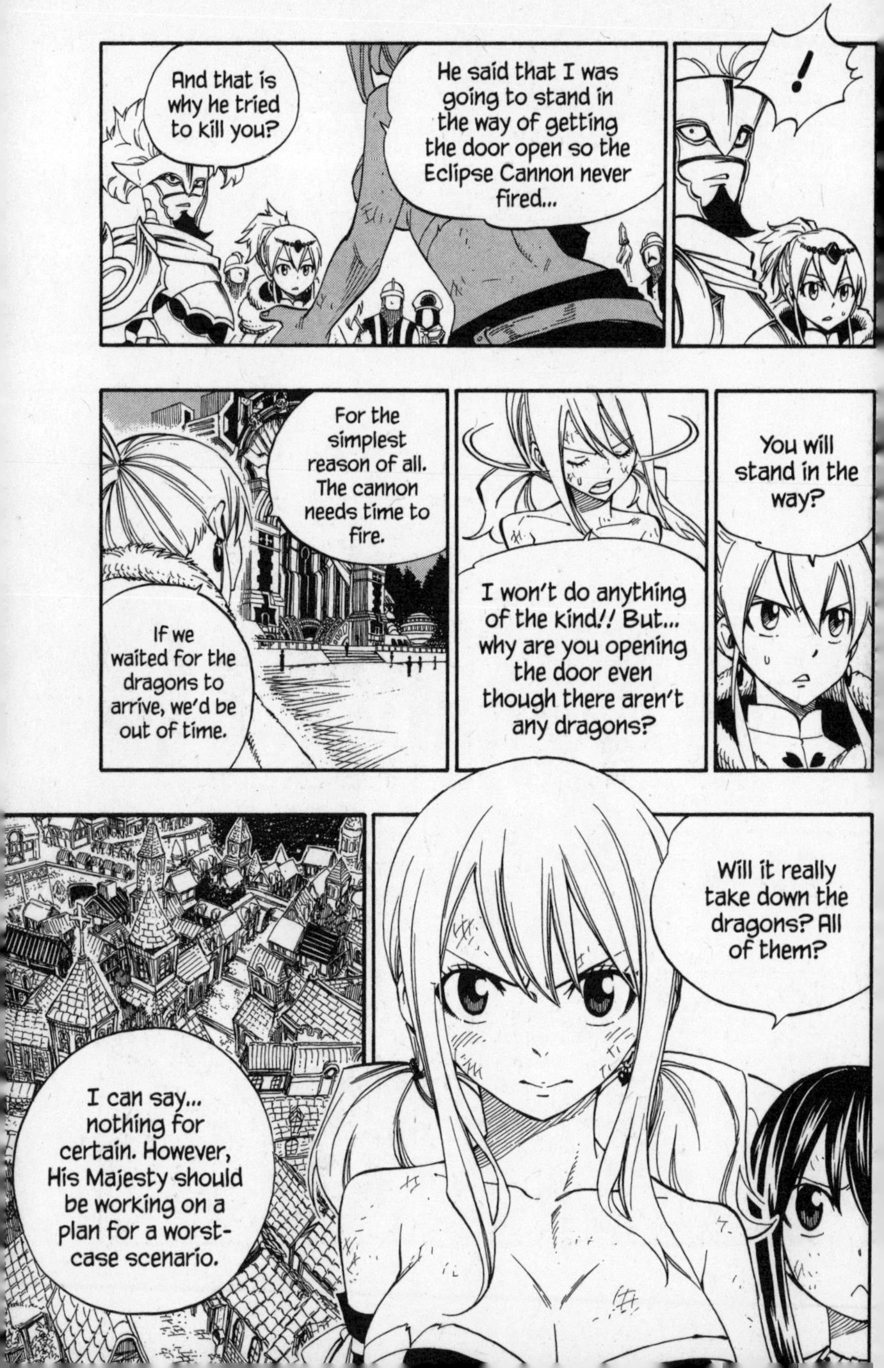
!
He said that I was going to stand in the way of getting the door open so the Eclipse Cannon never fired...
And that is why he tried to kill you?
You will stand in the way?
I won't do anything of the kind!! But... why are you opening the door even though there aren't any dragons?
For the simplest reason of all. The cannon needs time to fire.
If we waited for the dragons to arrive, we'd be out of time.
Will it really take down the dragons? All of them?
I can say... nothing for certain. However, His Majesty should be working on a plan for a worst-case scenario.

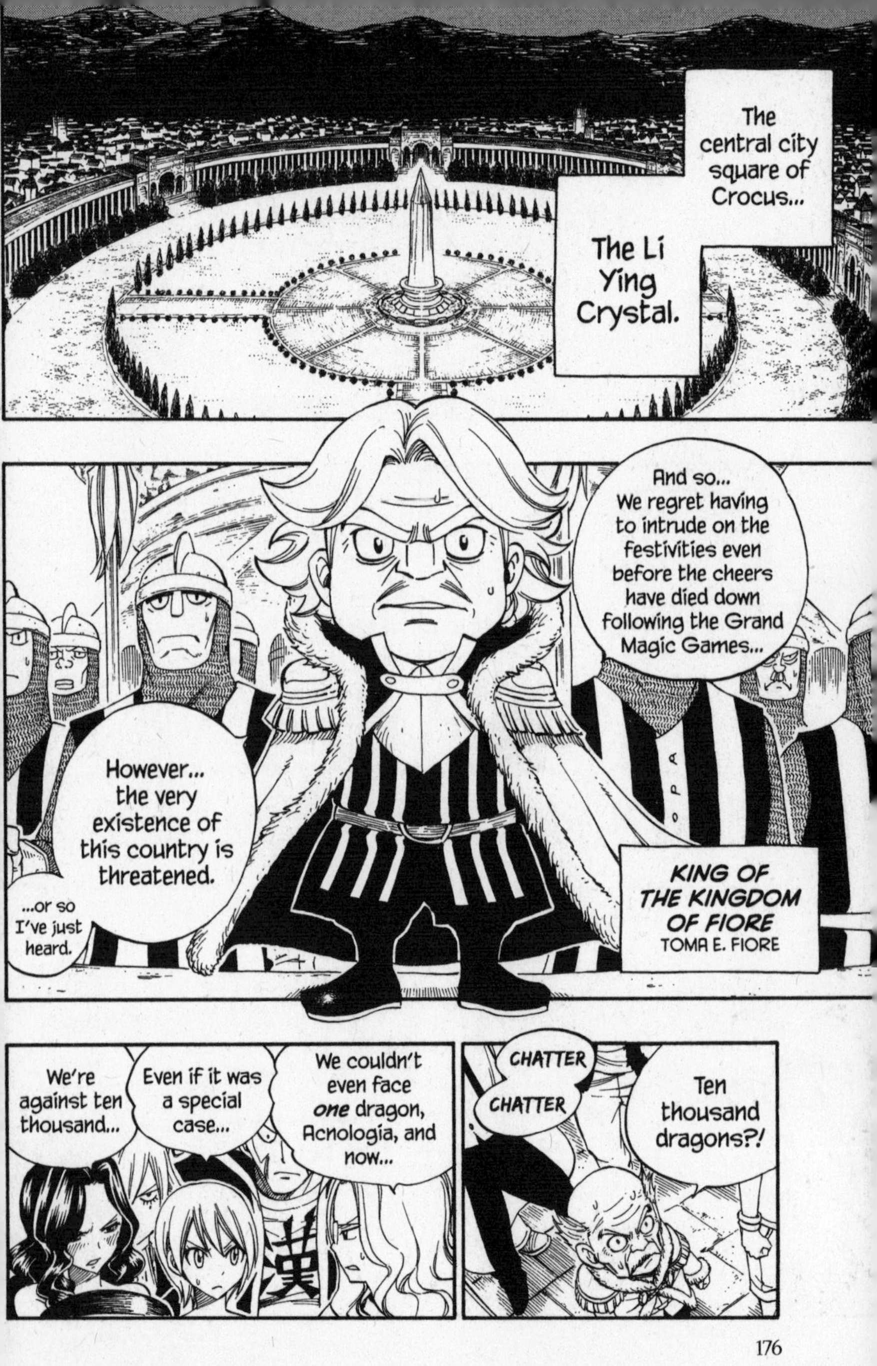
The central city square of Crocus...
The Li Ying Crystal.
And so... We regret having to intrude on the festivities even before the cheers have died down following the Grand Magic Games...
However... the very existence of this country is threatened.
...or so I've just heard.
KING OF THE KINGDOM OF FIORE
TOMA E. FIORE
Ten thousand dragons?!
CHATTER
CHATTER
We couldn't even face *one* dragon, Acnologia, and now...
Even if it was a special case...
We're against ten thousand...

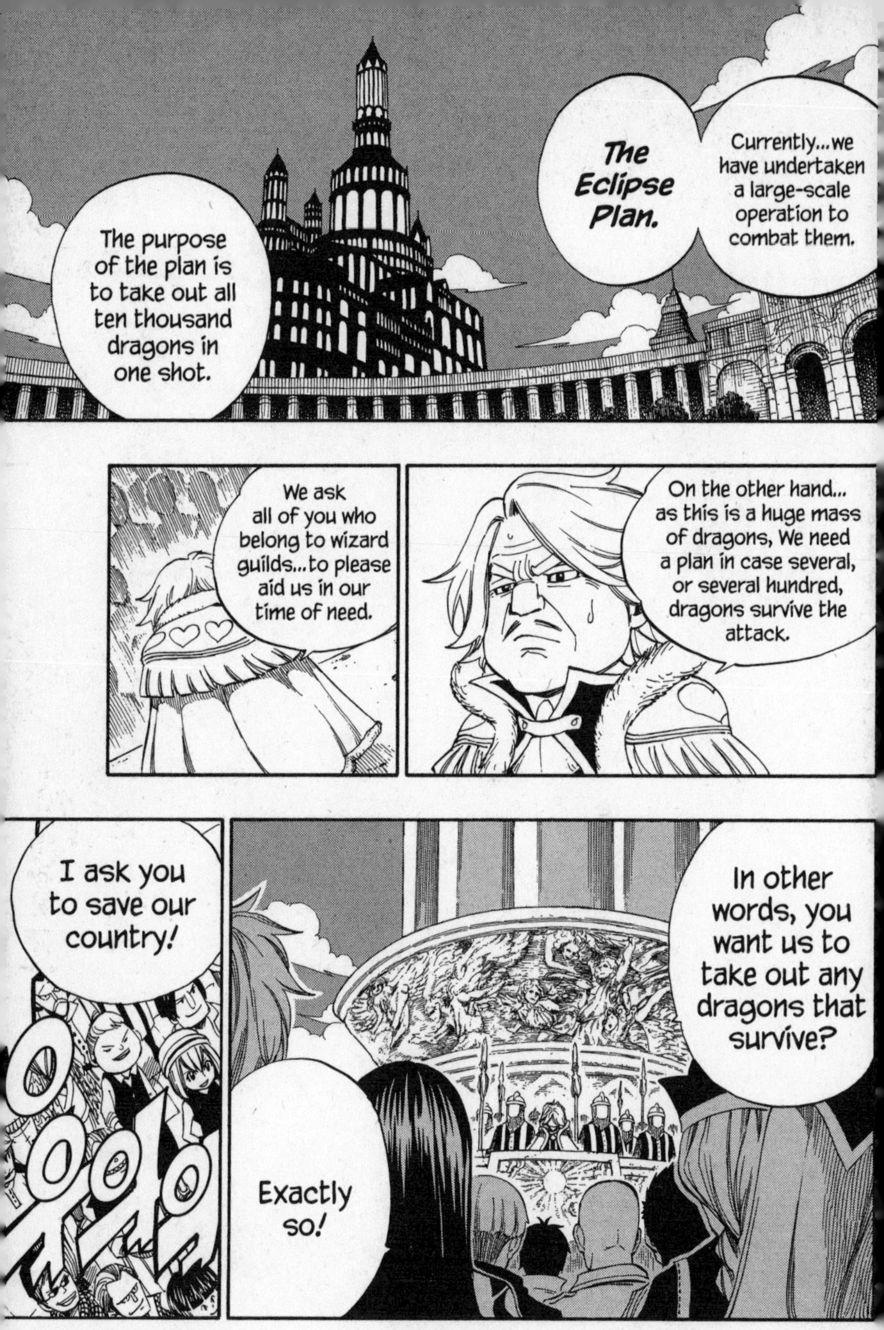

Currently...we have undertaken a large-scale operation to combat them.
The Eclipse Plan.
The purpose of the plan is to take out all ten thousand dragons in one shot.
On the other hand... as this is a huge mass of dragons, We need a plan in case several, or several hundred, dragons survive the attack.
We ask all of you who belong to wizard guilds...to please aid us in our time of need.
In other words, you want us to take out any dragons that survive?
Exactly so!
I ask you to save our country!

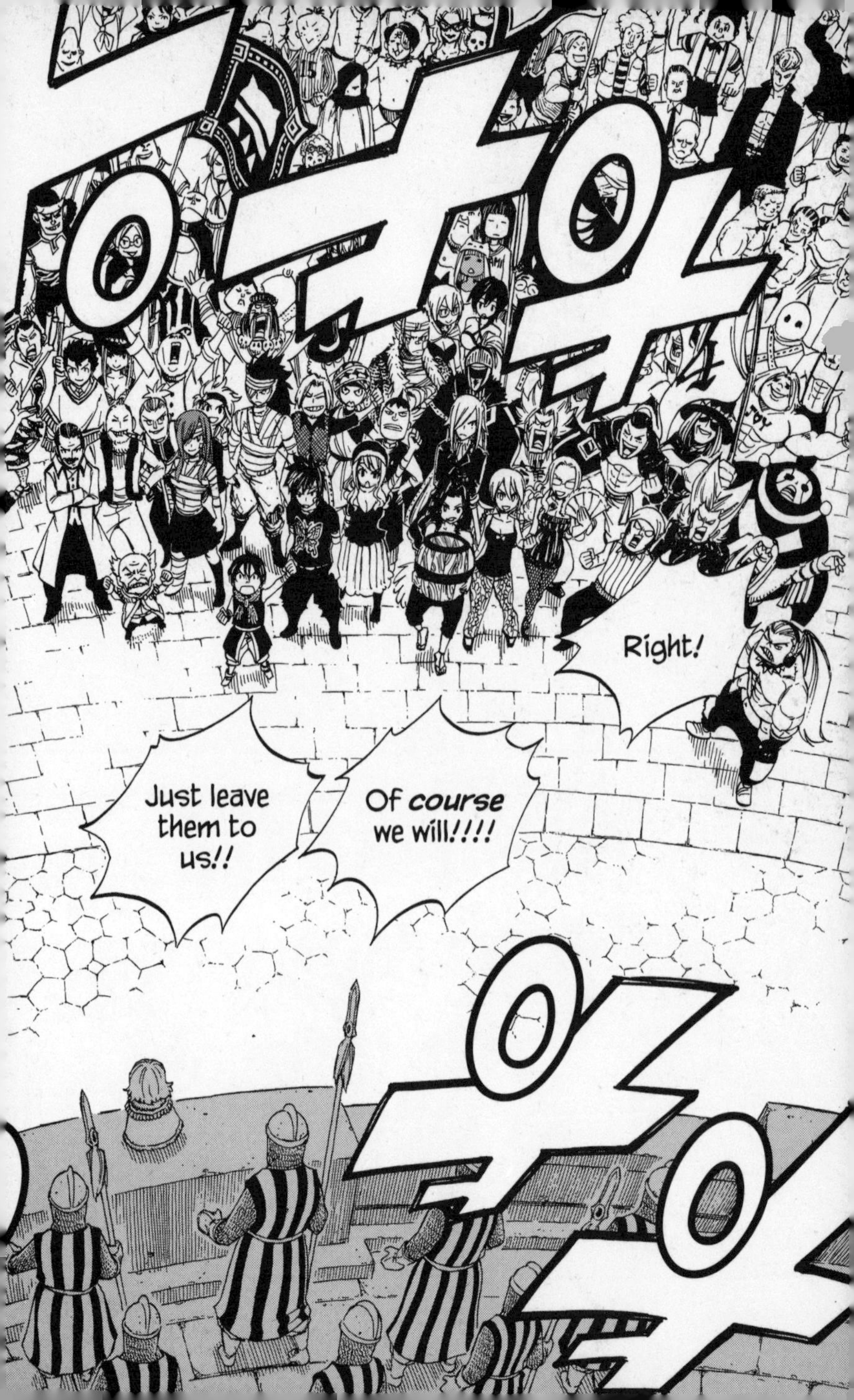
Right!
Of course we will!!!!
Just leave them to us!!

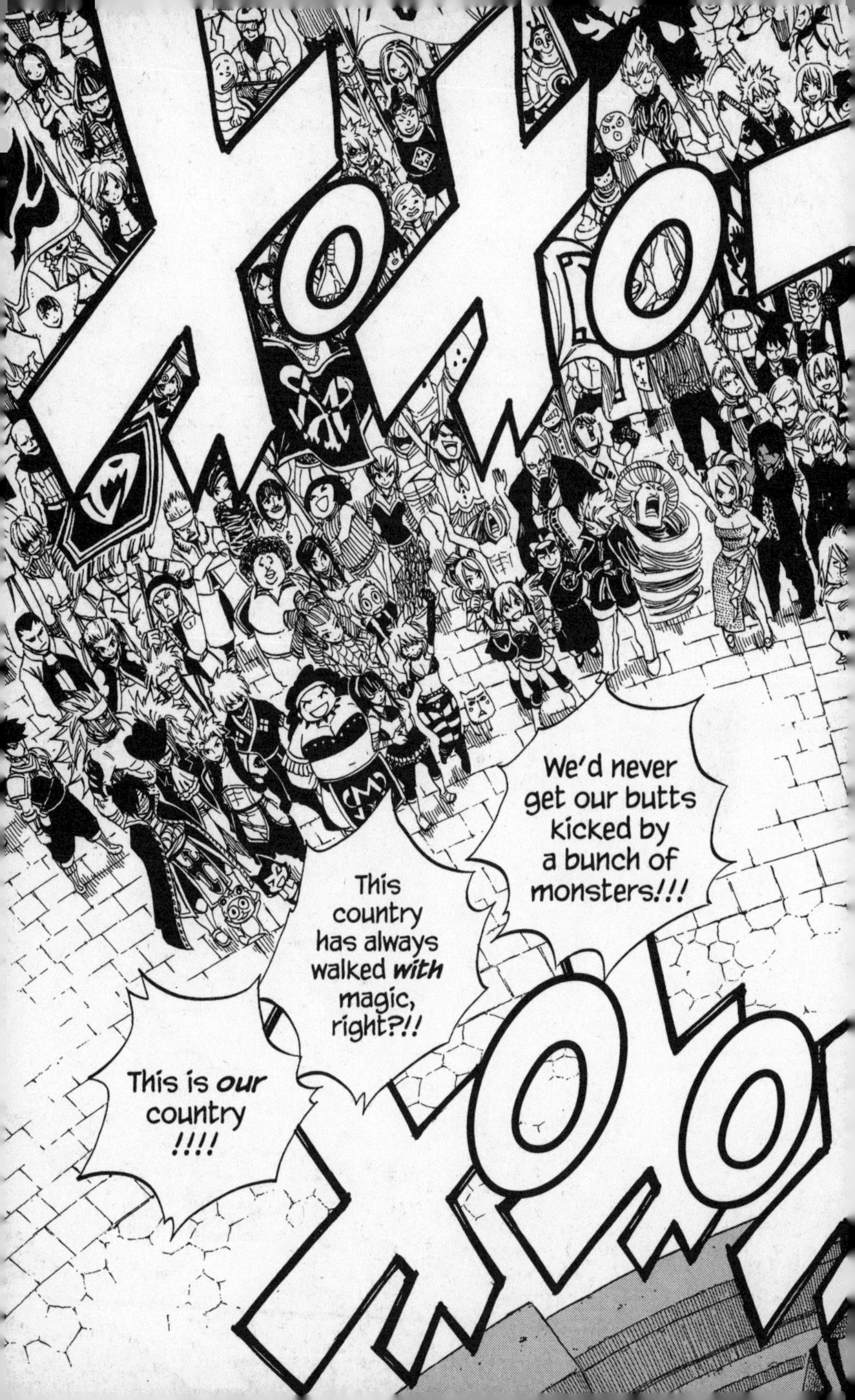
We'd never get our butts kicked by a bunch of monsters!!!
This country has always walked *with* magic, right?!!
This is *our* country !!!!

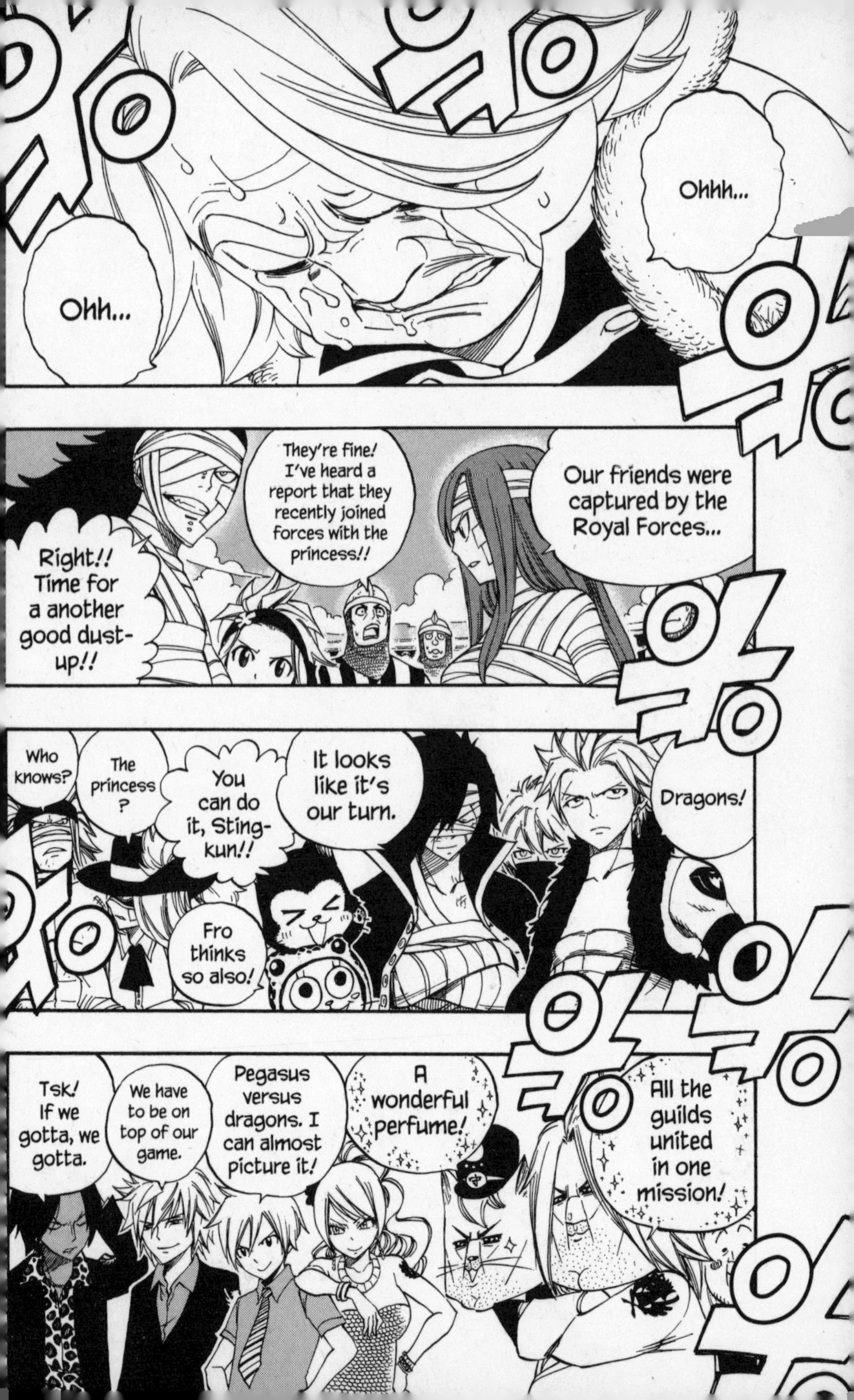
Ohhh...
Ohh...
Our friends were captured by the Royal Forces...
They're fine! I've heard a report that they recently joined forces with the princess!!
Right!! Time for a another good dust-up!!
Dragons!
It looks like it's our turn.
You can do it, Sting-kun!!
The princess?
Who knows?
Fro thinks so also!
All the guilds united in one mission!
A wonderful perfume!
Pegasus versus dragons. I can almost picture it!
We have to be on top of our game.
Tsk! If we gotta, we gotta.

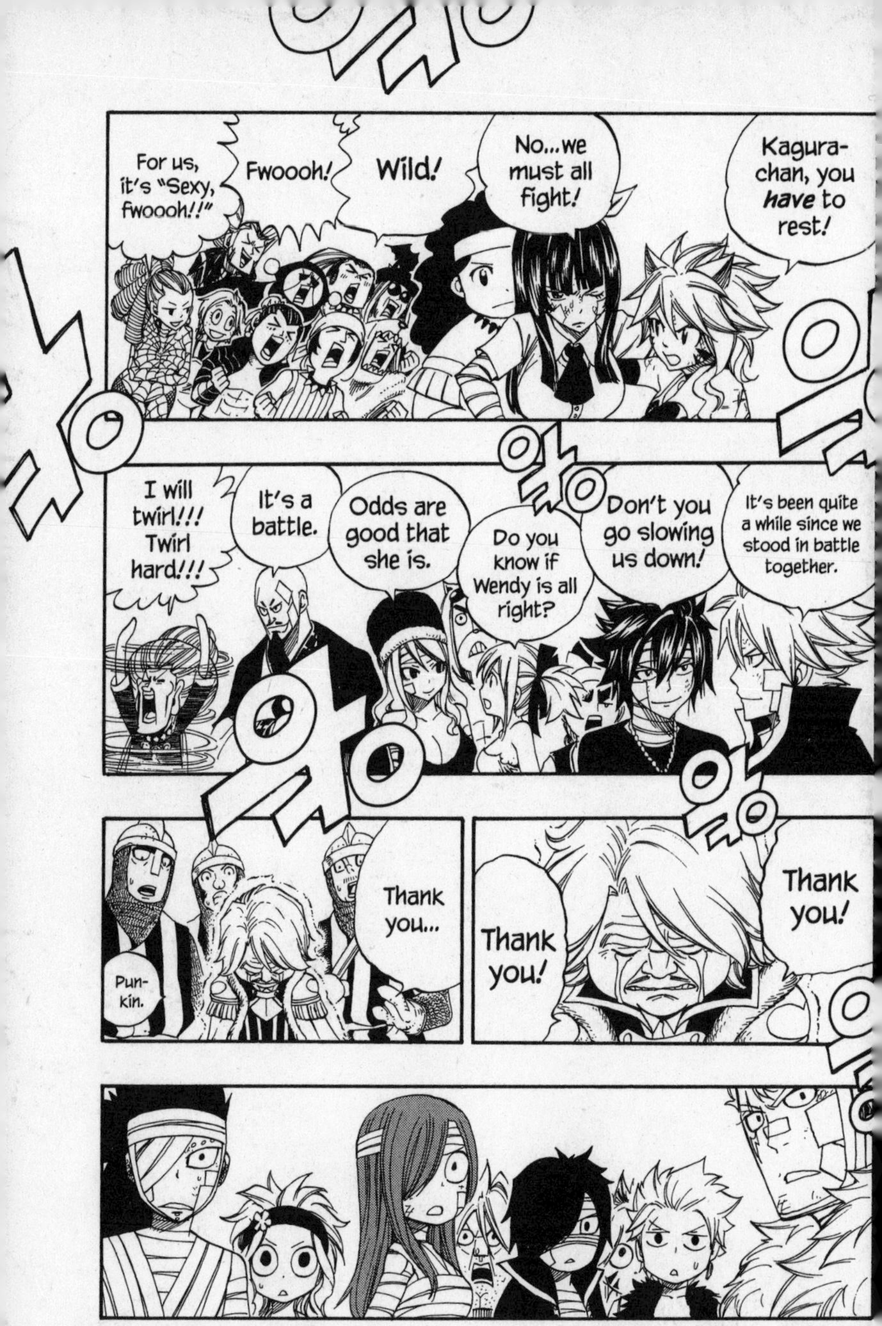
Kagura-chan, you *have* to rest!
No...we must all fight!
Wild!
Fwoooh!
For us, it's "Sexy, fwoooh!!"
It's been quite a while since we stood in battle together.
Don't you go slowing us down!
Do you know if Wendy is all right?
Odds are good that she is.
It's a battle.
I will twirl!!! Twirl hard!!!
Thank you!
Thank you!
Thank you...
Pun-kin.

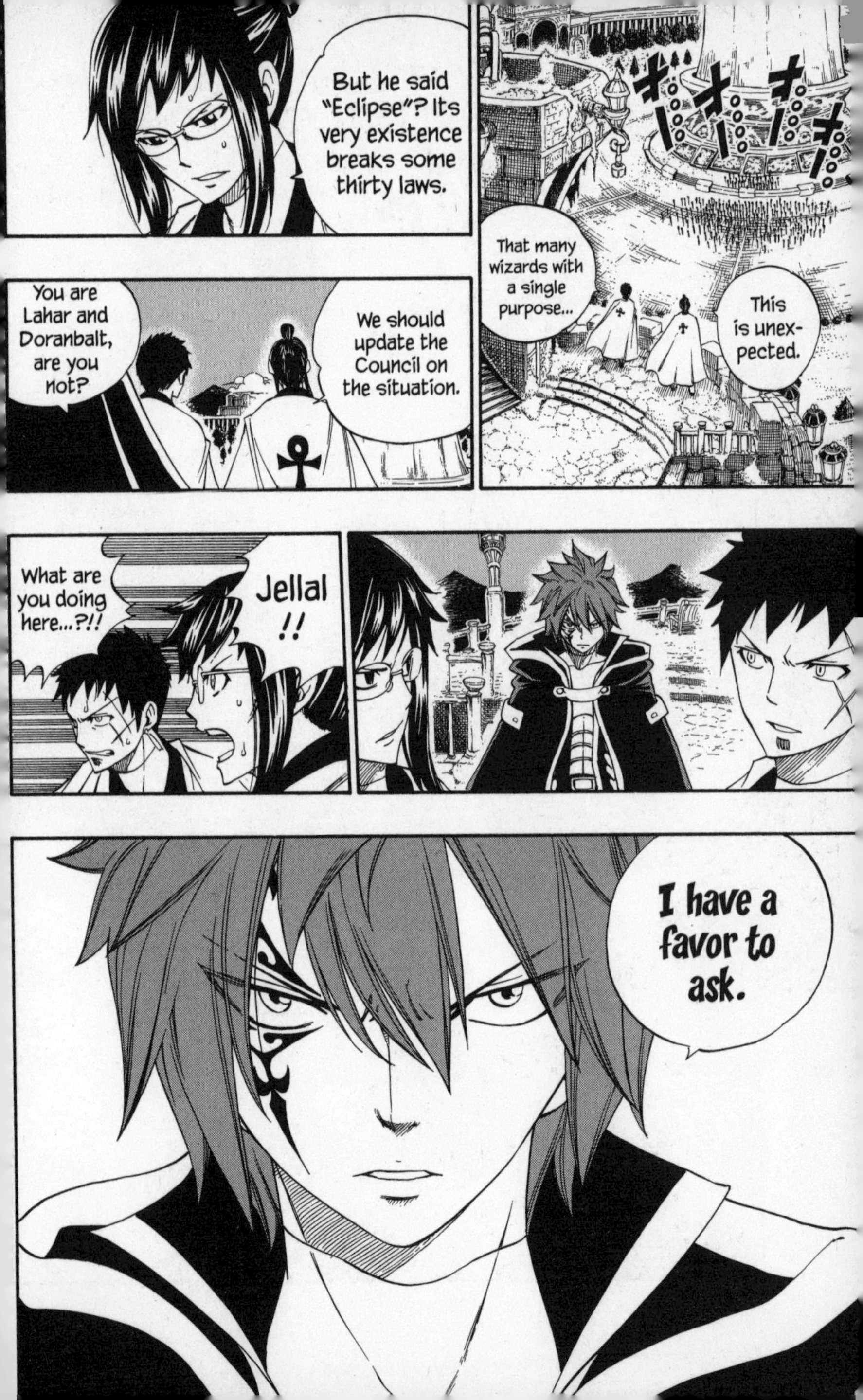
That many wizards with a single purpose...
This is unexpected.
But he said "Eclipse"? Its very existence breaks some thirty laws.
We should update the Council on the situation.
You are Lahar and Doranbalt, are you not?
Jellal !!
What are you doing here...?!!
I have a favor to ask.

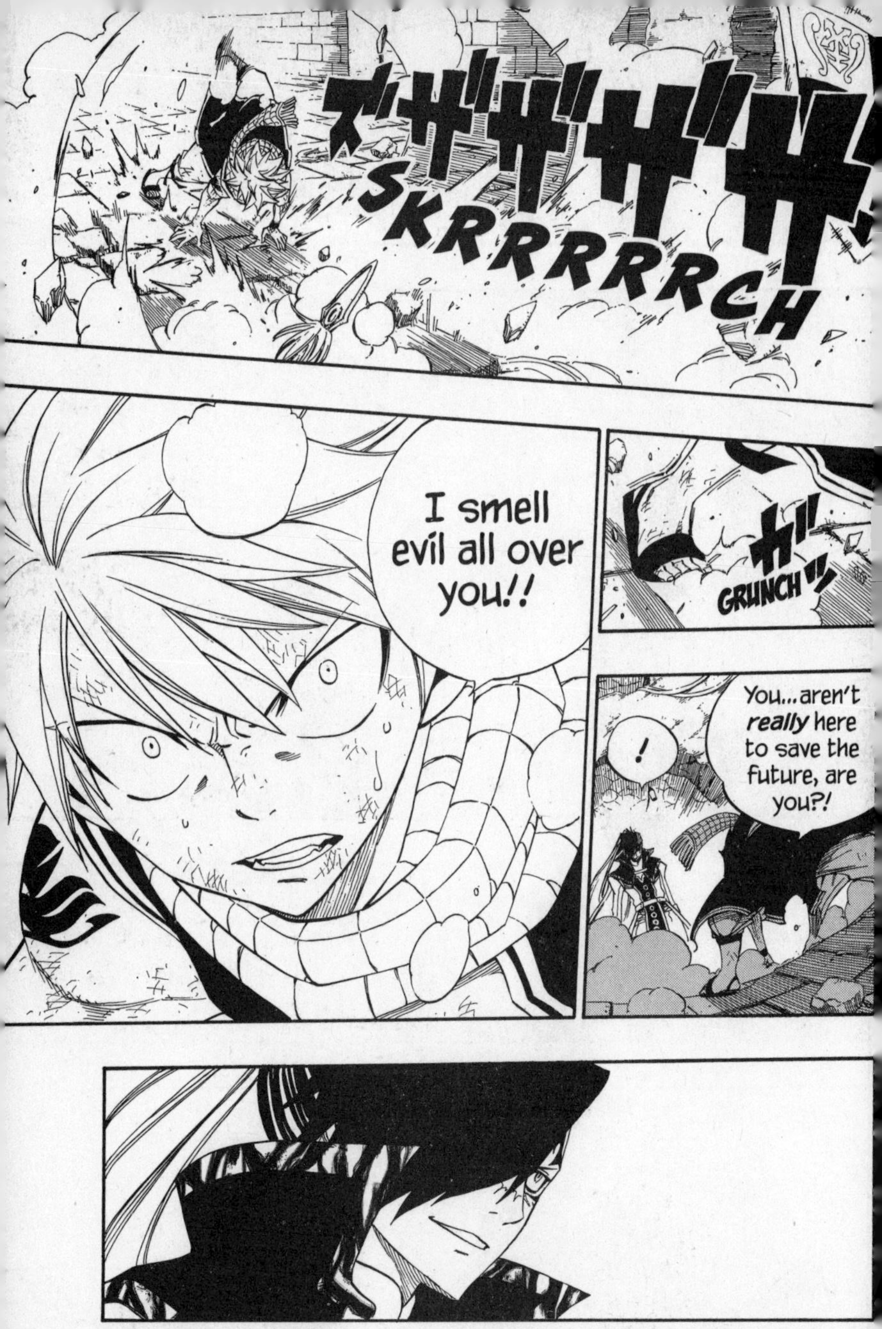
SKRRRRRRCH
GRUNCH!!
You...aren't *really* here to save the future, are you?!
!
I smell evil all over you!!

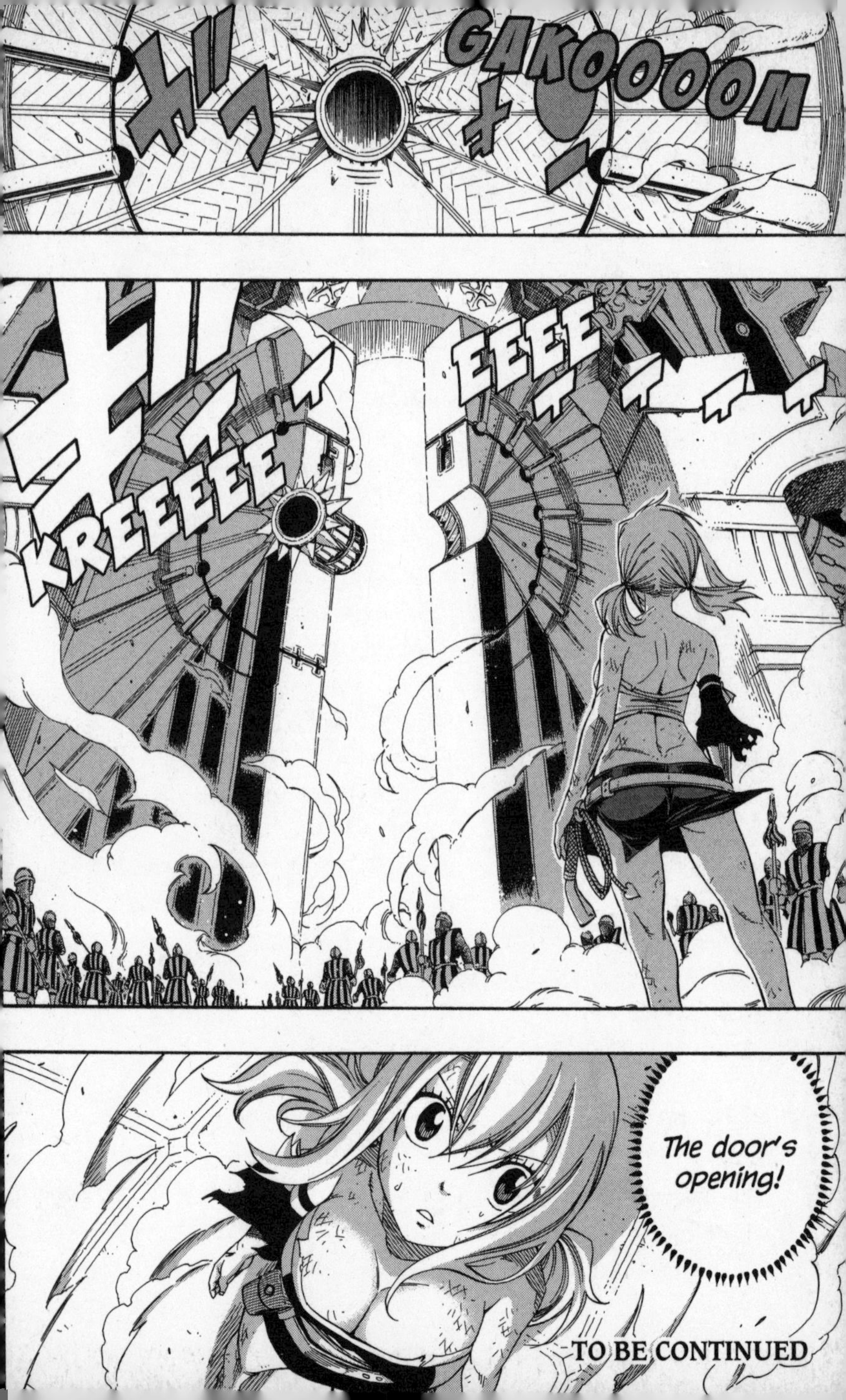
GAKOOOOM
KREEEEE
EEEE
The door's opening!
TO BE CONTINUED

Afterword

Ever since I was a kid, I loved manga with battles! I'd try to imagine if this character fought that one, which one would win (so exciting!), and it's probably because I spent my youth steeped in those fantasies that I wound up drawing battle manga myself. But there are plenty of other manga doing tournaments and competition stories, huh? And then they'd have great plot twists! Yeah, battle manga is the ultimate path for manga!

But I'm a little twisted myself, so even if I'm doing a tournament, I try to make sure that battles aren't all there is to it. Sure, I thought of plot lines that are just about the battles... But if I just did that, then the chances for the main character, Natsu, to show his stuff get drastically reduced. So I do battle, break, battle, and behind it all, I have another story going on (the Eclipse plan), until it becomes a really complicated plot. In fact, it was so complicated, there were a lot of places where my original ideas started to be inconsistent with how they actually went. So much so that as things went on, there were so many adjustments and rewrites to keep things on track in this story arc that it was wearing me out! I'll bet you can still find all sorts of contradictions that are still in there (sweat)!

Now, in the Japanese release of Volume 39 there will again be a normal version and a special edition. In the special edition, there will be an anime DVD that includes a collaboration between Fairy Tail and my previous work, Rave. After so long, we get to see moving versions of Haru and Elie!

X791 GRAND MAGIC GAMES IMPROMPTU AWARDS CEREMONY

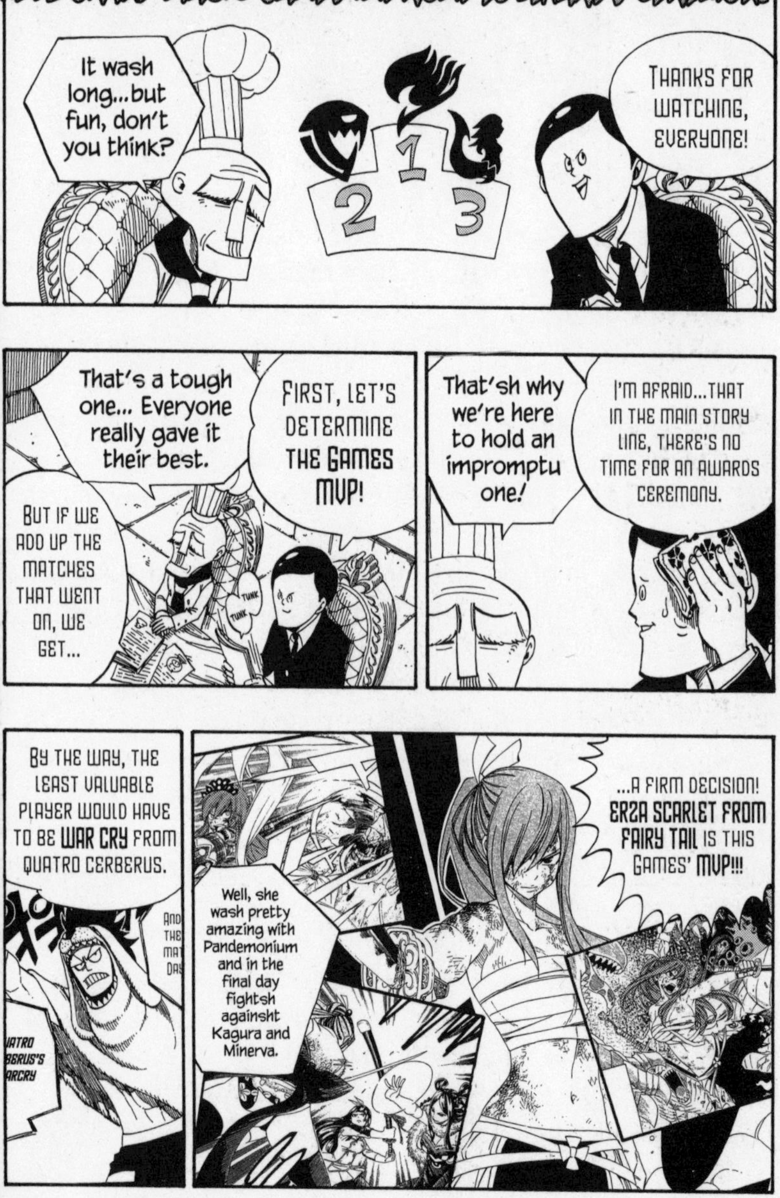
THANKS FOR WATCHING, EVERYONE!
It wash long...but fun, don't you think?
1
2
3
I'M AFRAID...THAT IN THE MAIN STORY LINE, THERE'S NO TIME FOR AN AWARDS CEREMONY.
That'sh why we're here to hold an impromptu one!
FIRST, LET'S DETERMINE THE GAMES MVP!
That's a tough one... Everyone really gave it their best.
BUT IF WE ADD UP THE MATCHES THAT WENT ON, WE GET...
TUNK
TUNK
...A FIRM DECISION! ERZA SCARLET FROM FAIRY TAIL IS THIS GAMES' MVP!!!
Well, she wash pretty amazing with Pandemonium and in the final day fightsh againsht Kagura and Minerva.
BY THE WAY, THE LEAST VALUABLE PLAYER WOULD HAVE TO BE WAR CRY FROM QUATRO CERBERUS.

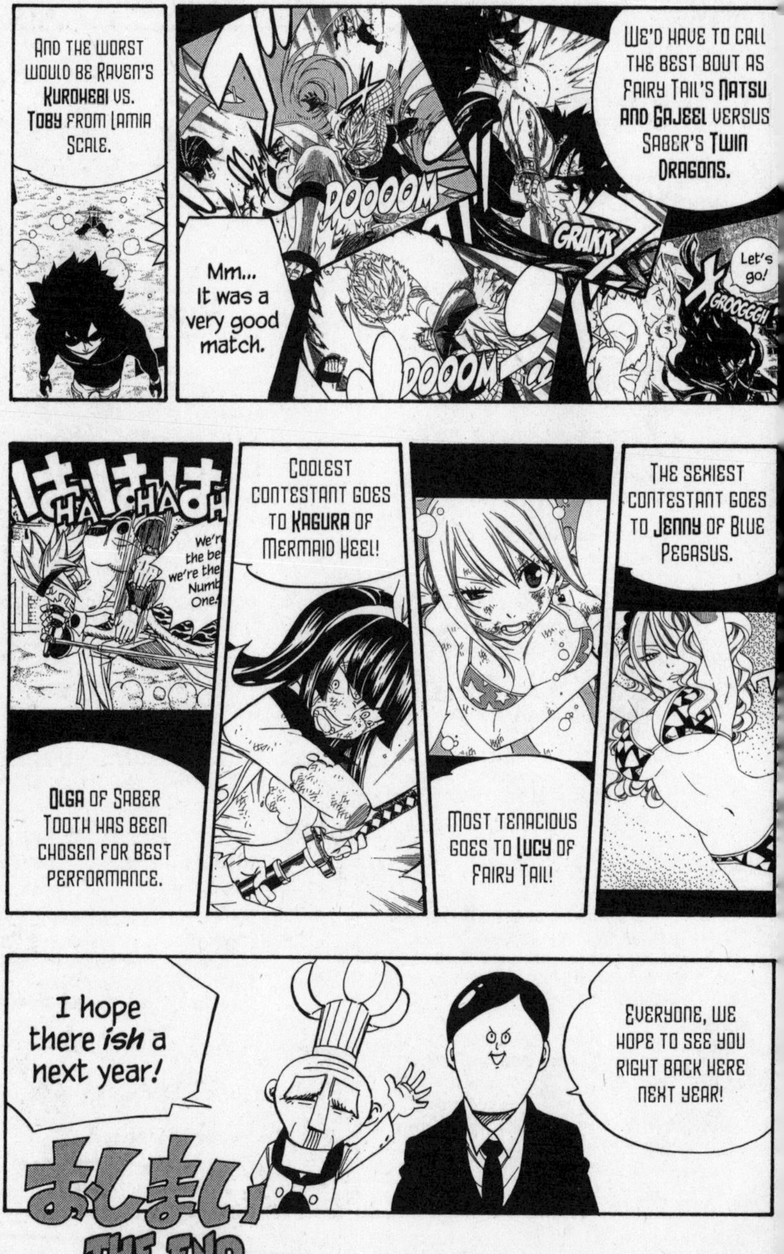

We'd have to call the best bout as Fairy Tail's Natsu and Gajeel versus Saber's Twin Dragons.
Let's go!
GROOGGGH
GRAKK
DOOOOM
Mm... It was a very good match.
DOOOM
And the worst would be Raven's Kurohebi vs. Toby from Lamia Scale.
The sexiest contestant goes to Jenny of Blue Pegasus.
Most tenacious goes to Lucy of Fairy Tail!
Coolest contestant goes to Kagura of Mermaid Heel!
HA HA
Olga of Saber Tooth has been chosen for best performance.
Everyone, we hope to see you right back here next year!
I hope there ish a next year!
おしまい
THE END

Continued from the left-hand page.

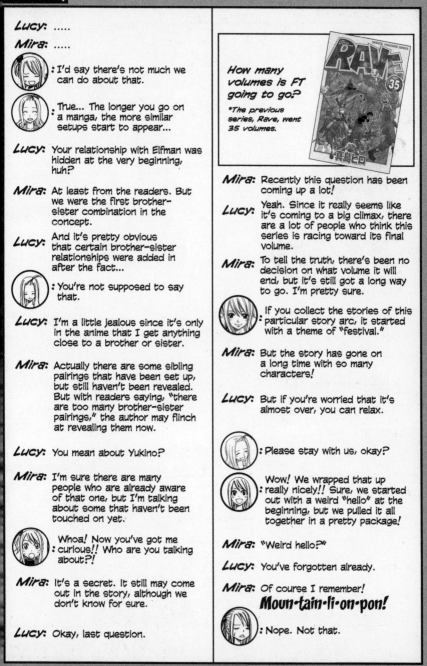

Lucy: .....

Mira: .....

: I'd say there's not much we can do about that.

: True... The longer you go on a manga, the more similar setups start to appear...

Lucy: Your relationship with Elfman was hidden at the very beginning, huh?

Mira: At least from the readers. But we were the first brother-sister combination in the concept.

Lucy: And it's pretty obvious that certain brother-sister relationships were added in after the fact...

: You're not supposed to say that.

Lucy: I'm a little jealous since it's only in the anime that I get anything close to a brother or sister.

Mira: Actually there are some sibling pairings that have been set up, but still haven't been revealed. But with readers saying, "there are too many brother-sister pairings," the author may flinch at revealing them now.

Lucy: You mean about Yukino?

Mira: I'm sure there are many people who are already aware of that one, but I'm talking about some that haven't been touched on yet.

: Whoa! Now you've got me curious!! Who are you talking about?!

Mira: It's a secret. It still may come out in the story, although we don't know for sure.

Lucy: Okay, last question.

How many volumes is FT going to go?

****The previous series, Rave, went 35 volumes.***

SHONEN MAGAZINE COMICS
RAVE
レイヴ
35
真島ヒロ

Mira: Recently this question has been coming up a lot!

Lucy: Yeah. Since it really seems like it's coming to a big climax, there are a lot of people who think this series is racing toward its final volume.

Mira: To tell the truth, there's been no decision on what volume it will end, but it's still got a long way to go. I'm pretty sure.

: If you collect the stories of this particular story arc, it started with a theme of "festival."

Mira: But the story has gone on a long time with so many characters!

Lucy: But if you're worried that it's almost over, you can relax.

: Please stay with us, okay?

: Wow! We wrapped that up really nicely!! Sure, we started out with a weird "hello" at the beginning, but we pulled it all together in a pretty package!

Mira: "Weird hello?"

Lucy: You've forgotten already.

Mira: Of course I remember!

Moun-tain-li-on-pon!

: Nope. Not that.

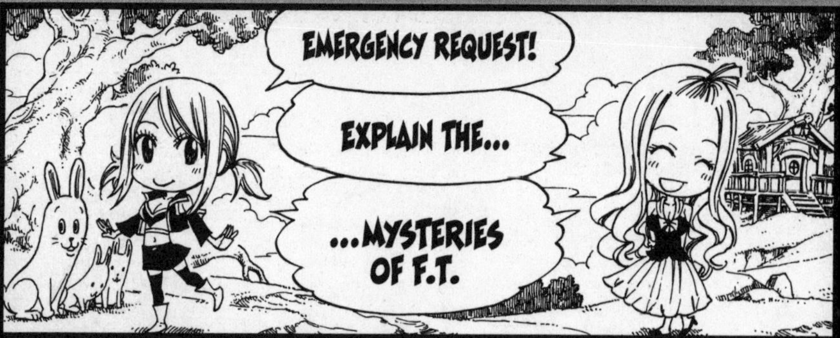
EMERGENCY REQUEST!
EXPLAIN THE...
...MYSTERIES OF F.T.

At some open space somewhere...

: Hellall!!♡

: What that, all of a sudden?

Mira: It's "Hello all" shortened. Hellall! ♡

Lucy: That is ***never*** going to catch on!

Mira: Let's have the first question of this column!

In Pandemonium, Erza defeated 100 monsters, but wouldn't she have won with just 51?

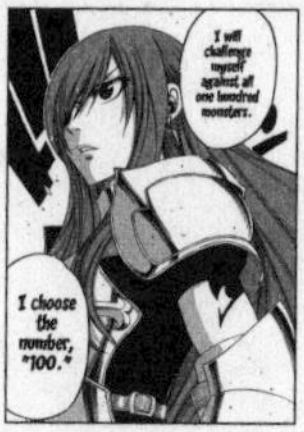
I will challenge myself against all one hundred monsters.
I choose the number, "100."

Lucy: We got a *lot* of this one!

Mira: It's a little on the "old" side, but since we got so many of them, we decided to pick it out and answer it.

Lucy: I'll bet nobody even remembers the rules to it.

Mira: There was an actual reason for her actions, from Erza's point of view. And it's a very Erza thing to do.

Lucy: Is that so?

Mira: Remember the order of players in the game.

: If I remember right, Erza was first, and the middle guys are a blur, and finally came Cana, I think.

Mira: That's it! That's the point. Sure, if she defeated 51 monsters, she'd win, but afterwards, the rest of the field would have to finish off the other 49.

: You're right! With everybody going in order and Cana last in line, it'd be very unlikely for Cana to come in second.

: She wouldn't have known that the next game would be "MPF," but she defeated all hundred monsters hoping to give Cana a better chance.

Lucy: That's Erza for you!

Mira: Next question!

I get the feeling there are too many brothers and sisters in this manga.

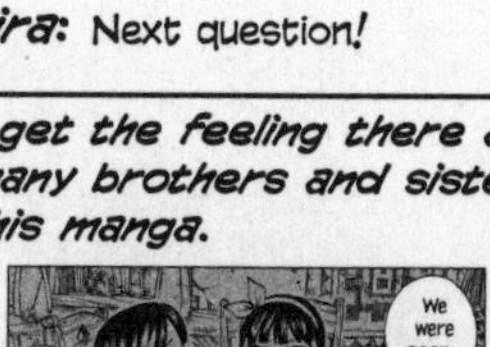
We were poor...
...but very happy.

Continued on the right-hand page.

TAIL d'ART

The Fairy Tail Guild is looking for illustrations! Please send in your art on a postcard or at postcard size, and do it in black pen, okay? Those chosen to be published will get a signed mini poster! ♪ Make sure you write your real name and address on the back of your illustration!

Yamaguchi Prefecture, Yuririn

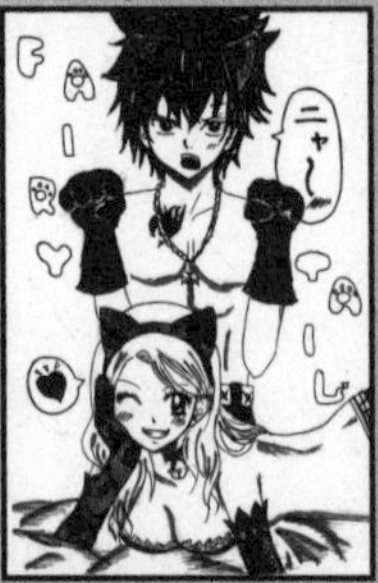

▲ Now this is adorable! I must say that Gray looks cute in a cat costume.

Saitama Prefecture, Ryōta Takada

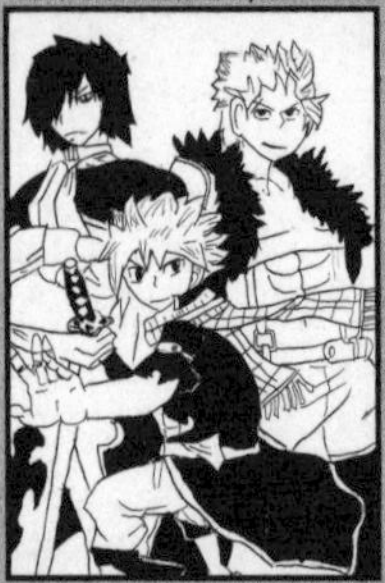

▲ Ohh! Natsu together with the Twin Dragons! Very cool!!

Saitama Prefecture, Ayaka Sato

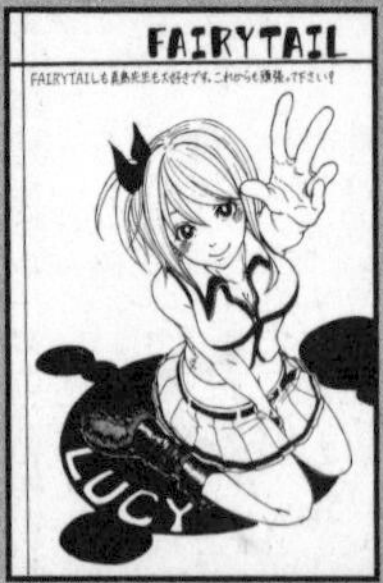
FAIRYTAIL
LUCY

▲ The composition and layout are quite professional. Very well done!!

Hyogo Prefecture, Choko

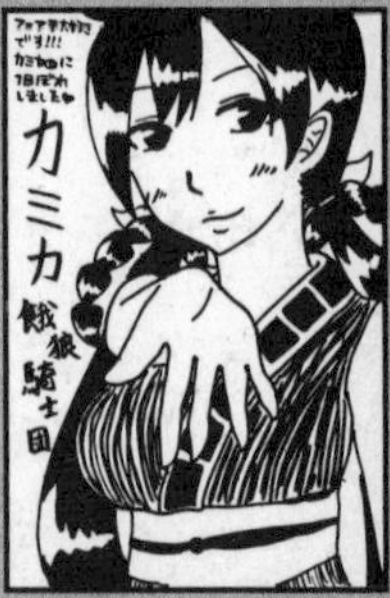
カミカ
餓狼騎士団

▲ Kamika-san. She doesn't stand out very much, but she is very tall.

Okayama Prefecture, King♪

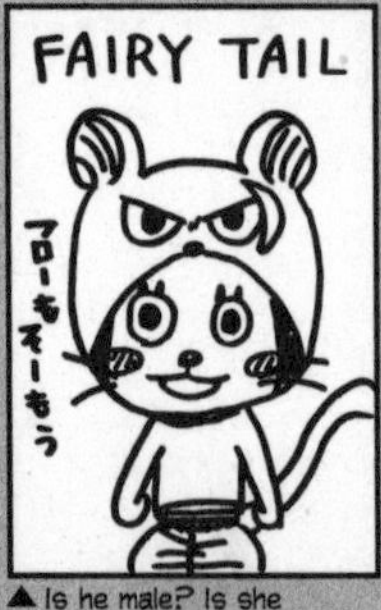
FAIRY TAIL

▲ Is he male? Is she female? Fro has a lot of mysteries. But the most basic is: Is this a cat or a frog?

Iwate Prefecture, Mameko

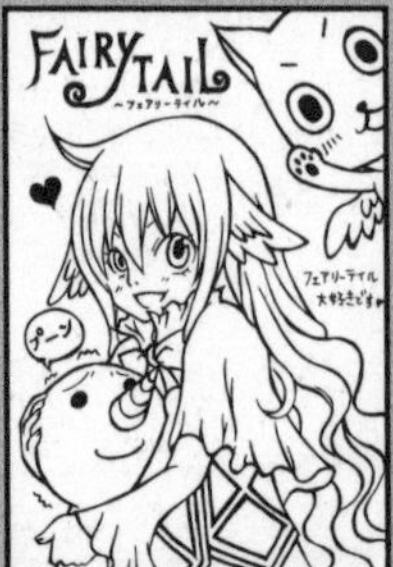
FAIRY TAIL
~フェアリーテイル~

▲ She's a ghost, but the first master shows up quite a lot. And she still has secrets.

Kanagawa Prefecture, Koro Koro

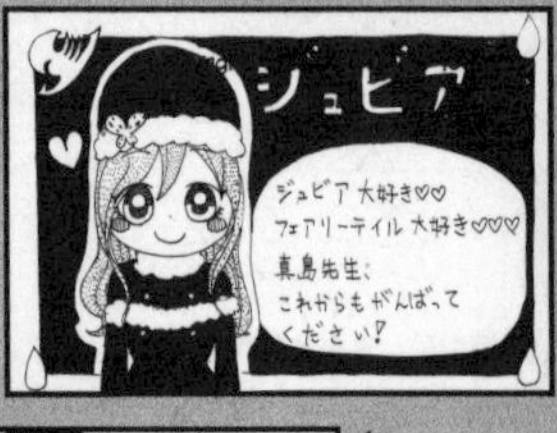
ジュビア
ジュビア大好き♡
フェアリーテイル大好き♡♡♡
真島先生、
これからもがんばって
ください!

Whoa! ▶ That is amazingly cute! I'll do my best! I can't help but do my best now!

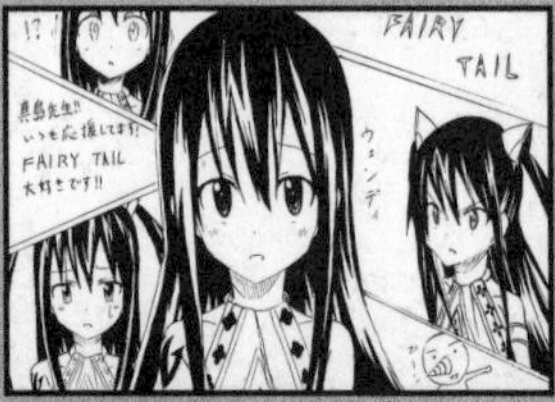
FAIRY TAIL
真島先生!!
いつも応援してます!
FAIRY TAIL
大好きです!!
ウェンディ

Hokkaido, Shinto Ishikawa

◀ Wendy making a bunch of different faces. So well done!! And for some reason Plue is there too.

Send to Hiro Mashima, Kodansha Comics
451 Park Ave. South, 7th Floor New York, NY 10016

FAIRY GUILD

Nagasaki Prefecture, Tomoka Sasano

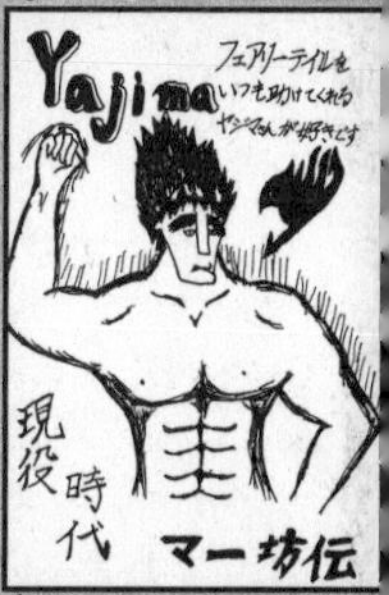
Yajima
現役時代
マー坊伝

▲He says this is how Yajima-san looked when he was a working wizard! Is that true?! (laughs)

Okayama Prefecture, Shiryū

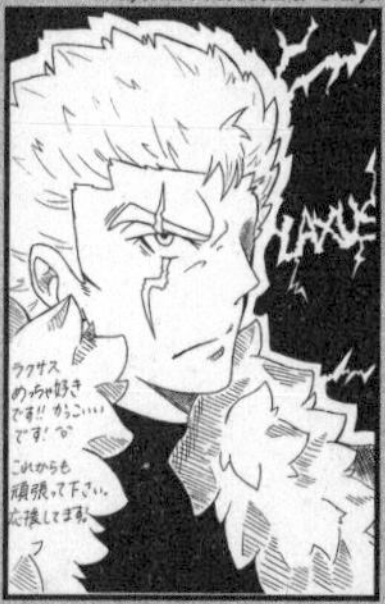

▲Big brother Thunder is strong and cool, huh? We gotta give him more chances to shine.

Ibaraki Prefecture, Mayonnaise ♡

They're ▶ always such a close family! I'm happy that people draw pictures like this!

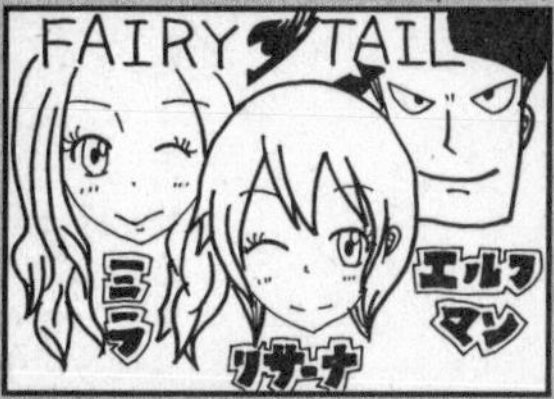
FAIRY TAIL
ミラ
エルフマン
リサーナ

I'm so ◀ thankful to the fans who came up with these characters!

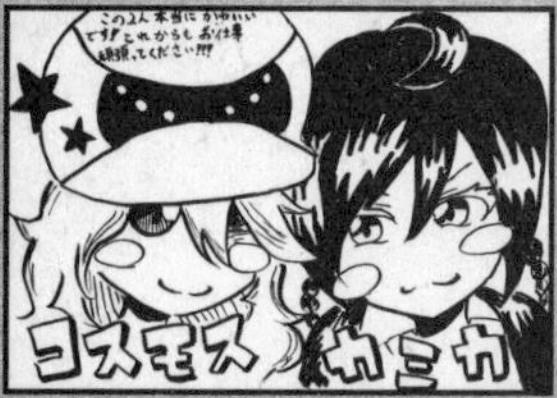
コスモス
カミカ

Fukuoka Prefecture, Akane Saji

Mie Prefecture, Kair

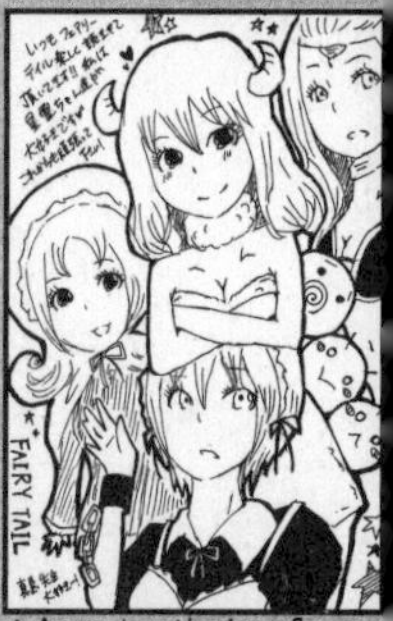
FAIRY TAIL

▲A great gathering of Celestial Spirits! Ah! Only the girls, huh?

Shimane Prefecture, Miina

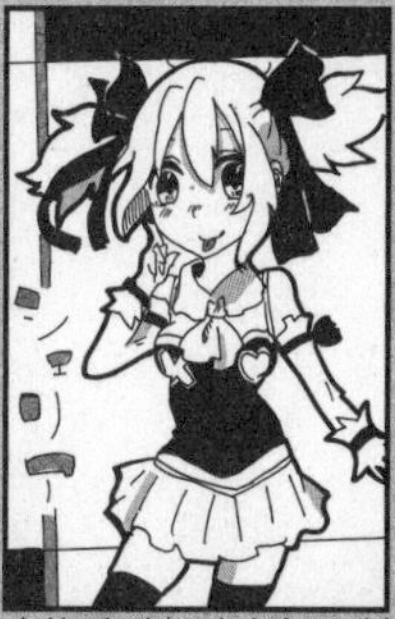

▲ Her impish grin is incredibly cute!

By sending in letters or postcards, you give us permission to give your name, address, postal code, and any other information you include to the artist as-is. Please keep that in mind.

REJECTION CORNER

One of the ▶ great things to have watched during the games was how Chapati coordinated his wigs!

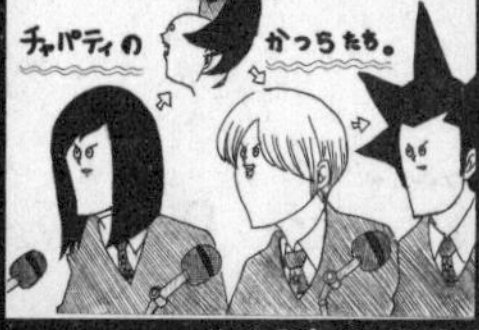
チャパティの
かつらたち。

Hyogo Prefecture, Yura Ikari

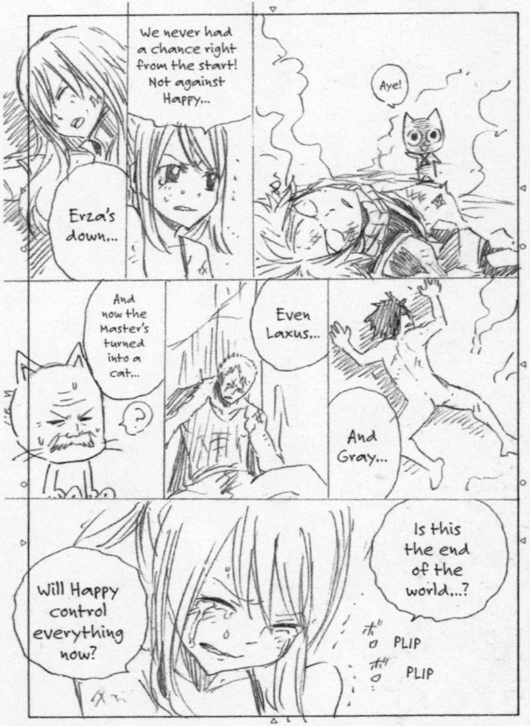
Aye!
We never had a chance right from the start! Not against Happy...
Erza's down...
And Gray...
Even Laxus...
And now the Master's turned into a cat...
?
Is this the end of the world...?
PLIP
PLIP
Will Happy control everything now?

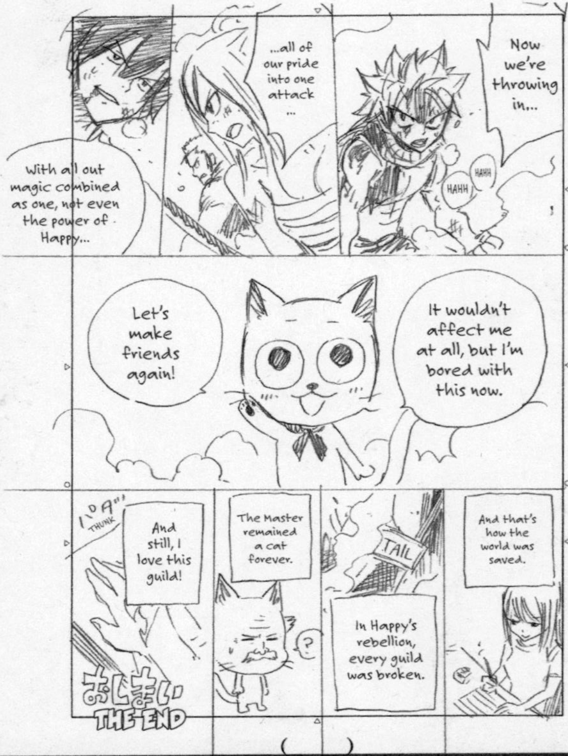
Now we're throwing in...
HAHH
HAHH
...all of our pride into one attack ...
With all out magic combined as one, not even the power of Happy...
It wouldn't affect me at all, but I'm bored with this now.
Let's make friends again!
And that's how the world was saved.
TAIL
In Happy's rebellion, every guild was broken.
The Master remained a cat forever.
?
And still, I love this guild!
THUNK
THE END

FAIRY TAIL

フェアリーテイル

38

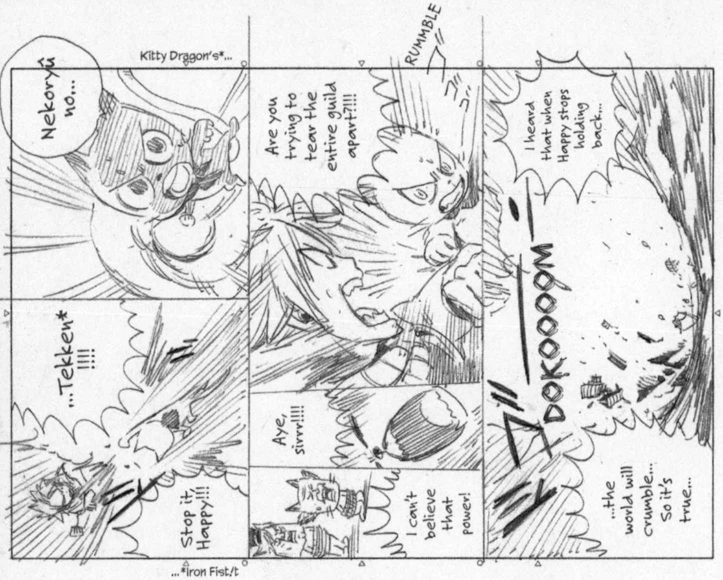

Kitty Dragon's*...
Nekoryū no...
...Tekken*!!!!
...*Iron Fist/t
Stop it, Happy!!!
RUMMBLE
Are you trying to tear the entire guild apart?!!!
Aye, sirrr!!!!
I can't believe that power!
I heard that when Happy stops holding back...
DOKOOOOOM
...the world will crumble... So it's true...

Twitter account: @hiro_mashima

HIRO 真島ヒロ MASHIMA

FROM HIRO MASHIMA

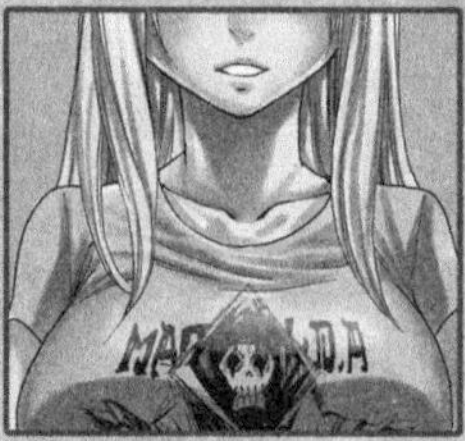
MAS LD.A

Recently, I've been trying out a lot of paint programs, but there still isn't any that I'd hold up and say, "This is my ideal paint program!!" While trying to color a drawing, I'm always frustrated that it doesn't have this feature or that feature. The drawing on the cover of this book has three types of coloring, all of them different.

Original Jacket Design: Hisao Ogawa

Translation Notes:

Japanese is a tricky language for most Westerners, and translation is often more art than science. For your edification and reading pleasure, here are notes on some of the places where we could have gone in a different direction with our translation of the work, or where a Japanese cultural reference is used.

Page 15, Waxwing

A waxwing is a small perching bird, varieties of which can be found in Japan, Asia, Europe, and North America. The Japanese variety is called *renjaku* by the Japanese.

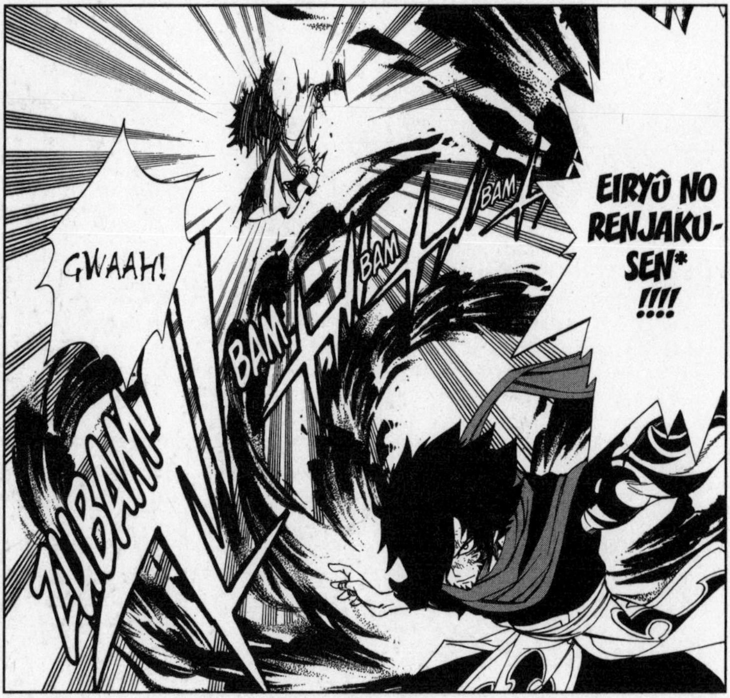
EIRYÛ NO RENJAKU-SEN* !!!!
BAM
BAM
BAM
GWAAH!
ZUBAM!

Page 55, Mizuchi

Lyon's attack, Mizuchi, refers to a dragon out of Japanese legends. The early legends regarding Mizuchi have been lost, so it is not known whether it originally referred to a single dragon or all dragons with a close relationship with water, however existing early legends connect them to rivers or the sea.

Page 71, Scree

Scree is the English word for Jura's *gaisui* attack. It refers to the pile of rocky debris that accumulates at the base of cliffs and other steep slopes. It is also known as a talus.

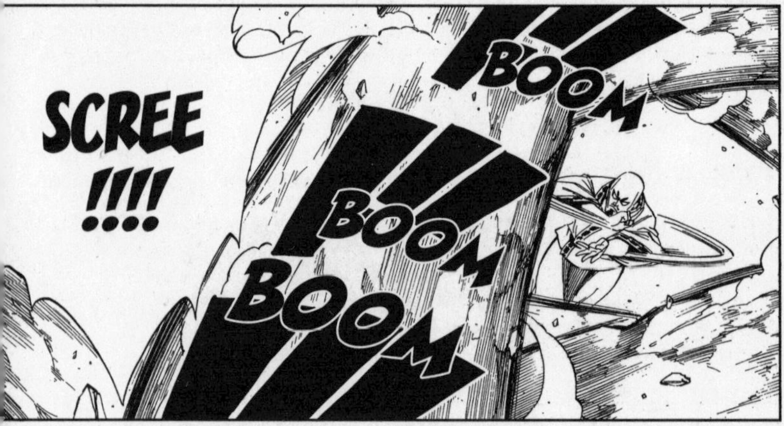
BOOM
BOOM
BOOM
SCREE !!!!

Page 83, Nakagami Armor

Nakagami, also known as Tenichijin or Tenitsujin, is one of the Twelve Generals of Heaven as described by the famous *onmyôji* (astrologer and mystic) Abe no Seimei during the Heian period a thousand years ago. The Twelve Generals refer to constellations, and among the twelve used in Abe no Seimei's astrology, Nakagami was the chief of the twelve god generals.

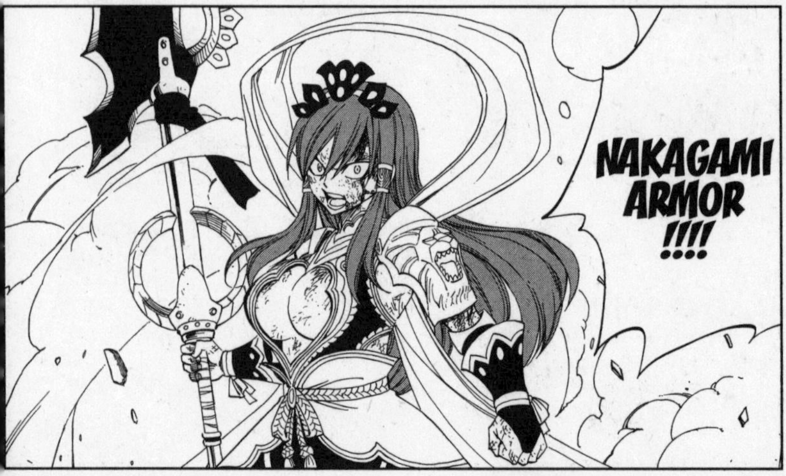
NAKAGAMI ARMOR !!!!

Page 86, Narumikazuchi

Although the normal word for thunder and lighting in Japanese is *kaminari*, there is another word, *ikazuchi*, which connotes to Japanese speakers lightning directed by a god. Indeed there is a god's name, Takemikazuchi, which uses the term *mikazuchi*, although this translator was not able to find any reference to a specific god named Narumikazuchi. *Naru* means a roar as in a lion's, and *mikazuchi* means thunder and lightning, so the translation is correct. Unfortunately, the English was not able to carry the nuance of god-directed lightning that is in the Japanese.

Page 101, Nakagami Asterism

As mentioned above, Nakagami was taken from the astrology of Abe no Seimei, and those relate to constellations in the night sky. However, technically some "constellations" such as the Big Dipper are not actual official constellations, but pictures that the stars make in the sky. (The stars of the big dipper are only a part of the Ursa Major constellation.) There is a word for the pictures the stars make in the sky, such as the big dipper or the teapot of Sagittarius: They are called "asterisms." The Japanese name for the attack, *seisai*, means "asterism."

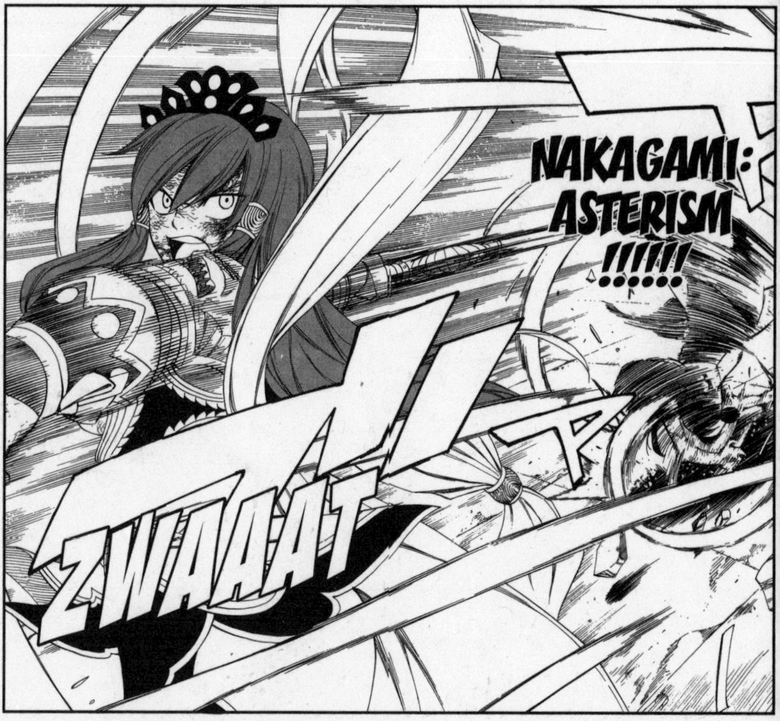
NAKAGAMI: ASTERISM !!!!!!
ZWAAAT

Page 125, There and Back Again

The Japanese words used in the title of this chapter are the same words that are found in the official Japanese title for the book, The Hobbit.

Chapter 323: The Shadow: There and Back Again

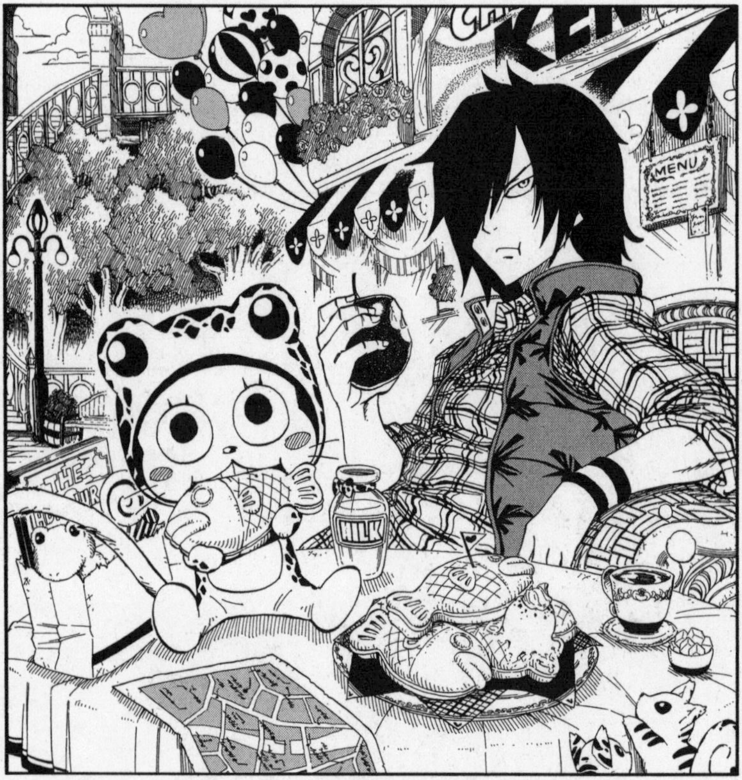
MENU
MILK

Preview of *Fairy Tail*, volume 39

We're pleased to present you with a preview from Fairy Tail, volume 39, now available on digital devices and coming to print in June 2014. See our Web site (www.kodanshacomics.com) for more details!

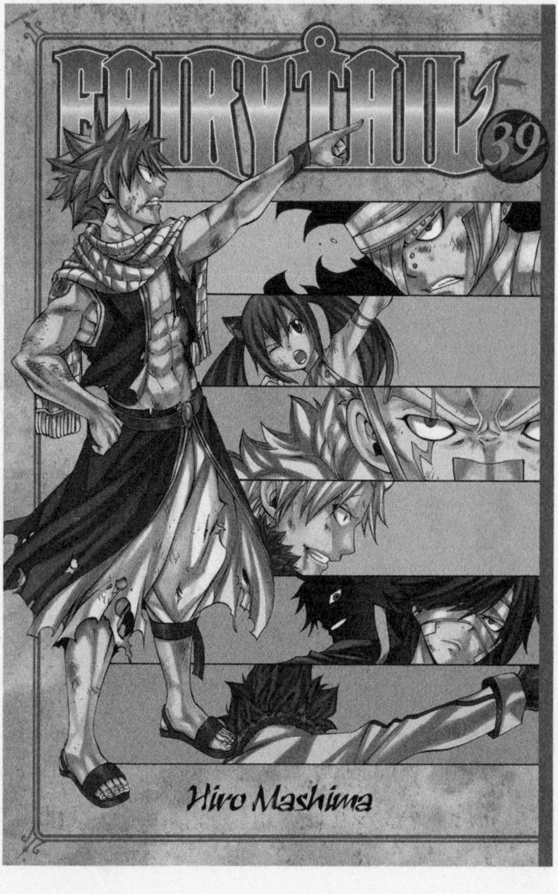
FAIRY TAIL
39
Hiro Mashima

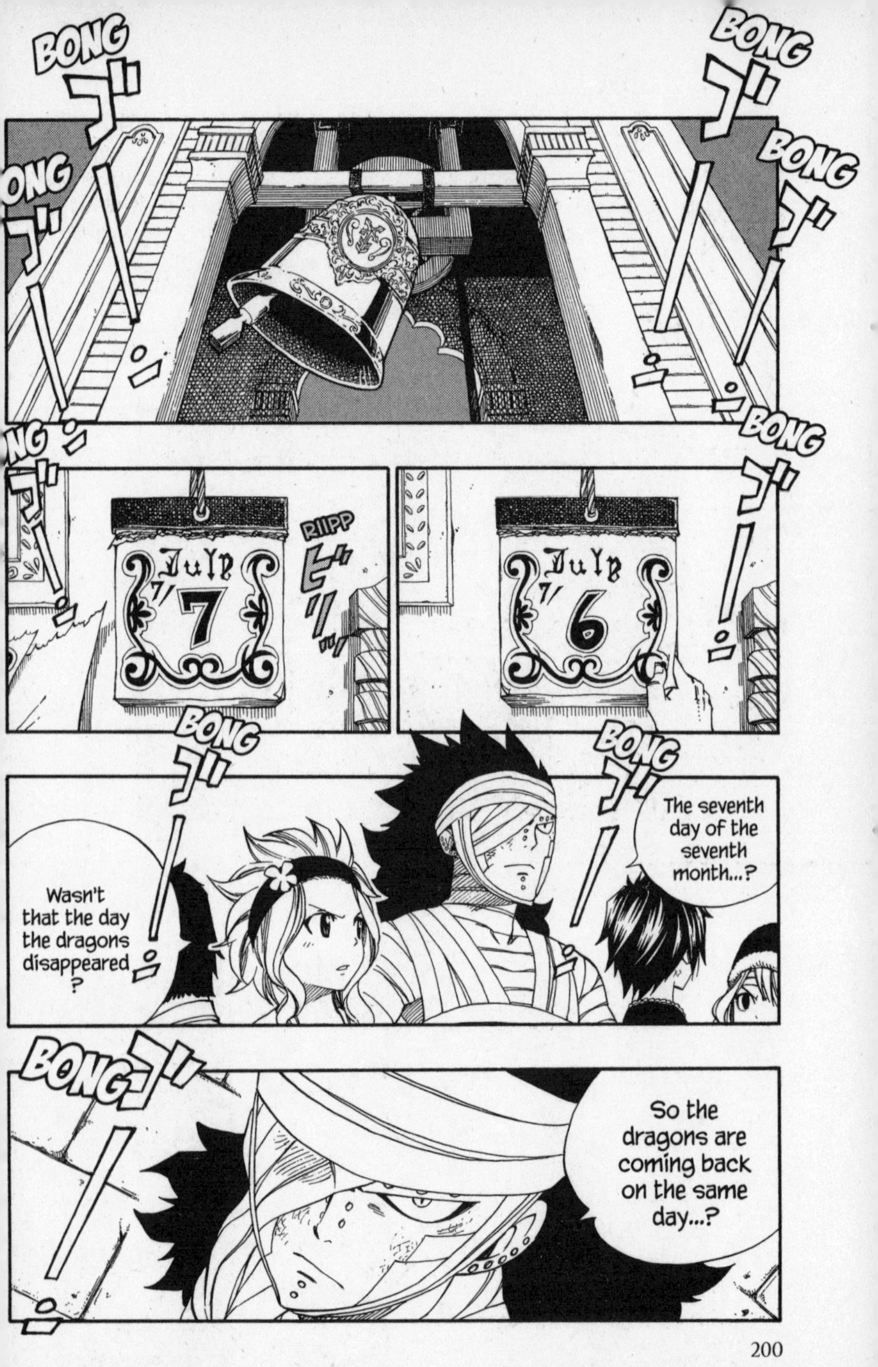
BONG
BONG
BONG
BONG
July
7/ 6
RIIPP
July
7/ 7
BONG
BONG
The seventh day of the seventh month...?
Wasn't that the day the dragons disappeared?
BONG
So the dragons are coming back on the same day...?

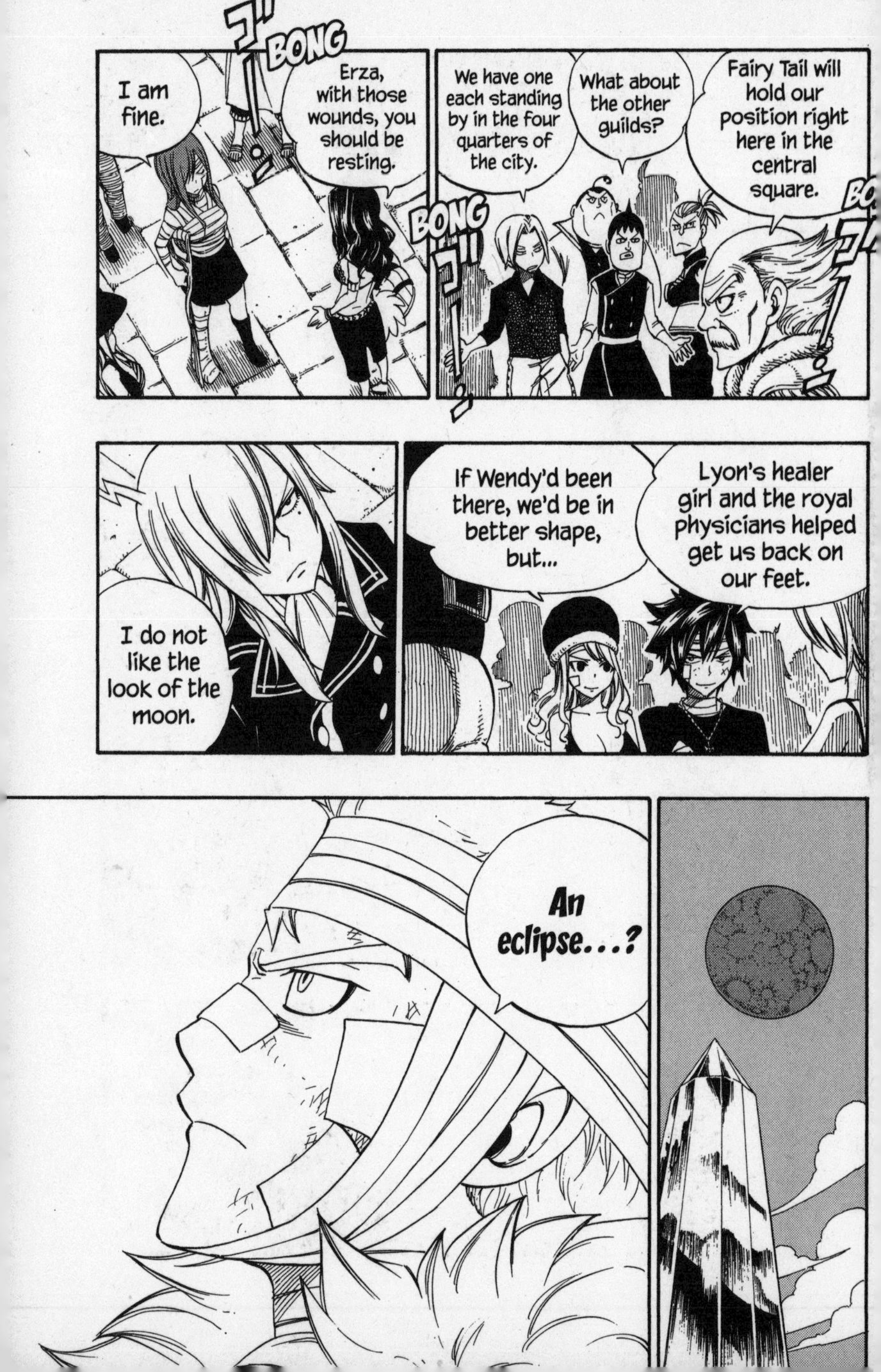
Fairy Tail will hold our position right here in the central square.
What about the other guilds?
We have one each standing by in the four quarters of the city.
BONG
BONG
Erza, with those wounds, you should be resting.
I am fine.
Lyon's healer girl and the royal physicians helped get us back on our feet.
If Wendy'd been there, we'd be in better shape, but...
I do not like the look of the moon.
An eclipse...?

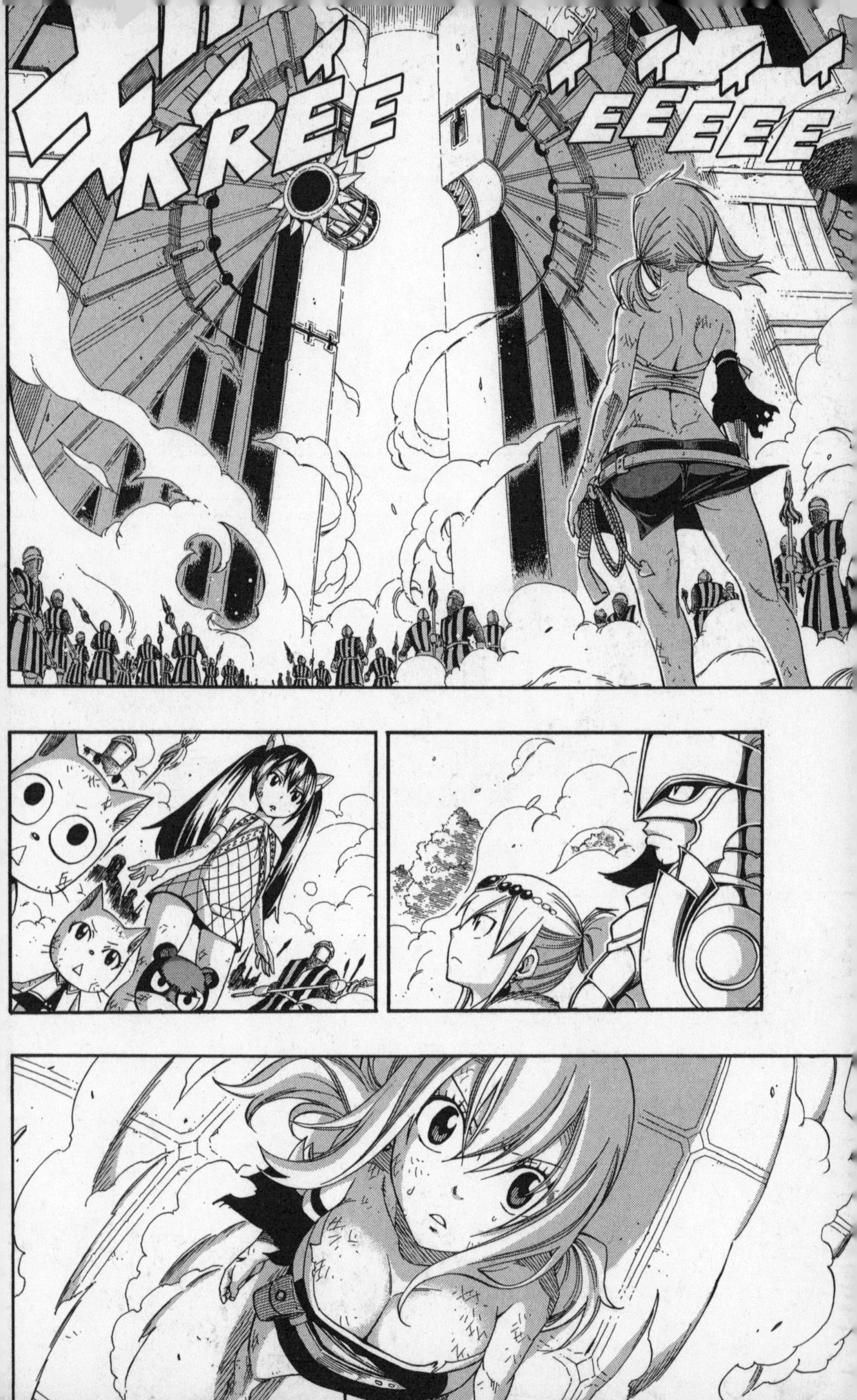
KREEEEEEE

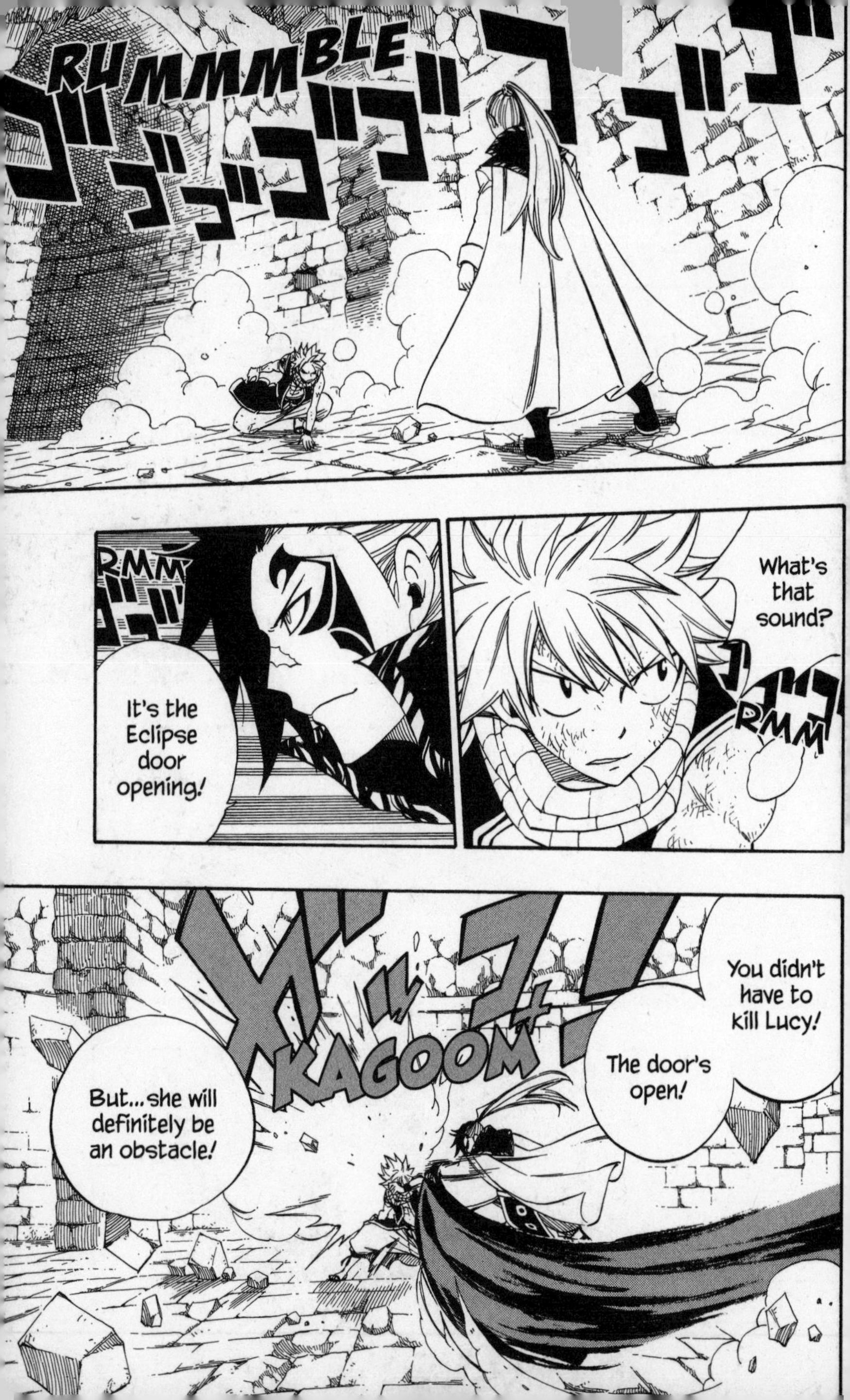
RUMMMBLE
What's that sound?
RMM
RMM
It's the Eclipse door opening!
You didn't have to kill Lucy!
The door's open!
KAGOOM
But...she will definitely be an obstacle!

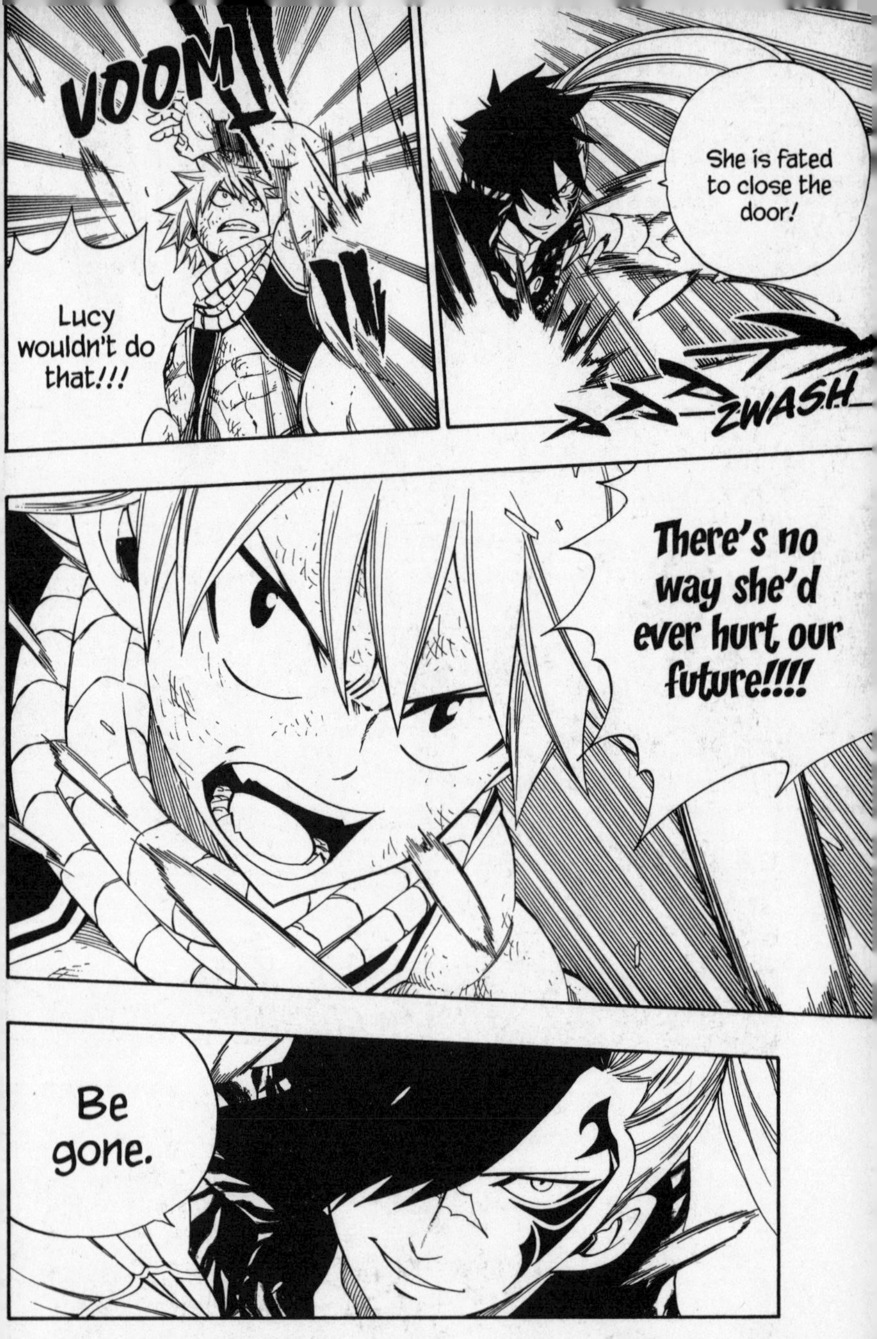
She is fated to close the door!
ZWASH
VOOM
Lucy wouldn't do that!!!
There's no way she'd ever hurt our future!!!!
Be gone.

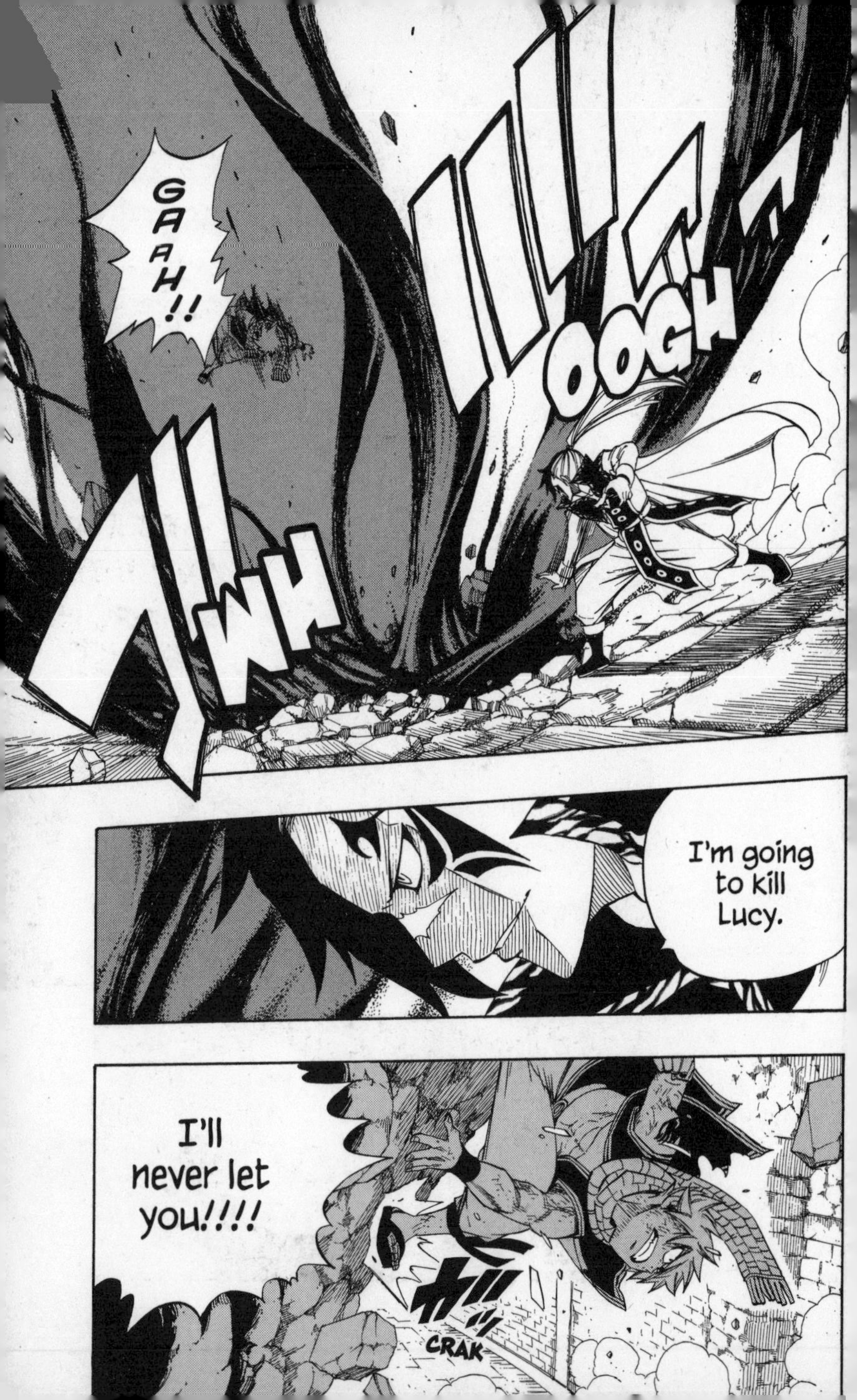
GAAH!!
OOGH
I'm going to kill Lucy.
I'll never let you!!!!
CRAK

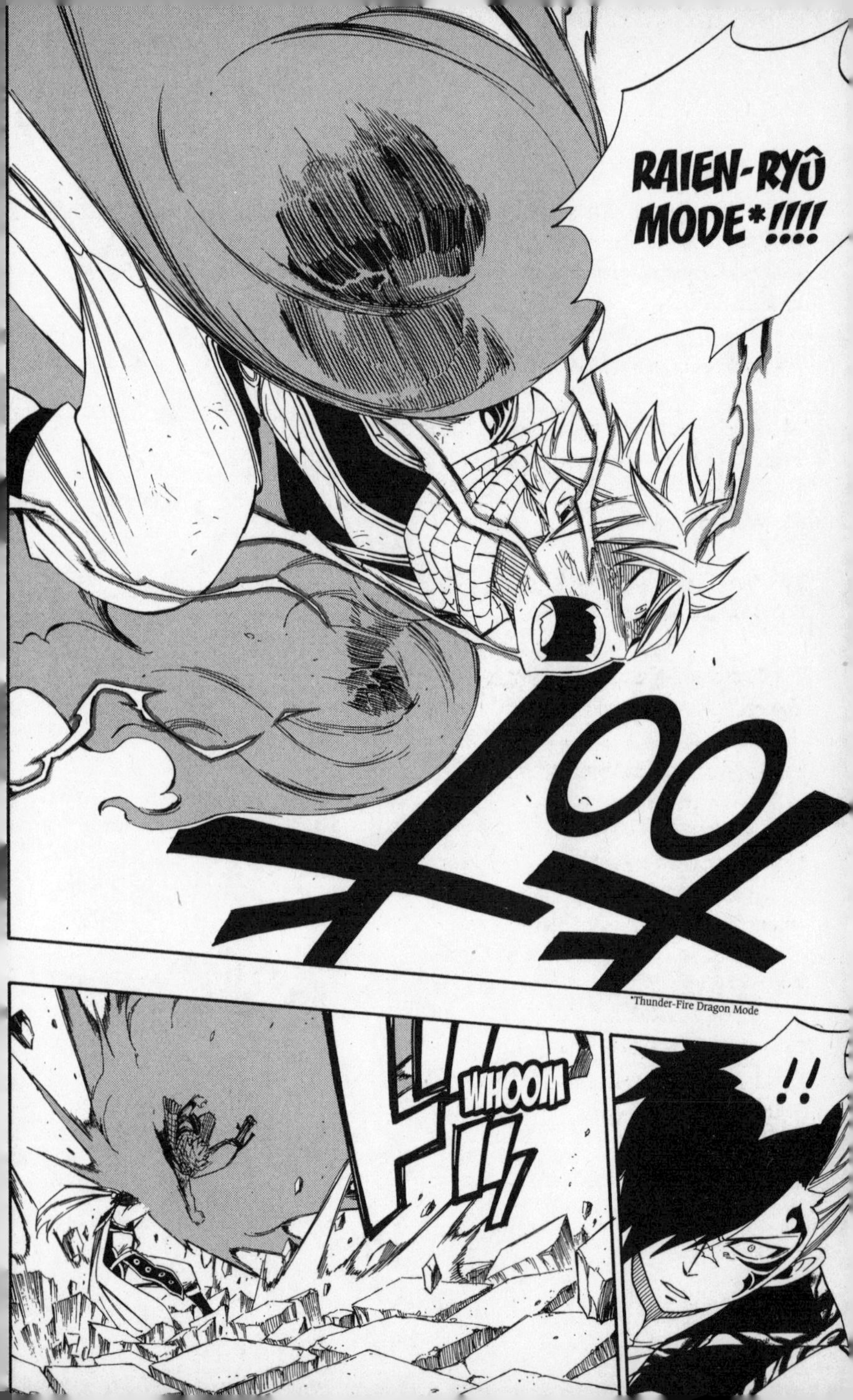
RAIEN-RYÛ MODE*!!!!
!!
WHOOM

*Thunder-Fire Dragon Mode

A Kodansha Comics Trade Paperback Original.

Fairy Tail volume 38 copyright © 2013 Hiro Mashima
English translation copyright © 2014 Hiro Mashima

Published in the United States by Kodansha Comics, an imprint of Kodansha USA Publishing, LLC, New York.

Publication rights for this English edition arranged through Kodansha Ltd., Tokyo.

First published in Japan in 2013 by Kodansha Ltd., Tokyo
ISBN 978-1-61262-434-1

Printed in the United States of America.

www.kodanshacomics.com

9 8 7 6 5 4 3 2 1

Translation: William Flanagan
Lettering: AndWorld Design
Editing: Ben Applegate

TOMARE!

止まれ
[STOP!]

You're going the wrong way!

Manga is a completely different
type of reading experience.

To start at the *beginning,*
go to the *end!*

That's right! Authentic manga is read the traditional Japanese way—from right to left, exactly the *opposite* of how American books are read. It's easy to follow: Just go to the other end of the book and read each page—and each panel—from right side to left side, starting at the top right. Now you're experiencing manga as it was meant to be!